Macmillan/McGraw-Hill READING

Macmillan
McGraw-Hill

New York   Farmington

Contributors

The Princeton Review, Time Magazine, Accelerated Reader

The Princeton Review is not
affiliated with Princeton
University or ETS.

RFB&D
learning through listening

Students with print disabilities may be eligible to obtain an accessible, audio version of the
pupil edition of this textbook. Please call Recording for the Blind & Dyslexic at 1-800-221-4792
for complete information.

Macmillan/McGraw-Hill

A Division of The McGraw·Hill Companies

Published by Macmillan/McGraw-Hill, a division of The McGraw-Hill Companies, Inc., Two Penn Plaza, NY, NY 10121

Printed in the United States of America

ISBN 0-02-188582-6/1, Bk.4

2 3 4 5 6 7 8 9   073/043 05 04 03 02

Macmillan/McGraw-Hill READING

Authors

James Flood

Jan E. Hasbrouck

James V. Hoffman

Diane Lapp

Donna Lubcker

Angela Shelf Medearis

Scott Paris

Steven Stahl

Josefina Villamil Tinajero

Karen D. Wood

Macmillan McGraw-Hill

New York   Farmington

Computer Center

Managing the

Art Center

Working with Words Center

Phonics Center

Reading and Listening Center

cat
dog

Writing Center

Classroom

TEACHING TIP

MANAGEMENT
Provide children in each group with their own list of centers they will go to. Children can check off each center after finishing their work. Early finishers can read a book from the Reading Center.

Math Center

1 2 3 4 5

Teacher Directed Small Group Instruction

Sample Management Plan

Group 1	Group 2	Group 3	Group 4
With Teacher	Phonics Center or Word Center	Writing Center or Reading Center	Cross-Curricular Center
Phonics Center or Word Center	**With Teacher**	Cross-Curricular Center	Writing Center or Reading Center
Writing Center or Reading Center	Cross-Curricular Center	**With Teacher**	Phonics Center or Word Center
Cross-Curricular Center	Writing Center or Reading Center	Phonics Center or Word Center	**With Teacher**

Creating CENTERS

Establishing independent Centers and other independent activities is the key to helping you manage the classroom as you meet with small groups.

Reading and Listening

Set up a classroom library that includes Theme Big Books, Leveled Books, and other independent reading titles on each group's independent reading level. Also, see the Theme Bibliography on pages T98 and T99 for suggested titles.

Children can use the Reading Center for:

- Self-selected reading
- Paired reading
- Listening to selections on audiocassette

Phonics

Children can practice the phonics skills they are learning. Phonics Center activities may include:

- Substituting consonants to build words
- Writing words with long vowels
- Reading and illustrating long vowel words
- Identifying and sorting vowel sounds

TEACHING TIP

WORD WALLS Write each letter of the alphabet on an index card. Place the cards on a wall.

Allow space underneath the cards for adding cards for words that begin with that letter. Add new vocabulary words to the Word Wall.

Writing

Children can practice their fine motor, handwriting, and writing skills.

Children can use the Writing Center for:

- Writing/drawing about their own experiences
- Practicing forming letters
- Responding to literature
- Journal writing

Working with Words

Children can practice reading and identifying high-frequency words. Place Word Building Manipulative Cards for the words *after, always, who, blue, were, work, because, buy, found, some, carry, been, clean, done, far, pretty, little, light, how, live,* and *clean* in the Center. Have pairs of children practice reading the words together.

Children can use the Working with Words Center for:

- Matching word cards
- Reading words
- Using words in sentences
- Playing word games

Cross-Curricular CENTERS

Set up Cross-Curricular Centers to help extend selection concepts and ideas. Suggestions for Cross-Curricular Centers can be found throughout the unit.

Science

- Recycling, 22
- Oil and Water, 38D
- Fish, 44
- Frogs, 80
- Terrific Trees!, 96D

3 + 2

Math

- How Many?, 8D
- Weight, 48
- Inch by Inch, 76
- Estimation, 110

Social Studies

- Food Mural, 8D
- Food Geography, 20
- Map Skills, 58
- Peaceful Solutions, 86
- Family Farming, 106
- Community Workers, 124D

Art

- Favorite Animals, 38D
- Color Theory, 104
- Fire Prevention Posters, 124D

Additional Independent Activities

The following independent activities are offered as a means to practice and reinforce concepts and skills taught within the unit.

PUPIL EDITION: READER RESPONSE

Story Questions to monitor student comprehension of the selection. The questions are leveled, progressing from literal to more critical thinking questions.

Story Activities related to the selection. Four activities are always provided: one Writing activity, two Cross-Curricular activities, and a Research and Inquiry activity in the "Find Out More" project, which encourages students to use the Internet for research.

LEVELED PRACTICE

Each week, Reteach, Practice, and Extend pages are offered to address the individual needs of students as they learn and review skills.

McGraw-Hill Reading

MULTI-AGE
Classroom

Using the same global themes at each grade level facilitates the use of materials in multi-age classrooms.

GRADE LEVEL	Experience Experiences can tell us about ourselves and our world.	Connections Making connections develops new understandings.
Kindergarten	**My World** We learn a lot from all the things we see and do at home and in school.	**All Kinds of Friends** When we work and play together, we learn more about ourselves.
Subtheme 1	At Home	Working Together
Subtheme 2	School Days	Playing Together
1	**Day by Day** Each day brings new experiences.	**Together Is Better** We like to share ideas and experiences with others.
2	**What's New?** With each day, we learn something new.	**Just Between Us** Family and friends help us see the world in new ways.
3	**Great Adventures** Life is made up of big and small experiences.	**Nature Links** Nature can give us new ideas.
4	**Reflections** Stories let us share the experiences of others.	**Something in Common** Sharing ideas can lead to meaningful cooperation.
5	**Time of My Life** We sometimes find memorable experiences in unexpected places.	**Building Bridges** Knowing what we have in common helps us appreciate our differences.
6	**Pathways** Reflecting on life's experiences can lead to new understandings.	**A Common Thread** A look beneath the surface may uncover hidden connections.

Themes: Kindergarten – Grade 6

Expression	Inquiry	Problem Solving	Making Decisions
There are many styles and forms for expressing ourselves.	By exploring and asking questions, we make discoveries.	Analyzing information can help us solve problems.	Using what we know helps us evaluate situations.
Time to Shine We can use our ideas and our imagination to do many wonderful things.	**I Wonder** We can make discoveries about the wonders of nature in our own backyard.	**Let's Work It Out** Working as part of a team can help me find a way to solve problems.	**Choices** We can make many good choices and decisions every day.
Great Ideas	**In My Backyard**	**Try and Try Again**	**Good Choices**
Let's Pretend	**Wonders of Nature**	**Teamwork**	**Let's Decide**
Stories to Tell Each one of us has a different story to tell.	**Let's Find Out!** Looking for answers is an adventure.	**Think About It!** It takes time to solve problems.	**Many Paths** Each decision opens the door to a new path.
Express Yourself We share our ideas in many ways.	**Look Around** There are surprises all around us.	**Figure It Out** We can solve problems by working together.	**Starting Now** Unexpected events can lead to new decisions.
Be Creative! We can all express ourselves in creative, wonderful ways.	**Tell Me More** Looking and listening closely will help us find out the facts.	**Think It Through** Solutions come in many shapes and sizes.	**Turning Points** We make new judgments based on our experiences.
Our Voices We can each use our talents to communicate ideas.	**Just Curious** We can find answers in surprising places.	**Make a Plan** Often we have to think carefully about a problem in order to solve it.	**Sorting It Out** We make decisions that can lead to new ideas and discoveries.
Imagine That The way we express our thoughts and feelings can take different forms.	**Investigate!** We never know where the search for answers might lead us.	**Bright Ideas** Some problems require unusual approaches.	**Crossroads** Decisions cause changes that can enrich our lives.
With Flying Colors Creative people help us see the world from different perspectives.	**Seek and Discover** To make new discoveries, we must observe and explore.	**Brainstorms** We can meet any challenge with determination and ingenuity.	**All Things Considered** Encountering new places and people can help us make decisions.

Let's Find Out!

*Looking for answers
is an adventure.*

THE SHOPPING LIST 8A

written by **Gary Apple**
illustrated by **Shirley Beckes**

SKILLS			
Phonics	**Comprehension**	**Vocabulary**	**Study Skill**
• **Introduce/Apply** Long *i: i-e*	• **Introduce** Cause and Effect	• **Review** Inflectional Ending -*s* and -*es*	• Charts
• **Review** Long *i-e, a-e*			

A HUMOROUS STORY

YASMIN'S DUCKS 38A

written by **Barbara Bottner**
illustrated by **Dominic Catalano**

SKILLS			
Phonics	**Comprehension**	**Vocabulary**	**Study Skill**
• **Introduce/Apply** Long *o: o-e*	• **Review** Cause and Effect	• **Review** Inflectional Ending -*ed*	• Charts
• **Review** Long *o-e, i-e, a-e*			

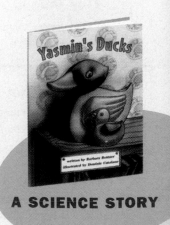

A SCIENCE STORY

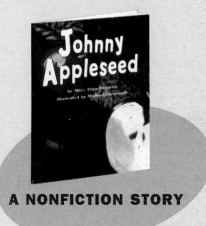

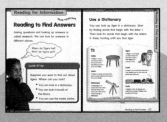

INFORMATIONAL TEXT

Unit Planner

	WEEK 1 The Shopping List	**WEEK 2** Yasmin's Ducks
Leveled Books	Easy: *A Pet for Max* Independent: *The Big Secret* Challenge: *Who Took the Farmer's Hat?*	Easy: *Spot's Trick* Independent: *Show and Tell Rose* Challenge: *My Best Friend*
✔ **Tested Skills**	✔ **Phonics** Introduce Long *i: i-e*, 8I–8J Review Long *i: i-e*, 37E–37F Review *i-e*, *a-e*, 37G–37H ✔ **Comprehension** Introduce Cause and Effect, 37I–37J ✔ **Vocabulary** Review Inflectional Endings *-s, es*, 37K–37L ✔ **Study Skills** Read a Chart, 36	✔ **Phonics** Introduce Long *o: o-e*, 38I–38J Review Long *o: o-e*, 65E–65F Review *o-e*, *i-e*, *a-e*, 65G–65H ✔ **Comprehension** Review Cause and Effect, 65I–65J ✔ **Vocabulary** Review Inflectional Ending *-ed*, 65K–65L ✔ **Study Skills** Graphic Aids, 64
Minilessons	**Phonics and Decoding:** Blends, 13; Short *a, i, o, u*, 19 **Make Inferences,** 17 **Context Clues,** 23 **Plot and Character,** 25 **Sequence of Events,** 27 **Summarizing,** 31	**Final Sound /k/ck,** 43 **Context Clues,** 47 **Make Inferences,** 51 **High-Frequency Words,** 55 **Main Idea,** 59
Language Arts	✎ **Writing:** Writing that Compares, 37M **Grammar:** *Was* and *Were*, 37O **Spelling:** Words with Long *i: i-e*, 37Q	✎ **Writing:** Writing that Compares, 65M **Grammar:** *Has* and *Have*, 65O **Spelling:** Words with Long *o: o-e*, 65Q

Activities

Curriculum Connections	Read Aloud: "General Store," 8G	Read Aloud: "The Ducks and the Fox," 38G
	Phonics Rhyme: "Wish List," 8/9	Phonics Rhyme: "My Phone," 38/39
	Math: How many? , 8D Shape Graphs, 12	Science: Oil and Water, 38D Fish, 44
	Social Studies: Food Mural, 8D Food Geography, 20	Math: Weight, 48
	Science: Recycling, 22	Social Studies: Map Skills, 58
	Music: Rhyme Song, 26	Art: Favorite Animals, 38D
CULTURAL PERSPECTIVES	Colors/Los Colores, 24	Down Feathers, 42

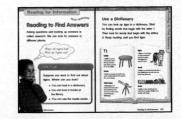

WEEK 3 The Knee-High Man	**WEEK 4** Johnny Appleseed	**WEEK 5** Ring! Ring! Ring! Put Out the Fire!	**WEEK 6** Review, Writing, Reading Information, Assessment
Easy: *Fun Run* **Independent:** *A Bigger House for June* **Challenge:** *Pete's Chicken*	**Easy:** *Fall is Fun!* **Independent:** *The Land* **Challenge:** *Down by the Bay*	Self-Selected Reading of Leveled Books	Self-Selected Reading

☑ **Phonics** Introduce Long *u: u-e*, 66I–66J Review Long *u: u-e*, 95E–95F Review *u-e, o-e, i-e, a-e*, 95G–95H	☑ **Phonics** Introduce Long *a: ay, ai*, 96I–96J Review Long *a: ay, ai*, 123E–123F Review *ai, ay; u-e, o-e*, 123G–123H	☑ **Phonics** Review *ai, ay; u-e, o-e, i-e, a-e*, 124I–124J	☑ **Assess Skills** Long *i: i-e* Long *o: o-e* Long *u: u-e* Long *a: ay, ai* Cause and Effect
☑ **Comprehension** Introduce Make Inferences, 95I–95J	☑ **Comprehension** Review Make Inferences, 123I–123J	☑ **Comprehension** Review Cause and Effect, 133E–133F Review Make Inferences, 133G–133H	Make Inferences Inflectional Endings *-s, -es* Inflectional Ending *-ed* Charts
☑ **Vocabulary** Introduce Inflectional Endings *-er, -est*, 95K–95L	☑ **Vocabulary** Review Inflectional Endings *-er, -est*, 123K–123L	☑ **Vocabulary** Review Inflectional Endings *-s, -es*, 133I–133J Review Inflectional Endings *-er, -est*, 133K–133L	☑ **Assess Grammar and Spelling** Review Verbs, 141A Review Spelling Patterns, 141B
☑ **Study Skills** Charts, 94	☑ **Study Skills** Apple Tree Chart, 122	☑ **Study Skills** Charts, 132	☑ **Unit Progress Assessment**
			☑ **Standardized Test Preparation**
Phonics and Decoding: *gr, fr, tr*, 73 **Context Clues,** 75 **High-Frequency Words,** 77 **Make Inferences,** 79 **Main Idea,** 89	**Context Clues,** 101 **Vowels,** 105 **Setting,** 107 **Character,** 109 **Cause and Effect,** 115 **Summarize,** 117		📖 **Reading to Find Answers** 136/137

✏ **Writing:** Writing that Compares, 95M **Grammar:** *Go* and *Do*, 95O **Spelling:** Words with Long *u: u-e*, 95Q	✏ **Writing:** Writing that Compares, 123M **Grammar:** *See* and *Say*, 123O **Spelling:** Words with Long *a: ai, ay*, 123Q	✏ **Writing:** Writing that Compares, 133M **Grammar:** Contractions with *Not*, 133O **Spelling:** Words from Social Studies, 133Q	✏ **Unit Writing Process:** Writing that Compares, 140A-140F

Read Aloud: "Timimoto," 66G	Read Aloud: "The Great Big Enormous Turnip," 96G	Read Aloud: "The Brave Ones," 124G	👥 **Cooperative Theme Project Research and Inquiry:** Places to Explore, 6J
Phonics Rhyme: "Duke the Ant," 66/67	Phonics Rhyme: "The Gift," 96/97	Phonics Rhyme: "Fire Pup," 124/125	
Math: How Tall Are You?, 66D Inch by Inch, 76	Science: Terrific Trees!, 96D Plant a Seed, 102	Art: Fire Prevention Posters, 124D	
Science: Green Grass Grows, 66D Frogs, 80	Art: Color Theory, 104	Social Studies: Community Workers, 124D	
Social Studies: Peaceful Solutions, 86	Social Studies: Family Farming, 106		
	Math: Estimation, 110		
	Music: Sing a Song of Science, 96D		
Corn Varieties, 72	Apples, 100		

Unit Resources

LITERATURE

LEVELED BOOKS

Easy:
- *A Pet For Max*
- *Spot's Trick*
- *Fun Run*
- *Fall is Fun!*

Independent:
- *The Big Secret*
- *Show and Tell Rose*
- *A Bigger House For June*
- *The Land*

Challenge:
- *Who Took the Farmer's Hat?*
- *My Best Friend*
- *Pete's Chicken*
- *Down by the Bay*

THEME BIG BOOK

Share *Fish Faces* to set the unit theme and make content-area connections.

LISTENING LIBRARY

For student book selections and poetry. Available on **compact disc** and **audiocassette.**

Macmillan/McGraw-Hill

i Intervention
Skills Intervention Guide
Easy Leveled Books

SKILLS

LEVELED PRACTICE

Practice: Student practice for phonics, comprehension, vocabulary and study skills; plus practice for instructional vocabulary and story comprehension. Take-Home Story included for each lesson.

Reteach: Reteaching opportunities for students who need more help with each assessed skill.

Extend: Extension activities for vocabulary, comprehension, story and study skills.

TEACHING CHARTS

Instructional charts for modeling vocabulary and tested skills. Also available as transparencies.

WORD BUILDING MANIPULATIVE CARDS

 Letter and word cards to utilize phonics and build instructional vocabulary.

LANGUAGE SUPPORT BOOK

ESL Parallel lessons and practice for students needing language support.

PHONICS/PHONEMIC AWARENESS PRACTICE BOOK

Additional practice on key phonetic elements.

FLUENCY PASSAGES
Practice for building reading fluency.

LANGUAGE ARTS

GRAMMAR PRACTICE BOOK
Provides practice for grammar and mechanics lessons.

SPELLING PRACTICE BOOK
Provides practice with the word list and spelling patterns. Includes home involvement activities.

DAILY LANGUAGE ACTIVITIES
Sentence activities that provide brief, regular practice and reinforcement of grammar, mechanics, and usage skills. Available as blackline masters and transparencies.

WRITING PROCESS TRANSPARENCIES
Transparencies that model each stage of the writing process.

HANDWRITING HANDBOOKS
Available for instruction and practice.

McGraw-Hill School
TECHNOLOGY

Phonics CD-ROM
Provides extra phonics support.

interNET CONNECTION Extends lesson activities through research and inquiry ideas. Visit **www.mhschool.com/reading.**

Handwriting CD-ROM
WRITING Provides practice activities.

Resources for Meeting Individual Needs

	EASY	INDEPENDENT	CHALLENGE	LANGUAGE SUPPORT
BOOK 4				
The Shopping List	**Leveled Book:** *A Pet for Max* **Reteach,** 127–134 **Alternate Teaching Strategies,** T64–T76 ✏ **Writing:** Draw a Map, 37M–37N 💿 CD-ROM ⓘ Intervention	**Leveled Book:** *The Big Secret* **Practice,** 127–134 **Alternate Teaching Strategies,** T64–T76 ✏ **Writing:** Write an Ad, 37M–37N 💿 CD-ROM	**Leveled Book:** *Who Took the Farmer's Hat?* **Extend,** 127–134 ✏ **Writing:** Make a Journal Entry, 37M–37N 💿 CD-ROM	**Teaching Strategies,** 10A, 10C, 11, 13, 15, 16, 19, 23, 28, 30, 37N **Language Support,** 136–144 **Alternate Teaching Strategies,** T64–T76 ✏ **Writing:** Write a Letter, 37M–37N 💿 CD-ROM
Yasmin's Ducks	**Leveled Book:** *Spot's Trick* **Reteach,** 135–142 **Alternate Teaching Strategies,** T64–T76 ✏ **Writing:** Draw a Scene, 65M–65N 💿 CD-ROM ⓘ Intervention	**Leveled Book:** *Show and Tell Rose* **Practice,** 135–142 **Alternate Teaching Strategies,** T64–T76 ✏ **Writing:** Write a Plan, 65M–65N 💿 CD-ROM	**Leveled Book:** *My Best Friend* **Extend,** 135–142 ✏ **Writing:** Make a Journal Entry, 65M–65N 💿 CD-ROM	**Teaching Strategies,** 40A, 40C, 41, 47, 53, 57, 65N **Language Support,** 145–153 **Alternate Teaching Strategies,** T64–T76 ✏ **Writing:** Write a Letter, 65M–65N 💿 CD-ROM
The Knee-High Man	**Leveled Book:** *Fun Run* **Reteach,** 143–150 **Alternate Teaching Strategies,** T64–T76 ✏ **Writing:** Draw a Scene, 95M–95N 💿 CD-ROM ⓘ Intervention	**Leveled Book:** *A Bigger House for June* **Practice,** 143–150 **Alternate Teaching Strategies,** T64–T76 ✏ **Writing:** Record a Dream, 95M–95N 💿 CD-ROM	**Leveled Book:** *Pete's Chicken* **Extend,** 143–150 ✏ **Writing:** Make a Journal Entry, 95M–95N 💿 CD-ROM	**Teaching Strategies,** 68A, 68C, 69, 71, 79, 85, 95N **Language Support,** 154–162 **AlternateTeaching Strategies,** T64–T76 ✏ **Writing:** Write a Letter, 95M–95N 💿 CD-ROM
Johnny Appleseed	**Leveled Book:** *Fall Is Fun!* **Reteach,** 151–158 **Alternate Teaching Strategies,** T64–T76 ✏ **Writing:** Draw Contrasting Scenes, 123M–123N 💿 CD-ROM ⓘ Intervention	**Leveled Book:** *The Land* **Practice,** 151–158 **Alternate Teaching Strategies,** T64–T76 ✏ **Writing:** Write a Handbook, 123M–123N 💿 CD-ROM	**Leveled Book:** *Down by the Bay* **Extend,** 151–158 ✏ **Writing:** Make a Journal Entry, 123M–123N 💿 CD-ROM	**Teaching Strategies,** 98A, 98C, 99, 107, 109, 115, 116, 123N **Language Support,** 163–171 **Alternate Teaching Strategies,** T64–T76 ✏ **Writing:** Write a Letter, 123M–123N 💿 CD-ROM
Ring! Ring! Ring! Put Out the Fire!	**Review** **Reteach,** 159–166 **Alternate Teaching Strategies,** T64–T76 ✏ **Writing:** Draw a Fire Scene, 133M–133N 💿 CD-ROM ⓘ Intervention	**Review** **Practice,** 159–166 **Alternate Teaching Strategies,** T64–T76 ✏ **Writing:** Write About Fighting a Fire, 133M–133N 💿 CD-ROM	**Review** **Extend,** 159–166 ✏ **Writing:** Make a Journal Entry, 133M–133N 💿 CD-ROM	**Teaching Strategies,** 126A, 126C, 127, 133N **Language Support,** 172–180 **Alternate Teaching Strategies,** T64–T76 ✏ **Writing:** Write a Speech, 133M–133N 💿 CD-ROM

INFORMAL

Informal Assessment

- Phonics, 8J, 33, 37F, 37H; 38J, 61, 65F, 65H; 66J, 91, 95F, 95H; 96J, 119, 123F, 123H; 124J, 129
- Comprehension, 32, 33, 37J; 60, 61, 65J; 90, 91, 95J; 118, 119, 123J; 129, 133F, 133H
- Vocabulary, 37L, 65L, 95L, 123L, 133J, 133L

Performance Assessment

- Scoring Rubrics, 37N, 65N, 95N, 123N, 133N, 135F
- Research and Inquiry, 6J, 135
- Listening, Speaking, Viewing Activities, 8G, 8H, 10A, 10–37, 37D, 37M–N; 38G, 38H, 40A, 40–65, 65D, 65M–N; 66G, 66H, 68A, 68–95, 95D, 95M–N; 96G, 96H, 98A, 98–123, 123D, 123M–N; 124G, 124H, 126A, 126–133, 133D, 133M–N
- Portfolio, 37N, 65N, 95N, 123N, 133N
- Writing, 37M–N, 65M–N, 95M–N, 123M–N, 133M–N, 140A–F
- Fluency, 32, 60, 90, 118, 128

Leveled Practice

Practice, Reteach, Extend

- **Phonics and Decoding**
  Long *i: i-e,* 127, 131, 132, 140, 148, 159
  Long *o: o-e,* 135, 139, 140, 148, 156, 159
  Long *u: u-e,* 143, 147, 148, 156, 159
  Long *a: ay, ai,* 151, 155, 156, 159
- **Comprehension**
  Cause and Effect, 133, 141, 163
  Make Inferences, 149, 157, 164
- **Vocabulary Strategies**
  Inflectional Endings *-s, -es,* 134, 165
  Inflectional Ending *-ed,* 142, 165
  Inflectional Endings *-er, -est,* 150, 158, 166
- **Study Skills**
  Charts, 130, 138, 146, 154, 162

FORMAL

Selection Assessments

- **Skills and Vocabulary Words**
  The Shopping List, 61–64
  Yasmin's Ducks, 65–68
  The Knee-High Man, 69–72
  Johnny Appleseed, 73–76
  Ring! Ring! Ring! Put Out the Fire! 77–78

Unit 4 Test

- **Phonics and Decoding**
  Long *i: i-e*
  Long *o: o-e*
  Long *u: u-e*
  Long *a: ay, ai*
- **Comprehension**
  Cause and Effect
  Make Inferences
- **Vocabulary Strategies**
  Inflectional Endings *-s, -es*
  Inflectional Ending *-ed*
  Inflectional Endings *-er, -est*

Grammar and Spelling Assessment

- **Grammar**
  Verbs, 101, 107, 113, 119, 125, 127–128
- **Spelling**
  Words with Long *i: i-e,* 102
  Words with Long *o: o-e,* 108
  Words with Long *u: u-e,* 114
  Words with Long *a: ay, ai,* 120
  Words from Social Studies, 126
  Unit Assessment, 127–128

Diagnostic/Placement Evaluation

- Phonemic Awareness Assessment
- Placement Tests
- Informal Reading Inventories
- Running Records

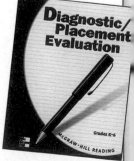

Test Preparation

- See also Test Power in Teacher's Edition, 37, 65, 95, 123, 133

- **Reading Test Generator** Assessment software

Assessment Checklist

Student .... Grade ....

Teacher ....

	The Shopping List	Yasmin's Ducks	The Knee-High Man	Johnny Appleseed	Put Out the Fire!	Assessment Summary
LISTENING/SPEAKING						
Participates in oral language experiences						
Listens and speaks to gain knowledge of culture						
Speaks appropriately to audiences for different purposes						
Communicates clearly						
READING						
Uses phonological awareness strategies, including						
• Identifying, segmenting, and combining strategies						
• Producing rhyming words						
• Identifying and isolating initial and final sounds						
Uses a variety of word identification strategies:						
• Phonics and decoding: long *i: i-e*						
• Phonics and decoding: long *o: o-e*						
• Phonics and decoding: long *u: u-e*						
• Phonics and decoding: long *a: ay, ai*						
• Inflectional Endings -s, -es						
• Inflectional Ending -ed						
• Inflectional Endings -er, -est						
Reads with fluency and understanding						
Reads widely for different purposes in varied sources						
Develops an extensive vocabulary						
Uses comprehension strategies: • Cause and Effect						
• Make Inferences						
Responds to various texts						
Analyzes the characteristics of various types of texts						
Conducts research using various sources: • Charts						
Reads to increase knowledge						
WRITING						
Writes for a variety of audiences and purposes						
Composes original texts using the conventions of written language such as capitalization and penmanship						
Spells proficiently						
Composes texts applying knowledge of grammar and usage						
Uses writing processes						
Evaluates own writing and writing of others						

+ Observed   − Not Observed

Introduce the Theme

Let's Find Out!

Looking for answers is an adventure.

DISCUSS THE THEME Write the theme Let's Find Out! on the board and have children read it aloud with you. Then read the theme statement to children. Have children discuss how they would go about finding answers to questions. Ask:

- How can looking for answers be an adventure?
- If you had a question, where would you start looking for answers?
- Who would you ask?
- What books would you look at?
- How would you use the computer to find answers?

SHARE A STORY Have children preview the unit by reading the table of contents and paging through the selections. Use the Big Book *Fish Faces* to help establish the unit

theme. Have children discuss how the book's presentation of so many different kinds of fish relates to the theme Let's Find Out!

PREVIEW UNIT SELECTIONS Have children preview the unit by reading the selection titles and looking at the illustrations. Ask:

- How do you think the stories, poems, and articles might relate to the theme?
- Which stories and illustrations look most interesting to you? Why?
- What do you see that might be a clue about what you'll be reading about?

As children proceed through the unit, encourage them to compare and contrast the characters, settings, and events that develop the unit theme Let's Find Out! Help children compare their original predictions with the actual literature.

THEME CONNECTIONS

Each of the five selections relates to the unit theme Let's Find Out! as well as to the global theme Inquiry. These thematic links will help children to make connections across texts.

The Shopping List People at a store help a boy recall what he was supposed to get.

Yasmin's Ducks A girl explains her interest in ducks to her friends.

The Knee-High Man A small man asks big animals how he can become big, too.

Johnny Appleseed A man helps settlers plant apple trees.

Ring! Ring! Ring! Put Out the Fire! Firefighting is an important job.

Research and Inquiry

Theme Project: Places to Explore Have small groups brainstorm lists of places they would like to find out about, such as a city or another planet. They will then choose a place as the basis for a project that will tell about the place, why they want to explore it, and what they hope to find out.

List What They Know Once children have picked a place to explore, have them list what they already know about it.

Ask Questions and Identify Resources Ask children to brainstorm some questions that tell what they want to know about the place they want to explore. Have them list possible resources. Remind children to take notes about any important details.

Create a Presentation When their research is complete, children will present their project to the class. Have children make a poster about their place, give a talk, or put on a play. Encourage children to use visuals.

QUESTIONS	POSSIBLE RESOURCES	ANSWERS
• What would it be like to walk on Mars? • How cold or hot is it there? • What does it look like there?	• Nonfiction books • Search on Internet	

See **Wrap Up the Theme,** page 135.

Research Strategies

As children search for information in various resources, emphasize the importance of taking notes. Share these note-taking tips:

- Create a research word web. In the middle circle, write the name of the place you'd like to explore. Then draw four larger circles, one in each of the four corners of your paper.

- Inside each circle, write something you have found out about your topic. Don't worry about complete sentences. Just jot down a few words to give the important facts. Writing it in your own words will help you remember it.

- In each circle, write the name of the book, CD-ROM, or Web site where you found your information.

- Keep your research word web. You may need to return to your notes as you develop your project.

interNET CONNECTION Students can learn more about storytelling by visiting **www.mhschool.com/reading**

6J

Poetry

Read the Poem

READ ALOUD Tell children that poems are often about people exploring, asking questions, or searching for answers. Read aloud "To the Top" by Sandra Liatsos. Afterward, ask:

- What kind of adventure is the author describing?
- What question does the poet ask about the adventure?
- How does the poem relate to the unit theme Let's Find Out!?

LISTENING LIBRARY The poem is available on **audiocassette** and on **compact disc.**

CHORAL READING Divide children into three groups to read the poem chorally. Talk about how the poet might feel (tired) and how children, as speakers, can use their voices to convey that to listeners.

Group 1:	lines 1 and 2
Group 2:	lines 3 and 4
Group 3:	lines 5 and 6
Together:	lines 7 and 8

Learn About Poetry

RHYTHM

Explain the following features of rhythm:

- Rhythm is the natural strong beat that some music or poetry has.
- A poet uses rhythm to convey different feelings or movements.
- Rhythm adds meaning to the words.
- The rhythm within a poem can change.
- Rhythm and rhyme are often used together in a poem to emphasize each other.

6

MEET THE POET

ABOUT SANDRA LIATSOS Sandra Liatsos lives in Pacific Palisades, California. Aside from her poetry for children, her work has appeared in numerous magazines, anthologies, and textbooks. She has also taught elementary school.

Let's Find Out

To the Top

We're climbing and climbing
The trail is so high
that I think we'll be climbing
right up to the sky.
I want it to end
and my poor feet to stop.
Oh, when will we reach
the mountaintop?

by Sandra Liatsos

7

Poetry

STEP TO THE RHYTHM Read "To the Top" to children, emphasizing the rhythm. Have children stomp or take make-believe "climbing" steps in time to the rhythm of the poem, slowing down as they get "tired," toward the end.

Oral Response

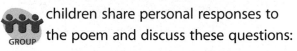

SMALL-GROUP DISCUSSIONS Have children share personal responses to the poem and discuss these questions:

- Why do you think the poet wants to get to the mountaintop? How will she feel when she gets there? What will she see at the top that she couldn't see at the bottom?

- What word does the poet repeat in the first line of the poem? Why do you think she repeats that word?

- When the poet says "I think I'll be climbing right up to the sky," what does she mean? Will she really reach the sky? Why do you think the poet chose these words?

- What places would you like to explore? Why?

RESPONDING TO POETRY

Ask children if they have ever taken a hike like the one described in the poem. Have children imagine themselves climbing a steep path. What kinds of things might they see along their way? What kinds of things would they take? Ask children to draw a picture showing themselves on such a hike. Have them write a sentence that tells about their picture.

Concept
- Shopping

Comprehension
- Cause and Effect

Phonics
- Long *i: i-e*

Vocabulary
- after
- always
- blue
- were
- who

Anthology

The Shopping List

Selection Summary Children will read about what happens when a boy forgets one item on his shopping list. With the help of other customers, the boy eventually remembers what he was supposed to get, but not before his father's store is turned upside down.

by Gary Apple
Illustrated by Shirley Beckes

Listening Library

Rhyme applies to Phonics

INSTRUCTIONAL pages 10–37

About the Author Gary Apple has always liked to write stories that are funny. "I like to write about things that make me laugh," he says. "I think that if something makes me laugh, then it will make other people laugh, too."

About the Illustrator Shirley Beckes is an illustrator of children's books, puzzles, and games. She and her husband live in Wisconsin, where they have their own design and illustration studio.

8A   *The Shopping List*

Same Concept, Skills and Vocabulary!

Leveled Books

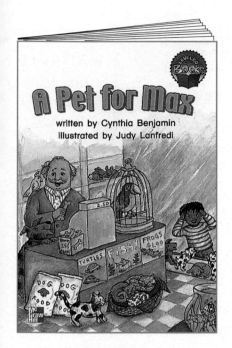

EASY
Lesson on pages 37A and 37D
`DECODABLE`

INDEPENDENT
Lesson on pages 37B and 37D

📖 *Take-Home version available*

`DECODABLE`

CHALLENGE
Lesson on pages 37C and 37D

Leveled Practice

EASY
Reteach, 127–134 Blackline masters with reteaching opportunities for each assessed skill

INDEPENDENT/ON-LEVEL
Practice, 127–134 Workbook with Take-Home Stories and practice opportunities for each assessed skill and story comprehension

CHALLENGE
Extend, 127–134 Blackline masters that offer challenge activities for each assessed skill

Quizzes Prepared by Accelerated Reader®

Center Activities

Social Studies . . .	Food Mural, *8D*
	Food Geography, *20*
Science	Recycling, *22*
Math	How Many, *8D*
	Shape Graphs, *12*
Music	Rhyme Song, *26*
Language Arts . .	Read Aloud, *8G*
Cultural Perspectives	Colors/Los Colores, *24*
Writing	A Food Label, *34*
Research and Inquiry	Find Out More, *35*
Internet Activities	www.mhschool.com/reading

Center Activities

Each of these activities takes 15-20 minutes.

Phonics

Build Long *i* Words

 Objective: Substitute consonants to build long *i* words.

◆ Have partners write "___ i ___ e" on paper.

◆ Children use the cards to build long *i* words.

◆ They may also draw pictures of the words, if appropriate.

MATERIALS
- Phonics Letter Cards (consonants) from the Word Building Manipulative Cards
- Crayons
- Construction paper

Writing

Food Favorites

Objective: Write and illustrate sentences about a favorite food.

◆ Display this sentence frame in the center: "My favorite food is _____."

◆ Have children draw a picture of themselves enjoying their favorite food.

◆ Children then use the frame to write a sentence below their drawing.

MATERIALS
- Drawing paper
- Crayons

Reading and Listening

Independent/Self-Selected Reading

 Objective: Listen and use illustrations to understand a story.

Fill the Center with books and corresponding audiocassettes or CD-ROMs children have read or listened to this week. You can also include books from the Theme Bibliography on pages T98 and T99.

Leveled Readers

◆ *A Pet for Max* by Cynthia Benjamin
◆ *The Big Secret* by Tim Kane
◆ *Who Took the Farmer's Hat?* by Joan L. Nodset

◆ Theme Big Book *Fish Faces* by Norbert Wu

◆ *The Shopping List* by Gary Apple

◆ "To the Top" by Sandra Liatsos

◆ Phonics Practice Reader, Vol. 2

Working with Words

Read and Find

Objective: Reinforce vocabulary words: *after, always, blue, were, who*

MATERIALS
- *The Shopping List* in the Student Anthology

◆ Display the words on paper.

◆ Have partners identify the sentences in the story that include the words.

◆ The child who finds and reads aloud each sentence first wins a point.

after
always
blue
were
who

Social Studies

Food Mural

Objective: Label food pictures for a class collage.

MATERIALS
- Mural paper
- Magazines
- Glue
- Crayons

◆ Display paper with the heading "Foods We Eat."

◆ Children look through magazines for photographs of foods.

◆ Then they classify the foods in categories of their choice and add their pictures to the collage.

Math 3+2

How Many?

Objective: Conduct an experiment and record results

MATERIALS
- Paper
- Dry cereal
- Small pretzels
- Measuring cup
- Construction paper

◆ Have partners measure out 1/4 or 1/2 of a cup of cereal and place it on a sheet of construction paper.

◆ Partners estimate and record the number of cereal pieces.

◆ Then children count and record the actual number of pieces.

◆ Repeat with the small pretzel twists.

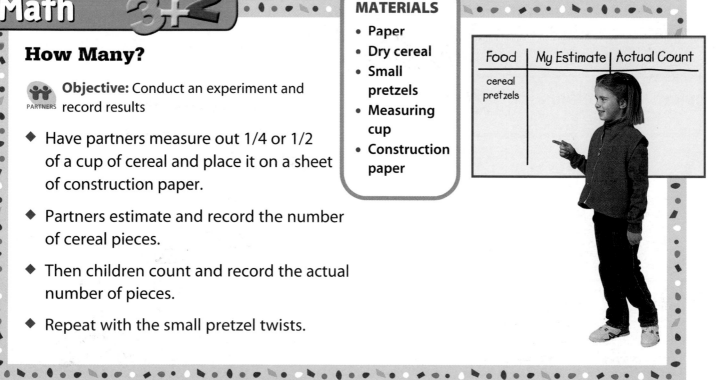

Food	My Estimate	Actual Count
cereal pretzels		

The Shopping List

READING AND LANGUAGE ARTS	**DAY 1** *Focus on Reading and Skills*	**DAY 2** *Read the Literature*
● **Phonics Daily Routines**	Daily Routine: Blending, 8J CD-ROM	Daily Routines: Segmenting, 10A CD-ROM

● **Phonological Awareness**
 	
● **Phonics** *Long i*
 	
● **Comprehension**
 	
● **Vocabulary**
 	
● **Study Skills**
 	
● **Listening, Speaking, Viewing, Representing**
	Read Aloud, 8G
	  "General Store"
	
	Develop Phonological Awareness, 8H
	
	☑ **Introduce Long *i: i-e*,** 8I–8J
	Reteach, Practice, Extend, 127
	Phonics/Phonemic Awareness Practice Book, 139–142
	
	 Apply Long *i: i–e*, 8/9
	  "Wish List"

	 **Intervention Program**
		Build Background, 10A
		  Develop Oral Language
		
		Vocabulary, 10B–10C
		<table><tr><td>after</td><td>always</td><td>blue</td></tr><tr><td>were</td><td>who</td><td></td></tr></table>**Teaching Chart 94**
		Word Building Manipulative Cards
		Reteach, Practice, Extend, 128
		
		 Read the Selection, 10-33
		  Guided Instruction
		    ☑ **Long *i: i-e***
		
		Genre: Story, 11
		
		Cultural Perspectives, 24
		
		Writer's Craft, 30

● **Curriculum Connections**	**Link** Language Arts, 8G	**Activity** Social Studies, 10A
● **Writing**	✏ **Writing Prompt:** Write about a time you went shopping. Tell how you found where everything was.	✏ **Writing Prompt:** Imagine that you were once a clerk in a store. Write about a child you watched shopping. **Journal Writing** Quick-Write, 33

● **Grammar**	**Introduce the Concept: *Was* and *Were*,** 37O
	  Daily Language Activity: Use *was* and *were* correctly.
	Grammar Practice Book, 97
		Teach the Concept: *Was* and *Were*, 37O
		  Daily Language Activity: Use *was* and *were* correctly.
		Grammar Practice Book, 98

● **Spelling** *Long i*	**Pretest: Words with Long *i: i-e*,** 37Q **Spelling Practice Book,** 97–98	**Explore the Pattern: Words with Long *i: i-e*,** 37Q **Spelling Practice Book,** 99

 ✔ = **Skill Assessed in Unit Test**

  Intervention Program Available

 **Read EVERY DAY**

DAY **3** *Read the Literature*	DAY **4** *Build Skills*	DAY **5** *Build Skills*

Daily  Phonics Routine:
Writing, 35

 **Phonics CD-ROM**

Daily Phonics Routine:
Fluency, 37F

Phonics CD-ROM

Daily Phonics Routine:
Rhyming, 37H

Phonics CD-ROM

Reread for Fluency, 32

Story Questions, 34
Reteach, Practice, Extend, 129

Story Activities, 35

Study Skill, 36

✔ **Charts**
Teaching Chart 95
Reteach, Practice, Extend, 130

 Read the Leveled Books, Guided Reading
✔ Long *i: i-e*
✔ High-Frequency Words

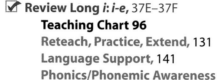 **Read the Leveled Books and Self-Selected Books**

✔ **Review Long *i: i-e*,** 37E–37F
Teaching Chart 96
Reteach, Practice, Extend, 131
Language Support, 141
Phonics/Phonemic Awareness
Practice Book, 139–142

✔ **Review *i-e, a-e*,** 37G–37H
Teaching Chart 97
Reteach, Practice, Extend, 132
Language Support, 142
Phonics/Phonemic Awareness
Practice Book, 139–142

Minilessons, 13, 17, 19, 23, 25, 27, 29

 Read Self-Selected Books

✔ **Introduce Cause and Effect,** 37I–37J
Teaching Chart 98
Reteach, Practice, Extend, 133
Language Support, 143

✔ **Review Inflectional Endings *-s, -es*,** 37K–37L
Teaching Chart 99
Reteach, Practice, Extend, 134
Language Support, 144

Listening, Speaking, Viewing, Representing, 37N
Illustrate the List
Convince the Class

Minilessons, 13, 17, 19, 23, 25, 27, 29

 Intervention Program

 Intervention Program

 Intervention Program

Activity Math, 8D, 12
Social Studies, 8D, 20

Activity Science, 22

Activity Music, 26

 Writing Prompt: Write a story about a cat who went to a store with a shopping list. What was the cat like? What did it buy?

 Journal Writing, 37D

Writing Prompt: Describe a holiday gift you bought for someone.

Writing that Compares, 37M
Prewrite, Draft

Meeting Individual Needs for Writing, 37N

Writing Prompt: Pretend you once stayed overnight in a store when nobody else was there. Write a story about how you felt and what you did.

Writing that Compares, 37M
Revise, Edit, Proofread, Publish

Review and Practice: *Was* and *Were*, 37P
Daily Language Activity: Use *was* and *were* correctly.

Grammar Practice Book, 99

Review and Practice: *Was* and *Were*, 37P
Daily Language Activity: Use *was* and *were* correctly.

Grammar Practice Book, 100

Assess and Reteach: *Was* and *Were*, 37P
Daily Language Activity: Use *was* and *were* correctly.

Grammar Practice Book, 101–102

Practice and Extend: Words with Long *i: i-e*, 37R

Spelling Practice Book, 100

Proofread and Write: Words with Long *i: i-e*, 37R

Spelling Practice Book, 101

Assess: Words with Long *i: i-e*, 37R

Spelling Practice Book, 102

Read Aloud

General Store
a poem by Rachel Field

Someday I'm going to have a
    store
With a tinkly bell hung over the
    door,
With real glass cases and coun-
    ters wide
And drawers all spilly with
    things inside.
There'll be a little of everything:
Bolts of calico; balls of string;
Jars of peppermint; tins of tea;
Pots and kettles and crockery;

Seeds in packets; scissors bright;
Kegs of sugar, brown and white;
Sarsaparilla for picnic lunches,
Bananas and rubber boots in
    bunches.
I'll fix the window and dust each
    shelf,
And take the money all in
    myself,
It will be my store and I will say:
"What can I do for you to-day?"

Oral Comprehension

LISTENING AND SPEAKING Motivate children to think about setting by reading this poem in which the poet imagines having a general store. Ask children to picture the store and everything in it as you read the poem aloud. When you are done, ask: "Where does the poem take place? What are some things that are in the store? Would you like to have a store like that? Why or why not?"

Activity Ask children to draw the scene described in "General Store." Help children by bringing in pictures of items with which they may not be familiar, such as calico. Encourage them to include as many details as they can from the poem. When children have finished, have them compare their pictures. ▶ **Visual**

GENRE STUDY: POEM Explain to children that a poem is a type of writing with lines that sometimes rhyme. In a poem, words are often chosen because of how they sound as well as because of what they mean. As you read the poem aloud, ask children to listen for interesting words, such as *tinkly* and *Sarsaparilla*.

Develop Phonological Awareness

Blend Sounds **Phonemic Awareness**

MATERIALS
- Phonics Picture Posters

Teach Tell children you will say some sounds. Tell them to help you blend the sounds together to say a word. Say: /k/-/ī/-/t/. *Let's say the sounds together—kite.* Hold up the Phonics Picture Poster for *kite* and have children say the word with you. Repeat using the Phonics Picture Poster for *nine*.

Practice Say the individual sounds for the following words and have children blend the sounds to say the words: *chime, dine, five, hide, mine, ripe, tide,* and vine.

Segment Sounds **Phonemic Awareness**

MATERIALS
- colored blocks (four per child)

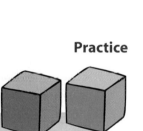

Teach Say the word *slide*. Tell children you are going to count the number of sounds in the word *slide*. Say the sounds /s/-/l/-/ī/-/d/ and place a block to show each sound in a row. Tell children the word *slide* has four sounds in a row.

Practice Have children practice segmenting the sounds in the following words: *bribe, dime, file, fine, hide, grime, nine, slime,* and *spine*. Then have them identify where they hear the /ī/ sound in each word by holding up the correct block.

Delete Sounds **Phonemic Awareness**

MATERIALS
- puppet
- Phonics Picture Card (star)

Teach Have the puppet say: *I'm thinking of something that shines in the sky. It is a _tar. Instead of* star, *I left out the |s| sound and said _tar.* Display the Phonics Picture Card for *star* and have children say the following with you: *star, tar.* Repeat with *bread.*

Practice Have volunteers continue the game by giving clues and saying the answer without its beginning sound. As you call on each volunteer, whisper one of the following words in his or her ear: *drive* (rive), *prize* (rize), *slide* (lide), *bread* (read), *plum* (lum), *smile* (mile), *crown* (rown), *blue* (lue).

INFORMAL ASSESSMENT Observe children as they blend sounds, segment sounds, and delete initial phonemes. If children have difficulty, see Alternate Teaching Strategies on page T64.

OBJECTIVES

Children will:

- identify long *i: i-e* words.
- blend and read long *i: i-e* words.
- review consonants, blends, and digraphs.
- learn strategies for decoding multisyllabic words.

MATERIALS

- letter cards, long *i* cards, and word building boxes from the **Word Building Manipulative Cards**

Skills Finder

Long *i: i-e*

Introduce	B4: 8I-J
Review	B4: 37E-F, 37G-H, 65G-H, 95G-H, 124I-J
Test	Book 4

SPELLING/PHONICS CONNECTIONS

Words with long *i-e*: See the 5-Day Spelling Plan, pages 37Q–37R.

TEACHING TIP

MULTISYLLABIC WORDS Write and say the word *shopping*. Explain that *shopping* has two parts or syllables. Explain that each syllable has a vowel sound. Model clapping out the parts or syllables in the word. Then have children clap the syllables. Cover *ping* and read *shop*. Cover *shop* and read *ping*. Repeat with: *chopping, slipping,* and *clipping*.

81   *The Shopping List*

Introduce **Long *i: i-e***

> **TEACH**

Identify *i-e* as a Symbol for /ī/   Let children know they will learn to read words with the letters *i-e* where the letter *i* sounds like /ī/ and the *e* on the end is silent.

- Display the *i-e* letter card. Point to the *i* and say /ī/.
- Explain to children that a consonant needs to go in the space between the two letters.

BLENDING
Model and Guide Practice with Long *i-e* Words

- Point to the *i* on the letter card, say /ī/, and have children repeat after you.
- Place the *p* letter card on the space between the *i* and the *e*.
- Point to the letters as you blend the sounds to read *ipe*. Have children repeat after you.

- Place the *r* letter card in front of the letter *i*.
- Have children blend the sounds and read the word *ripe* with you as you move your hand below the word. Remind children that the final *e* is silent.

Use the Word in Context
- Use the word in context to reinforce its meaning. Example: *The ripe apples fell from the tree.*

Repeat the Procedure   Use the following words to continue modeling and guided practice with long *i: i-e*.

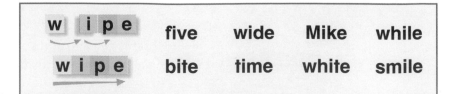

	five	wide	Mike	while
	bite	time	white	smile

Daily Routines

PRACTICE

LETTER SUBSTITUTION
Build Long *i-e* Words with Letter Cards

GROUP

Display the *i-e* letter card. Point to the *i* and say /ī/. Remind children that the *e* is silent. Add a *t* between the *i* and *e*, and a *k* at the beginning. Build and read the word *kite,* then ask children to read it. Continue by having children substitute letters and build, read, and write the following words: *bite, bike, like, life, wife, wipe, dive.*

▶**Linguistic/Kinesthetic**

ASSESS/CLOSE

Read and Write Long *i-e* Words

To assess children's ability to blend and read long *i-e* words, observe them as they build and read the words in the Practice activity. Have children write a sentence using one of the words.

ADDITIONAL PHONICS RESOURCES

Phonics/Phonemic Awareness Practice Book, pages 139–142

PHONICS KIT
Hands-on Activities and Practice

McGraw-Hill School
TECHNOLOGY

Phonics CD-ROM
activities for practice with Blending and Segmenting

Meeting Individual Needs for Phonics

EASY	ON-LEVEL	CHALLENGE

EASY

Name_____ Date_____ Reteach **127**

Long *i*: *i-e*

Read the sentence.
Would you **like** to **bite** a **lime**?

Circle the word that completes the sentence. Then write the word.

1. I _____smile_____ when I am glad.
   (smile) bite gripe

2. He _____likes_____ to write letters.
   (likes) times lives

3. I like her _____white_____ dress.
   mile drive (white)

4. My cat had _____five_____ kittens.
   rice bride (five)

Book 1.4
The Shopping List   **At Home:** Say a long *i* word, such as **wipe**. Have children name words that rhyme with it such as **pipe** or **stripe**.   127

ON-LEVEL

Name_____ Date_____ Practice **127**

Long *i*: *i-e*

Use the words in the box to answer the riddles.

five	smile	time	bike	ripe

1. Six is after me. What am I? ___five___

2. You do this with your lips. What am I? ___smile___

3. A good plum is this way. What am I? ___ripe___

4. A clock tells you about me. What am I? ___time___

5. You can ride me. What am I? ___bike___

Book 1.4
The Shopping List   **At Home:** Have children make up sentences using each of the words in the box.   127

CHALLENGE

Name_____ Date_____ Extend **127**

Long *i*: *i-e*

Read the words in the box. Find them in the puzzle. Circle them.

like	white	ride	ripe	Mike	nine	smile

```
A N I N E N O
M I K E E I M
I R I D E K L
V F R I P E X
E C W H I T E
L I K E O C P
S M I L E Z A
```

Choose a word from the box. Write a sentence with that word.

Answers will vary but should include a word from the box.

Think of your own **i-e** word. Use it in a sentence.

Possible answers include price, pile, and lime.

Book 1.4
The Shopping List   **At Home:** Write -ile, -ipe, -ike, -ive, -ike, and -ile on separate cards. Take turns picking cards and filling in letters to create new words. Example: -ipe, pipe; and -ile, bile.   127

Reteach, 127   Practice, 127   Extend, 127

OBJECTIVES

Children will read a poem with words containing long *i: i-e*.

Apply Long *i: i-e*

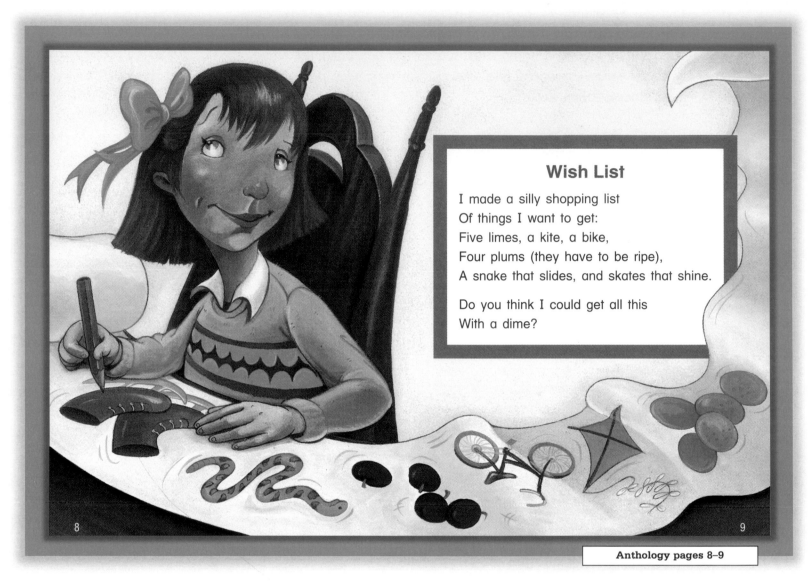

Wish List

I made a silly shopping list
Of things I want to get:
Five limes, a kite, a bike,
Four plums (they have to be ripe),
A snake that slides, and skates that shine.

Do you think I could get all this
With a dime?

Anthology pages 8–9

Read and Build Fluency

READ THE POEM Tell children they will now read a poem called *Wish List*. Model reading the alliterative words in the fifth line. Model asking the question at the end. Track print with your finger. Have children read with you.

REREAD FOR FLUENCY Have children pretend the poem is their "wish list." Tell them to do repeated readings of the poem.

READ A DECODABLE STORY For additional practice reading and to develop fluency, have children read *Mike and Ike* from **Phonics Practice Reader, Vol. 2.**

Dictate and Spell

DICTATE WORDS Segment the word *five* into its three individual sounds. Repeat the word aloud and use it in a sentence: *I want five limes.* Then have children say the word and write the letter or letters that represent each sound until they make the entire word. Repeat with *limes, kite, bike, ripe, slides, shine,* and *dime* from the poem. Then repeat with long *i* words not from the poem, such as: *bite, chime, dive, fire, hike, line, quite, side, smile, wipe,* and *wire.*

i Intervention Skills Intervention Guide,
Book A, for direct instruction and extra practice in Long *i: i-e*

Build Background

ial Studies

Concept: Shopping

Evaluate Prior Knowledge

CONCEPT: SHOPPING Ask children to share their experiences going to the grocery store. Use the following activity to give them more information about grocery shopping.

MAKE A SHOPPING LIST Help children record items they would like to buy at the grocery store. Work with children to categorize their items. For example, list all dairy products together, fruits, etc.

▶ **Visual/ Linguistic**

DRAW A PICTURE Invite children to draw pictures of something they would like to get at the grocery store. Encourage them to use the list for ideas. Have children label drawings with the sentence: *I like to get ___ at the store.*

Develop Oral Language

CONNECT WORDS AND ACTIONS Have

ESL children follow simple instructions to act out a trip to the grocery store. For example:

- *Write a list.*
- *Drive to the store.*
- *Push the cart.*
- *Pay the money.*

Encourage children to talk about their trip as they act it out. Ask:

- *What are you doing?*
- *Where are you right now?*
- *Who are you paying?*

▶ **Kinesthetic/Linguistic**

DAILY Phonics ROUTINES

DAY 2 **Letter Substitution** Give children the *i-e* an consonant letter cards. Say *dime* aloud and show how to build the word. Have children listen to the sounds and replace consonant cards to build the words *time* and *hive.*

Phonics CD-ROM

LANGUAGE SUPPORT

To build more background, see pages 136–139 in the **Language Support Book.**

OBJECTIVES

Children will:

- identify high-frequency words *after, blue, always, were,* and *who.*

MATERIALS

- Teaching Chart 94
- Word Building Manipulative Cards *after, blue, always, were, who*

TEACHING TIP

The following chart indicates words from the upcoming story that children have learned to decode as well as high-frequency words that have been taught in this lesson.

Decodable		High-Frequency
five	while	after
Mike	time	always
ripe	wide	blue
smile		were
		who

SPELLING/VOCABULARY CONNECTIONS

The words *after, blue, were,* and *who* are Challenge Words. See page 37Q for Day 1 of the 5-Day Spelling Plan.

---

after

blue

always

were

who

Vocabulary
High-Frequency Words

Shopping

I always take a shopping list.
It helps me not forget.
I got red grapes. I got blue plums.
But I'm not finished yet.
Milk and chips were jotted down.
And after them, a bun.
Who gets to eat this soup I got?
I bet it will be good and hot.
I like my shopping list a lot.
Shopping is such fun!

Teaching Chart 94

Auditory

LISTEN TO WORDS Without displaying it, read aloud "Shopping" on **Teaching Chart 94.** Ask children to imagine what other things were on the poet's shopping list. Then have them talk about their own experiences shopping with a list.

FIND ANTONYMS FOR HIGH-FREQUENCY WORDS Have children aurally identify each high-frequency word using the following activity:

- Say aloud one of the high-frequency words. Read a line of the poem where the word appears.

- Ask children if they can think of a word that means the opposite of the high-frequency word. (always/never, were/weren't, after/before) Then have them use the words in a sentence.

- Repeat this activity with other high-frequency words.

Visual

READ WORDS Display "Shopping" on **Teaching Chart 94.** Read the poem, tracking the print with your finger. Next, point to and say the word *after.* Ask children to hold up the vocabulary card for *after* and say it. Repeat with *blue, always, were,* and *who.* Hold up a vocabulary card for each word. Have volunteers read the words and circle them on the chart.

Word Building Manipulative Cards

MAKING A SHOPPING LIST OF WORDS

GROUP Have each group make a shopping list of the vocabulary words. Then put the vocabulary cards in different places in the room. Have groups go "shopping" for the cards.

Activities

Word Wall

Jar of Words Write the word wall words on slips of paper and put the papers in a jar. Give the jar to a child, and have him or her draw a slip of paper from the jar and read the word. The child sitting next to the "reader" points to the word on the Word Wall. Have the "pointer" place the paper back in the jar, and then draw the next word.

Clap it Out To help children practice spelling the word wall words, say a word from the Word Wall. Say the first letter in the word. Then tell children you will clap for each of the remaining letters in the word. Ask volunteers to finish the spelling of the word, clapping as they say each letter.

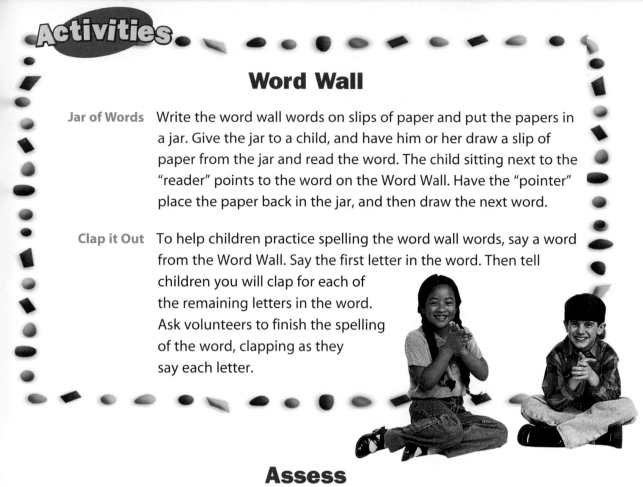

LANGUAGE SUPPORT

To help children develop understanding and recognition of high-frequency words, see page 136 in the **Language Support Book.**

Assess

Word Train Have children stand in line and form a train. The train moves around the room, with each child stopping at the teacher "station." At the station, the teacher asks each child to spell a word. The train continues until each child has a turn.

Meeting Individual Needs for Vocabulary

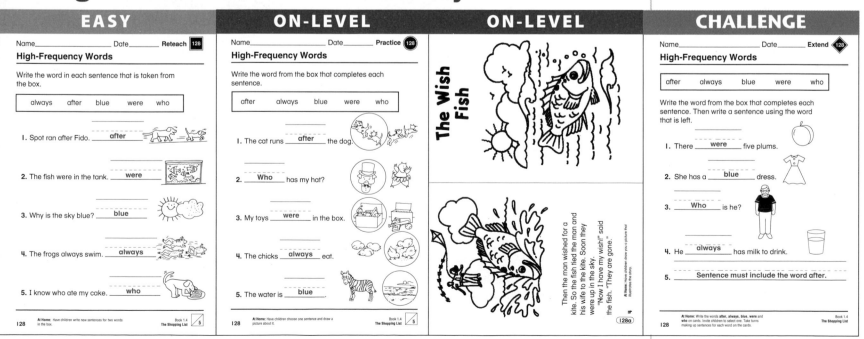

EASY	ON-LEVEL	ON-LEVEL	CHALLENGE
Reteach, 128	Practice, 128	Practice, 128a Take-Home Story	Extend, 128

Comprehension

Prereading Strategies

PREVIEW AND PREDICT Point to and read aloud the names of the author and the illustrator. Take a **picture walk** to discuss what children see, stopping after eight or ten pages. Using words from the story, talk about the illustrations. Point out a few long *i: i-e* words as you go *(Mike, ripe)*. Have children make predictions about the story. Discuss questions such as these:

• Who do you think the story is about?

• What do you think is going to happen?

Chart children's predictions about plot and character and read them aloud.

PREDICTIONS	WHAT HAPPENED
The story is about a boy.	
People try to help the boy remember what he forgot.	

SET PURPOSES Ask children what they want to find out by reading the story. For example:

• Why does the store get so untidy?

• What did the boy forget?

READ TOGETHER

Meet Gary Apple

When Gary Apple was a little boy, he liked to write funny stories. Now that he is grown up, he still likes to write funny stories. Today, he writes funny books, plays, and TV shows.

Meet Shirley Bec

Shirley Beckes is an illustrator of children's books, puzzles, and gam She owns her own design studio in Wisconsin.

10

Meeting Individual Needs • Grouping Suggestions for Strategic Reading

EASY	ON-LEVEL	CHALLENGE
Shared Reading Read the story aloud as you model directionality and track print with your finger. Invite children to join in on words and phrases they recognize. As you read each page, discuss the illustrations.	**Guided Instruction** Read the story with children, using the Comprehension questions. Monitor any reading difficulties that children have in order to determine which parts of the Comprehension section to emphasize. After reading the story with children, have them reread it, using the rereading suggestions on page 32.	**Independent Reading** Have children set purposes before they read. After reading, have children retell the story. Children can use the questions on page 34 for a group discussion.

The Shopping List

by Gary Apple

illustrated by Shirley Beckes

11

Comprehension

☑ **Phonics** Long *i: i-e*

STRATEGIC READING Tell children that paying attention to what characters say in a story will help them understand what happens. Explain that they will use a map of a grocery store to keep track of the information in the story.

① We are going to read *The Shopping List* by Gary Apple. Do you think Mr. Apple used his own experiences in grocery stores to write this book? Now let's read about Shirley Beckes. Do you think she visited grocery stores to plan her illustrations? *Concept of a Book: Author/Illustrator*

② Do people in your family write lists? Why do you think it is a good idea? (You won't forget things.) *Make Connections*

Genre

Story

Remind children that a story:

- is a fictional piece containing the elements of character, plot, and setting.
- focuses on one or more characters who must solve a problem.

Activity After reading *The Shopping List*, discuss the setting of this story. Have volunteers tell about their own experiences shopping at grocery stores. Ask children to compare how the store in the story is alike or different from the stores they have been in. Have children identify the different areas of the store they see in the story.

LANGUAGE SUPPORT

A blackline master for a map of a grocery store can be found in the **Language Support Book.** Children will draw items on the different types of shelves shown.

LANGUAGE SUPPORT, 140

11

Comprehension

3 **Phonics** **LONG i: i-e** "One day . . . " the next word looks like it might be someone's name. Let's see what it is. I'm going to read it as a long *i*, silent *e* word. I can say the letter sounds and blend them together: M i k(e) Mike. The name is *Mike.* *Graphophonic Cues*

4 Look at the picture. Why do you think Mike is holding a list? (It is probably a shopping list. He will use it to remember what he wants to buy at the store.) *Make Inferences*

5 Why did Mike go to the store? (to shop for his mom) Why did he find Dad there? (It's his dad's store.) *Analyze Plot and Character*

TEACHING TIP

MANAGEMENT When you use the Math activity below, if containers are limited, children can work in pairs or in small groups. You may also invite volunteers to draw and label their own containers (box or can).

3

4

5 12

One day Mike went to his dad's store with a list.

Activity

Cross Curricular: Math

SHAPE GRAPHS Display empty food boxes and cans of various sizes.

• Have children name each shape as you sort it: *This is a ___.* (box/can)

• Make a graph on the chalkboard to show how many of each shape. Use the graph to talk about *more, fewer.*

Activity Make a grid on the floor with a large piece of paper and a marker. Have each child select one of the empty containers. Invite children to create a floor graph to show whether more boxes or more cans were chosen.

▶ **Visual/Spatial**

Dad was always glad to see Mike.

"Hi, there, Mike!" said Dad with a grin.

"Hi!" said Mike. "Mom sent me to get some things."

13

Comprehension

6 What can you tell about Dad from the way his store looks? (He's neat; he works hard; he likes things to look nice and tidy.) *Analyze Character/Use Illustrations*

7 Why is Dad grinning? (He's glad to see Mike.) *Cause and Effect*

Minilesson

REVIEW/MAINTAIN

Blends

Tell children you want to play a game called "What is the beginning? What is the ending?" Tell them you will say a word and ask one of the two questions. Use the following words:

- *list (st)*
- *glad (gl)*
- *grin (gr)*
- *sent (nt)*

Once children identify the blend, write the word on the board and underline the blend.

Activity Write a sentence on the board using the blend words and ask children to find the blends.

LANGUAGE SUPPORT

ESL Help children with the concept of *always* by contrasting it with *sometimes* and *never*. Use the three words orally in context. Invite children to make up sentences or stories using the words. Examples: *I always brush my teeth at night. Sometimes I also take a shower. My dog never takes a shower. She always shakes off the water when she's wet.*

Have children draw pictures to illustrate their sentences or stories.

13

Comprehension

8 **Phonics** **LONG** *i: i-e* There are some long *i* words on this page. The first one is *Mike*. Let's look at the last sentence. Who can spot the first long *i* word? Let's blend the sounds to read it: f i v(e) five. Now let's blend the other long *i* word: r i p(e) ripe. *Graphophonic Cues*

p/i **VOCABULARY STRATEGIES** Point to the word in the first sentence that tells what Mike is doing. *(checked)* What is the root word of *checked*? *(check)* Semantic Cues

Mike checked his list. "Let's see," he said. "Mom wants me to get jam and rice.

8 She needs five ripe plums, too."

14

---

p/i **PREVENTION/INTERVENTION**

VOCABULARY STRATEGIES Help children decode *-ed* words by reminding them that the *-ed* ending signals time: it says that an action happened in the past. The rest of the word tells the action. Write *-ed* words and ask children to find and read the action word with the *-ed* ending. Then have them read the whole word. Examples: *asked (ask), mixed (mix), locked (lock), bumped (bump), thanked (thank).* Semantic Cues

Dad got the rice, the jam, and the five ripe plums.
"Thanks a lot!" said Mike.
Mike packed them in a big bag.

15

Comprehension

9 Why did Dad get the rice, jam, and plums? (Mike asked for them; Mom wanted them.) ***Cause and Effect***

10 Why do rice and jam come in containers? (It makes them easier to carry.) Why is Mike's dad putting the plums in a bag? (to make them easier to carry) Why don't plums come in a container? (so customers can buy the exact number they want; fresh fruit might spoil more quickly) ***Make Connections***

11 Now it's time to draw the rice, jam, and five plums on our map of Dad's grocery store. Look at the illustration. Who can tell me where the rice, jam, and plums should go? ***Use Illustrations/Story Props***

LANGUAGE SUPPORT

ESL The long *i* sound may be difficult for some children to identify. Reinforce the sound of long *i* by giving children rhyming words. Write these words on the chalkboard: *bike, hike, like, Mike, spike, strike*. Let children say or chant pairs of words together.

15

Comprehension

 Which sentence helps us know why Mike cannot remember what Mom wants? (*"I didn't write it down."*) *Cause and Effect*

 How do you think Mike is feeling? (He is puzzled/upset/confused because he forgot what Mom wants.) *Make Inferences*

"There was something else I had to get," said Mike

"What is it?" asked Dad.

 "I didn't write it down," said Mike. "I can't remember now."

16

"I can help you," said Dad. "Did Mom ask for fresh fish?"

"No, it was not fish," said Mike.

14

17

Comprehension

14 What does Dad think that Mike forgot? (fish) Why are the fish lying on ice? (so they will stay fresh) Find the fish section on your map of Dad's store. Draw some fish in the empty space. *Make Connections/Story Props*

P/i **BLENDING SHORT *i* WORDS** What short *i* words can you read on this page? *(did, it, fish)* Graphophonic Cues

Minilesson

REVIEW/MAINTAIN

Make Inferences

Remind children that they can look at people's expressions and actions to learn more about what is happening in a story.

• How do you think Dad is feeling? (glad/happy) How does the picture help you know? (Dad is smiling. He has his arm around Mike.)

• Mike seems proud of his dad in the picture. Why do you think so? (Dad can help; Dad owns a clean and tidy store.)

Activity Have children draw a picture of someone feeling happy, sad, angry, or scared. Have children label the pictures and display them under the appropriate heading on the bulletin board.

P/i **PREVENTION/INTERVENTION**

BLENDING SHORT *i* WORDS
Review with children the sound of short *i*. Then write the word *fish* on the chalkboard. Review the blending process as you run your finger under the sounds in the word f i sh fish.

Then give children short *i* word cards and ask them to work in pairs. One child shows a word card and the other blends the sounds to read the word aloud. Have children take turns. Examples: *wish, this, hid, lick.* *Graphophonic Cues*

Comprehension

15 What foods do you see here? (grapes, strawberries, apples, oranges, bananas, pears) **Where would you see these in a grocery store?** (in the fruit section) *Use Picture Clues*

15 "Well, did Mom want you to get some grapes?" asked Dad.

"No, she didn't ask for grapes," said Mike.

18

"Is it punch? Is it milk? Is it something to drink?" **17**
asked Dad.

"No. It was not something to drink," said Mike.

19

Comprehension

16 Is Dad taking the containers out of the case or putting them back in? (taking them out) Why do you think so? (He is showing them to Mike.) *Make Inferences*

17 Which new foods does Dad think Mike is forgetting? (grapes, milk, punch) Where do these go in the grocery store? (in the fruit section; in the cooler) Find the fruit section on your map and draw in some grapes. Then find a section for drinks and draw in some milk and punch. *Story Props*

Minilesson

REVIEW/MAINTAIN

Short *a, i, o, u*

Have children identify and sort short *a, i, o, u* words on this page. Ask them to find:

- 2 short *a* words (asked, Dad)
- 5 short *i* words (is, it, milk, drink, something)
- 1 short *o* word (not)
- 1 short *u* word (punch)

Activity Ask children to draw a picture of four things they like to eat or drink that have the short *a, i, o,* and *u* sound. Have them label their pictures.

Phonics CD-ROM Have children use the interactive activities for reinforcement of these short vowels.

LANGUAGE SUPPORT

ESL As you read through the story, have children identify the areas of the store on their maps of Dad's grocery store. Use this opportunity to build vocabulary about food and other grocery store items.

Comprehension

18 How does Miss Lin know that something is "going on"? (Mike's expression)
Make Inferences

19 What does the word *can't* tell us in the third sentence? (Mike is unable to remember.)

Ⓢ ELF-MONITORING STRATEGY

REREAD Remind children that rereading part of the story can help them understand the main idea.

MODEL I read that Miss Lin came in and asked what was going on. She can see that Mike and Dad are upset. Then she says, "Maybe I can help." I don't remember how she knows what is going on. Oh, I see. Dad says, "Mike can't remember what he came to get." So Dad explains the problem to Miss Lin.

18

Just then, Miss Lin came in.

"What's going on?" she asked.

19 "Mike can't remember what he came to get," said Dad.

20

Activity

Cross Curricular: Social Studies

FOOD GEOGRAPHY Explain that many foods we think of as ordinary are not native to North America. Potatoes come from South America. Rice was first grown in Asia. Broccoli is native to Europe. Peanuts are from Africa. Help children find these continents on a map or globe.

▶ **Visual/Linguistic**

RESEARCH AND INQUIRY Let children look through cookbooks and other books and magazines about food.

interNET CONNECTION To access sites about foods grown around the world, have children log on to **www.mhschool.com/reading.**

"Maybe I can help," said Miss Lin. "Does it come in a big box?" **20**

"Does it come in a small sack?" asked Dad. **21**

21

Comprehension

20 Do Miss Lin and Dad name a food? (no) What do they suggest? (possible containers: box and sack)

21 How are a box and a sack alike? (Both hold things.) How are they different? (A box is harder and has square corners.) *Compare and Contrast*

p/i **BLENDING SHORT *a*, *o* WORDS** Find and read the short *a* words on this page. *(can, sack, Dad)* Now find and read the short *o* word on this page. *(box)* *Graphophonic Cues*

TEACHING TIP

MANAGEMENT Observe which children are having difficulty with the Prevention/Intervention prompt. After reading the story with children, reinforce blending of short *a* and *o* words with these children. Have the rest of the class reread the story for fluency development.

---

p/i **PREVENTION/INTERVENTION**

BLENDING SHORT *a*, *o* WORDS Have children blend the sounds in *box* and *sack* as you move your hand beneath the letters in each word. Give children word-building boxes and write these incomplete words on the chalkboard: *gl-d, th-t, p-th, fl-g, st-p, ch-p, tr-t, l-g.* Ask children to blend and fill in a missing short *o* or short *a*. Read the words together. *Graphophonic Cues*

Comprehension

22 Let's look back through the pictures up to page 22. What has happened to the store? (It is getting untidy.) Why does it look so different from the way it did at the beginning? (People are searching for what Mike forgot.) *Use Illustrations*

23 Do you think Mike will remember what Mom wanted him to get? (yes/no) Why or why not? Let's add a new prediction to our chart. *Make Predictions*

24 Look at the picture. How would you describe the expression on Mike's face? (confused) On Dad's face? (frustrated) *Use Illustrations*

22
23
24

"Does it come in tin cans or glass jars?" asked Miss Lin.

But Mike still could not remember.

22

Activity

Cross Curricular: Science

RECYCLING Recycling turns garbage into something useful. Children can see recycled glass sparkling in roads and sidewalks. Paper waste finds new life in roofing and building materials. Recycling conserves our planet's natural resources and reduces pollution.

RESEARCH AND INQUIRY Have children find out and draw pictures to show where waste goes and how to recycle at school. ▶ **Visual**

interNET CONNECTION To access links to various sites about recycling, log on to **www.mhschool.com/reading.**

Then Fran and Ann Gomez came in. **26**

Soon, they were trying to help, too.

23

Comprehension

25 Why did Fran and Ann Gomez come into the store? (to get groceries) What happened to change their plan? (They found out about Mike's problem and decided to stay and help.) *Sequence of Events*

26 What do you notice about Fran and Ann's last name? (It is the same.) Does this mean they are in the same family? (probably) How do you think they are related? (They are sisters/sisters-in-law/mother and daughter/cousins.) *Make Inferences*

25

Minilesson

REVIEW/MAINTAIN

Context Clues

Remind children that they can use clues in the story and the first or last sounds of a word to help identify and read it. Ask:

• Which word on page 23 is *Gomez*?

• What is the sound of the first letter? (/g/)

• How do you know it is a character's last name? (It comes after the name *Ann*; it is capitalized.)

Activity Ask children to write their first names on slips of paper. Put all the names in a hat. Have a volunteer pull a name from the hat and read it by using the first and/or last sounds in the word and the names they know of children in the classroom.

LANGUAGE SUPPORT

ESL Have children look at the illustrations of the messy store. Have them name the items that are out of place and show where they should go on their own map.

23

Comprehension

27 Help me blend the sounds to read the seventh word in the second sentence: b l a ck black. *Graphophonic Cues*

28 When Fran asks *What color is it?* what is the *it* she is talking about? (the thing Mike can't remember)

29 **Phonics** LONG *i: i-e* Hmm . . . I know red and blue are colors, maybe this word names a color too. The word begins with /wh/. Then I see *i-t-e*. I'm going to blend this word as a long *i*, silent *e* word. wh i t(e) white *Graphophonic Cues*

TEACHING TIP

MANAGEMENT You may wish to pair children who speak different languages so they can guide each other in the Cultural Perspectives activity. Have other children form a chorus to chant the English word after each new language word.

27 "What color is it?" asked Fran.
"Is it red, blue, white, or black?" asked Ann.

28

29 24

 ## CULTURAL PERSPECTIVES

COLORS/LOS COLORES Ask children who know a second language to share the words for *red*, *blue*, *white*, or *black*.

Activity On the chalkboard write:

red   blue   white   black
rojo   azul   blanco   negro

Teach children these words in Spanish. (Say: *ro-ho, ah-ssul, blahnk-o, nay-gro.*) Point out that all four Spanish words have two syllables, while the four color words in English have one syllable. Then pick one word and play "I Spy Something ___ " (*rojo*).

▶ **Auditory/Linguistic**

Then Miss Lin jumped in. "Is it carrots, muffins, or bread?"

"No, no, and no!" said Mike.

 30

 31

25

Comprehension

30 Why does Mike say *no* three times? (Miss Lin asks about three foods, but they are not what Mike forgot.) How do you think Mike feels at this point in the story? (sad; angry; more confused by other people's help) *Analyze Character and Plot*

PHONOLOGICAL AWARENESS Listen to the second sentence. Which word starts with the same sound that *Miss* and *Mike* start with? (*muffins*)

31 What are the foods Miss Lin suggests? (Miss Lin said carrots, muffins, and bread.) Let's find the bakery section on our maps of Dad's store and add muffins and bread to the picture. Where would the carrots go? (in the vegetable section) Let's add carrots to our map as well. *Story Props*

Minilesson

REVIEW/MAINTAIN

Plot and Character

Help children see how the story plot develops because of what people do *not* do (as well as what people do). Ask:

- Tell something that Mike did *not* do that made him forget. (He did *not* write everything down.)
- What problem has Mike created by *not* remembering? (Everyone is messing up the store and getting excited.)
- What could Mike do now to change the situation? (Remember what he forgot!)

Activity Briefly describe an unusual event. For example: A gigantic tub of ice cream is found floating in the pool. Invite children to suggest what happened just before the event and what might (not) happen after it. Let children draw their "plot."

PREVENTION/INTERVENTION

PHONOLOGICAL AWARENESS Ask children to identify words in sentences you say aloud that begin with the same sounds. Examples: What word in the sentence "Is it carrots, muffins, or bread?" starts with the same sound as *color*? (*carrots*) What word begins with the same sound as *bright* and *break*? (*bread*) Encourage children to contribute other words that start with the /k/c or /br/ sounds: *cut, came, corn, cake; brook, bring, brown, brave.*

25

Comprehension

(32) As we read the last two lines, show me how you are going to "cut" and "chop." This is how I do it. Watch me cut and chop as I read the last line. Now we'll read it again and cut and chop together. *Pantomime*

(33) How are the ideas of "cut" and "chop" alike? (Both are ways of preparing food.) How do cut and chopped foods look the same? (Both are in pieces.) How are they different? (They have different shapes and sizes.) *Compare and Contrast*

TEACHING **TIP**

CAPITAL LETTERS FOR NAMES Help children see that names begin with a capital letter, but they do not always start a sentence. Invite volunteers to point out names within the sentence.

Then together, Fran, Ann, Dad, and Miss Lin spoke. "Is it this or that?
(32) Is it that or this? Do you cut it?
(33) Do you chop it?"

26

Activity

Cross Curricular: Music

RHYME SONG Write the words *pipe* and *ripe* on the board. Read them aloud. Sing the following poem to the tune of "Twinkle, Twinkle, Little Star."

We know a word that rhymes with ___. (pipe)

But it's not another ___. (pipe)

You are right if you guess ___. (ripe)
That's a word that rhymes with ___. (pipe)

Repeat with other rhyming long *i: i-e* words on the chalkboard. Examples: *five, hive, drive; file, mile, pile; ripe, pipe, stripe; spike, bike, hike.* ▶ **Auditory**

"I know!" said Miss Lin. "You were sent to get dog food!"

"Who needs that?" asked Mike.

"We do not have a dog!"

27

Comprehension

34 Why doesn't Mike need dog food? (He has no dog.)

 **CONCEPTS OF PRINT** How many sentences are there on page 26? (five) How many are on page 27? (four) How do you know when a new sentence begins? (The first word starts with a capital letter.) *Syntactic Cues*

PREVENTION/INTERVENTION

TRACKING PRINT Have children use self-stick notes to mark the first word in each sentence on pages 26–27. Read the pages aloud and ask children to pause when they see a period at the end of a sentence and to clap when a new sentence starts. *Syntactic Cues*

Minilesson

REVIEW/MAINTAIN

Sequence of Events

Remind children that they can understand a story by thinking about what happened first, next, and so on.

- Ask children to tell the first thing that happened to Mike.
- Ask them to continue telling the main events in sequence.
- Help children differentiate between main events and details.
- Lead a discussion about how the separate events are building up to create a feeling of frustration.

Activity Invite children to draw a picture of something that could happen next.

27

Comprehension

35 Why is everyone running around and showing things to Mike? (They're trying to jog his memory.) *Make Inferences*

36 How is the store different from the way it was at the beginning of the story? (It is now topsy-turvy.) What do you think Dad will be doing in his store tomorrow? (cleaning up) *Make Predictions*

35

36

Dad looked in every row.

Miss Lin looked on every shelf.

Fran looked up and down.

Ann looked down and up!

28

Visual Literacy

VIEWING AND REPRESENTING

Discuss the illustration on page 28. What view do you get of the store? Explain. (The artist drew it like a tunnel to show the entire store.) Why is Miss Lin's face so much larger than the other faces? (For perspective: People look bigger when they are standing in front of other people or objects.)

Ask: Why do you think the illustrator drew the picture from this point of view? (to show that all the people are looking; to show the amount of chaos up and down the store)

LANGUAGE SUPPORT

ESL Invite children to look up and down along with the characters to reinforce what those words mean. Make sure children understand what "I give up!" means by restating it: *Miss Lin can't* *help anymore. She doesn't know what Mike needs.*

Then, have children reread pages 28–29 with you. Encourage vocal inflection for the exclamation and dialogue.

After they had looked everywhere,
Miss Lin said, "I give up!"
"And we give up, too!" said Ann and Fran.

29

Comprehension

 When did Miss Lin give up? (after they had looked everywhere) Did Ann and Fran give up before or after Miss Lin? (after Miss Lin) *Sequence of Events*

CONCEPTS OF PRINT What do Ann and Fran say? ("And we give up, too!") How do you know they are saying this? (There are quotation marks before and after what they say.) *Syntactic Cues*

PREVENTION/INTERVENTION

CONCEPTS OF PRINT Remind children that quotation marks, or "quotes," are used before and after what someone says to show that someone is speaking. Ask children how they like the story. Then, on the chalkboard, write *"We think this story is*

funny!" said the children. Have two volunteers come to the board. Have one child point to the beginning quotes and the other child point to the ending quotes to frame the sentence. Invite the class to read the sentence aloud. *Syntactic Cues*

Minilesson

REVIEW/MAINTAIN

Make Predictions

Tell children that they can sometimes guess how a person is going to act by how that person has acted or felt in the past. Ask: At this point, which person in the story is most likely to help Mike? Why?

- Is it Miss Lin, Ann, or Fran? (No. They've given up; they've become too frustrated by looking everywhere.)
- What about Dad? (Maybe. He's been calmer than everyone; he knows what his family usually buys.)
- How about Mom? (Sure, but she's not there.)
- Who does that leave? (Mike himself!)

Activity Invite the class to brainstorm ideas about what people can do to remember or help others remember.

Comprehension

38 Look closely at the illustration. How does it help you know that Mike is thinking? (His hand is on his chin.) **What shows you that Dad is upset?** (His glasses are not straight; his hair is not as neat as it was at the beginning; he looks frustrated.) *Use Picture Clues*

39 Why do you think the artist drew this picture as a close-up of Mike and Dad? (to show the characters' facial expressions) *Concept of a Book: Illustrator*

38 "Think, Mike, think!" said Dad. "What were you sent to get?"

39 Mike said, "Let me think."

30

Mike looked at the messy store.
Then Mike looked at Dad.
A wide smile filled Mike's face.

31

Comprehension

40 Why is Mike smiling? (He just remembered what he forgot.) When was the last time he looked this happy? (when he first came into the store) *Make Inferences*

CONCEPTS OF PRINT The name *Mike* appears three times on this page. The third *Mike* has a mark and the letter *s* after it. What does this ending tell us? (Mike has or owns the thing that follows.) *Syntactic Cues*

Summarizing

Remind children that summarizing means telling a story's main parts and leaving out the details. They should include the main idea, the most important events, and how the story ends. Ask:

• In a summary, do you mention every suggestion that people made to Mike? (no)

• Do you mention Dad in the story? (yes)

• Do you mention that Mike didn't own a dog? (no)

• Do you mention that Mike remembered what Mom wanted? (yes)

Activity Have children form news teams to make up a headline that tells the entire story. Example: "Mike Remembers Food, Forgets Dad!" Let children write their headlines on banner paper.

PREVENTION/INTERVENTION

CONCEPTS OF PRINT Remind children that apostrophe -s shows possession. In this case, it tells us that the face belongs to Mike. Help children find the possessive on page 12.

(dad's store) Encourage children to then think of something they own and say their name and the item. Example: *Mary's dog. Syntactic Cues*

Comprehension

41 So what was it that Mike finally remembered? (his dad)

42 Let's look at our maps of Dad's store. Where would be a good place to draw Dad? (next to Mike) Let's add Dad to the picture. *Story Props*

RETELL THE STORY Ask children to work in groups of five to act out the story. After they decide on what to say in their retelling, have them choose roles. One child can retell the story as the others act out the events. Remind children to refer to the map of Dad's store to help them remember specific grocery items and what happened in the store. *Summarize/Story Props*

STUDENT SELF-ASSESSMENT

Have children ask themselves the following questions to assess how they are reading:

- How did I use what I already know about grocery shopping to understand the story?

- How did I use letters and sounds I already know to help me read the words?

- How did I use the pictures and words to understand what is happening?

TRANSFERRING THE STRATEGIES

- How can I use these strategies to help me read other stories?

"Mom wanted me to get...!" he said.

"What is it?" yelled Miss Lin.

"Tell us!" yelled Fran and Ann.

32

REREADING FOR *Fluency*

GROUP Children who need fluency practice can read along silently or aloud as they listen to the story being read.

READING RATE When you evaluate reading rate, have children read aloud from the story for one minute. Place a stick-on note after the last word read. Count words read. To evaluate children's performance, see the Running Record in the **Fluency Assessment** book.

i Intervention For leveled fluency lessons, passages, and norms charts, see **Skills Intervention Guide**, Part 5, Fluency.

Mike smiled and said, "Mom asked me to get YOU, Dad. It's time for supper!"

33

Comprehension

Return to Predictions and Purposes

Reread children's predictions about the story and discuss them. Ask if they need to revise any predictions about the story, and if their questions were answered.

Have children talk about the strategy of using the map of Dad's store. Did it help them follow what the characters said, where the story took place, and what happened in the story?

PREDICTIONS	WHAT HAPPENED
The story is about a boy.	The story is about Mike, who visits his dad's grocery store.
People try to help the boy find something.	People give Mike many ideas, but they are unsuccessful.
In the end, Mike does not remember what he forgot.	Mike finally remembers on his own: Get Dad!

INFORMAL ASSESSMENT

HOW TO ASSESS

Phonics LONG *i: i-e* Have children find and read three long *i: i-e* words in the story. *(Possible answers: five, Mike, ripe, time, white, smile, wide, smiled, rice, write)*

FOLLOW UP

Phonics LONG *i: i-e* Continue to model blending the sounds in long *i: i-e* words in the story for children who are having difficulty.

LITERARY RESPONSE

QUICK-WRITE Have children write in their journals about a character or a part of the story they found interesting. They can use the map of Dad's store or ask for help with difficult words.

JOURNAL

ORAL RESPONSE Have children use their journal entries to discuss these questions:

- Choose a role from the story. Why do you want to be this character?
- Imagine you are Mike telling Mom what happened. What do you say?

SENTENCE STRIPS Children can use strips 1–77 to retell the story:

> 1
> One day Mike went to his dad's store

> 2
> with a list.

Story Questions

Tell children that now they will read some questions about the story. Help children read the questions. Discuss possible answers.

Answers:

1. jam, rice, 5 ripe plums *Literal*

2. Dad's store became a big mess. *Inferential/Make Inferences*

3. Answers may vary. (One response: because the item Mike forgot was not food.) *Inferential/Make Inferences*

4. Accept appropriate responses. *Critical/Summarize*

5. Meg forgot to bring her rain gear when she went outside in the rain to catch the bus. *Critical/Reading Across Texts*

Draw Two Kinds of Fruits For a full writing-process lesson related to this writing suggestion, see the lesson on writing that compares on pages 37M–37N.

Story Questions & Activities

1. What foods were on Mike's list?

2. What happened to Dad's store?

3. Why do you think Mike forgot?

4. Pretend you are Mike and tell about your day.

5. Tell how Meg from "Splash!" also forgot something.

Draw Two Kinds of Fruit

Choose two fruits from the story. Draw a picture of each one. Write how they are alike.

Both are red.

Meeting Individual Needs

EASY	ON-LEVEL	CHALLENGE
Name_____ Date_____ Reteach 129	Name_____ Date_____ Practice 129	Name_____ Date_____ Extend 129
Story Comprehension	**Story Comprehension**	**Story Comprehension**
Think about "The Shopping List." Fill in the chart below.	Think about what happened in "The Shopping List." Write **T** if the sentence is **true**. Write **F** if the sentence is **false**.	What do you put on a shopping list? Look at the pictures. Make a list of things to buy. Then add more things. Draw a picture, too.

EASY — Reteach:

First: Mike goes to the store with a shopping list.

Then: Mike can't remember one thing he had to get.

Next: Miss Lin, Fran, and Ann try to help Mike.

Finally: Mike remembers what is not on the list. Mom wants Dad to come home with Mike.

ON-LEVEL — Practice:

1. __T__ Mike has a list.

2. __F__ His dad drives a bus.

3. __T__ Dad wants to know what Mike forgot.

4. __T__ Dad hunts and hunts.

5. __T__ Fran and Ann try to help Mike.

6. __T__ At last, Miss Lin gives up.

7. __F__ Mike gets sad and goes away.

8. __T__ Mom wants Mike to tell Dad it is time to eat.

CHALLENGE — Extend:

SHOPPING LIST

cake

milk

grapes

Reteach, 129	Practice, 129	Extend, 129

Play a Memory Game

Play in a group.
One person begins:

"I went to the store to buy soap."

The next person says:

"I went to the store to buy soap and bananas."

Keep playing.
See how many items you remember.

Find Out More

Find out about one food that is good for you.
Tell about the food and how it helps you.

35

Story Activities

Memory Game

Read the directions aloud. Help children who have questions. Are there any things they want to buy at the store? Are these items for the kitchen or another room in the house?

GROUP After the children have played the memory game in groups, have them make a list of the items they "bought" at the store. Then have them illustrate their shopping lists.

Find Out More

RESEARCH AND INQUIRY Again, read the directions aloud, and help children who have questions. Then have them work in pairs.

PARTNERS

Partners should choose one food together that is good for them. Have them write a list about why this food helps them grow and stay healthy. Invite children to illustrate their findings and present them to the class.

*inter*NET CONNECTION Have children log on to **www.mhschool.com/reading**, where they can access sites about food.

FORMAL **ASSESSMENT**

See the Selection Assessment for Book 1.4.

DAILY  ROUTINES

DAY 3 **Writing** Have children write labels on simple pictures using the appropriate word from this list: *kite, tire, bike, five.*

 **CD-ROM**

35

Read the Literature

Study Skills

CHARTS

OBJECTIVES

Children will:

• learn to read a chart to gather information.

PREPARE Preview the chart with children, pointing out that a chart presents information in columns or lists. Display **Teaching Chart 95**.

TEACH Review how to get information from a chart. Have children read the labels and look at the illustrations.

PRACTICE Have children answer questions 1–2. Review the answers with them.
1. a peach, a plum, and a cherry **2.** a carrot

ASSESS/CLOSE Have children draw conclusions from the chart and write their conclusions in a sentence or two.

STUDY SKILLS

Fruit or Vegetable?

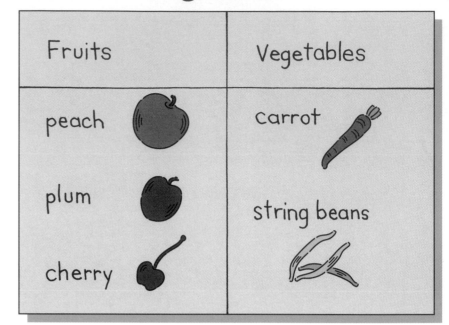

Fruits	Vegetables
peach	carrot
plum	string beans
cherry	

Look at the Chart

1 Which are listed as fruits?

2 Name an orange vegetable.

Meeting Individual Needs

EASY	ON-LEVEL	CHALLENGE

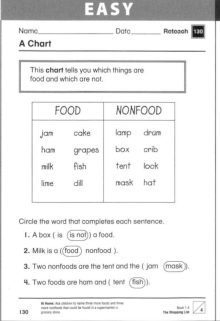

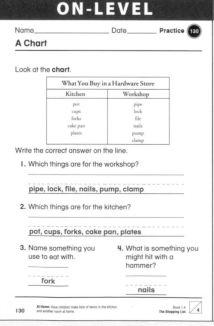

Reteach, 130   Practice, 130   Extend, 130

TEST POWER

Mike's Pet

Mike has a fish.

It lives in a fish tank.

Mike feeds his fish everyday.

The food sits on top of the water.

The fish swims to the top to eat the food.

Then, it swims back down to the bottom.

Why does the fish swim to the top?

○ To say hello to Mike

● To eat the food

Ask yourself: "What does the story tell me?"

37

Test Power

THE PRINCETON REVIEW

Read the Page

Explain to children that you will be reading this story as a group. You will read the story, and they will follow in their books.

Request that children put pens, pencils, and markers away, since they will not be writing in their books.

Discuss the Question

Discuss with children what constitutes an answer to a "why" question. Have them reread the story, find the place where the fish swims to the top, and put their fingers on the reason why the fish swims to the top.

Test-Tip

Always look back to the story to find the answer. The answer is always somewhere in the passage.

ITBS/TEST PREPARATION

TERRA NOVA/TEST PREPARATION

SAT 9/TEST PREPARATION

Leveled Books

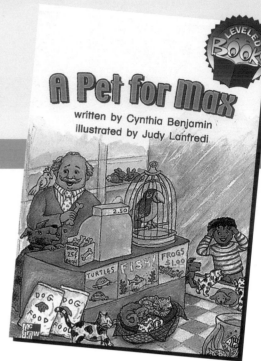

EASY

A Pet for Max

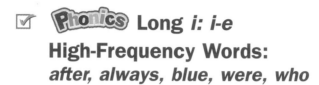 ☑ **Phonics** Long *i: i-e*
High-Frequency Words:
after, always, blue, were, who

Answers to Story Questions
1. a pet
2. a bird (parrot)
3. Answers will vary.
4. Kim had a cat. Dave had a dog. Nick had a duck.
5. *Max, the Cat; Quack; One Good Pup; Splash*

The Story Questions and Activity below appear in the Easy Book.

Story Questions and Activity
1. What did Max want?
2. Who said, "Look at me!"?
3. Why do a lot of people like pets?
4. Tell about the pets Max's friends had.
5. What other stories have you read about pets?

A Pet Page
Find pictures of pets in magazines, or use pictures of a pet you know. Cut and paste them onto a page. Write a sentence for your Pet Page.

from A Pet for Max

Guided Reading

PREVIEW AND PREDICT Discuss each illustration up to page 9, using the high-frequency words. As you take the **picture walk,** have children predict what the story will be about and chart their ideas.

SET PURPOSES Have children write or draw why they want to read *A Pet for Max.* For example: *I want to find out what pet Max got.*

READ THE BOOK Use questions like the following as children read or once they have read the story independently.

Pages 2–3: Model: The second sentence on page 2 says, *A pet is …* I'm not sure what this word is, but I can blend the letters together to read it. The first letter is *f.* It stands for the sound /f/. The middle letter is *i.* It has the long *i* sound, /ī/. The next letter is *n,* for the /n/ sound. The final letter is silent *e.* I can blend the sounds together f i n(e) fine. The word is *fine.* Who sees another word with long *i* and silent *e* on page 3? *(like) Phonics and Decoding*

Pages 4–5: What does Max want after visiting Kim? (a cat) Why? (because she has one) *Cause and Effect*

Pages 8–11: What pet does Max want after visiting Nick? (a duck) Why? (because Nick says it's a fun pet) Who sees a word with long *i* and silent *e* on page 8? *(bike)* On page 10? *(dive) Cause and Effect, Phonics and Decoding*

Pages 12–16: Who sees a vocabulary word we just learned on page 14? *(who)* On page 15? *(blue)* Where does Max finally see the pet he wants? (in a pet store) *High-Frequency Words/Use Illustrations*

RETURN TO PREDICTIONS AND PURPOSES Discuss children's predictions and review their purposes for reading. Ask which were close to the story and why. Did they find out what pet Max got?

LITERARY RESPONSE Focus children's responses by asking:

• Why do people have all kinds of pets?

• Do you have a pet? Tell about it.

Also see the story questions and writing activity in *A Pet for Max.*

See the **Phonics** CD-ROM for practice with long *i: i-e.*

Leveled Books

INDEPENDENT

The Big Secret

☑ **Phonics** Long *i: i-e*
High-Frequency Words:
after, always, blue, were, who

The Big Secret
by Tim Kane
Illustrated by Kristine Goeters

Guided Reading

PREVIEW AND PREDICT Discuss each illustration up to page 9, using the high-frequency words. As you take the **picture walk**, have children predict what the story will be about and chart their ideas in their journals.

SET PURPOSES Have children write or draw why they want to read *The Big Secret*. For example: *I want to find out what the big secret is.*

READ THE BOOK Ask questions like the following as children read or once they have read the story independently.

Pages 2–7: Let's look at the pictures and read the third sentence on page 3. Model: *I don't have … I'm not sure what this word is, but I can blend the letters together to read it. The first letter is t. It stands for the sound /t/. The middle letter is i. It has the long i sound. The next letter is m, for the /m/ sound. The final letter is silent e. I can blend the sounds together t i m(e) time. The word is time.* Why do you think everyone is busy? (getting ready for Dan's party) Why? (It's his birthday.) *Phonics and Decoding/Draw Conclusions*

Pages 8–13: Who sees a vocabulary word we just learned on page 9? *(blue)* Who has a big white box? (Meg) Who has two red boxes? (Miss Kent) *High-Frequency Words/ Use Illustrations*

Pages 14–16: What was the big secret? (There is a birthday party for Dan.) What does Dan get that he wanted? (a blue bike) *Confirm Predictions/Use Illustrations*

RETURN TO PREDICTIONS AND PURPOSES Discuss children's predictions and review their purposes. Ask which were close to the story and why. Did they find out what the big secret was?

LITERARY RESPONSE Focus children's responses by asking:

- How did Dan help with his own party?

- Have you ever kept a secret?

Also see the story questions and writing activity in *The Big Secret*.

See the **Phonics** CD-ROM for practice with long *i: i-e.*

Answers to Story Questions
1. shopping
2. There was a party for Dan.
3. Answers will vary.
4. Dan wakes up, goes outside, goes shopping, sees a bike in a shop, sees Meg, and sees Miss Kent.
5. Answers may vary: *The Shopping List.*

The Story Questions and Activity below appear in the Independent Book.

Story Questions and Activity
1. Where did Dan go with Gran?
2. What was the big secret?
3. Why do people sometimes keep party secrets?
4. Tell four things about Dan's day.
5. In what other story that you have read did someone go to a store?

Make a Birthday Card
Make a birthday card.
Use construction paper and markers.
Make a birthday card for someone whose birthday is this month.

from The Big Secret

Leveled Books

WHO TOOK THE FARMER'S HAT?

by Joan L. Nodset pictures by Fritz Siebel

CHALLENGE

Who Took the Farmer's Hat?

☑  Long *i: i-e*

Guided Reading

PREVIEW AND PREDICT Discuss each illustration up to page 15. As you take the **picture walk**, have children predict what the story is about and chart their ideas in their journals.

SET PURPOSES Have children write or draw why they want to read *Who Took the Farmer's Hat?* For example: *I want to find out who took that hat.*

READ THE BOOK Ask questions like the following as children read or once they have read the story independently:

Pages 2–13: Model: *Oh, how he … I'm not sure what this next word is, but I can blend the letters together. The first letter is *l*. It stands for the /l/ sound. The next letter is *i*. It has the long *i* sound. The next letter is *k*. It has the /k/ sound. The ending is *ed*. Let's blend the sounds of these letters to read the word l i k(e) d liked. The word is liked.* *Phonics and Decoding*

Pages 15–21: Who did the farmer ask after the duck? (the bird) Did the bird see the hat? (No, but she saw a nice brown nest that was really the hat.) *Analyze Character and Plot/Details*

Pages 22–29: Did the farmer ever find his hat? (No, he got a new one.) *Use Illustrations, Main Idea and Details*

RETURN TO PREDICTIONS AND PURPOSES Discuss children's predictions. Ask which were close to the story and why. Have children review their purposes for reading. Did they find out who took the farmer's hat?

LITERARY RESPONSE Focus children's responses by asking:

- Why didn't the farmer take his hat away from the bird?
- Have you ever lost something you liked a lot? Tell about it.

Also see the story questions and writing activity in *Who Took the Farmer's Hat?*

See the **CD-ROM** for practice with long *i: i-e.*

Answers to Story Questions

1. the wind
2. A bird used it for a nest.
3. Answers will vary.
4. The wind took the farmer's hat. He looked for the hat. None of the animals he asked saw the hat. Bird had the hat and used it as a nest. The farmer got a new hat.
5. Both stories are about friendship.

The Story Questions and Activity below appear in the Challenge Book.

Story Questions and Activity

1. Who took the farmer's hat?
2. Why does the farmer get a new hat?
3. What does this story tell you about sharing?
4. Tell the story in your own words.
5. How is this story like *The Cow That Went OINK*?

Make a Card

Pretend you are a bird. Write a thank-you card for the farmer.

from Who Took the Farmer's Hat?

Bringing Groups Together

Anthology and Leveled Books

Connecting Texts

STORY CHARTS
Write the story titles on the chalkboard. Discuss with children what the characters in each story are shopping for. Have children construct a word web that describes the shopping items in each story.

Use the chart to talk about shopping.

The Shopping List
jam, rice, five ripe plums

A Pet for Max
a pet bird

Shopping

The Big Secret
**birthday gifts
a blue bike**

Who Took the
Farmer's Hat?
a hat

Viewing/Representing

GROUP PRESENTATIONS Divide the class into groups, one for each of the four books. (For *The Shopping List,* combine children of different reading levels.) Have each group draw pictures of the shopping items and orally summarize the book. Have each group present its pictures and summary.

AUDIENCE RESPONSE
Ask children to pay attention to each group's presentation. Allow time for questions after each group presents.

Research and Inquiry

MORE ABOUT SHOPPING Have children ask themselves: What else would I like to know about shopping? Then invite them to do the following:

- Bring in shopping catalogues from home.

- Ask a grown-up who works in the retail industry to come and speak about it.

inter NET CONNECTION Have children log on to **www.mhschool.com/reading** for links to Web pages about shopping.

 Children can draw pictures representing what they learned in their journals.
JOURNAL

OBJECTIVES

Children will:
- identify long *i: i-e* words.
- blend and read long *i: i-e* words.
- review consonants.

....

MATERIALS
- **Teaching Chart 96**
- long *i* cards from the **Word Building Manipulative Cards**

Skills Finder	
Long *i: i-e*	
Introduce	B4: 8I-J
Review	B4: 37E-F, 37G-H, 38E-F, 65G-H, 95G-H, 124I-J
Test	Book 4

ALTERNATE TEACHING STRATEGY
....

PHONICS: LONG *i: i-e*

For a different approach to teaching this skill, see pages T64 and T65.

37E *The Shopping List*

Review Long *i: i-e*

PREPARE

Listen for the Long *i* Sound
Read the following sentence aloud and ask children to tap their feet when they hear a word with the long *i: i-e* sound:

If you like, we will dine on grape jam and lime ice.

TEACH

Review the Letters *i-e* as Symbols for /ī/
- Tell children that they will review the vowel pattern *i-e* and the long *i* sound it makes.
- Display the letter card *i-e*. Remind children that the space between the letters *i-e* is for a consonant letter. Together the letters make a long *i* sound.

BLENDING
Model and Guide Practice with Long *i* Words
- Say /ī/. Have children repeat after you. Display **Teaching Chart 96.**
- Run your hand under the letters *ive* and blend them together. Have children repeat after you. i̮ ve ive

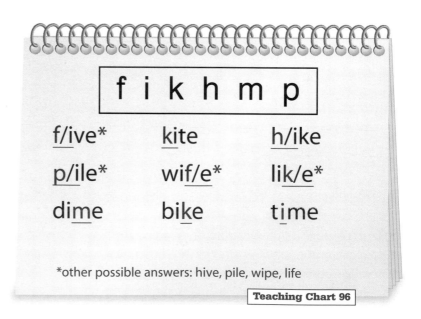

f i k h m p

f/ive*	kite	h/ike
p/ile*	wif/e*	lik/e*
dime	bike	time

*other possible answers: hive, pile, wipe, life

Teaching Chart 96

- Write the letter *f* in the blank space. Run your hand under the letters again, blending them to read the word *five*. f i̮ ve five
- Erase the *f* and have the children choose another letter from the box to complete the word.

Use the Word in Context
Have volunteers say the word in a sentence to reinforce its meaning. Example : *I saw five bee hives in the park.*

Repeat the Procedure
Continue by having children substitute other letters to complete words on the chart.

PRACTICE

BLENDING
Build and Sort
Long *i: i-e* Words
with Letter Banks

PARTNERS

Write the following letter banks on the chalkboard:

b f l		i _ e		d f k
p s h				l n t

Ask children to work in pairs. One child writes *i-e* on the paper and then chooses a letter from the first letter bank to begin a long *i: i-e* word. The partner chooses another letter from the third letter bank to complete the long *i: i-e* word. Partners can then reverse roles. Have children keep a list of the words they make. Then have children sort the words into rhyming groups. ▶ **Auditory/Linguistic**

ASSESS/CLOSE

Read Long *i: i-e*
Words

To assess children's mastery of blending and reading long *i: i-e* words, check the words they built in the Practice activity. Ask them to read some of the words from their lists.

ADDITIONAL PHONICS RESOURCES

**Phonics/Phonemic Awareness
Practice Book,
pages 135–142**

PHONICS KIT
Hands-on Activities and Practice

McGraw-Hill School
TECHNOLOGY
 **CD-ROM**

activities for practice with
Blending and Building

DAILY **Phonics** ROUTINES

DAY 4
Fluency Write the following list of long *i-e* words on the chalkboard: *mine, hike, drive, smile, ride.* Ask children to first read the list silently and then read it aloud.

 Phonics CD-ROM

**SPELLING/PHONICS
CONNECTIONS**
Words with long *i: i-e;* See the 5-Day Spelling Plan, pages 37Q-37R.

i Intervention ▶ **Skills**
Intervention Guide, for direct instruction and extra practice in long *i: i-e*

Meeting Individual Needs for Phonics

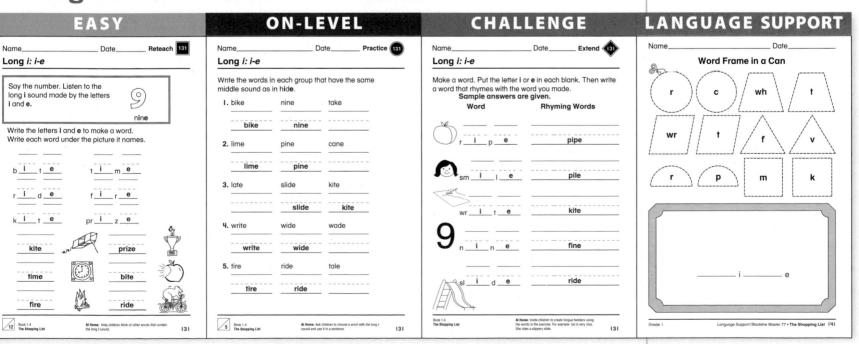

EASY	ON-LEVEL	CHALLENGE	LANGUAGE SUPPORT
Reteach, 131	**Practice, 131**	Extend, 131	Language Support, 141

37F

OBJECTIVES

Children will:

- review long *a: a-e* and long *i: i-e*.

- blend and read long *a: a-e* and long *i: i-e* words.

- cumulative review: consonants, blends, and digraphs.

MATERIALS

- **Teaching Chart 97**

- letter cards long *a* and long *i* cards from the **Word Building Manipulative Cards**

- **Phonics Practice Reader, Volume 2**

Skills Finder	
Long *i: i-e*	
Introduce	B4: 8I-J
Review	B4: 37E-F, 37G-H, 38E-F, 65G-H, 95G-H, 124I-J
Test	Book 4

ALTERNATE TEACHING STRATEGY

PHONICS: LONG *i: i-e*

For a different approach to teaching this skill, see pages T64 and T65.

Review Long *i-e, a-e*

PREPARE

Identify *i-e* and *a-e* as Symbols for /ī/, /ā/   Write the letters *a-e* and *i-e* on the chalkboard and say their sounds aloud. Have children repeat the sounds after you.

Discriminate Between /ā/ *a-e* and /ī/ *i-e* Words   Display the word cards or list words on the chalkboard for *a-e* and *i-e*. Ask volunteers to read the words with the /ā/ sound. Do the same for words with the /ī/ sound.

TEACH

BLENDING
Model and Guide Practice with Long *a* and Long *i* Words   **Display Teaching Chart 97.** Point to the letters *a* and *i* at the top.

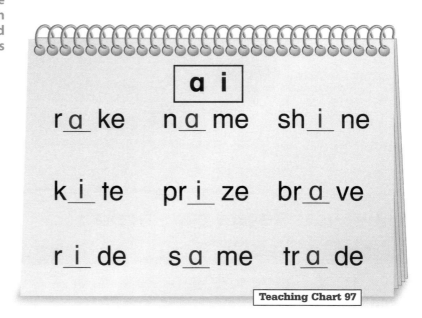

r a̲ ke   n a̲ me   sh i̲ ne

k i̲ te   pr i̲ ze   br a̲ ve

r i̲ de   s a̲ me   tr a̲ de

Teaching Chart 97

- Write the letter *a* in the blank space: r_ke. Cover the first letter *r* and blend the remaining sounds, a ke ake. Have children repeat after you. Uncover the letter *r* and blend the whole word together. Have children repeat.

  r ake   rake

- Replace the letter *a* with *i* and repeat the blending process.

- Ask which letter forms a real word. (*a*)

Use the Word in Context   - Invite volunteers to use the word in a sentence to reinforce its meaning. Example: *I like to rake leaves in the fall.*

Repeat the Procedure   - Continue by asking volunteers to complete words and blend sounds together to read the words aloud.

PRACTICE

BLENDING
Build and Sort
Long *a-e, i-e*
Words

PARTNERS

Have children work in pairs using the letter cards and long vowel cards to build words. One child builds long *a: a-e* words and the partner builds long *i: i-e* words. Have children write two lists for the words they build. Pairs can switch lists to see if they can think of any new words their partner may have missed. ▶ **Linguistic/Kinesthetic**

ASSESS/CLOSE

Draw and Label
a Picture

Use your observations from the Practice activity to determine if children need more reinforcement with long *ai, a-e,* and long *i: i-e* words. Have children choose a word, draw a picture of it, and label it with the word.

Read a Decodable
Story

For additional practice reading words with long *i* and to develop fluency, direct children to read the story *Nate's Kite* from the **Phonics Practice Reader, Volume 2.**

ADDITIONAL PHONICS RESOURCES

Phonics/Phonemic Awareness Practice Book, pages 135–142

PHONICS KIT
Hands-on Activities and Practice

McGraw-Hill School
TECHNOLOGY
Phonics CD-ROM
activities for practice with Blending and Building

DAILY Phonics ROUTINES

DAY 5
Rhyming Using the *i-e* and consonant cards, have pairs of children build sets of rhyming words.

 **Phonics CD-ROM**

ⓘ **Intervention** ▶ **Skills Intervention Guide,** for direct instruction and extra practice in Long *i: i-e*

Meeting Individual Needs for Phonics

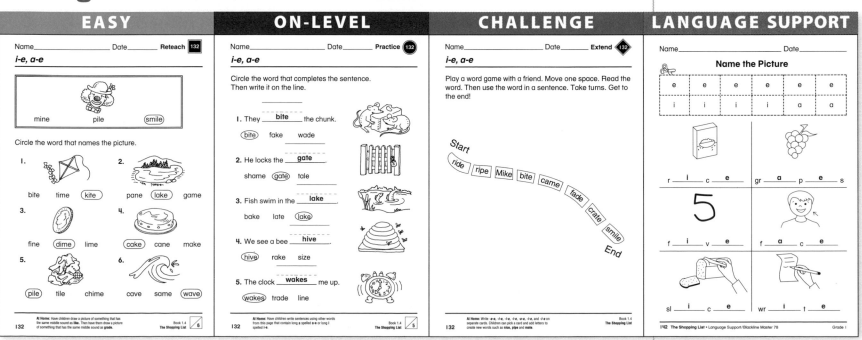

EASY	ON-LEVEL	CHALLENGE	LANGUAGE SUPPORT
Reteach, 132	Practice, 132	Extend, 132	Language Support, 142

OBJECTIVES

Children will use words and pictures to identify cause and effect.

MATERIALS

• Teaching Chart 98

TEACHING TIP

CAUSE AND EFFECT
Encourage children to share examples of cause-and-effect events in their own lives by making a drawing that depicts a cause-and-effect event.

Skills Finder

Cause & Effect

Introduce	B4: 37I–J
Review	B4: 65I–J, 133E–F
Test	Book 4
Maintain	B5: 17, 251, 267

SELF-SELECTED Reading

Children may choose from the following titles.

ANTHOLOGY

• *The Shopping List*

LEVELED BOOKS

• *A Pet for Max*

• *The Big Secret*

• *Who Took the Farmer's Hat?*

Bibliography, pages T98–T99

Introduce Cause and Effect

PREPARE

Introduce the Concept of Cause and Effect
Tell children that they can understand a story better by seeing that some things happen as a result of other things that happened before them.

TEACH

Identify Cause and Effect
Display **Teaching Chart 98**. Encourage children to look carefully at the first set of pictures and think about the cause-and-effect relationship.

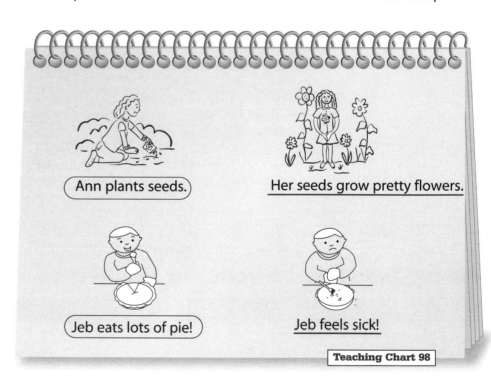

Ann plants seeds.

Her seeds grow pretty flowers.

Jeb eats lots of pie!

Jeb feels sick!

Teaching Chart 98

MODEL I can tell why the boy is looking sick in the second set of pictures by looking at the first picture. The first picture shows him getting ready to eat a very big pie. The second picture shows him after he has eaten all the pie, and now he has a tummy ache. When I read the sentences, they tell the same story.

Have children look at the second set of pictures on the chart. Point out to children how the first picture shows *why* something happened—the cause—and the second picture shows *what* happened—the effect. Invite children to tell in their own words the events shown in that set of pictures. Encourage them to identify the cause and the effect. Ask volunteers to circle the "cause" sentences and underline the "effect" sentences.

PRACTICE

Act Out Cause and Effect

GROUP

Have children think about another cause-and-effect event, such as some things that could happen as a result of a snowfall. (building a snowman, shoveling the sidewalk, and so on.) Have volunteers act out possible effects based on the cause. Invite the class to guess what the volunteers are pantomiming. ▶ **Visual/Kinesthetic**

ASSESS/CLOSE

Think of a Different Cause or Effect

Review children's skits to determine how well they have understood the concept of cause and effect. To reinforce understanding, ask them to look again at the pictures on **Teaching Chart 98.** Invite volunteers to make up a different cause or effect than the obvious one. Example: *Jeb is upset because someone else ate his lime pie.*

ALTERNATE TEACHING STRATEGY

················

CAUSE AND EFFECT

For a different approach to teaching this skill, see page T67.

i **Intervention** ▶ **Skills Intervention Guide,** for direct instruction and extra practice in Cause and Effect

Meeting Individual Needs for Comprehension

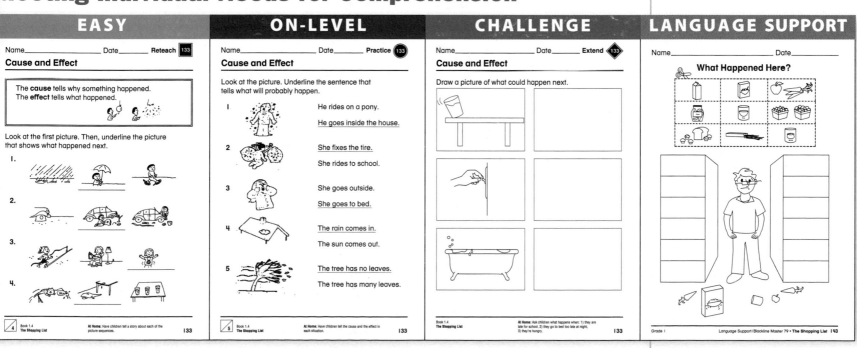

EASY	ON-LEVEL	CHALLENGE	LANGUAGE SUPPORT

Reteach, 133   Practice, 133   Extend, 133   Language Support, 143

OBJECTIVES

Children will:

• read words that end in -s and -es.

• understand the concept of root words and suffixes.

MATERIALS

• Teaching Chart 99

• index cards

Skills Finder

Inflectional Endings -s, –es

Introduce	B4: 31K-L
Review	B4: 37K-L, 133I-J
Test	Book 4

TEACHING TIP

PHONICS TEACHING TIP

Point out to children that when a word ends in *sh*, *ch*, *x*, or *ss*, the plural is always formed by adding -es. Remind children that the *s* at the end of a word that names more than one stands for the sound /z/. The *es* at the end of a word that names more than one stands for the sound /əz/. Write and say the word *dish*. Add *es* and say *dishes*. Have children repeat after you.

Review Inflectional Endings -s, -es

PREPARE

Review the Concept of Endings -s, -es

Write the word *can* on the chalkboard. Ask a volunteer to pantomime handing you one can, then another. Say: *I had one can. Now I have two cans.* Point out that the word *can* is the root or base word. Write -s after *can* and explain that we add the suffixes -s or -es to many words to show more than one. A suffix is a letter or set of letters added to the end of a word. Pretend to pull a nut from one can and eat it. Say: *I ate one nut.* Then repeat your action and say: *I ate two nuts.* Write the root word *nut* on the board, then add the letter -s.

TEACH

Identify Root Words

Track each sentence on **Teaching Chart 99** as you read it with children. Invite volunteers to identify the words ending in -s or -es and then underline the root word in each. Model for children how understanding inflectional endings can help them read.

Here are <u>cans</u> of <u>nuts</u>.

Here are <u>bunches</u> of <u>grapes</u>.

Here are <u>dishes</u> of <u>plums</u>.

Teaching Chart 99

MODEL I can use what I know to help me recognize -s and -es words. I know the word *can.* I can see the root word *can* with the suffix -s at the end. I know that sometimes when this letter appears at the end of a word, it means more than one. The word is *cans.*

PRACTICE

Add -s, -es

PARTNERS

Distribute index cards to children. Then write *benches, dresses, frogs, boxes, dolls,* and *wishes* on the chalkboard. Have children read each word, identifying the root word. Then ask children to write each word on an index card. Direct them to turn the card over and write the root word, leaving off the suffix *–s* or *–es.* Have pairs practice reading all the words and using them in sentences. ▶ **Visual/Representing**

ASSESS/CLOSE

Use the Words in Context

Invite pairs of children to make up stories using their words. Children can tell their stories. They may wish to act them out as well. Call on other children to identify the root words.

ALTERNATE TEACHING STRATEGY

INFLECTIONAL ENDINGS
-s, -es

For a different approach to learning this skill, see page T68.

ⓘ Intervention ▶ Skills

Intervention Guide, for direct instruction and extra practice in Inflectional Endings *–s* and *–es*

Meeting Individual Needs for Vocabulary

EASY	ON-LEVEL	CHALLENGE	LANGUAGE SUPPORT

EASY

Name_____ Date_____ Reteach 134

Inflectional Ending -s, -es

Add **-s** or **-es** to tell what one person or thing does.

Dan and Pam hike up the hill.
hike + s = hike**s**
Dad hike**s** up the hill.

If the word ends in **e** or most consonants, add **-s**.
If the word ends in **sh, ch, x,** or **ss**, add **-es**.

Underline the word that finishes each sentence.

1. Dan ___ to see Pam.
   want   <u>wants</u>

2. He ___ to Pam's house.
   run   <u>runs</u>

3. Pam ___ in.
   dash   <u>dashes</u>   sits

4. Dan ___ Pam an apple.
   pass   <u>passes</u>

134   At Home: Choose two more verbs with -s or -es endings, and help children to use them in sentences.   Book 1.4
The Shopping List

ON-LEVEL

Name_____ Date_____ Practice 134

Inflectional Endings -s, -es

Add **-s** or **-es** to tell what only one person or thing does.

When a word ends in **e** or most consonants, add **-s**.
When a word ends in **sh, ch, x,** or **ss**, add **-es**.

Circle the word that completes each sentence.
Then write the word on the line.

1. Nick __brushes__ his pup.
   brush (brushes)

2. She __gives__ me a ring.
   give (gives)

3. They __shop__ for food.
   (shop) hops

4. The mouse __munches__.
   munch (munches)

5. Bob and Jen __wish__ for fish.
   (wish) wishes

6. The boy __yanks__ the gate.
   yank (yanks)

134   At Home: Challenge children to use three of the uncircled word choices in sentences.   Book 1.4
The Shopping List

CHALLENGE

Name_____ Date_____ Extend 134

Inflectional Endings -s, -es

Choose one of the two words. Use it in a sentence.
Circle the word you used.   Sample answers are given.

can   cans

I will buy a can of soup.

grape   grapes

Here are the red grapes.

muffin   muffins

I like corn muffins.

plum   plums

Plums taste good.

Look at the picture. Write a sentence about it. Use one of the words in the box.

duck   ducks

The mother duck swims in the front.

134   At Home: Have children use words such as bench/benches, doll/dolls, wing/wings, and frog/frogs in sentences.   Book 1.4
The Shopping List

LANGUAGE SUPPORT

Name_____ Date_____

Pick an Ending

s	s	s	es	es

1. ___ ate the grape__s__.

2. ___ has five can__s__.

3. ___ has two box__es__.

4. ___ takes the ripe plum__s__.

5. ___ puts away a can of peach__es__.

144   The Shopping List • Language Support/Blackline Master 80   Grade 1

Reteach, 134   **Practice, 134**   **Extend, 134**   **Language Support, 144**

37L

Handwriting CD-ROM

GRAMMAR/SPELLING CONNECTIONS

See the 5-Day Grammar and Usage Plan on *was* and *were,* pages 370–37P.

See the 5-Day Spelling Plan on Words with Long *i: i-e (silent e rule),* pages 37Q–37R.

TEACHING TIP

Technology
Introduce children to the "Save" icon on the toolbar. Encourage them to use it to save what they have written every few minutes.

Organization
Explain to children that it is important to organize details in an order that makes sense. It is easier for the reader to understand what he or she is reading if the details are in an order that makes sense.

Writing That Compares

Prewrite

WRITE A LETTER Present this writing assignment: Write a letter to a family member that compares two healthy snacks. Name the two snacks and tell why each is a good choice.

BRAINSTORM IDEAS Have children brainstorm ideas for healthy snacks they would like to eat.

STRATEGY: MAKE A LIST Have children list the healthy snacks they would like to eat. Suggest the following:

- In one column, list several healthy snacks.
- In another column, list the characteristics of each snack.

Draft

USE THE LIST Have children choose two snacks from their list. Guide them to write complete sentences telling about each snack and elaborating on what makes them similar and different. As they write their letters, they should include a heading with their address, the date, a greeting, and a closing signature.

WRITE PARAGRAPHS Tell children that a group of sentences that tells about one main idea is called a paragraph. The sentences in a paragraph give details that support the main idea. Explain that the sentences telling about each item make up a paragraph. Point out that the first line of a paragraph is indented, or starts to the right of the other lines below it. Indenting paragraphs helps readers know where each paragraph begins.

Revise

SELF-CORRECTION Ask children to assess their drafts.

- Did I explain how the snacks are alike and different?
- Are the paragraphs indented? Do they each have one main idea and supporting details?

PARTNERS Have children trade letters with a partner. Have partners make sure the letters compare the snacks.

Edit/Proofread

CHECK FOR ERRORS Children should reread their letters for spelling, grammar, punctuation, paragraphs, and letter format.

Publish

SHARE LETTERS Children can read their letters to one another. The class can compare the two snacks.

Joe Kidd
18 Main Street
Anytown, TX 99999
January 11, 20__

Dear Mom,

   I like to eat oranges and carrots for a snack. They are both good for you to eat.

   An orange and a carrot are the same color. But an orange is a fruit and a carrot is a vegetable.

   You have to peel an orange to eat it. You have to peel a carrot, too. You can peel an orange with your fingers. But you need a vegetable peeler to peel a carrot.

   But they both taste very good and are good for you!

Love,
Joe

Presentation Ideas

ILLUSTRATE THE CHOICES Have children draw pictures of the two snacks they like to eat. Encourage children to consult their letters as they draw their pictures.

▶ **Viewing/Representing**

CONVINCE THE CLASS Have children bring in the snacks they compared. Volunteers can tell which snack they prefer.

▶ **Speaking/Listening**

Scoring Rubric

Excellent	Good	Fair	Unsatisfactory
4: The writer • crafts full sentences for each snack, with vivid descriptions. • provides accurate descriptions of the snacks' similarities and differences. • uses correct letter format.	**3:** The writer • presents clear, full sentences for each snack. • provides good descriptions of the snacks' similarities and differences. • uses letter format.	**2:** The writer • lists each snack, but may not use full sentences. • may give vague or unconvincing descriptions of the snacks' similarities and differences. • may use only partial letter format.	**1:** The writer • may not present two different snacks. • may offer few or no descriptions of the snacks' similarities and differences. • does not use letter format.

0: The writer leaves the page blank or fails to respond to the writing task. The writer does not address the topic or simply paraphrases the prompt. The response is illegible or incoherent.

Meeting Individual Needs for Writing

EASY	ON-LEVEL	CHALLENGE
Draw a Scene Have children draw a picture of themselves sharing a healthy snack with a friend.	**Write an Ad** Have children write an ad for a grocery store, naming two or three snacks and comparing them to show why shoppers might want to buy the healthy snacks.	**Make a Journal Entry** Have children write a journal entry about their favorite healthy meal. What did they eat? Who prepared the meal? How was the meal prepared? Who shared the meal with them?

Listening and Speaking

LISTENING STRATEGIES

Encourage children to listen to the speakers' descriptions carefully, and to try to picture the two objects that the speaker is comparing. They should ask questions that will give them more details about the snacks. Remind children to raise their hand and wait for their turn to speak if they have a question.

SPEAKING STRATEGIES

Remind children to make eye contact with their listeners as they tell about their favorite snack.

LANGUAGE SUPPORT

ESL ESL children may not have developed the vocabulary necessary to compare two things. Support those who need additional help by sharing examples of other children's work. Allow ESL children to "borrow" ideas for their own list.

PORTFOLIO Invite children to include their letters about their healthy snacks in their portfolios.

5 Day Grammar and Usage Plan

DAILY LANGUAGE ACTIVITIES

Write the Daily Language Activities on the chalkboard each day or use **Transparency 1**. Have children correct the sentences orally.

Day 1

1. The store were small. was
2. Mike were glad. was
3. Dad were happy, too. was

Day 2

1. The boxes was neat. were
2. The sisters was twins. were
3. The bag were big. was

Day 3

1. Miss Lin were old. was
2. The twins was girls. were
3. They was not old. were

Day 4

1. The plums was ripe. were
2. The jam were red. was
3. The cans was full. were

Day 5

1. The sack were tan. was
2. The store were a mess. was
3. They was late. were

Daily Language Transparency 1

DAY 1 — Introduce the Concept

Oral Warm-Up Say the following sentences aloud: *The boy is fine. Yesterday, the boy was fine.* Ask children what changed in the second sentence. (*is* changed to *was*) Repeat with these sentences: *The boys are fine. Yesterday, the boys were fine.* (*are* changed to *were*)

Introduce *Was* and *Were* Discuss with children:

Was and *Were*

- The words *was* and *were* are verbs that tell about the past.
- The word *was* tells about one person, one place, or one thing.

Present the Daily Language Activity and have students correct the sentences orally. Then have children write a sentence using *was*.

WRITING Assign the daily Writing Prompt on page 8E.

Name_____ Date_____ GRAMMAR 97

Was and Were

- The words *was* and *were* are verbs that tell about the past.
- The word *was* tells about one person, place, or thing.
  Mike **was** in his Dad's store.

Read the sentences. Write *was* in each sentence.

1. Dad _____ was _____ happy.
2. Mike _____ was _____ in the store.
3. No one _____ was _____ home.
4. Miss Lin _____ was _____ with Mike.
5. The store _____ was _____ full of people.

EXTENSION: Ask students to use the words was and were to write sentences about what they did yesterday.

Book 1.4 The Shopping List   97

GRAMMAR PRACTICE BOOK, PAGE 97

DAY 2 — Teach the Concept

Introduce *Were* Remind children that yesterday they learned about using *was*.

Review *Was* Write the following sentence on the chalkboard: *Meg was fast.* Ask children which word is a verb and tells something about Meg. (was)

Introduce *Were* Write the following sentences on the chalkboard: *The ham was thick. The hams were thick.* Read the sentences aloud. Ask children which sentence tells about one thing (the first) and which tells about more than one thing (the second). Discuss with children:

Was and *Were*

- The word *were* tells about more than one person, place, or thing.

Present the Daily Language Activity. Have students correct the sentences orally. Then have children write a sentence using *were*.

WRITING Assign the daily Writing Prompt on page 8E.

Name_____ Date_____ GRAMMAR 98

Was and Were

- The words *was* and *were* are verbs that tell about the past.
- The word *was* tells about one person, place, or thing.
- The word *were* tells about more than one person, place, or thing.
  Gran and Ann **were** in the store.

Read the sentence about each picture. Circle the verb for more than one person, place, or thing.

1. Mom and Dad (were) happy.
2. The jam and rice (were) for supper.
3. Mike and Dad (were) smiling.
4. The five plums (were) in a bag.
5. Grapes (were) on the list.

EXTENSION: Have the children think of sentences about shopping for groceries. The sentences should be about more than one person, place, or thing.

Book 1.4 The Shopping List   98

GRAMMAR PRACTICE BOOK, PAGE 98

Was and Were

DAY 3 — Review and Practice

Learn from the Literature Review *was* and *were* with children. Then read the first sentence on page 12 of *The Shopping List:*

Dad was always glad to see Mike.

Ask children why *was* is used instead of *were*. (Dad is only one person, so the correct verb is *was*.) Then write this: The twins _____ always glad to see Mike. Ask children to fill in the blank orally using *was* or *were*. Then ask them why *were* is the correct choice. (The twins are more than one person, so the correct verb is *were*.)

Use *Was* and *Were* Present the Daily Language Activity and have children correct orally. Then have children write two sentences using *was* and *were* about people or things in *The Shopping List*.

WRITING Assign the daily Writing Prompt on page 8F.

DAY 4 — Review and Practice

Review *Was* and *Were* Write the following sentence on the chalkboard: *The jets was fast.* Ask children if the sentence is correct. (no) Why not? (The verb should be *were*.) Why? (because there is more than one jet) Correct the sentence on the chalkboard, then present the Daily Language Activity for Day 4.

Mechanics and Usage Before children begin the daily Writing Prompt on page 8F, review proper nouns. Display and discuss:

> **Proper Nouns**
>
> - The name of each day begins with a capital letter.
> - The name of each month begins with a capital letter.
> - The name of a holiday begins with a capital letter.

WRITING Assign the daily Writing Prompt on page 8F.

DAY 5 — Assess and Reteach

Assess Use the Daily Language Activity and page 101 of the **Grammar Practice Book** for assessment.

Reteach Have children look through magazines and find two pictures: one of one person, place, or thing and one of more than one person, place, or thing. Then have children write a sentence describing each picture, using *was* or *were*.

Children can create a classroom word wall with the sentences they have written.

Use page 102 of the **Grammar Practice Book** for additional reteaching.

WRITING Assign the daily Writing Prompt on page 8F.

Name_____ Date_____ PRACTICE AND WRITE GRAMMAR 99

Was and Were

- The words *was* and *were* are verbs that tell about the past.
- The word *was* tells about one person, place, or thing.
  Mike **was** smiling.
- The word *were* tells about more than one person, place, or thing.
  Fran and Ann **were** smiling.

Read the sentences. Write *was* for one person, place, or thing. Write *were* for more than one person, place, or thing.

1. Mike _____ was _____ in the store.

2. Fran _____ was _____ in the store.

3. Fran and Ann _____ were _____ there.

4. Tin cans and glass jars _____ were _____ on the shelves.

5. Fran and Ann _____ were _____ trying to help.

EXTENSION: Have the children change the sentences with one person, place, or thing to sentences with more than one.

Book 1.4 The Shopping List 99

GRAMMAR PRACTICE BOOK, PAGE 99

Name_____ Date_____ MECHANICS GRAMMAR 100

Capital Letters

- The name of each day begins with a capital letter.
- The name of each month begins with a capital letter.
- The name of a holiday begins with a capital letter.

Read the sentences. Circle each word that should begin with a capital letter.

1. Ann Gomez was home on (thursday).

2. Last (april) was Mike's birthday.

3. Ann and Fran were at the (thanksgiving) dinner.

4. Miss Lin was celebrating (new year's day).

5. Mike was looking for birthday presents on (sunday).

6. It was cold last (november).

EXTENSION: Have the students write sentences that use names of days, months, and holidays.

100 Book 1.4 The Shopping List 6

GRAMMAR PRACTICE BOOK, PAGE 100

Name_____ Date_____ TEST GRAMMAR 101

Was and Were

Circle and write *was* or *were* to complete each sentence.

1. Mike _____ was _____ glad to see Mom.
   (was) were

2. Miss Lin and Dad _____ were _____ helping.
   was (were)

3. Ann and Fran _____ were _____ helping.
   was (were)

4. There _____ was _____ something else to get.
   (was) were

5. It _____ was _____ not milk.
   (was) were

Book 1.4 The Shopping List 101

GRAMMAR PRACTICE BOOK, PAGE 101

5Day Spelling Plan

ESL ESL children may have difficulty hearing the difference between the long and short *i*. Provide lots of listening practice of pairs of short and long *i* words, such as *hid/hide, bit/bite, bid/bide, will/while*. Once children can identify the difference, proceed with the spelling lessons.

DICTATION SENTENCES

Spelling Words

1. She likes your smile.
2. I have a white cat.
3. The path is wide.
4. We can look while we ride.
5. The cat could bite.
6. We can hide in the shed.

Challenge Words

7. You can ride after me.
8. Look at the blue hat!
9. What were you looking for?
10. Who said we could go?

DAY 1 Pretest

Assess Prior Knowledge Use the Dictation Sentences at left and **Spelling Practice Book** page 97 for the pretest. Allow children to correct their own papers. If children have trouble, have partners give each other a midweek test on Day 3. Children who require a modified list may be tested on the first eight words.

Spelling Words		Challenge Words	
1. **smile**	4. while	7. **after**	9. **were**
2. **white**	5. bite	8. **blue**	10. **who**
3. **wide**	6. hide		

*Note: Words in **dark type** are from the story.*

Word Study On page 98 of the **Spelling Practice Book** are word study steps and an at-home activity.

DAY 2 Explore the Pattern

Sort and Spell Words Say *hid* and *hide*. Ask children what vowel sound they hear in each word. Write the words on the chalkboard and circle the *i-e* pattern as you repeat the word *hide*. Repeat with the following pairs: *bit/bite; kit/kite; fin/fine; pin, pine*.

Ask children to read aloud the six spelling words before sorting them according to the spelling pattern.

Words ending with		
-ite	*-ile*	*-ide*
bite	smile	wide
white	while	hide

Word Wall As children read other stories and texts, have them look for new words with long-vowel sounds that follow the silent *e* rule. Add them to a classroom word wall, underlining the vowel and the silent *e*.

Name_____ Date_____ PRETEST SPELLING **97**

Words with Long i : i-e

Pretest Directions
Fold back the paper along the dotted line. Use the blanks to write each word as it is read aloud. When you finish the test, unfold the paper. Use the list at the right to correct any spelling mistakes. Practice the words you missed for the Posttest.

1. _____ 1. smile
2. _____ 2. white
3. _____ 3. wide
4. _____ 4. while
5. _____ 5. bite
6. _____ 6. hide

To Parents
Here are the results of your child's weekly spelling Pretest. You can help your child study for the Posttest by following these simple steps for each word on the list:
1. Read the word to your child.
2. Have your child write the word, saying each letter as it is written.
3. Say each letter of the word as your child checks the spelling.
4. If a mistake has been made, have your child read each letter of the correctly spelled word aloud, and then repeat steps 1-3.

Challenge Words

_____ after
_____ blue
_____ were
_____ who

Book 1.4
The Shopping List   97

SPELLING PRACTICE BOOK, PAGE 97

WORD STUDY STEPS AND ACTIVITY, PAGE 98

Name_____ Date_____ EXPLORE THE PATTERN SPELLING **99**

Words with Long i : i-e

Look at the spelling words in the box.

| smile white wide while bite hide |

Write the two letters that are found in every spelling word.

1. ____i____ 2. ____e____

Write the words that end with **ite**.

3. ___white___ 4. ___bite___

Write the words that end with **ile**.

5. ___smile___ 6. ___while___

Write the words that end with **ide**.

7. ___wide___ 8. ___hide___

Book 1.4
The Shopping List   99

SPELLING PRACTICE BOOK, PAGE 99

Words with Long *i*: *i-e*

DAY 3 Practice and Extend

Word Meaning: Add -s Remind children that we can add -s to a verb to show an action that one person or thing does now. Ask children to add -s to the following spelling words and write sentences using the words: *smile, bite, hide.*

Identify Spelling Patterns Write this sentence on the chalkboard: *Who can smile for a while?* Have a volunteer read it and tell which words follow the *-ile* spelling pattern and which word is a Challenge Word. Repeat with the spelling patterns *-ite, ide,* using these sentences:

The cat does not bite after she eats.

The sky is blue and wide.

Then have children write other sentences using the Challenge Words.

DAY 4 Proofread and Write

Proofread Sentences Write these sentences on the chalkboard, including the misspelled words. Ask children to proofread, circling incorrect spellings and writing the correct spellings. There are two errors in each sentence.

We can (hid) for a (whil). (hide, while)

I made a (wid)(smil). (wide, smile)

I took a (bit) of (whit) bread. (bite, white)

Have children create additional sentences with errors for partners to correct.

WRITING Have children use as many Spelling Words as possible in the daily Writing Prompt on page 8F. Remind children to proofread their writing for errors in spelling, grammar, and punctuation.

DAY 5 Assess

Assess Children's Knowledge Use page 102 of the **Spelling Practice Book** or the Dictation Sentences on page 37Q for the posttest.

Personal Word List If children have trouble with any words in the lesson, have them create a personal list of troublesome words in their journals. Have children write a short poem with the words.

Children should refer to their word lists during later writing activities.

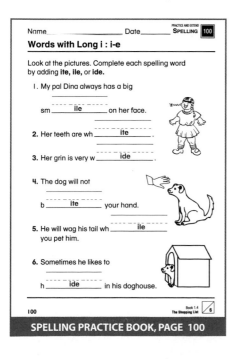

Name_____ Date_____ **PRACTICE AND EXTEND SPELLING 100**

Words with Long i : i-e

Look at the pictures. Complete each spelling word by adding **ite, ile,** or **ide.**

1. My pal Dina always has a big

   sm _____ile_____ on her face.

2. Her teeth are wh _____ite_____

3. Her grin is very w _____ide_____

4. The dog will not

   b _____ite_____ your hand.

5. He will wag his tail wh _____ile_____ you pet him.

6. Sometimes he likes to

   h _____ide_____ in his doghouse.

100

Book 1.4 The Shopping List

SPELLING PRACTICE BOOK, PAGE 100

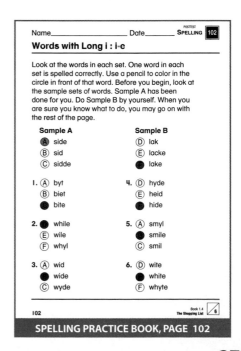

Name_____ Date_____ **PROOFREAD AND WRITE SPELLING 101**

Words with Long i : i-e

Finding Mistakes
Read the poem. There are six spelling mistakes. Circle the mistakes. Write the words correctly on the lines.

A tent that is (whide)
Is a good place to (hyd).
All the (whyle),
I sit and (smil)
I take a (bitte)
Of cake so (wite).

1. _____wide_____ 2. _____hide_____

3. _____while_____ 4. _____smile_____

5. _____bite_____ 6. _____white_____

Write a sentence using two words you wrote.

_____

_____

Book 1.4 The Shopping List

101

SPELLING PRACTICE BOOK, PAGE 101

Name_____ Date_____ **POSTTEST SPELLING 102**

Words with Long i : i-e

Look at the words in each set. One word in each set is spelled correctly. Use a pencil to color in the circle in front of that word. Before you begin, look at the sample sets of words. Sample A has been done for you. Do Sample B by yourself. When you are sure you know what to do, you may go on with the rest of the page.

Sample A
- (A) side
- (B) sid
- (C) sidde

Sample B
- (D) lak
- (E) lacke
- (●) lake

1.
- (A) byt
- (B) biet
- (●) bite

4.
- (D) hyde
- (E) heid
- (●) hide

2.
- (●) while
- (E) wile
- (F) whyl

5.
- (A) smyl
- (●) smile
- (C) smil

3.
- (A) wid
- (●) wide
- (C) wyde

6.
- (D) wite
- (●) white
- (F) whyte

102

Book 1.4 The Shopping List

SPELLING PRACTICE BOOK, PAGE 102

Reaching All Learners

Concept
- Teaching

Comprehension
- Cause and Effect

Phonics
- Long *o: o-e*

Vocabulary
- work
- because
- buy
- found
- some

Anthology

Yasmin's Ducks

Selection Summary Yasmin discovers the value and joy of teaching as she tells her friends what she has learned about ducks.

Listening Library

Rhyme applies to Phonics

INSTRUCTIONAL pages 40–65

About the Author As a young woman, Barbara Bottner dreamed of becoming an actress. While recovering from a broken leg, Ms. Bottner realized how much she loved to draw. She began to illustrate children's books. Soon she was writing stories, too.

About the Illustrator Dominic Catalano has illustrated several children's books. He is also a musician. Mr. Catalano owns his own design studio.

Same Concept, Skills and Vocabulary!

Leveled Books

EASY
Lesson on pages 65A and 65D
DECODABLE

INDEPENDENT
Lesson on pages 65B and 65D

📖 *Take-Home version available*
DECODABLE

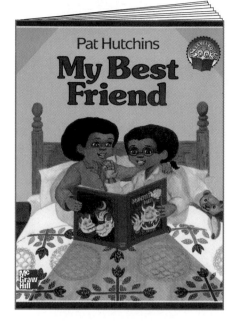

CHALLENGE
Lesson on pages 65C and 65D

Leveled Practice

EASY
Reteach, 135-142 Blackline masters with reteaching opportunities for each assessed skill

INDEPENDENT/ON-LEVEL
Practice, 135-142 Workbook with Take-Home Stories and practice opportunities for each assessed skill and story comprehension

CHALLENGE
Extend, 135–142 Blackline masters that offer challenge activities for each assessed skill

Quizzes Prepared by 📘 Accelerated Reader®

Social Studies ...	Map Skills, *58*
Science	Oil and Water, *38D*
	Fish, *44*
Math	Weight, *48*
Art	Favorite Animals, *38D*
Cultural Perspectives	Down Feathers, *42*
Language Arts ..	Read Aloud, *38G*
Writing	A Letter, *62*
Research and Inquiry	Find Out More, *63*
Internet Activities	www.mhschool.com/reading

Center Activities

> Each of these activities takes 15-20 minutes.

Phonics

MATERIALS
- Large index cards
- Crayons

Long *o* Flashcards

PARTNERS **Objective:** Make flashcards to reinforce long *o* words.

◆ Have partners look through *Yasmin's Ducks* to find long *o* words with the *o-e* pattern: *home, hose, globe, joke, nope.*

◆ Children write each word on an index card to make a set of flashcards.

◆ Partners take turns displaying the flash-cards and reading the words aloud.

Writing

MATERIALS
- Construction paper
- Crayons

Show and Tell

ONE **Objective:** Write sentences about a drawing.

◆ Have children draw something they would like to share on show-and-tell day.

◆ Children can write a sentence or two that tells about their picture.

◆ You may wish to have children use the story pattern for ideas: "I like to show _____."

Reading and Listening

Independent/Self-Selected Reading

ONE **Objective:** Listen and use illustrations to understand a story.

Fill the Center with books and corresponding audiocassettes or CD-ROMs children have read or listened to this week. You can also include books from the Theme Bibliography on pages T98 and T99.

Leveled Books

- *Spot's Trick* by Judy Nayer
- *Show and Tell Rose* by Josie Lee
- *My Best Friend* by Pat Hutchins

◆ Theme Big Book *Fish Faces* by Norbert Wu
◆ *Yasmin's Ducks* by Barbara Bottner
◆ "To The Top" by Sandra Liatsos
◆ Phonics Practice Reader, Vol. 2

Working with Words

Write Sentences

 Objective: Reinforce vocabulary words: *work, because, buy, found, some.*

◆ Have partners write each word on a card.

◆ Children match each word card with a word in the story.

◆ Partners take turns reading the sentences.

MATERIALS
- *Yasmin's Ducks* in the Student Anthology
- Index cards
- Pencils

some   buy   work

because   found

Art

Favorite Animals

 Objective: Draw and label a picture of a favorite animal.

◆ Have children draw a picture of a favorite animal.

◆ Children can use the story title as a model for labeling their pictures.

◆ Have children share their pictures and one interesting fact about the animal.

MATERIALS
- Drawing paper
- Crayons

Pam's Penguin

Science

Oil and Water

 Objective: Conduct a simple experiment and draw the results.

◆ One partner uses a paintbrush to brush oil on one paper bag.

◆ The other partner uses a paintbrush to brush water on both bags.

◆ Have partners draw a picture and write a sentence summarizing their experiment.

MATERIALS
- Lunch bags
- small jar of water
- Bowl of salad oil
- 2 paint-brushes
- Pencil

READING AND LANGUAGE ARTS	**DAY 1** *Focus on Reading and Skills*	**DAY 2** *Read the Literature*
● **Phonics Daily Routines**	Daily  Routine: Segmenting, 38J  CD-ROM	Daily  Routine: Blending, 40A  CD-ROM

● **Phonological Awareness**
 	
● **Phonics** *Long o*
 	
● **Comprehension**
 	
● **Vocabulary**
 	
● **Study Skills**
 	
● **Listening, Speaking, Viewing, Representing**
	Read Aloud, 38G "Drawing Ducks"
	
	☑ **Develop Phonological Awareness,** 38H
	
	☑ **Introduce Long *o: o-e,*** 38I–38J
	   Reteach, Practice, Extend, 135
	   Phonics/Phonemic Awareness
	   Practice Book, 143–146
	
	 Apply Long *o: o-e,* 38/39 "My Phone"
	
	ⓘ Intervention Program
		Build Background, 40A
		   Develop Oral Language
		
		Vocabulary, 40B–40C

		| work
			because	buy

found	some	|
		
		   Teaching Chart 100
		   Word Building Manipulative Cards
		   Reteach, Practice, Extend, 136
		
		 Read the Selection, 40–61
		   Guided Instruction
		   ☑ **Long *o: o-e***
		   ☑ **Cause and Effect**
		
		Genre: Informational Story, 41
		
		Cultural Perspectives, 42

● **Curriculum Connections**	Art, 38D, 38G	Social Studies, 40A
● **Writing**	**Writing Prompt:** Write about the pets you have, or the pets you would like to have.	**Writing Prompt:** Write a short article comparing a dog and a duck. 📓 **Journal Writing** Quick-Write, 61
● **Grammar**	**Introduce the Concept: *Has* and *Have,*** 65O Daily Language Activity: Use *has* and *have* correctly. **Grammar Practice Book,** 103	**Teach the Concept: *Has* and *Have,*** 65O Daily Language Activity: Use *has* and *have* correctly. **Grammar Practice Book,** 104
● **Spelling** *Long o*	**Pretest: Words with Long *o: o-e,*** 65Q **Spelling Practice Book,** 103, 104	**Explore the Pattern: Words with Long *o: o-e,*** 65Q **Spelling Practice Book,** 105

Meeting Individual Needs

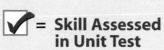 ☑ = **Skill Assessed in Unit Test**

 ⓘ **Intervention Program Available**

DAY 3 — *Read the Literature*

 Daily **Phonics** Routine:
Fluency, 63

💿 **Phonics CD-ROM**

Reread for Fluency, 60

Story Questions, 62
  Reteach, Practice, Extend, 137

Story Activities, 63

Study Skill, 64
  ☑ **Charts**
  Teaching Chart 101
  Reteach, Practice, Extend, 138

Test Power, 65

 **Read the Leveled Books, Guided Reading**
  ☑ Words with Long *o: o-e*
  ☑ Cause and Effect
  ☑ High-Frequency Words

 Intervention Program

 Activity   Science, 38D, 44

 **Writing Prompt:** Think of an art project you could do with your friends. Which friends own art supplies? Write about your project, and tell what your friends have that they can use.

🖥 **Journal Writing,** 65D

Review and Practice: *Has* and *Have*, 65P
  Daily Language Activity: Identify the correct use of *has* and *have*.

Grammar Practice Book, 105

Practice and Extend: Words with Long *o: o-e*, 65R

Spelling Practice Book, 106

DAY 4 — *Build Skills*

 Daily **Phonics** Routine:
Writing, 65F

💿 **Phonics CD-ROM**

 Read the Leveled Books and Self-Selected Books

  ☑ **Review Long *o: o-e*,** 65E–65F
    Teaching Chart 102
    Reteach, Practice, Extend, 139
    Language Support, 150
    Phonics/Phonemic Awareness
      Practice Book, 143–146

  ☑ **Review *o-e, i-e, a-e*,** 65G–65H
    Teaching Chart 103
    Reteach, Practice, Extend, 140
    Language Support, 151
    Phonics/Phonemic Awareness
      Practice Book, 143–146

  Minilessons, 43, 47, 51, 55, 59

 Intervention Program

 Activity   Math, 48

Writing Prompt: Interview a friend. Ask about your friend's pets. Write your questions and his or her answers.

Writing that Compares, 65M
  Prewrite, Draft

Meeting Individual Needs for Writing, 65N

Review and Practice: *Has* and *Have*, 65P
  Daily Language Activity: Identify the correct use of *has* and *have*.

Grammar Practice Book, 106

Practice and Write: Words with Long *o: o-e*, 65R

Spelling Practice Book, 107

DAY 5 — *Build Skills*

Daily **Phonics** Routine:
Letter Substitution, 65H

💿 **Phonics CD-ROM**

 Read Self-Selected Books

  ☑ **Review Cause and Effect,** 65I–65J
    Teaching Chart 104
    Reteach, Practice, Extend, 141
    Language Support, 152

  ☑ **Review Inflectional Endings -*ed*,** 65K–65L
    Teaching Chart 105
    Reteach, Practice, Extend, 142
    Language Support, 153

  Listening, Speaking, Viewing, Representing, 65N

  Minilessons, 43, 47, 51, 55, 59

 **Intervention Program**

Activity   Social Studies, 58

Writing Prompt: Pretend you're a duck planning a poster about people. Describe how people are different from you.

Writing that Compares, 65M
  Revise, Edit/Proofread, Publish

Assess and Reteach: *Has* and *Have*, 65P
  Daily Language Activity: Identify the correct use of *has* and *have*.

Grammar Practice Book, 107–108

Assess and Reteach: Words with Long *o: o-e*, 65R

Spelling Practice Book, 108

Language Arts

Read Aloud

The Ducks and the Fox
a fable retold by Arnold Lobel

Two Duck sisters were waddling down the road to the pond for their morning swim.

"This is a good road," said the first sister, "but I think, just for a change, we should find another route. There are many other roads that lead to the pond."

"No," said the second sister, "I do not agree. I really do not want to try a new way. This road makes me feel comfortable. I am accustomed to it."

One morning the Ducks met a Fox sitting on a fence along the road.

"Good morning, ladies," said the Fox. "On the way to the pond, I suppose?"

"Oh, yes," said the sisters, "we come along here every day."

"Interesting," said the Fox with a toothy smile.

When the sun came up the next morning, the first sister said, "We are sure to meet that Fox again if we go our usual way. I did not like his looks. Today is the day that we must find another road!"

Continued on page T2

Oral Comprehension

LISTENING AND SPEAKING Ask children to think about sequence of events as they listen to this story. Ask children what happens the first time that the ducks meet the fox. Then ask what happens at the end of the story. Can children explain why the story ended as it did?

Activity Divide the class in half. Assign half the children to be ducks, the other half to be foxes. Explain that ducks waddle slowly, while foxes walk quickly. Have the "ducks" try to waddle away as the "foxes" chase them. Have children switch roles. Encourage them to imagine how difficult it must be for waddling ducks to run away from quick foxes.

GENRE STUDY: FABLE Explain to children that a fable is a short story that teaches a moral or a lesson. The characters are often animals that speak and act like people. Ask: *What is the moral of this story? What does it teach us?* Have children discuss the lesson they learned from *The Ducks and the Fox.* ▶ **Kinesthetic**

Develop Phonological Awareness

Blend Sounds

MATERIALS
- puppet

Teach   Tell children that the puppet will say some mystery sounds. Tell children they will have to blend these sounds together to find out what the words are. Have the puppet say: *Listen as I say these sounds—/k/-/ō/-/n/. Help me blend the sounds together to say the word—*cone.

Practice   Have the puppet say the sounds for the words below. Have children blend the sounds together. Use the words: *broke, clove, cope, home, joke, nope, pose, rope, stove, vote.*

Segment Sounds

Phonemic Awareness

/b/-/ō/-/n/

MATERIALS
- Word Building Boxes

Teach   Tell children you will say a word. They will listen carefully and then say the word with you, sound by sound. Say: *hope—/h/-/ō/-/p/.* As you say each sound in the word, point to a word box. Then ask children if they hear the /ō/ sound in the word *hope.* (yes)

Practice   Tell children they will play a new version of Simon Says. Have children segment the sounds in the words Simon Says only if they have the /ō/ sound in them. Begin by saying, "Simon Says" to say the sounds for the word *bone.* Continue using these words: *hope, hop, mop, mope, not, note, globe, robe.*

Delete Sounds

Phonemic Awareness

Teach   Say to children: *Listen as I say this word—*broke. *It has four sounds: /b/-/r/-/ō/-/k/. If I take off the /b/ sound, the sounds that are left are /r/-/ō/-/k/.* Have children say the following with you: *broke, roke.*

Practice   Have children delete the initial sounds for the following words. Ask them to say the whole word, then say the word without the initial sound: *close, drove, globe, grove, probe, scope, slope,* and *spoke.*

 **ASSESSMENT**   Observe children as they blend sounds, segment sounds, and delete initial sounds. If children have difficulty, see Alternate Teaching Strategies on page T69.

38H

OBJECTIVES

Children will:

• identify words with long *o: o-e*.

• blend and read words with long *o: o-e*.

• review consonants.

....

MATERIALS

• letter cards and long *o* cards, and word building boxes from the **Word Building Manipulative Cards**

Skills Finder

Long *o: o-e*

Introduce	B4: 38I-J
Review	B4: 65E-F, 65G-H, 95G-H, 123G-H, 124I-J
Test	Book 4

SPELLING/PHONICS CONNECTIONS

Words with long *o: o-e* see 5-Day Spelling Plan, pages 65Q–65R.

Introduce Long *o: o-e*

TEACH

Identify the Letter *o* as the Symbol for the Sound /ō/

Let children know they will learn to read words with the letters *o-e*, where the letter *o* makes the sound /ō/ and the *e* on the end is silent.

• Display the *o-e* letter card and say /ō/.

BLENDING Model and Guide Practice with Long *o* Words

• Point to the *o* on the letter card and say /ō/. Have children repeat after you.

• Remind children that a consonant belongs in the space between the two letters and the *e* at the end is silent.

• Place the *m* letter card in the space between *o* and *e*.

• Blend the sounds together and have children repeat after you.

• Place the *h* letter card before the *o _e* letter card.

• Blend the sounds to read the word *home*. Have children repeat after you.

 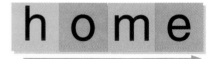

Use the Word in Context

• Use the word in context to reinforce its meaning. Example: *I walk home from school.*

Repeat the Procedure

• Use the following words to continue modeling and guided practice with long *o*.

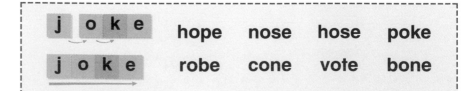

hope	nose	hose	poke
robe	cone	vote	bone

PRACTICE

LETTER SUBSTITUTION
Build Long *o* Words with Letter Cards

ONE

Build the word *mope,* asking children to repeat after you. Change the word to *hope* by replacing the *m* with *h.* Have children repeat after you. Next, ask children to build and read the following words, substituting the appropriate letter: *hose, nose, rose, rope, robe.*

▶ **Spatial/Kinesthetic**

ASSESS/CLOSE

Read and Write Long *o* Words

To assess children's ability to blend and read long *o* words, observe children as they build words in the Practice activity. Have children turn to page 39 and read "My Phone."

ADDITIONAL PHONICS RESOURCES

Phonics/Phonemic Awareness Practice Book, pages 143–146

PHONICS KIT
Hands-on Activities and Practice

McGraw-Hill School
TECHNOLOGY
Phonics CD-ROM

activities for practice with Blending and Segmenting

Daily Routines

DAY 1 **Segmenting** Distribute word building boxes. Say a word with long *o* and silent *e.* Have children write the spelling of each sound in the appropriate box. (Use *hope, nope, joke, home, vote.*)

DAY 2 **Blending** Write the spelling of each sound in *cone* as you say it. Ask children to blend the sounds to read the word. Repeat with *poke* and *woke.*

DAY 3 **Fluency** Write a list of words with long *o* and silent *e.* Point to each word, asking children to blend the sounds silently. Ask a volunteer to read each word aloud.

DAY 4 **Writing** Have children choose three words with long *o* and silent *e* and write a sentence using each word.

DAY 5 **Letter Substitution** Using the letter and long *o* cards, have pairs of children build *bone.* Taking turns, one child is to change a letter to build a new word, asking the partner to read it.

Meeting Individual Needs for Phonics and Decoding

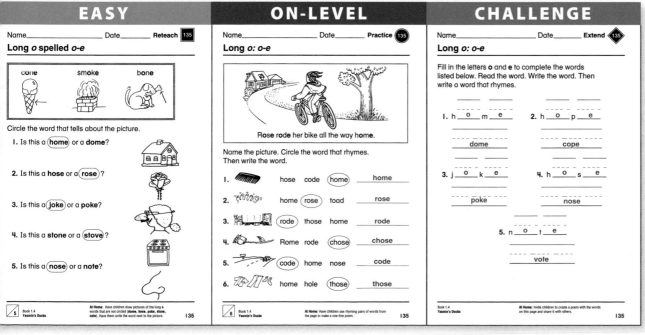

EASY	ON-LEVEL	CHALLENGE

Reteach, 135   Practice, 135   Extend, 135

TESTED OBJECTIVES

Children will read a poem with words containing long *o: o-e*.

Apply Long *o: o-e*

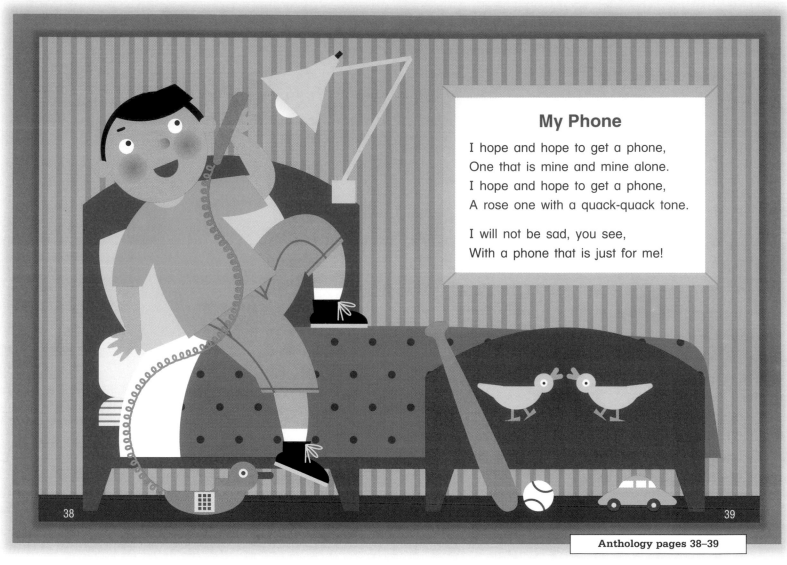

My Phone

I hope and hope to get a phone,
One that is mine and mine alone.
I hope and hope to get a phone,
A rose one with a quack-quack tone.

I will not be sad, you see,
With a phone that is just for me!

Anthology pages 38–39

Read and Build Fluency

READ THE POEM Tell children they will read a poem called *My Phone*. Model pausing at commas. Read the exclamatory sentence with excitement. Model reading repetitive words and lines with emphasis. Have children listen for long *o* words. Have children read with you.

REREAD FOR FLUENCY Have children pretend they are using a telephone. They can do repeated read-ings of the poem. Have them use extra feeling when reading the exclamatory sentence.

READ A DECODABLE STORY For additional practice reading to develop fluency, have children read *The Mole Zone* from **Phonics Practice Reader, Vol. 2.**

The Mole Zone

Dictate and Spell

DICTATE WORDS Segment the word *hope* into its three individual sounds. Repeat the word aloud and use it in a sentence: *I hope to get a phone.* Then have children say the word and write the letter or letters that represent each sound until they make the entire word. Repeat with *rose* and *tone* from the poem. Then repeat with long *o* words not from the poem, such as: *bone, close, globe, hole, joke, nose, rope, smoke, vote, woke,* and *zone.*

ⓘ Intervention **Skills Intervention Guide,** Book A, for direct instruction and extra practice in Long *o: o-e*

Build Background

ial Studies

Concept: Teaching

Evaluate Prior Knowledge

CONCEPT: TEACHING Ask children to think of something they can do. How would they teach this to someone else? Have children perform the following activities to help them become more aware of the teaching and learning process.

MAKE A WORD WEB FOR TEACHING Ask the class to brainstorm a list of actions and items they can use to help teach a fact or skill. Make a word web of their ideas.

▶ **Linguistic/Visual**

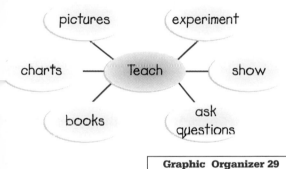

pictures   experiment

charts — Teach — show

books   ask questions

Graphic Organizer 29

MAKE A TEACHING-AID PICTURE Ask children to choose one of the actions or items from the word web. Invite them to draw a picture of themselves using it to teach a fact or skill. Then have children write a sentence under their illustration to explain how they are using that item to teach.

Develop Oral Language

CONNECT WORDS AND ACTIONS

ESL Have children pretend to be schoolteachers and follow simple instructions such as:

• Greet the class.

• Tell the class what you will teach today.

• Write some facts on the board.

Prompt children to say what they are doing by asking:

• What are you doing?

• What will you teach today?

• What items will you use to help you teach the class?

▶ **Kinesthetic/Linguistic**

Horses

I will use a book to teach about horses.

DAILY **Phonics** ROUTINES

DAY 2 **Blending** Write the spelling of each sound in *cone* as you say it. Ask children to blend the sounds to read the word. Repeat with *poke* and *woke*.

Phonics CD-ROM

LANGUAGE SUPPORT

ESL To build more background, see pages 145–148 in the **Language Support Book.**

OBJECTIVES

Children will:

- identify high-frequency words *work, found, because, some,* and *buy.*

MATERIALS

- Teaching Chart 100
- Word Building Manipulative Cards *work, found, because, some, buy*

TEACHING TIP

The following chart indicates words from the upcoming story that children have learned to decode, as well as high-frequency words that have been taught in this lesson.

Decodable	High-Frequency
globe	because
home	buy
hoses	found
joke	some
hope	work
Rome's	

SPELLING/VOCABULARY CONNECTIONS

The words *work, because, buy,* and *some* are Challenge Words. See page 65Q for Day 1 of the 5-Day Spelling Plan.

---

work

found

because

some

buy

Vocabulary

High-Frequency Words

Yum!

I (found) a pal who could teach me to bake.

We had to (buy) (some) sugar for cake.

We went to (work) and we made no mistake.

And now we will eat (because) we have cake!

Teaching Chart 100

Auditory

LISTEN TO WORDS Without displaying it, read aloud "Yum!" on **Teaching Chart 100.** Ask children if they ever had a friend who taught them something, or if they ever taught a friend something. What was it? How did they teach it?

SAY "YUM" FOR HIGH-FREQUENCY WORDS Have children aurally identify each high-frequency word using the following activity:

- Say aloud one of the high-frequency words. Read a line of the poem where the word appears.
- Before you read the line again, ask children to say the high-frequency word with you, and then say "Yum!" Then read the line again, pausing at the word.
- Repeat this activity with each of the high-frequency words.

Visual

TEACH WORDS Display "Yum!" on **Teaching Chart 100.** Read the poem, tracking the print with your finger. Point to and say the word *work.* Have them say the word with you. Ask them to hold up the vocabulary card for *work* and say the word. Repeat with *found, because, some,* and *buy.*

Hold up vocabulary cards for *work, found, because, some,* and *buy* one at a time. Have volunteers read the words and then circle them on the chart.

work found because

buy some

Word Building Manipulative Cards

CREATE SENTENCES Have partners write the vocabulary words on index cards. **PARTNERS** Have them turn the cards upside-down, take turns picking a card, reading the word, and then using it in a sentence.

Activities

Word Wall

Mystery Word Tell children that you are going to give them clues about a word. The first clue is always that the word is on the Word Wall. Other clues can be:

> *The word has _____ parts. The word begins like _____. The word ends like _____. The word rhymes with _____.*

Tap and Say Choose a word wall word and say it aloud. Then tap and say the first two letters of that word: some, s-o. Have a child spell the rest of the word out loud as he or she taps out each letter. (m-e) Repeat with each of this week's word wall words.

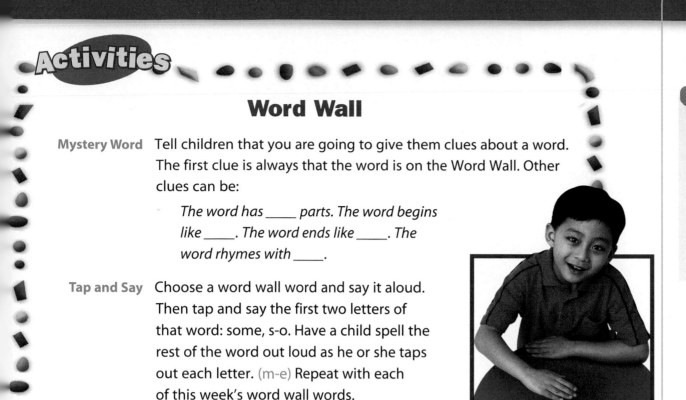

LANGUAGE SUPPORT

To help children develop understanding and recognition of high-frequency words, see page 145 in the **Language Support Book.**

Assess

Tell Me A Sentence Ask children to tell a sentence using each of the word wall words. Children should then spell the word wall word that's in the sentence they said aloud.

Meeting Individual Needs for Vocabulary

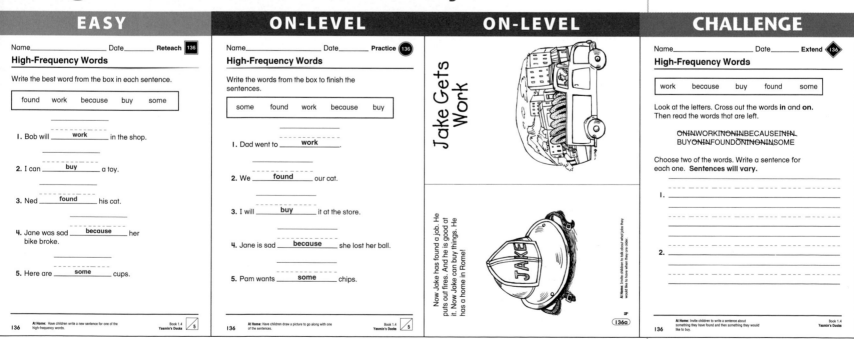

EASY	ON-LEVEL	ON-LEVEL	CHALLENGE
Reteach, 136	Practice, 136	Practice, 136a Take-Home Story	Extend, 136

Comprehension

Prereading Strategies

PREVIEW AND PREDICT Point to and read aloud the names of the author and the illustrator. Discuss the roles of each person. Then take a **picture walk** through the illustrations, stopping at page 48. Using words from the story, talk about the details of each illustration.

- What do you think this story will be about?
- What animal might we learn facts about?
- Will this story be a realistic one or a fantasy? (The drawings suggest a realistic story.)
- Where does this story take place?

Have children make predictions about the story using the class chart.

PREDICTIONS	WHAT HAPPENED
The story will be about why a girl likes ducks.	
We will learn facts about ducks.	

SET PURPOSES Ask children what they want to find out.

- What do Yasmin and her friends talk about?
- Why is Yasmin drawing pictures of ducks?

Meet Barbara Bottner

When Barbara Bottner was a young woman, she was an actress. When she was touring with a group of actors, she broke her leg. While she was getting better, Bottner realized how much she loved to draw. She began to illustrate children's books. Soon she was writing stories to go along with her pictures. Now Bottner loves to write and she spends most of her time writing.

①

Meet Dominic Catalano

Dominic Catalano has illustrated several children's books. He is also a musician. Catalano owns a design studio.

40

Meeting Individual Needs · Grouping Suggestions for Strategic Reading

EASY

Shared Reading Read the story aloud as you track print and model directionality. As you read with children, model using the strategy of understanding cause and effect. Use the Comprehension questions and other intervention prompts for additional help with decoding, vocabulary, and comprehension.

ON-LEVEL

Guided Instruction Ask children to read the story with you. Monitor children to identify any difficulties with reading they may have and to determine which prompts from the Comprehension section to emphasize. After reading the story, have children reread it alone, using the rereading suggestions on page 60.

CHALLENGE

Independent Reading Have children set purposes before they read. Remind them that thinking about why things happen can help them understand the story. After reading, have children tell why Yasmin likes ducks and why ducks don't get wet. Children can use the questions on page 62 for group discussion.

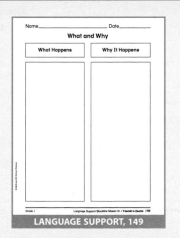

②

Yasmin's Ducks

written by Barbara Bottner
illustrated by Dominic Catalano

41

LANGUAGE SUPPORT

A blackline master of this Cause-and-Effect chart can be found in the **Language Support Book.**

Name_____ Date_____
What and Why

What Happens	Why It Happens

Comprehension

☑ **Phonics** Long *o: o-e*
☑ **Apply Cause and Effect**

STRATEGIC READING Explain to children that to help them understand the story, they can think about how one event causes another event to happen.

① Let's look at page 40 again. What did the author do before she became a writer? (She was an actress.) What does the illustrator do besides draw pictures? (He is a musician.) *Concept of a Book: Author/ Illustrator*

② **CAUSE AND EFFECT** Let's make Cause-and-Effect charts. We will fill them in as we read the story. *Graphic Organizer*

What Happens	Why It Happens

Genre

Informational Story

Remind children that an informational story:

- gives information in an easy-to-understand way.
- has characters and a setting that are usually realistic.

Activity After reading *Yasmin's Ducks*, have volunteers give examples of how the author used paper bags, water, and oil to present the information of how ducks stay dry. Discuss how the illustrations added to the information about ducks.

Comprehension

3 How does Yasmin feel about her drawing? (proud, happy) **How can you tell?** (She looks happy. She says the ducks are the best she has ever made.) **Why do you think she chose to draw ducks?** (Answers will vary.) *Use Illustrations/Analyze Character*

4 How do you think Yasmin feels about ducks? (She is interested in ducks; she likes ducks.) **How do you know?** (Yasmin has drawn ducks more than once; these are the best ducks she has ever drawn.) *Make Inferences*

3 "These are the best ducks I have ever made!" said Yasmin.
"I can just see them in the lake. They swim around and quack. Quack, quack, quack," said Yasmin.

42

CULTURAL PERSPECTIVES

DOWN FEATHERS Tell children that small feathers from ducks and geese, called down, are often used for warmth in blankets and clothing. In Scandinavian countries, where it can get very cold, eiderdown is collected from ducks. Display a world map or globe and point out Norway, Sweden, and Denmark.

Activity Invite children to find out more about Scandinavian customs and clothing. Ask each child to illustrate and label an item that has down feathers.
▶ **Visual/Logical**

My blanket is puffy.

My coat keeps me warm

"Ducks, ducks, ducks!" said Ben.
"I like your ducks."

43

Comprehension

⑤ CAUSE AND EFFECT Look back at Yasmin on page 42. What did she make? (a picture of ducks) Why do you think she draws ducks? (because she likes them) Let's write this on our Cause-and-Effect charts. *Graphic Organizer*

What Happens		Why It Happens
Yasmin draws a picture of ducks.		She likes ducks.

⑥ Look at the first thing Ben says. How many commas are there? (2) What does the comma show? (a pause) Point out the similar use of commas in the last line of page 42. *Concepts of Print*

43

Comprehension

7 Let's read the first sentence on page 44 again. What punctuation mark comes after the word *ducks*? (question mark) What does a question mark mean? (Someone is asking a question.) *Concepts of Print*

8 What is the first thing Yasmin did in the story? (drew a picture of ducks) What has she done now? (showed the picture to her mother) What will she do next? (take the picture to school to show to her class) *Sequence of Events*

7 "Look, Mom, do you like my ducks?" asked Yasmin.

"Yes, they are fine ducks," she said.

"I will take them to class. It's show-and-tell day," said Yasmin.

44

Activity

Cross Curricular: Science

FISH After children read page 45, have them name different fish they have heard of or seen. Prompt them by asking:

• What are some very big fish?

• What are some very small fish?

▶ **Linguistic/Logical**

RESEARCH AND INQUIRY Invite children to look through nonfiction books and magazines to find some examples of different fish.

interNET CONNECTION For more information about fish, help children log on to **www.mhschool.com/reading**.

Miss Rome's class held up their work. ⑨

Tim made pictures of fish with fins.
"I like to make my fish with lots of colors,"
said Tim. "I have five blue and white fish
at home. I hope to buy a red fish."

45

Comprehension

⑨ Phonics **LONG** *o: o-e* "*Miss...*"
I'm not sure what this word is. Let's blend the sounds of the letters together to read it. R o m(e)s Rome's Let's read the word *hope* the same way. *Graphophonic Cues*

⑩ Let's look at the pictures that Yasmin and Tim drew. **How are the pictures alike?** (They both show animals.) **How are the pictures different?** (Yasmin's picture shows ducks. Tim's picture shows fish.) *Compare and Contrast*

NOUNS Let's look at the second sentence on page 45. **How many nouns, or naming words, are there?** (4) **What are they?** (*Tim, pictures, fish, fins*) *Syntactic Cues*

PREVENTION/INTERVENTION

NOUNS Remind children that a noun is a word that names a person, place, or thing. Write the sentence *The boy made pictures of fish with fins* on the chalkboard. Invite a volunteer to the board to circle one noun in the sentence and explain why it is a noun. (*boy* is a person; *pictures, fish,* and *fins* are things.) Repeat this activity until all four nouns in the sentence have been circled. Continue to identify nouns by pointing to objects in the classroom, and ask children to call out the name of each object and explain why it is a noun. Explain to children that in the second sentence, *Tim* is a special kind of noun. It is a proper noun because it names the boy. *Syntactic Cues*

Comprehension

(11)  **LONG** *o: o-e* Look at the last word in the first sentence and point to it with your finger. Let's blend the sounds of the letters together to read it. h o s e s hoses. *Graphophonic Cues*

(12) **CAUSE AND EFFECT** Why does Kate like to make big red fire trucks? (Her dad is a fireman.)

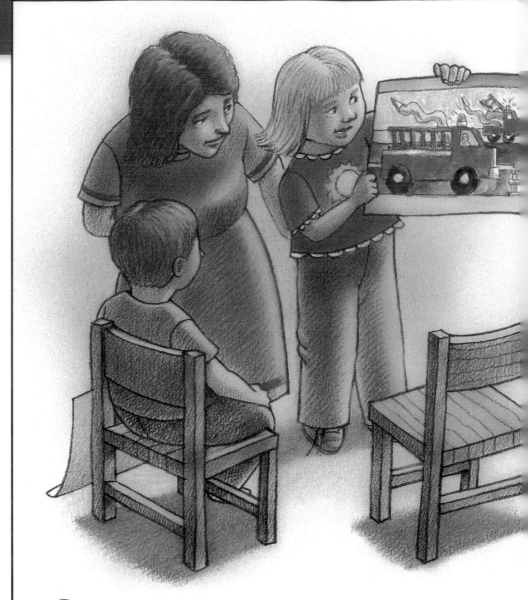

(11) Kate made fire trucks with big hoses. "I like to make big, red fire trucks. My dad **(12)** is a fireman. He is very brave," said Kate.

46

Fluency

READ WITH EXPRESSION

GROUP Point out the punctuation marks at the ends of Mack's sentences on page 47. Discuss the differences between a statement and an exclamation.

Have children read Mack's statement aloud.

Then ask them to read Mack's exclamation aloud, reminding them to show excitement.

Invite children to read the two sentences again, displaying the proper changes in expression.

Mack said, "I like to make rocket ships.
They can go around the globe and back!" (14)

47

Comprehension

(13) Look at the picture of Max. Now look
at the punctuation mark at the end of
the second sentence on this page. What is it?
(exclamation mark) What does that tell you?
(Mack is excited to talk about his picture.)
Concepts of Print

(14) **Phonics** LONG *o: o-e* "They
can go around the . . ." I'm not sure
what this word is. Let's blend the sounds
of the letters together to read it.
g l o b(e), globe *Graphophonic Cues*

Minilesson

REVIEW/MAINTAIN

Context Clues

Tell children that sometimes they will see
words they don't know. Remind them that
they can use pictures and other words in the
sentence to help them figure out new words.

Have children look at page 46. Point out the
word *hoses*. Ask children to point to the
hoses in the picture. Invite volunteers to
explain what a hose is.

Activity Point out the word *globe*. Ask
children to write a definition of the word
globe. Then invite children to draw a picture
above their definition.

LANGUAGE SUPPORT

ESL Some children may have
difficulty pronouncing
/sh/ in words. Ask children to sound
out /sh/ and draw it out, as if they
were hushing someone. Then invite
them to slowly add a vowel sound
after /sh/. Practice saying *rocket ship*
with children until they are comfort-

able blending the letters *sh* with the
short *i*.

Invite children to write their own
tongue twisters with /sh/. Remind children that correct pronunciation of
each sound is more important than
speed in reciting their tongue twisters.

Comprehension

15 What is Yasmin doing on this page? (She is showing her picture of ducks to the class.) *Use Illustrations*

16 How does Yasmin feel as she talks about ducks? (excited) **How do you know?** (Her sentences end with exclamation marks.) *Analyze Character/Concepts of Print*

15

16

Yasmin held up her ducks. "I like ducks the best," she said. "I want to make ducks with wings that shine! I want to make ducks that swim and quack!"

48

Activity

Cross Curricular: Math

WEIGHT Explain that most ducks weigh between two and four pounds.

Create a chart with the following heads: Weighs More than a Duck, Weighs Less than a Duck. Have children cut out pictures of animals to place in their charts.

▶ **Logical/Visual**

RESEARCH AND INQUIRY Have children research the actual weights of the animals in their charts.

***inter*NET** **CONNECTION** To find out about animals, have children log on to *www.mhschool.com/reading*.

"Why do you like to make ducks?"
Tim, Kate, and Mack asked.

49

Comprehension

17 Look at the picture on this page. What do you see? (children, a slide, the sun, and the grass) Where are the children? (at a playground) *Analyze Setting/Use Picture Clues*

18 Who are Tim, Kate, and Mack talking to on this page? (Yasmin) *Make Inferences*

P/i CONCEPTS OF PRINT Look at the first part of the sentence. There are punctuation marks at the beginning and end of it. What do these marks mean? (They are quotation marks. They show that someone is talking.) *Syntactic Cues*

P/i PREVENTION/INTERVENTION

CONCEPTS OF PRINT Write the sentence *"Why do you like to make ducks?" Tim asked.* on the chalkboard and read it with children. Ask children who is speaking. (Tim) Ask children to read what he is saying. To reinforce the separation between what is being said and the speaker, invite a volunteer to come to the board and frame the words between the quotation marks. Repeat this activity with other examples from the story. *Syntactic Cues*

Comprehension

(19) CAUSE AND EFFECT What did Yasmin just do? (She read a good book on ducks.) Why did she read a book about ducks? (because she wanted to learn more about them) Let's write this in our Cause-and-Effect charts. *Graphic Organizer*

What Happens		Why It Happens
Yasmin draws a picture of ducks.		She likes ducks.
Yasmin read about ducks.		She wanted to learn about them.

(20) MULTISYLLABIC WORDS Look at the picture on page 50. What things can you find in the picture that have more than one syllable in their name? (Possible answers: Yasmin, overalls, bushes, mountain, eyeglasses)

TEACHING TIP

CAUSE AND EFFECT To help children focus more closely, help them understand that in filling in their Cause-and-Effect chart, this process names the effect and then looks for its cause. Stress that they are "working backwards" by stating what happened and then asking why it happened. Make sure that children realize that the cause always occurs first and the effect always follows.

(19) "Well, I just read a good book on ducks. I found out a lot about them," said Yasmin.

"What did you learn?" Kate asked.

50

50 *Yasmin's Ducks*

Comprehension

21 Yasmin tells her friends that ducks don't get wet. Are Yasmin's friends surprised? (yes) How do you know? (They say "Wow.") *Make Inferences*

CONTRACTIONS Look at the last sentence on page 51. Point to the word *don't*. What does the apostrophe mean? (One or more letters have been taken out of the word.) Read it with me. *Semantic Cues*

"Did you know that ducks don't get wet?" Yasmin asked.

"Wow," Yasmin's pals said. **21**

"It's no joke," Yasmin added.

"How come they don't get wet?" Kate asked.

51

PREVENTION/INTERVENTION

CONTRACTIONS Write the word *don't* on the chalkboard. Invite children to read it with you. Then write the words *do not* below it. Ask children what letter was removed from *do not* and replaced by the apostrophe in *don't.* (the second o) Ask children to use

don't and then replace it with *do not* in the same sentence. Repeat this procedure with the words *can't, it's,* and *I'm.* *Semantic Cues*

Minilesson

REVIEW/MAINTAIN

Make Inferences

Remind children that they can use clues from illustrations to understand how characters are feeling.

Have children look carefully at the expressions on the characters' faces on pages 50 and 51.

Then ask them to brainstorm a list of words describing how each character might be feeling.

Activity Invite a volunteer to pantomime a character's expression. Suggest that the volunteer refer to the illustration as well as the list of words the class just brainstormed. The rest of the class can infer what the volunteer is feeling and call out descriptions of the volunteer's expression.

Comprehension

(22) **CAUSE AND EFFECT** What do ducks do to their feathers? (Ducks wipe oil on their feathers.) What effect does this have? (It keeps the ducks dry because oil and water don't mix.) Let's write this in our Cause-and-Effect charts. *Graphic Organizer*

What Happens		Why It Happens
Yasmin draws a picture of ducks.		She likes ducks.
Yasmin read about ducks.		She wanted to learn about them.
Ducks wipe oil on their feathers.		The oil keeps them dry.

(23) How does Yasmin know so many facts about ducks? (She has just read a book about ducks.) *Analyze Character/Plot*

(p/i) **RHYMING WORDS** Ask children to find a word on the page that rhymes with *sack*. (back) *Graphophonic Cues*

ⓈELF-MONITORING STRATEGY

ASK FOR HELP Sometimes you might not understand what you read. You can ask questions about what you don't understand. First think of the things you do understand, then ask a friend or ask your teacher to explain what you don't understand.

MODEL I understand that a duck has oil next to its tail. I have heard that oil and water don't mix. But I don't know how the duck wipes the oil on its feathers in order to keep dry. I wipe with my hands, but ducks don't have hands. How does a duck wipe oil on its feathers without hands? I will ask the teacher to explain it to me.

(23)

(22) "A duck has oil next to its tail," said Yasmin. "It wipes the oil all around its feathers. The duck's feathers don't get wet because water and oil don't mix. The water rolls off its back," Yasmin said.

52

(p/i) **PREVENTION/INTERVENTION**

RHYMING WORDS Write the words *sack* and *back* on the chalkboard. Ask a volunteer to underline the part of each word that is the same. (-ack) Then ask children to name other words that rhyme with *sack* and *back*. (Jack, pack, quack, rack, tack) *Graphophonic Cues*

Comprehension

24 Where was Yasmin at the beginning of the story? (at home) Where did she go next? (to school) Where will Yasmin and her friends go after school? (to Yasmin's house)
Sequence of Events

25 What do you think Yasmin and her friends will do at Yasmin's house?
(Maybe they will try to mix water and oil.)
Make Predictions

"That's cool," Mack said.

"Let's all go to my house after school,"
Yasmin said. "I'll show you how ducks
don't get wet."

53

LANGUAGE SUPPORT

ESL Make sure ESL children understand how oil and water don't mix by rubbing petroleum jelly on the back of your hand and then placing your hand in a bowl of water. You may wish to place this experiment at the Science Center for children to do.

Comprehension

26 **Phonics** **LONG** *o: o-e* Read the first sentence aloud. Ask children to raise their hands when they hear a long *o* word as you reread the sentence slowly. (*home*) Still using the first sentence, have children read silently as you track print and ask them to raise their hands when you reach the long *o* word. *Nonverbal Response*

p/i **BLENDING WITH SHORT** *o* Look at the first sentence. Find the word *got* and point to it with your finger. Now read the word with me, using your finger to help you remember to blend the sounds of the letters together. *Graphophonic Cues*

26

When they got home, Yasmin got out her book on ducks. "We need two bags and salad oil," said Yasmin.

54

---

p/i **PREVENTION/INTERVENTION**

BLENDING WITH SHORT *o* Write the following words on a piece of chart paper: *got, not, dot, mop,* and *hop.* Cover the first and last letters of each word with a self-stick note so that only the short *o* shows. Have children practice saying the short *o* sound. Then, starting with the first word, have a volunteer pull off one of the self-stick notes and blend the letters together. Invite another child to pull off the second note and blend all the letters together to read the word. Then have children smoothly read the word with you as you run your hand underneath it. Repeat this activity with the rest of the words. *Graphophonic Cues*

First, you put the oil on one lunch bag. **27**
Then you put some water on both bags,"
aid Yasmin.

"Look at that!" Tim said.

"That bag isn't wet," Kate said. **28**

"The water drips off!" Tim said.

55

Comprehension

27 Let's go through Yasmin's demonstration again. What materials did she get first? (her book on ducks, two paper lunch bags, and some oil) What did Yasmin do next? (put oil on one bag) After she put oil on one bag, what did she do? (put some water on both of the bags) *Sequence of Events*

28 What happened to the paper bags? (One got wet and one stayed dry.) How do you know? (Kate says, *"That bag isn't wet."*) *Draw Conclusions*

TEACHING **TIP**

DOUBLE NEGATIVES Focus children's attention on the sentence Kate said on page 55. Have a volunteer read Kate's words aloud and then ask if anyone can say the words in a different way with the same meaning. *(That bag is not wet.)* Show children that if Kate had said an extra *not* by mistake *(That bag isn't not wet.)*, she really would have meant the *opposite: That bag isn't* "not wet," or "dry." Remind children to use only one *no/not* word at a time to express a negative idea.

Minilesson
REVIEW/MAINTAIN

High-Frequency Words

Write each of the following high-frequency words on index cards: *you, said, the.* Distribute sets of cards to children.

Have pairs of children show each other the index cards in turn and practice reading them. Then have them find these words on pages 54–55.

Activity Give children a page from a newspaper or children's magazine. Ask them to circle any of these high-frequency words that they find.

Comprehension

(29) CAUSE AND EFFECT Let's write about Yasmin's demonstration in our Cause-and-Effect charts. What did she put on one paper bag? (oil) What happened when she put water on that bag? (The water rolled off the bag; the bag stayed dry.) *Graphic Organizer*

What Happens		Why It Happens
Yasmin draws a picture of ducks.		She likes ducks.
Yasmin read about ducks.		She wanted to learn about them.
Ducks wipe oil on their feathers.		The oil keeps them dry.
Yasmin puts oil on a paper bag.		She shows how oil keeps it dry.

TEACHING TIP

MANAGEMENT Discuss with children questions about the story that can be answered with an experiment or demonstration. Set up materials for the experiments in the Science Center. Have children label each set of materials by writing the question that the experiment will answer.

As children complete experiments, have them write notes about their results so that other children who use the center after them can compare their results.

"Water and oil really don't mix," Mack said.

56

30

31

"What about this? Did you know that ducks can dive to the bottom of very deep lakes?" Yasmin asked.

"And they don't get wet!" Yasmin's pals said.

"Nope! They don't," Yasmin said.

57

Comprehension

30 Look at the picture in Yasmin's book on this page. What does the picture show? *(a duck diving to the bottom of a deep lake)* When the duck dives underwater, why doesn't it get wet? *(because of the oil on its feathers)* *Use Illustrations/Draw Conclusions*

31 **INFLECTIONAL ENDING** *-ed* Find the word in the first sentence that tells about Yasmin's action. *(asked)* What is the root word? *(ask)* What is the ending? *(-ed)* Tell children that adding *-ed* to the end of an action word shows action that happened in the past.

LANGUAGE SUPPORT

ESL As children read, have them place self-stick notes on any words they do not know. Remind children that to help understand these words, they can use pictures on the page, think about the sentence that the word is in, or ask a partner or the teacher. You may wish to model using context clues to help children figure out the meaning of the word *dive* on page 57. Have children figure out what *dive* means by looking at the illustration. Ask children:

• What is the duck doing? (swimming downward in the water)

• What do you think the word *dive* means, based on what you see in the picture? (swim down or swim underwater)

57

Comprehension

32 **CAUSE AND EFFECT** What happens to the lake in the fall? (It gets cold.) How does this affect the ducks? (They have no plants to eat so they fly south.) Let's write this in our Cause-and-Effect charts. *Graphic Organizer*

What Happens		Why It Happens
Yasmin draws a picture of ducks.		She likes ducks.
Yasmin read about ducks.		She wanted to learn about them.
Ducks wipe oil on their feathers.		The oil keeps them dry.
Yasmin puts oil on a paper bag.		She shows how oil keeps it dry.
Ducks fly south in the fall.		It is cold and there's no food.

33 Why do you think ducks would fly south rather than north to find plants to eat? (because the south is usually warmer and plants grow where it is warm) *Make Inferences*

"Did you know that ducks fly south in the fall?" asked Yasmin.

32 "When it's fall, the ducks can't get plants to eat because the lake is cold. They go
33 south where they can eat."

58

Activity

Cross Curricular: Social Studies

MAP SKILLS Display a map of your state. Label North, East, South, and West around the edges of the map. (Example: Texas) Point out the major cities, such as Austin, Dallas, Houston, Ft. Worth, and El Paso. Invite a volunteer to the map to find a city in the western part of the state.

Repeat this activity for all directions.

Activity Locate your town on the map. Then invite children to locate towns or points that are north, south, west, and east of your town.
▶ **Visual/Spatial**

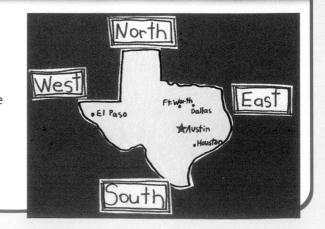

"They fly in a big flock," said Mack.
"I saw them last fall."

59

Comprehension

34 Look at the picture on this page. Do you think Yasmin's friends are now interested in ducks? (yes) How do you know? (They are drawing pictures of ducks.) *Make Inferences*

35 What else do you see in this picture? (children, art supplies, a book, nuts, and figs) Where do you think Yasmin and her friends are? (in the kitchen) *Use Picture Clues*

Minilesson

REVIEW/MAINTAIN

Main Idea

Remind children that the main idea describes what a story is about and can be told in two or three sentences. Work with children to write a few sentences that tell the main idea of the story. Guide results by asking the following questions:

- What is the title of the story?
- What does Yasmin do with her friends?
- How do her friends feel about ducks at the end of the story?

Activity Ask children to write the title of the story and the main idea sentences on a piece of paper. Then invite them to illustrate their sentences by drawing three separate pictures underneath. You may wish to hang these "mini book reports" in a bulletin-board display.

Comprehension

CAUSE AND EFFECT Why do you think Tim and Kate have started to like ducks? (because Yasmin has taught them about ducks) Let's write this information in our Cause-and-Effect charts. *Graphic Organizer*

What Happens		Why It Happens
Yasmin draws a picture of ducks.		She likes ducks.
Yasmin read about ducks.		She wanted to learn about them.
Ducks wipe oil on their feathers.		The oil keeps them dry.
Yasmin puts oil on a bag.		She shows how oil keeps it dry.
Ducks fly south.		It is cold and there's no food.
Tim and Kate like ducks.		Yasmin taught them about ducks.

RETELL THE STORY Using their Cause-and-Effect charts, have small groups of children talk about what happens in the story and why. *Summarize*

^{STUDENT} SELF-ASSESSMENT

Have children ask themselves the following questions to assess how they are reading:

- How did I use what Yasmin taught her friends to help me understand the story?
- How did I make sure I understood why things happened in the story?
- How did I use the pictures and the letters and the sounds I know to help me read the words in the story?

TRANSFERRING THE STRATEGIES

- How can I use these strategies to help me read other stories?

"I think I like ducks, too," Tim said.

"Me, too. I wish I didn't have to go home now," said Kate.

"It's raining out," Yasmin said.

60

REREADING FOR *Fluency*

PARTNERS Have partners take turns reading every page aloud while practicing appropriate rate and pausing.

READING RATE When you evaluate reading rate, have children read aloud from the story for one minute. Place a stick-on note after the last word read. Count words read. To evaluate children's performance, see

the Running Record in the **Fluency Assessment** book.

i Intervention For leveled fluency lessons, passages, and norms charts, see **Skills Intervention Guide**, Part 5, Fluency.

"Too bad we're not ducks!" Tim said.
"Then we would not get wet!"

Yasmin and her pals smiled.
"Quack, quack, quack, quack!"

61

Comprehension

Return to Predictions and Purposes

Reread children's predictions about the story. Ask children whether the story answered all the questions they had before they read it. Discuss their predictions, noting which needed to be revised.

Have children talk about the strategy of listing causes and effects in a chart. How did using their charts help them understand what and why things happened in the story?

INFORMAL ASSESSMENT

HOW TO ASSESS

Phonics LONG *o: o-e* Have children turn to page 51. Have them point to and read the word *joke*. Then have them turn to page 57 and repeat the activity with the word *Nope*.

CAUSE AND EFFECT Have children describe an event in the story. Ask them to state one cause and its effect that they learned by referring to their Cause-and-Effect charts.

FOLLOW UP

Phonics LONG *o: o-e* Continue to model blending long *o* words that end in silent *e* for children who are having difficulty.

CAUSE AND EFFECT Children who are having difficulty can review the story and ask themselves "What happened?" to pinpoint one effect. To find the cause, children should then ask themselves "Why did it happen?"

LITERARY RESPONSE

QUICK-WRITE Have children draw a picture of a duck in their journals. Ask them to describe what they find interesting about ducks and why. Then invite children to write about how Yasmin has inspired them.

ORAL RESPONSE Have children use their journal entries to discuss these questions:

- What is most interesting to you about ducks? Why?
- What words would you use to describe Yasmin?

SENTENCE STRIPS Children can use strips 1–80 to retell the story.

> 1
> "These are the best ducks

> 2
> I have ever made!" said Yasmin.

61

Story Questions

Tell children that now they will read some questions about the story. Help children read the questions and discuss possible answers.

Answers:

1. fly south *Critical/Sequence of Events*

2. to demonstrate that oil and water don't mix *Inferential/Make Inferences*

3. Answers will vary. Possible answer: It is raining and they will get wet. *Inferential/Make Inferences*

4. Reading helped Yasmin learn interesting facts about ducks. *Critical/Summarize*

5. In both stories, children learn about nature. *Critical/Reading Across Texts*

Write About the Experiment For a full writing process lesson related to writing a letter, see the lesson on writing that compares on pages 65M–65N.

Story Questions & Activities

1. What do ducks do in the fall?

2. Why does Yasmin need two bags and salad oil?

3. Why don't the children want to go home?

4. What did you learn from this story?

5. Is "What Bug Is It?" like this story?

Write About the Experiment

Yasmin puts oil on one bag.
Then she puts water on both bags.
Write what happens to each bag.

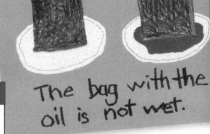

The bag with the oil is not wet.

Meeting Individual Needs

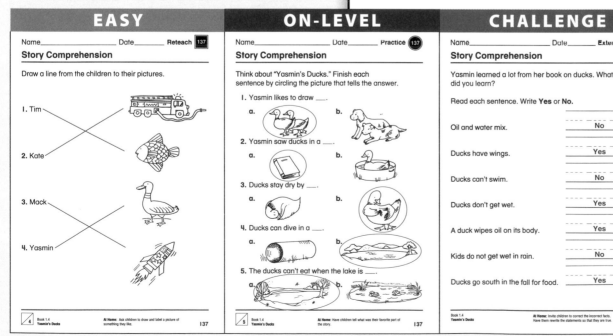

EASY	ON-LEVEL	CHALLENGE

Name_____ Date_____ Reteach **137**
Story Comprehension

Draw a line from the children to their pictures.

1. Tim
2. Kate
3. Mack
4. Yasmin

Book 1.4
Yasmin's Ducks
At Home: Ask children to draw and label a picture of something they like.
137

Name_____ Date_____ Practice **137**
Story Comprehension

Think about "Yasmin's Ducks." Finish each sentence by circling the picture that tells the answer.

1. Yasmin likes to draw ___.
   a.   b.
2. Yasmin saw ducks in a ___.
   a.   b.
3. Ducks stay dry by ___.
   a.   b.
4. Ducks can dive in a ___.
   a.   b.
5. The ducks can't eat when the lake is ___.
   a.   b.

Book 1.4
Yasmin's Ducks
At Home: Have children tell what was their favorite part of the story.
137

Name_____ Date_____ Extend **137**
Story Comprehension

Yasmin learned a lot from her book on ducks. What did you learn?

Read each sentence. Write **Yes** or **No**.

Oil and water mix.	No
Ducks have wings.	Yes
Ducks can't swim.	No
Ducks don't get wet.	Yes
A duck wipes oil on its body.	Yes
Kids do not get wet in rain.	No
Ducks go south in the fall for food.	Yes

Book 1.4
Yasmin's Ducks
At Home: Invite children to correct the incorrect facts. Have them rewrite the statements so that they are true.
137

Reteach, 137   Practice, 137   Extend, 137

Play Duck, Duck, Goose

Sit in a circle.

Think of names of birds.

Play Duck, Duck, Goose.

Play again and use other bird names.

Have fun!

Find Out More

Find out about another water bird.

How is it like a duck?

How is it different from a duck?

63

Story Activities

Play "Duck, Duck, Goose"

GROUP Read the directions aloud. Have volunteers explain how to play "Duck, Duck, Goose." Invite children to name different birds and to list them on the chalkboard.

Find Out More

Brainstorm a list of other birds that live on or near the water. Select one of the birds listed and create a Venn diagram with its name above one circle and "Duck" above the other circle. Then ask children to compare and contrast the two birds by calling out features that each one has. (For instance, a "Duck" has a bill and short legs; "Both" have feathers; a "Crane" has a beak and long legs.)

GROUP **RESEARCH AND INQUIRY** Ask children how they could find out more about ducks and other water birds. Is there a place nearby where children could observe them? Have any children gone on nature hikes and watched water birds? Invite volunteers to describe water birds they have seen.

inter NET CONNECTION For more information on water birds, go to *www.mhschool.com/reading*.

FORMAL ASSESSMENT

After page 63, see the Selection Assessment.

DAILY Phonics ROUTINES

DAY 3 **Fluency** Write a list of words with long *o* and silent *e*. Point to each word, asking children to blend the sounds silently. Ask a volunteer to read each word aloud.

Phonics CD-ROM

Study Skills

CHARTS

ⓋOBJECTIVES

Children will practice reading a tally chart of a class vote.

Remind children that they have just read a story about some friends who like to draw different things. Tell them that they will now read a tally chart that shows what some children like to draw. Explain that the tally chart shows the actual number of votes made for the thing the children liked to draw. Demonstrate by taking a quick vote on how many students enjoy drawing ducks.

Display **Teaching Chart 101.** Have children read the sentences and the title of the tally chart with you. Review how to read tallies and how to use tallies to show "5" (draw 4 vertical lines with a diagonal slash through them). Point to the column for "Fish" and ask how many children on the tally chart like to draw fish (2). Then help them read the questions below the diagram.

STUDY SKILLS

A Class Vote

This chart shows what some children draw.
Count the lines.
See how many children draw each thing.

What Do You Like to Draw?	
ducks	IIII
fish	II
fire trucks	HHH HHH
jets	HHI
hats	IIII

Look at the Chart

1 How many children like to draw jets?

2 Which thing do the most children like to draw?

Meeting Individual Needs

EASY	ON-LEVEL	CHALLENGE

EASY

Name_____ Date_____ Reteach 138

A Chart

This **chart** shows some children's toys.
Under the name of each toy are **tally marks**.
Each mark stands for a child who chose that toy as his or her favorite.

What Toy Do I Like Best?					
Kites	Bikes	Trucks	Planes	Dolls	Drums
IIIIII	IIIIIIII	IIIII	IIII	IIIIII	IIIII

Underline the word or words that answer the question.

1. Which two toys had five tally marks each?
bikes and planes   drums and trucks

2. Which two toys had six marks?
dolls and planes   dolls and kites

3. Which toy was the favorite of eight children?
bikes   trucks

4. Which toy was the favorite of the most children?
bikes   kites

138   At Home: Ask children to name each toy and count the number of tally marks under it.   Book 1.4 Yasmin's Ducks 4

ON-LEVEL

Name_____ Date_____ Practice 138

A Chart

Look at the tally chart below.

What Pets Do You Like Best?			
Mice	IIIIII	Rats	IIIII
Cats	IIIIIIIII	Birds	IIII
Dogs	IIIIII	Fish	IIIII

This chart shows some children's favorite pets. Count the marks next to each item. Then you will know which pets the children like best.

Write the correct word to complete each sentence.

1. The favorite pet of most of the children is a __cat__.

2. __Five__ children like rats best.

3. Mice and dogs each have __six__ tally marks.

4. Birds have __four__ tally marks.

138   At Home: Help children to make a tally sheet to record people's preferences about something that interests them.   Book 1.4 Yasmin's Ducks 4

CHALLENGE

Name_____ Date_____ Extend 138

Use a Chart

Take a class vote. Find what children like to draw.

What Do You Like to Draw?

Look at the chart. What do children like to draw best?

__Answer should be based on the chart.__

138   At Home: Ask children other questions about the chart they made, such as: How many children chose ducks to draw?   Book 1.4 Yasmin's Ducks

Reteach, 138   Practice, 138   Extend, 138

TEST POWER

Jasmin and Her Kite

Jasmin takes her kite outside.

She finds a place with no trees.

She unrolls her kite string.

She holds her kite up high.

The wind picks up the kite.

The kite begins to fly.

Soon it is high in the sky.

Why does Jasmin's kite fly?

● The wind picks it up.

○ There are no trees.

Ask yourself the question in your own words.

65

Test Power

THE PRINCETON REVIEW

Read the Page

Explain to children that you will be reading this story as a group. You will read the story, and they will follow in their books.

Request that children put pens, pencils, and markers away, since they will not be writing in their books.

Discuss the Question

Discuss with children what constitutes an answer to a "why" question. Have them reread the story, find the place where the kite starts to fly, and put their fingers on the reason why the kite flies.

Test-Tip

It's a good idea to restate the question in your own words to make sure that you understand it completely.

Leveled Books

Intervention ▶ **Skills**
Intervention Guide, for direct instruction and extra practice in vocabulary and comprehension

EASY

Spot's Trick

☑ **Phonics** Long *o: o-e*
☑ **Cause and Effect**
High-Frequency Words:
work, because, buy, found, some

by Judy Nayer
illustrated by Key Wilde

Guided Reading

PREVIEW AND PREDICT Discuss each illustration up to page 9, using the high-frequency words. As you take the **picture walk**, have children predict what the story will be about and record their ideas in their journals.

SET PURPOSES Have children write or draw why they want to read *Spot's Trick*. For example: *I want to find out what trick Spot can do.*

READ THE BOOK Use questions like the following to guide children's reading or after they have read the story independently.

Pages 2–4: Who sees some vocabulary words we just learned on page 2? *(buy, found, because)* On page 4? *(work)* *High-Frequency Words*

Page 7: Point to the word on this page that tells what Kate wants Spot to dig up. Model: If I don't recognize this word, I can read it by blending the sounds of the letters together as I run my finger under the word. 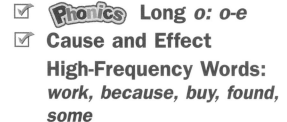 b o n(e) bone The word is *bone.*

Now read the word with me. Now let's use this strategy to find out what Spot dug up. r o s e s roses. *Phonics and Decoding*

Pages 8–13: What is happening so far in the story? (Kate wants Spot to do tricks, but he won't.) Is Kate proud of Spot? Why or why not? (No, she wants her dog to do tricks.) *High-Frequency Words/Main Idea and Details*

Pages 14–16: What happens when Spot jumps up on the bench with paint on his paws? (He makes paw prints on the bench; he paints the bench.) *Cause and Effect*

RETURN TO PREDICTIONS AND PURPOSES Discuss children's predictions. Ask which were close to the story. Have children review their purposes for reading. Did they find out what Spot's trick was?

LITERARY RESPONSE The following questions will help focus children's responses:

• Was Spot a good dog? What do you think would help Kate teach Spot a trick?

• Has someone ever wanted you to do something you couldn't do? Tell about it.

Also see the story questions and activity in *Spot's Trick.*

See the **Phonics** CD-ROM for practice with long *o: o-e.*

Answers to Story Questions

1. a trick
2. frustrated, upset
3. no
4. Kate got a dog and tried to teach him tricks. He didn't learn any. The next day, when Greg came over, Kate asked Spot to do a trick. Spot jumped up on the bench Kate was painting and that was his trick.
5. Answers will vary.

The Story Questions and Activity below appear in the Easy Book.

Story Questions and Activity

1. What does Kate want Spot to do?
2. How does Kate feel when Spot does not do those things?
3. Did Kate tell Spot to paint?
4. Tell what happened in the story.
5. What other pets have you read about?

Pick a Pet

Your Mom and Dad say you can have a pet!

What pet do you want? Draw a picture of it.

Give it a name.

Tell what it is and why you picked it.

from *Spot's Trick*

Leveled Books

INDEPENDENT

Show and Tell Rose

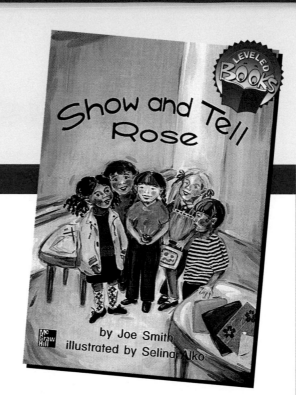

by Joe Smith
illustrated by Selina Alko

☑ **Long *o*: *o-e***

☑ **Cause and Effect**
High-Frequency Words:
work, because, buy, found,
some

Guided Reading

PREVIEW AND PREDICT Discuss each illustration up to page 9, using the high-frequency words. As you take the **picture walk**, have children predict what the story will be about and chart their ideas in their journals.

SET PURPOSES Have children write or draw why they want to read *Show and Tell Rose*. For example: I want to find out what Rose shows and tells.

READ THE BOOK Use questions like the following to guide children's reading or after they have read the story independently.

Pages 2–3: How many words can you find on page 3 with long *o* and silent *e*? (four) Read them for me. Remember to blend the sounds of the letters together if you need to. (Rose, hope, drove, home) *Phonics and Decoding*

Pages 4–7: Who sees some vocabulary words we just learned on page 4? *(found)* On page 5? *(because, some)* Page 6? *(work)* *High-Frequency Words*

Pages 8–13: Why was Rose happy to meet Mr. Lin Chan? (She liked his cooking; he taught her to make paper things.) What will Rose bring for show and tell? (a paper flower) *Cause and Effect/Make Predictions*

Pages 14–16: How did learning how to make paper things help Rose? (It gave her a new skill she liked; it gave her a new friend at home and friends at school.) *Cause and Effect*

RETURN TO PREDICTIONS AND PURPOSES Discuss children's predictions. Ask which were close to the story and why. Have children review their purposes for reading. Did they find out what Rose brought for show and tell?

LITERARY RESPONSE The following questions will help focus children's responses:

• How did Mr. Lin Chan help Rose?

• Have you ever taught anyone to do something new? Tell about it.

Also see the story questions and writing activity in *Show and Tell Rose*.

See the **Phonics CD-ROM** for practice with long *o: o-e*.

Answers to Story Questions

1. make something for show and tell
2. She was new and she hadn't made any friends yet.
3. make paper roses
4. She feels good.
5. Answers will vary.

The Story Questions and Activity below appear in the Independent Book.

Story Questions and Activity

1. What does Rose have to do for class?
2. Why is Rose a bit sad in class?
3. What does Rose learn how to do?
4. How does Rose feel about her new school now?
5. What are some things you can bring for show and tell?

Make Something with Paper

Get some paper.

Work with a partner.

Show your partner how to make something with paper.

You can write, color, or cut the paper.

Then your partner can take a turn.

from Show and Tell Rose

Leveled Books

CHALLENGE

My Best Friend

☑   Long *o: o-e*
☑ Cause and Effect

Guided Reading

PREVIEW AND PREDICT Discuss each illustration up to page 15. As you take the **picture walk**, have children predict what the story will be about and list their ideas.

SET PURPOSES Have children write or draw why they want to read *My Best Friend*. For example: *I want to find out more about the best friend.*

READ THE BOOK Use questions like the following to guide children's reading or after they have read the story independently.

Pages 2–9: Let's read these pages together and look at the pictures. What is this book about? (two best friends) Why is the girl glad to have a best friend? (Her friend knows how to do things she can't do.) What can her friend do? (run fast, climb high) *Use Illustrations/Make Inferences*

Pages 14–25: What else can the best friend do well? (untie her shoelaces, do up her buttons) What about the girl? (She can't do those things very well.) What is the friend afraid of? (monsters) Is the girl afraid? (no) *Details*

Pages 20–25: What made the monster? (the wind blowing the curtains) How does the girl make the monster go away? (She closes the window.) *Cause and Effect*

Page 24: Find the long *o* word on this page and point to it. *(close)* Let's read it together. Remember that *s* can sometimes make the sound /z/.

RETURN TO PREDICTIONS AND PURPOSES Discuss children's predictions. Ask which were close to the story and why. Have children review their purposes for reading. Did they find out more about the best friends?

LITERARY RESPONSE The following questions will help focus children's responses:

- Are you good at something no one else can do? Tell about it.

- Can your friend do something you can't? Do you like that? Why or why not?

Also see the story questions and activity in *My Best Friend*.

See the **CD-ROM** for practice with long *o: o-e.*

Answers to Story Questions

1. jump, eat spaghetti, paint
2. She thinks the wind is a monster.
3. Answers will vary.
4. two best friends
5. Both stories are about children who are friends.

The Story Questions and Activity below appear in the Challenge Book.

Story Questions and Activity

1. Name three things the friends do.
2. Why is the girl in the story afraid?
3. What makes a friend special?
4. What is this story about?
5. How is this story like *Big Brother Little Brother*?

Your Special Friend

Draw a picture of a special friend. Write a sentence that tells why your friend is special.

from *My Best Friend*

Bringing Groups Together

Anthology and Leveled Books

Connecting Texts

CLASS DISCUSSION	CHARACTER WEB
Lead a discussion of how the unit theme of Teaching applies to each of the stories. Have children construct a word web that describes what characters teach or what they learn from their own experiences or from others.	Have children create a web to compare the characters from their stories, their traits and what they do.

Yasmin's Ducks
Yasmin teaches her friends about ducks.

Spot's Trick
Kate works hard to teach Spot a trick.

Teaching

Show and Tell Rose
Mr. Lin Chan teaches Rose to make origami.

My Best Friend
A girl teaches her best friend not to be afraid.

Viewing/Representing

GROUP PRESENTATIONS Divide the class into groups, one for each of the four books. (For *Yasmin's Ducks,* combine children of different reading levels.) Have each group draw pictures of the main events and orally summarize the book. Have each group present its pictures and summary.

AUDIENCE RESPONSE
Ask children to pay attention to each group's presentation. Allow time for questions after each group presents.

Research and Inquiry

MORE ABOUT TEACHING Have children ask themselves: What is something I would like a friend or relative to teach me? Then invite them to:

- have show and tell in class, describing something that can be taught and who could teach it.

- ask a teacher of music, dance, or art to come and speak about it.

interNET CONNECTION Have children log on to **www.mhschool.com/reading** for more information about teachers.

JOURNAL Children can draw pictures representing what they learned in their journals.

OBJECTIVES

Children will:

- identify /ō/o words with final *e*.
- blend and read long *o* words.
- review consonants.

MATERIALS

- **Teaching Chart 102**
- long *o* vowel card from the **Word Building Manipulative Cards**

Skills Finder	
Long o: o-e	
Introduce	B4: 38I-J
Review	B4: 65E-F, 65G-H, 95G-H, 123G-H, 124I-J
Test	Book 4

ALTERNATE TEACHING STRATEGY

LONG *o: o-e*

For a different approach to teaching this skill, see pages T69 and T70.

Review **Long** *o: o-e*

PREPARE

Listen for Long *o* Read the following sentences and have children raise their hands whenever they hear a word with the long *o* sound.

- I <u>wrote</u> a <u>note</u>. It has lots of <u>jokes</u>. I <u>hope</u> my <u>note</u> is funny.

TEACH

Review the letters *o-e* as symbols for the sound /o/

- Tell children they will review vowel pattern *o_e* and the long *o* sound it makes.
- Display the long vowel card *o_e*. Remind children that the space between the letters is for a consonant letter. Together the letters make a long *o* sound.

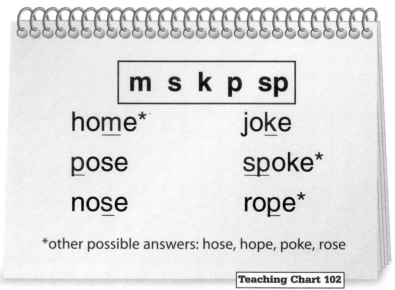

m s k p sp

home*   joke

pose   spoke*

nose   rope*

*other possible answers: hose, hope, poke, rose

Teaching Chart 102

BLENDING
Model and Guide Practice with Long *o* Words

- Display **Teaching Chart 102**. Cover the letter *h* in the first example. Run your finger under the letters *o-e* and say /ō/.
- Choose the letter *m* from the box at the top of the chart and write it in the blank space. Blend the sounds together to say *o me*.
- Uncover the letter *h*. Run your finger under the letters again and have children blend the sounds and read the word *home*. home

Use the Word in Context   Have volunteers use the word in a sentence to reinforce its meaning. Example: *Let's go home.*

Repeat the Procedure   Erase *m* and model blending with *s* and the word *hose*. Continue by having children substitute other letters to complete words on the chart.

PRACTICE

BLENDING
Build long _o_
Words with Letter
Banks

PARTNERS

Write the following letter banks on the chalkboard as shown:

h	j	r
p	w	n

o

ke	me	de
pe	le	se

Have a child choose a letter from the first bank, write it down, and then write the letter _o_. Have another child choose a pair of letters from the third bank to form a word. Ask children to read the word. Then have the children sort the words into rhyming groups.

▶ **Spatial/Linguistic**

ASSESS/CLOSE

Read Long _o_
Words

To assess children's mastery of blending and reading long _o_ words, observe them as they build words in the Practice activity. Ask each child to read three or four words aloud from their list.

ADDITIONAL PHONICS RESOURCES

Phonics/Phonemic Awareness
Practice Book,
pages 143–146

McGraw-Hill School
TECHNOLOGY

PHONICS KIT
Hands-on Activities and Practice

 **CD-ROM**
activities for practice with
Blending and Building

DAY **4** **Writing** Have children choose three words with long _o_ and silent _e_ and write a sentence using each word.

 **CD-ROM**

SPELLING/PHONICS CONNECTIONS

Words with long _o_: See 5-Day Spelling Plan, pages 65Q–65R.

i **Intervention** **Skills**
Intervention Guide, for direct instruction and extra practice in Long _o: o-e_

Meeting Individual Needs for Phonics

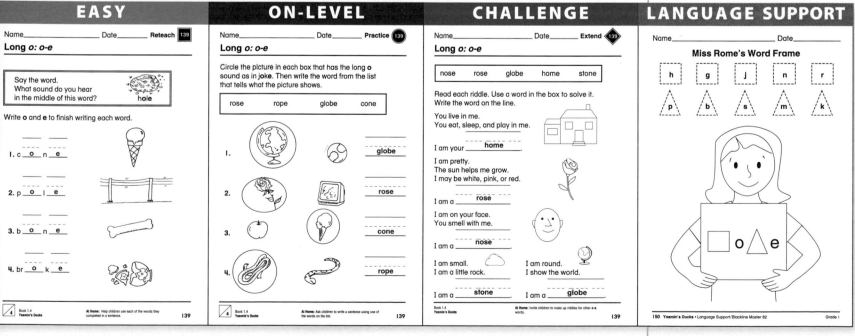

EASY	ON-LEVEL	CHALLENGE	LANGUAGE SUPPORT
Reteach, 139	Practice, 139	Extend, 139	Language Support, 150

**OBJECTIVES**

Children will:

- review /ō/o, /ī/i, /ā/a in words with final *e*.
- blend and read long *o, i,* and *a* in words with final *e*.
- cumulative review: discriminate between long and short *o, i,* and *a* sounds.

MATERIALS

- **Teaching Chart 103**
- **Phonics Practice Reader, Volume 2**

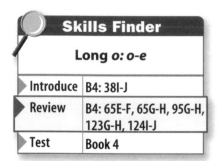

Skills Finder
Long *o: o-e*

Introduce	B4: 38I–J
Review	B4: 65E–F, 65G–H, 95G–H, 123G–H, 124I–J
Test	Book 4

ALTERNATE TEACHING STRATEGY

DISCRIMINATION BETWEEN LONG AND SHORT *o, i,* AND *a*

For a different approach to teaching this skill, see pages T64, T68, and T72.

Review *o-e, i-e, a-e*

PREPARE

Discriminate Between Long and Short *o, i, a*
Write the following long *o, i,* and *a* words with final *e* on the chalkboard: *rope, bike,* and *cake.* Ask a volunteer for a word that has the same /ō/ sound as in *rope.* Then ask another volunteer for a word in which *o* makes the short sound. Repeat the activity for long and short *i* and *a.*

TEACH

BLENDING Model and Guide Practice in Discriminating Long and Short *o, i,* and *a*

- Display **Teaching Chart 103**. Explain that the chart shows nine words. Children can make nine more words by adding *e* to the end of each word.
- Blend the first word on the chart with children.

  h o p   hop

- Write an *e* at the end of the first word and blend the word with children.

  h o pe   hope

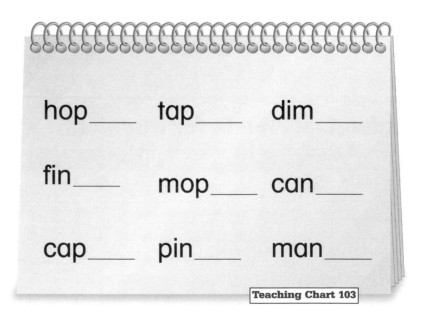

hop____   tap____   dim____

fin____   mop____   can____

cap____   pin____   man____

Teaching Chart 103

Use the Word in Context
Ask a volunteer to use both words in a sentence to reinforce their meanings. Example: *I hope I can hop on one foot.*

Repeat the Procedure
Continue with **Teaching Chart 103**. Have children blend the sounds aloud and say the word. Then add an *e* to the end of the word and have them blend the sounds to say the new word.

PRACTICE

BLENDING
Build Words with Long and Short o, i, and a

PARTNERS

Have children work in pairs. Ask one partner to write as many words with long o as possible, while the other partner writes as many words with short o as possible. Have partners check each other's work. Repeat with long and short i and a. Have partners compare their word lists to lists that other pairs have created.

▶ **Linguistic/Interpersonal**

ASSESS/CLOSE

Read Words with Long and Short o, i, a

Use your observations from the Practice activity to determine if children need more reinforcement discriminating between long and short o, i, and a.

Read A Decodable Story

For additional practice reading words with long o; o-e and to develop fluency, direct children to read the story *Dad's Kite Kit* from the **Phonics Practice Reader, Volume 2.**

ADDITIONAL PHONICS RESOURCES

Phonics/Phonemic Awareness Practice Book, pages 143–146

PHONICS KIT
Hands-on Activities and Practice

McGraw-Hill School
TECHNOLOGY

Phonics **CD-ROM**
activities for practice with Blending and Building

DAILY Phonics ROUTINES

DAY 5   **Letter Substitution**
Using the letter and long o cards, have pairs of children build *bone.* Taking turns, one child is to change a letter to build a new word, asking the partner to read it.

Phonics **CD-ROM**

ⓘ **Intervention** ▸ **Skills Intervention Guide,** for direct instruction and extra practice in Long o: o-e

---

Meeting Individual Needs for Phonics

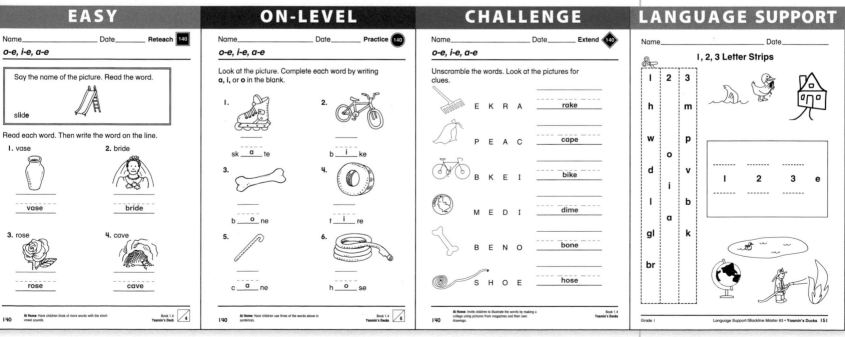

EASY	ON-LEVEL	CHALLENGE	LANGUAGE SUPPORT
Reteach, 140	Practice, 140	Extend, 140	Language Support, 151

BJECTIVES

Children will identify cause and effect.

MATERIALS
• Teaching Chart 104

Skills Finder

Cause & Effect

Introduce	B4: 37I-J
Review	B4: 65I-J, 133E-F
Test	Book 4
Maintain	B5: 17, 251, 267

TEACHING TIP

CAUSE AND EFFECT

Say a simple cause-and-effect statement aloud. As you repeat the sentence, ask children to raise their hands when they hear the cause and clap their hands when they hear the effect. For example, *It was snowing* (cause) *so I stayed at home.* (effect)

SELECTION
Connection

Children may choose from the following titles for independent reading.

• *Yasmin's Ducks*

• *Spot's Trick*

• *Show and Tell Rose*

• *My Best Friend*

Bibliography, pages T98–T99

Review Cause and Effect

PREPARE

Review Cause and Effect Remind children that as they read or listen, they should think about how one thing can cause another thing to happen.

TEACH

Identify Cause and Effect Display **Teaching Chart 104**. Read the first set of sentences aloud, tracking the print as you read. Ask children to think about why Yasmin put on her coat.

1. It is cold.
   Yasmin puts on her coat.

2. It is raining.
   Yasmin brings her umbrella.

3. It is sunny.
   Yasmin puts on her hat.

Cause	Effect
1. It is cold.	1. Yasmin puts on her coat.
2. It is raining.	2. Yasmin brings her umbrella.
3. It is sunny.	3. Yasmin puts on her hat.

Teaching Chart 104

MODEL As I read the first two sentences, I need to figure out why Yasmin put on her coat. She put on her coat because it is cold. So the cause is the cold, and the effect is that Yasmin put on her coat.

Follow the same procedure for the other sets of sentences on the chart. Have volunteers write the causes and effects on **Teaching Chart 104**.

PRACTICE

Create a Cause and Effect Chart

GROUP

Have children reread *Yasmin's Ducks,* or other stories they have read, and look for causes and effects. Make another cause and effect chart. Ask children to write sentences on the chart showing causes and effects. ▶ **Logical/Logistic**

ASSESS/CLOSE

Identify Cause and Effect

Brainstorm with children events that happen each day. Then write sentences on the chalkboard that tell each event and its effect. For example: *The alarm clock went off and I woke up. I was hot so I opened the window.* Have volunteers circle the cause and underline the effect in each sentence. Ask if there were any clue words that helped them to determine which was the cause and which was the effect.

ALTERNATE TEACHING STRATEGY

CAUSE AND EFFECT
For a different approach to teaching this skill, see page T67.

Intervention Skills
Intervention Guide, for direct instruction and extra practice in Cause and Effect

Meeting Individual Needs for Comprehension

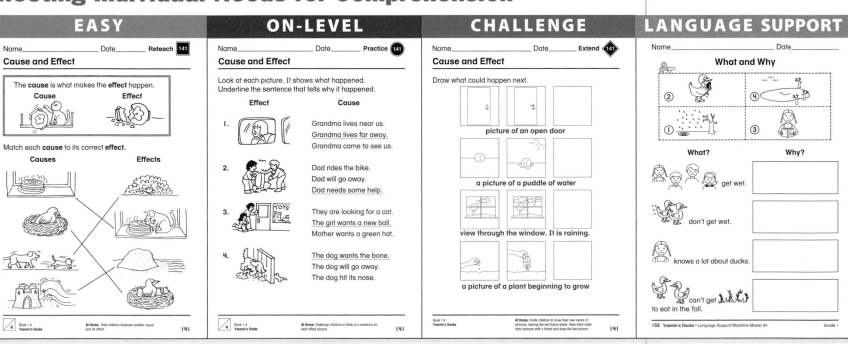

Reteach, 141   Practice, 141   Extend, 141   Language Support, 152

65J

OBJECTIVES

Children will:

- review reading words with the inflectional ending -*ed*, including words with a double consonant or a dropped -*e*.
- understand the concept of root words and suffixes.

....

MATERIALS
- **Teaching Chart 105**
- index cards

Skills Finder

Inflectional Ending -*ed*	
Introduce	B2: 35K-L
Review	B2: 65K-L, 137I-J; B4: 65K-L
Test	Book 2, Book 4

LANGUAGE SUPPORT

ESL If children are having difficulty remembering rules for the -*ed* ending, have them list only words that need a double consonant on one page. Then have them list only words that drop the final -*e* on a separate page.

Review Inflectional Ending -ed

PREPARE

Review the Concept

Write the word *flap* on the chalkboard. Have children pretend they are ducks and are flapping their wings. As they tell what they just did, add -*ped*. Explain that often -*ed* is added to words that show that something already happened. Explain that -*ed* is a suffix. Point out that with some words, like *flap*, the last letter must be doubled before the -*ed* is added.

Repeat the procedure with the word *smile*. Explain that with some words, like *smile*, the final *e* must be dropped before the -*ed* is added.

TEACH

Identify Root Words

Track the first sentence on **Teaching Chart 105** as you read it with children. Then point to the word *flapped* on the chart. Ask children if they recognize the root word. (*flap*) Model for children how understanding inflectional endings can help them read.

I Like Ducks

The duck <u>flap</u>ped its wings.

I <u>smile</u>d at the ducks.

The ducks <u>race</u>d.

Teaching Chart 105

MODEL I can use what I already know to help me read words I don't recognize. I know the root word *flap*. I know that sometimes when you add the suffix -*ed* to the end of a word, you have to double the last letter of the word. That's where the extra *p* comes from. The suffix -*ed* shows that the action happened in the past. The word is *flapped*.

Repeat this activity with the other two sentences. Then call on children to come up and draw a line under the base word in each sentence.

PRACTICE

Add -ed
PARTNERS

Write *added, hiked,* and *smiled* on the chalkboard. Have partners read each word and write it on an index card so that the *-ed* appears after a dotted line. Then have them turn the card over and write the root word without the *-ed* ending. Invite volunteers to explain how the words *hiked* and *smiled* are spelled without the *-ed* ending. Then write *stop* and *care* on the chalkboard. Call on children to add *-ed* to each root word, making sure either to double the final consonant or drop the final *e*.

▶ **Linguistic**

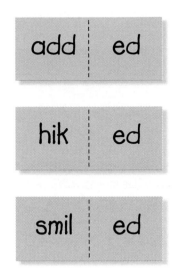

ASSESS/CLOSE

Identify More Root Words

Use your observations from the Practice activity to determine if children need more reinforcement with *-ed* words with double consonants or dropped *-e* endings. Provide children with other *-ed* words such as *sipped, voted,* and *talked.* Have children circle the part of the word that they know and explain how each word changes when *-ed* is added.

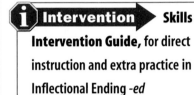

Intervention **Skills**
Intervention Guide, for direct instruction and extra practice in Inflectional Ending *-ed*

Meeting Individual Needs for Vocabulary

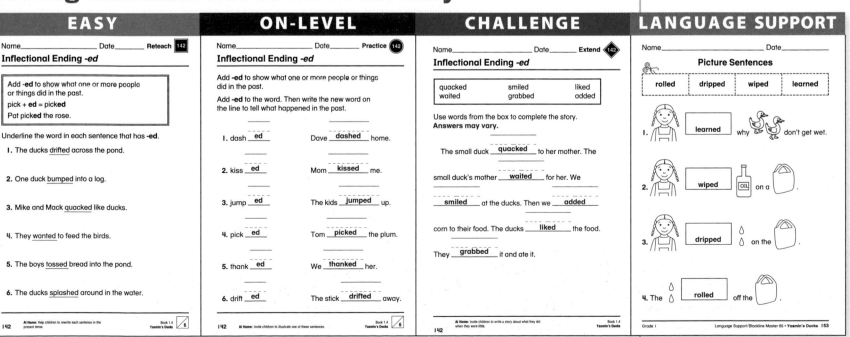

EASY	ON-LEVEL	CHALLENGE	LANGUAGE SUPPORT

Reteach, 142   **Practice, 142**   **Extend, 142**   **Language Support, 153**

65L

GRAMMAR/SPELLING
CONNECTIONS

See the 5-Day Grammar and Usage Plan on *Has* and *Have*, pages 65O–65P.

See the 5-Day Spelling Plan on Words with Long *o: o-e* (silent *e* rule), pages 65Q–65R.

TEACHING TIP

Technology
Never clean a computer with water. Use cleaning products specifically designed for computers. Turn the computer off to clean it, and wait a few moments to allow the computer to dry before you turn it back on.

Handwriting
If children are having difficulty with directionality, or with forming letters or numbers correctly, refer to pages T78–T91 for specific instruction.

Writing That Compares

Prewrite

WRITE A LETTER Present this writing assignment: Pretend you are in Yasmin's and Tim's class. Write a letter to your friends telling what you learned about ducks and fish from Yasmin's and Tim's work.

BRAINSTORM IDEAS Have children brainstorm ideas for things they know about ducks and fish.

STRATEGY: MAKE A CHART Have children make a two-column chart. Suggest the following:

- Label one column "ducks." Under the heading, list what you know about ducks.
- Label the other column "fish." Write what you know about fish in this column.

Draft

USE THE CHART In their letters, children should write full sentences describing the similarities and differences between ducks and fish. They should describe each animal in separate paragraphs. Remind children to include their address, a greeting, and a closing in their letter.

Revise

SELF-CORRECTION Have children use these questions as a revising checklist:

- Did I describe each animal clearly?
- What other details about ducks and fish could I include?
- Did I use words that compare in my writing?

Edit/Proofread

CHECK FOR ERRORS Children should reread their letters for spelling, grammar, punctuation, and letter format.

Publish

SHARE LETTERS Children can "mail" their letters to classmates. Have each recipient describe the animal they like more.

Maria Lopez
21 Elm St.
Somewhere, FL 99999

March 3, 20__

Dear Sharon, Kenny, and Heather,

Tim told us about fish in school today. Yasmin talked about ducks. This is what I learned.
A fish is an animal that lives in the water. A fish has scales covering its body. It swims to move around.
A duck lives in the water, but it lives on land too. A duck has feathers, not scales. A duck swims, but it can fly, too.
Fish and ducks are the same in some ways. They are both animals that live in the water, and they both swim. A duck is different from a fish because it has feathers instead of scales. It can fly, too.

Sincerely,
Maria

Presentation Ideas

SKETCH THE ANIMALS Have children draw a pond that has fish and ducks swimming in it. Display their sketches in the school library. ▶ **Viewing/Representing**

PUT ON A SKIT Have volunteers pretend that they're trying to persuade the rest of the class that either a fish or a duck would make a better class pet.
▶ **Speaking/Listening**

Consider children's creative efforts, possibly adding a plus (+) for originality, wit, and imagination.

Scoring Rubric

Excellent	Good	Fair	Unsatisfactory
4: The writer	**3:** The writer	**2:** The writer	**1:** The writer
• presents accurate details about each animal.	• presents clear details about each animal.	• attempts to present clear details about each animal.	• may not present details about each animal.
• organizes details about each animal in separate paragraphs.	• attempts to organize details about each animal in separate paragraphs.	• may not organize details about each animal in separate paragraphs.	• may not organize details about each animal in paragraph form.
• vividly describes the animals using full, clear sentences in letter form.	• describes the animals using full, clear sentences in letter form.	• may not follow through with a clear plan.	• may not describe the animals using full, clear sentences in letter form.

0: The writer leaves the page blank or fails to respond to the writing task. The writer does not address the topic or simply paraphrases the prompt. The response is illegible or incoherent.

Meeting Individual Needs for Writing

EASY	ON-LEVEL	CHALLENGE
Draw a Scene Have children draw a picture of a duck and a fish swimming together in a river. Ask them to write a short sentence about each animal.	**Write a Plan** Have children pretend that they will have a fish and a duck for class pets. Have them write, in full sentences, a detailed plan about what both animals will need.	**Make a Journal Entry** Have children write about a pet they have or would like to have. What is the pet? Describe it. What makes your pet special?

Viewing and Speaking

VIEWING STRATEGIES
Have children tell what they like best about each other's drawings. Children may also suggest more details to include in the drawings.

SPEAKING STRATEGIES
Encourage children to speak slowly and clearly as they discuss one another's pictures.

LANGUAGE SUPPORT

ESL It may benefit ESL children to focus their writing on another animal found in their native country. Have them review their drafts with a fluent classmate.

Invite children to include PORTFOLIO their letters about the animals in their portfolios.

65N

5 Day Grammar and Usage Plan

Provide extra listening practice for your English learners to hear correct usage of *has* and *have*. Do the Grammar Practice Book pages as oral lessons to help English learners develop an "ear" for how to use *have* and *has*.

DAILY LANGUAGE ACTIVITIES

Write the Daily Language Activities on the chalkboard each day or use **Transparency 17**. Have children correct the sentences orally, using the correct form of the verb *to have*.

Day 1
1. Yasmin have a duck. has
2. Tim have a fish. has
3. Kate have a red truck. has

Day 2
1. The girls has fun. have
2. They has cars. have
3. The children has pens. have

Day 3
1. Ducks has wings. have
2. The lady have a hat. has
3. My parents has a lot of work. have

Day 4
1. Miss Rome have a wish. has
2. The boys has toys. have
3. The truck have a hose. has

Day 5
1. A fish have fins. has
2. We has many ducks. have
3. Yasmin have a new dress. has

Daily Language Transparency 17

DAY 1 — Introduce the Concept

Oral Warm-Up Read aloud the following: *The cat has a mouse. The cats have a mouse.* Ask children to tell which words changed in the sentences. (cat, has; cats, have)

Introduce *Has* and *Have* Tell children that a *verb* is a word that shows action. Discuss with children:

Has and Have

- The words *has* and *have* are verbs that tell about the present.

- The word *has* tells about one person, place, or thing.

Present the Daily Language Activity and have children correct the sentences orally. Then have children write a sentence using *has*.

 WRITING Assign the daily Writing Prompt on page 38E.

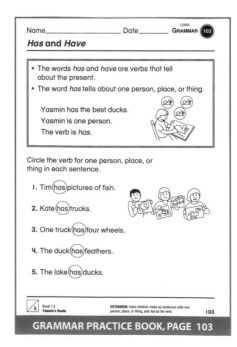

Name_____ Date_____ LEARN **GRAMMAR** 103
Has and Have

- The words *has* and *have* are verbs that tell about the present.
- The word *has* tells about one person, place, or thing.

Yasmin has the best ducks.
Yasmin is one person.
The verb is *has*.

Circle the verb for one person, place, or thing in each sentence.

1. Tim (has) pictures of fish.
2. Kate (has) trucks.
3. One truck (has) four wheels.
4. The duck (has) feathers.
5. The lake (has) ducks.

Book 1.4 *Yasmin's Ducks* EXTENSION: Have children make up sentences with one person, place, or thing, and *has* as the verb. 103

GRAMMAR PRACTICE BOOK, PAGE 103

DAY 2 — Teach the Concept

Review *Has* Remind children that yesterday they learned about the word *has*, a verb that tells something in the present about one person, place, or thing. Write the following sentence on the chalkboard: *Meg has a new dress.* Ask children which word is a verb that tells about Meg. *(has)*

Introduce *Have* Read the following sentences aloud: *The boy has a big dog. The boys have a big dog.* Ask children to tell which words changed in the sentences. *(boy, has; boys, have)* Discuss with children:

Have

- The word *have* tells about more than one person, place, or thing.

Present the Daily Language Activity. Have children correct the sentences orally. Then have children write a sentence using have.

 WRITING Assign the daily Writing Prompt on page 38E.

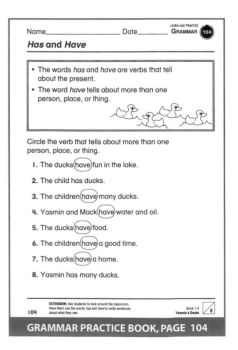

Name_____ Date_____ LEARN AND PRACTICE **GRAMMAR** 104
Has and Have

- The words *has* and *have* are verbs that tell about the present.
- The word *have* tells about more than one person, place, or thing.

Circle the verb that tells about more than one person, place, or thing.

1. The ducks (have) fun in the lake.
2. The child has ducks.
3. The children (have) many ducks.
4. Yasmin and Mack (have) water and oil.
5. The ducks (have) food.
6. The children (have) a good time.
7. The ducks (have) a home.
8. Yasmin has many ducks.

EXTENSION: Ask students to look around the classroom. Have them use the words *has* and *have* to write sentences about what they see.
104 Book 1.4 *Yasmin's Ducks*

GRAMMAR PRACTICE BOOK, PAGE 104

Has and Have

DAY 3 Review and Practice

Learn from the Literature Review *has* and *have* with children. Read the excerpt from the first sentence on page 54 of *Yasmin's Ducks.*

> **These dresses have dots.**

Point out the word *have*. Ask why *have* is correct and not *has*. (*Have* tells about more than one thing.) Then write: *This dress _____ dots.* Ask children whether they would use *has* or *have* in this sentence and why. (*Has* because there is only one dress.)

Use *Has* and *Have* Present the Daily Language Activity and have children correct the sentences orally. Then have children write a sentence using *have*. Ask children to exchange papers with a partner. Have children rewrite their partners sentences, changing the verb from *have* to *has*. For example, *The girls have red shoes. The girl has red shoes.*

 WRITING Assign the daily Writing Prompt on page 38F.

DAY 4 Review and Practice

Review *Has* and *Have* Write the following sentence on the chalkboard: *The boys has a bat.* Ask children if the sentence is correct. (no) Why not? (The verb should be *have*.) Why? (Because *The boys* are more than one person) Correct the sentence on the chalkboard, then present the Daily Language Activity for Day 4.

Mechanics and Usage Before children begin the daily Writing Prompt on page 38F, review sentence punctuation. Display and discuss:

Sentence Punctuation

- Begin every sentence with a capital letter.
- End every sentence with a period.
- End every question with a question mark.

 WRITING Assign the daily Writing Prompt on page 38F.

DAY 5 Assess and Reteach

Assess Use the Daily Language Activity and page 107 of the **Grammar Practice Book** for assessment.

Reteach Help children write each rule about *has* and *have* on an index card. Have children write a sentence using *has* or *have*. Ask them to draw a picture to illustrate their sentences. Then have children attach the index card with the appropriate rule to the drawings.

Have children create a word wall with the pictures they have made, underlining *has* or *have* in each sentence.

Use page 108 of the **Grammar Practice Book** for additional reteaching.

 WRITING Assign the daily Writing Prompt on page 38F.

Name_____ Date_____ PRACTICE AND WRITE **GRAMMAR** 105

Has and Have

- The words *has* and *have* are verbs that tell about the past.
- The word *has* tells about one person, place, or thing.
- The word *have* tells about more than one person, place, or thing.

Read each sentence. Then write *has* for one person, place, or thing. Write *have* for sentences with more than one person, place, or thing.

1. This duck ____**has**____ fun with the children.
2. The duck ____**has**____ plenty of food.
3. Yasmin ____**has**____ a book about ducks.
4. Ducks ____**have**____ oil on their feathers.
5. Yasmin and Tim ____**have**____ ducks.

Book 1.4
Yasmin's Ducks   105

GRAMMAR PRACTICE BOOK, PAGE 105

Name_____ Date_____ MECHANICS **GRAMMAR** 106

Correcting Sentences with Has and Have

- Begin every sentence with a capital letter.
- End every sentence with a period.
- End every question with a question mark.

Write each sentence correctly.

1. the children have show and tell

     The children have show and tell.
2. Does Tim have pictures of fish

     Does Tim have pictures of fish?
3. mom has ducks too

     Mom has ducks too.
4. Kate has a picture of fire trucks

     Kate has a picture of fire trucks.
5. do Kate and Mack have pictures for show and tell

     Do Kate and Mack have pictures for show and tell?

106   EXTENSION: Have children write additional statements and   Book 1.4
                         questions without end marks. Then have them exchange   **Yasmin's Ducks**
                         sentences and put in the end marks.

GRAMMAR PRACTICE BOOK, PAGE 106

Name_____ Date_____ TEST **GRAMMAR** 107

Test

Read each sentence. Circle the correct verb for each sentence.

1. Yasmin _____ a duck.

   (has)   have   do

2. Ducks _____ oil next to their tails.

   has   (have)   are

3. The duck _____ a friend.

   (has)   have   are

4. That duck _____ food.

   can   (has)   have

5. The ducks _____ fun.

   do   has   (have)

Book 1.4
Yasmin's Ducks   107

GRAMMAR PRACTICE BOOK, PAGE 107

5 Day Spelling Plan

To help children who have difficulty with the long *o* and the silent *e* rule, write the words *rope, nose, home,* and *hole* on the chalkboard. Pronounce each word slowly as you underline *o* and *e* in each word. Have children repeat the words after you.

DICTATION SENTENCES

Spelling Words

1. We came <u>home</u> after school.
2. I <u>hope</u> we win.
3. My cat can dig a <u>hole</u>.
4. She blew her <u>nose</u>.
5. The <u>rope</u> is in the shed.
6. <u>Those</u> pigs live on a farm.

Challenge Words

7. He goes to <u>work</u> every morning.
8. We took the bus <u>because</u> it rained.
9. I can <u>buy</u> you that toy.
10. They want to have <u>some</u> cake.

DAY 1 Pretest

Assess Prior Knowledge Use the Dictation Sentences at left and **Spelling Practice Book** page 103 for the pretest. Allow children to correct their own papers. If children have trouble, have partners give each other a midweek test on Day 3.

Spelling Words		Challenge Words
1. **home**	4. nose	7. **work**
2. **hope**	5. rope	8. **because**
3. hole	6. those	9. **buy**
		10. **some**

*Note: Words in **dark type** are from the story.*

Word Study On page 104 of the **Spelling Practice Book** are word study steps and an at-home activity.

DAY 2 Explore the Pattern

Sort and Spell Words Say *hop* and *hope*. Ask children what sound they hear in each word. Write the words on the chalkboard and circle the *o-e* pattern as you repeat the word *hope*. Repeat with the following pairs: *not/note; mop/mope; rod/rode.*

Ask children to read aloud the six Spelling Words before sorting them according to the spelling pattern.

Words ending with

-ope	-ole	-ose	-ome
hope	hole	nose	home
rope		those	

Word Wall As children read other stories and texts, have them look for new words with long vowel sounds that follow the silent *e* rule. Add them to a classroom word wall, underlining the vowel and the silent *e*.

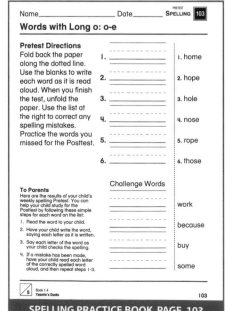

SPELLING PRACTICE BOOK, PAGE 103

WORD STUDY STEPS AND ACTIVITY, PAGE 104

SPELLING PRACTICE BOOK, PAGE 105

Words with Long *o: o-e*

DAY 3 — Practice and Extend

Word Meaning: Riddles Have children solve the riddle by answering with a Spelling Word.

This is in the middle of your face. nose

A doughnut has one of these in the middle. hole

This is the place where you live. home

When you wish for something, you do this. hope

This is used to tie things up. rope

This word means *that*, but for more than one. those

Identify Spelling Patterns Write this sentence on the chalkboard: *I hope to buy a new home.* Have a volunteer read it aloud. Ask children to tell which words have the spelling pattern *o-e* and which word is the Challenge Word. Then have children make up new sentences, using the Spelling and Challenge Words.

DAY 4 — Proofread and Write

Proofread Sentences Write these sentences on the chalkboard, including the misspelled words. Ask children to proofread, circling incorrect spellings and writing the correct spellings. There are two errors in each sentence.

I (hop) my mom is (hom). (hope, home)

The (rop) is in the (hol). (rope, hole)

Have children create additional sentences with errors for partners to correct.

 WRITING Have children use as many Spelling Words as possible in the daily Writing Prompt on page 38F. Remind children to proofread their writing for errors in spelling, grammar, and punctuation.

DAY 5 — Assess and Reteach

Assess Children's Knowledge Use page 108 of the **Spelling Practice Book** or the Dictation Sentences on page 65Q for the posttest.

Personal Word List If children **JOURNAL** have trouble with any words in the lesson, have them create a personal list of troublesome words in their journals. Have children write riddles for the Spelling Words.

Children should refer to their word lists during later writing activities.

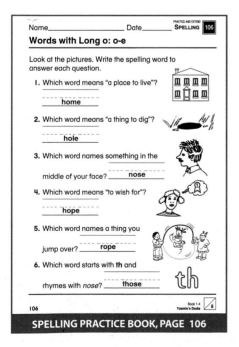

Name_____ Date_____ PRACTICE AND EXTEND SPELLING 106

Words with Long o: o-e

Look at the pictures. Write the spelling word to answer each question.

1. Which word means "a place to live"?
   home

2. Which word means "a thing to dig"?
   hole

3. Which word names something in the middle of your face?
   nose

4. Which word means "to wish for"?
   hope

5. Which word names a thing you jump over?
   rope

6. Which word starts with **th** and rhymes with **nose**?
   those

106   Book 1.4 Yasmin's Ducks / 6

SPELLING PRACTICE BOOK, PAGE 106

Name_____ Date_____ PROOFREAD AND WRITE SPELLING 107

Words with Long o: o-e

Read the poem. There are six spelling mistakes. Circle the mistakes. Write the words correctly on the lines.

Look at that (hol).
It is (hom) to a mouse.
He packs it with (roep).
To make a house.
He adds thin sticks.
Can you see (thoze)?
I (hop) we see him.
Look! There is his (noze).

1. ___hole___   2. ___home___

3. ___rope___   4. ___those___

5. ___hope___   6. ___nose___

Writing Activity
Write a story telling about an animal you like.
Use three spelling words in your story.

9   Book 1.4 Yasmin's Ducks   107

SPELLING PRACTICE BOOK, PAGE 107

Name_____ Date_____ POSTTEST SPELLING 108

Words with Long o: o-e

Look at the words in each set. One word in each set is spelled correctly. Use a pencil to color in the circle in front of that word. Before you begin, look at the sample sets of words. Sample A has been done for you. Do Sample B by yourself. When you are sure you know what to do, you may go on with the rest of the page.

Sample A   Sample B
Ⓐ● hose   Ⓓ bitte
Ⓑ hoze   ● bite
Ⓒ hoose   Ⓕ byt

1. ● home   4. Ⓓ hopp
   Ⓑ hom   ● hope
   Ⓒ hoem   Ⓕ hoope

2. Ⓓ nos   5. ● rope
   ● nose   Ⓑ rop
   Ⓕ noze   Ⓒ roope

3. Ⓐ whol   6. Ⓓ thoz
   Ⓑ hol   ● those
   ● hole   Ⓕ thos

108   Book 1.4 Yasmin's Ducks / 6

SPELLING PRACTICE BOOK, PAGE 108

65R

Concept
• Self-Acceptance

Comprehension
• Cause and Effect

Phonics
• Long *u*: *u-e*

Vocabulary
• carry
• been
• clean
• done
• far

Reaching All Learners

Anthology

The Knee-High Man

Selection Summary Sam, the Knee-High Man, wants to be something other than what he is. He solicits advice about how he can become bigger, until a wise owl teaches him about self-acceptance.

INSTRUCTIONAL pages 68–95

Duke the Ant

Duke the ant is quite a dude.
He is very polite and never rude.
Duke the ant is small and cute.
He plays music on his new flute.
Duke the ant is always in tune!
He gave a concert just last June.
Duke can make a tone that's pure.
Duke the bug is cool, for sure!

Rhyme applies to Phonics

Listening Library

About the Author Ellen Dreyer has always loved writing. She gets many ideas for her books from talking with children. Ms. Dreyer says it is important for writers to write down what they see and hear.

About the Illustrator Tim Raglin illustrates children's books, magazines, and advertisements. Raglin especially likes to draw animals. He tells boys and girls, "If you like to draw, just keep practicing. Talent is just one small part, the rest is work."

Same Concept, Skills and Vocabulary!

Leveled Books

by Rachel Patrick
illustrated by Jane Sanders

EASY
Lesson on pages 95A and 95D
`DECODABLE`

A Bigger House for June

written by Anna Smyth
illustrated by Kathy Wilburn

INDEPENDENT
Lesson on pages 37B and 37D

📖 *Take-Home version available*
`DECODABLE`

PETE'S CHICKEN

Harriet Ziefert • Laura Rader

CHALLENGE
Lesson on pages 95C and 95D

Leveled Practice

EASY
Reteach, 143–150 Blackline masters with reteaching opportunities for each assessed skill

INDEPENDENT/ON-LEVEL
Practice, 143–150 Workbook with Take-Home Stories and practice opportunities for each assessed skill and story comprehension

CHALLENGE
Extend, 143–150 Blackline masters that offer challenge activities for each assessed skill

Quizzes Prepared by Accelerated Reader®

CENTER Activities

Social Studies . . . **Peaceful Solutions,** 86

Science . . . . **Green Grass Grows,** 66D
                         Frogs, 80

Math . . . . **How Tall Are You?,** 66D
                         Inch By Inch, 76

Language Arts . . **Read Aloud,** 66G

Cultural
Perspectives . . . . . **Corn Varieties,** 72

Writing . . . . **Help Sam,** 92

Research
and Inquiry . . . . . . **Find Out More,** 93

Internet
Activities . . . . **www.mhschool.com/reading**

66B

Center Activities

Each of these activities takes 15-20 minutes.

Phonics

Listen for Long and Short *u*

PARTNERS

Objective: Sort picture cards according to the long *u* and short *u* sounds.

◆ Provide children with copies of the cards.

◆ Children sort the cards according to their vowel sounds, then think of other short and long *u* words, draw or write them, and sort them.

MATERIALS
- Phonics Picture Cards (*umbrella, sun, thumb, cube*)
- Paper

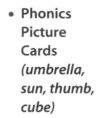

Writing

Animal Advice

PARTNERS

Objective: Write and illustrate sentences from an animal's point of view.

◆ Have partners choose a big animal and talk about the food it eats.

◆ Children work together to write and illustrate sentences from the animal's point of view, telling what the Knee-High Man should eat to get big.

MATERIALS
- Drawing paper
- Crayons

Reading and Listening

Independent/Self-Selected Reading

ONE

Objective: Listen and use illustrations to understand a story.

Fill the Center with books and corresponding audiocassettes or CD-ROMs children have read or listened to this week. You can also include books from the Theme Bibliography pages T98 and T99.

Leveled Readers

◆ *Fun Run* by Rachel Patrick
◆ *A Bigger House for June* by Anna Smyth
◆ *Pete's Chicken* by Harriet Ziefert

◆ Theme Big Book *Fish Faces* by Norbert Wu
◆ *The Knee-High Man* by Ellen Dreyer
◆ "To the Top" by Sandra Liatsos
◆ Phonics Practice Reader, Vol. 2

Working with Words

Write Sentences

 Objective: Reinforce vocabulary words: *carry, been, clean, done, far.*

◆ Have children use self-stick notes to mark the sentences in the story that include the vocabulary words.

◆ Children can record themselves reading the story sentences.

MATERIALS
- *The Knee-High Man* in the Student Anthology
- Self-stick notes
- Tape recorder

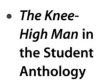

Science

Green Grass Grows

Objective: Plant grass seed and observe seed growth.

◆ Remind children that Bob Bull eats grass to grow big. Tell children they will grow grass.

◆ Children spoon soil into the cup, sprinkle grass seeds on top, add water, and put the cups by a window.

MATERIALS
- Foam cups
- Potting soil
- Grass seed
- Spoons
- Markers

Math

How Tall Are You?

Objective: Use a common unit to measure and record height.

◆ Hang a large sheet of mural paper on the wall, with its bottom edge along the floor.

◆ One child stands against the paper while a partner marks his or her height.

◆ Children choose classroom objects, such as an eraser or a pencil, to use to measure their height.

MATERIALS
- Mural paper
- Various classroom objects
- Markers
- Drawing paper

Kate is about 12 erasers tall.

READING AND LANGUAGE ARTS	**DAY 1** *Focus on Reading and Skills*	**DAY 2** *Read the Literature*
● **Phonics Daily Routines**	Daily  Routine: **Segmenting,** 66J Phonics **CD-ROM**	Daily  Routine: **Blending,** 68A Phonics **CD-ROM**

● **Phonological Awareness**
 	
● **Phonics** *Long u*
 	
● **Comprehension**
 	
● **Vocabulary**
 	
● **Study Skills**
 	
● **Listening, Speaking, Viewing, Representing**
	Read Aloud, 66G
	"Timimoto"
	
	Develop Phonological Awareness, 66H
	
	☑ **Introduce Long *u: u-e*,** 66I–66J
	Reteach, Practice, Extend, 143
	Phonics/Phonemic Awareness Practice Book, 147–150
	
	 Apply Long *u: u-e*, 66/67
	"Duke the Ant"
	
	ℹ **Intervention Program**
		Build Background, 68A
		Develop Oral Language
		
		Vocabulary, 68B–68C
		
		carry been clean
		done far
		
		Teaching Chart 106
		Word Building Manipulative Cards
		Reteach, Practice, Extend, 144
		
		 Read the Selection, 68–91
		Guided Instruction
		    ☑ **Long *u: u-e***
		    ☑ **Cause and Effect**
		
		Genre: Play, 69
		
		Cultural Perspectives, 72
		
		Writer's Craft, 72

● **Curriculum Connections**	Language Arts, 66G	Science, 68A
● **Writing**	**Writing Prompt:** Write about the places you could go if you were very, very short.	**Writing Prompt:** Write some dos and don'ts for growing. 📓 **Journal Writing** Quick-Write, 91
● **Grammar**	**Introduce the Concept: *Go and Do*,** 95O Daily Language Activity: Use the correct form of *go* and *do* in sentences. **Grammar Practice Book,** 109	**Teach the Concept: *Go and Do*,** 95O Daily Language Activity: Use the correct form of *go* and *do* in sentences. **Grammar Practice Book,** 110
● **Spelling** *Long u*	**Pretest: Words with Long *u: u-e*,** 95Q **Spelling Practice Book,** 109–110	**Explore the Pattern: Words with Long *u: u-e*,** 95Q **Spelling Practice Book,** 111

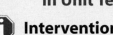
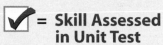

DAY 3 Read the Literature	DAY 4 Build Skills	DAY 5 Build Skills

Daily  Routine:
Fluency, 93

 CD-ROM

Daily  Routine:
Writing, 95F

 CD-ROM

Daily Routine:
Letter Substitution, 95H

 CD-ROM

Reread for Fluency, 90

Story Questions, 92
Reteach, Practice, Extend, 145

Story Activities, 93

Study Skill, 94
☑ **Charts**
Teaching Chart 107
Reteach, Practice, Extend, 146

 Read the Leveled Books, Guided Reading
☑ **Read Words with Long** *u: u-e*
☑ **Cause and Effect**
☑ **High-Frequency Words**

 Read the Leveled Books and Self-Selected Books

☑ **Review Long** *u: u-e*, 95E–95F
Teaching Chart 108
Reteach, Practice, Extend, 147
Language Support, 159
Phonics/Phonemic Awareness
Practice Book, 147–150

☑ **Review** *u-e, o-e, i-e, a-e*, 95G–95H
Teaching Chart 109
Reteach, Practice, Extend, 148
Language Support, 160
Phonics/Phonemic Awareness
Practice Book, 147–150

Minilessons, 73, 75, 77, 79, 89

 Read Self-Selected Books

☑ **Introduce Make Inferences,** 95I–95J
Teaching Chart 110
Reteach, Practice, Extend, 149
Language Support, 161

☑ **Introduce Inflectional Endings** *-er, -est*, 95K–95L
Teaching Chart 111
Reteach, Practice, Extend, 150
Language Support, 162

Listening, Speaking, Viewing Representing, 95N

Minilessons, 73, 75, 77, 79, 89

 Intervention Program

 Intervention Program

Intervention Program

 Math, 66D, 76

Activity Science, 66D, 80

Activity Social Studies, 86

Writing Prompt: Write a letter to a friend about something silly you think he or she should do.

Journal Writing, 95D

Writing Prompt: Name a place you went to. Write about what you did there.

Writing that Compares, 95M
Prewrite, Draft

Meeting Individual Needs for Writing, 95N

Writing Prompt: Write about a place you would like to go to when you get bigger.

Writing that Compres, 95M
Revise, Edit/Proofread, Publish

Review and Practice: *Go* and *Do,* 95P
Daily Language Activity: Use the correct form of *go* and *do* in sentences.

Grammar Practice Book, 111

Review and Practice: *Go* and *Do,* 95P
Daily Language Activity: Use the correct form of *go* and *do* in sentences.

Grammar Practice Book, 112

Assess and Reteach: *Go* and *Do,* 95P
Daily Language Activity: Use the correct form of *go* and *do* in sentences.

Grammar Practice Book, 113, 114

Practice and Extend: Words with Long *u: u-e,* 95R

Spelling Practice Book, 112

Proofread and Write: Words with Long *u: u-e,* 95R

Spelling Practice Book, 113

Assess and Reteach: Words with Long *u: u-e,* 95R

Spelling Practice Book, 114

Read Aloud

Timimoto
a folktale retold by Margaret H. Lippert

Once upon a time in Japan there lived an old man and an old woman. They were very lonely because they had no children. One day the old woman said to her husband, "I wish we had a child. I would like a little boy, even if he is no bigger than my finger."

That day as the old woman went to fetch water, she heard crying by the side of the path. She looked in the grass and there lay a tiny baby, only one inch long, wrapped in a red handkerchief.

The old woman was overjoyed. She took the baby home and showed him to her husband. "My wish has come true," she said. "Now we will never be lonely again." They named the baby Timimoto.

Timimoto grew up, but not very much. When he was five years old, he was as tall as his mother's thumb. At fifteen, he was only as tall as his mother's middle finger.

One morning Timimoto said, "I am going on a journey to see the world.

Continued on page T3

Oral Comprehension

LISTENING AND SPEAKING Encourage children to think about cause-and-effect relationships by reading this story about a tiny Japanese boy. When you finish reading the story, ask, "Why did Timimoto leave his parents?" Then ask, "What happened when Timimoto stabbed the giant's tongue? Why did the town have a feast in Timimoto's honor?"

 Help children to make their own cartoon strip version of Timimoto's journey. Have children divide a piece of paper into six equal squares. In the first square, ask children to draw Timimoto in his boat. Remind them to include Timimoto's sword and paddle. In the other squares, have children include events from the journey. ▶ **Visual**

GENRE STUDY: FOLKTALE Explain to children that a folktale is a story that comes from a particular culture or geographic area. It is usually passed down from generation to generation through storytelling. Ask children what elements of this folktale make it a fictional story. (Timimoto is as big as a thumb, there is a giant in the story.) Tell children that the rice bowl and chopsticks in the story reflect Japanese culture. They are common Japanese utensils. Japanese children use them like we use plates and forks.

Develop Phonological Awareness

Blend Sounds
Phonemic Awareness

MATERIALS
• puppet

Teach Tell children the puppet is going to say some sounds. Have the puppet say: /k/-/ū/-/t/. *Let's blend these sounds together and say the word*—cute.

Practice Have children practice blending the sounds for the following words: *cure, fume, fuse, mule, pure, rule, tube.*

Segment Sounds
Phonemic Awareness

MATERIALS
• Word Building Boxes
• colored felt squares or counters

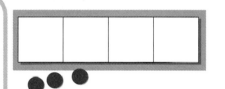

Teach Tell children you will say a word and then count the number of sounds in the word. Display the Word Building Boxes with four sections. Place a counter in a box as you say each sound. Say: *cube*: /k/-/ū/-/b/. The word *cube* has three sounds. Have children say the three sounds as you point to each box and say each sound. Have them Identify where the long *u* sound is.

Practice Distribute the Word Building Boxes and counters to each child. Have children place a counter in a box for each sound they hear in these words: *brute, cure, dude, flute, fuse, mule, pure, tune.*

Substitute Sounds
Phonemic Awareness

Teach Say: *Listen carefully to this word*—cube. *If I take away the /k/ sound and add the /t/ sound, I make the word* tube. Repeat the word *cube,* take off the /b/ sound, and add the /t/ sound. Have children sound out and blend the word *cute* with you.

Practice Using the following sets of words, have children change the beginning or ending sounds to make new words: *brute/flute, dude/duke, cute/mute, tune/dune, June/prune, fume/fuse, pure/cure, mule/rule, tube/tune, rude/rule.*

 **INFORMAL ASSESSMENT** Observe children as they blend sounds, segment sounds, and substitute beginning and ending sounds. If children have difficulty, see Alternate Teaching Strategies on page T71.

Introduce Long *u*: *u-e*

TESTED OBJECTIVES

Children will:

- identify long *u-e* words.
- blend and read long *u-e* words.
- review consonants.

MATERIALS

- letter and long *u* cards and word building boxes from the **Word Building Manipulative Cards**

Skills Finder

Long *u*: *u-e*	
Introduce	B4: 66I-J
Review	B4: 95G-H, 123G-H, 124I-J
Test	Book 4

SPELLING/PHONICS CONNECTIONS

Words with long *u*: See the 5-Day Spelling Plan, pages 95Q–95R.

TEACHING TIP

LONG *u* You may point out to children that the long *u* sound spelled *u-e* often makes slightly different long *u* sounds, as in the words *rude* and *mule*.

TEACH

Identify the Letter *u* as the Symbol for /ū/

Explain to children that they will learn to read words with the letters *u-e* where the letter *u* sounds like /ū/ and the *e* on the end is silent.

- Display the *u-e* letter card and say /ū/. Have children repeat.

BLENDING Model and Guide Practice with Long *u-e* Words

- Explain that many words with long *u* end in *e*.
- Point to the long *u* letter card and say /ū/. Remind children that the space between the letters *u* and *e* is a place for a consonant.
- Place the *t* letter card between the letters *u* and *e*. Blend the sounds together.

- Now place the *c* letter card before the *u t e*. Have children blend the sounds together to read *cute*.

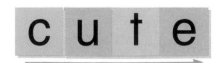

Use the Word in Context

Use the word in context to reinforce its meaning. Example: *The little dog is so cute.*

Repeat the Procedure

Use the following words to continue modeling and guided practice with long *u*.

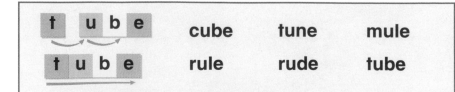

	cube	tune	mule
	rule	rude	tube

PRACTICE

LETTER SUBSTITUTION
Build Long *u* Words with Letter Cards

PARTNERS

Have children work in pairs. Build the word *mule* with letter cards and have one child in each pair do the same. Then ask the partner to replace the *m* with an *r* letter card. Ask children to read the new word. Have partners switch roles, and continue with the following word pairs: *tune/dune; use/fuse; pure/cure.* Ask partners to present their rhyming pairs of words to the group. For example, one partner holds up a card for *mule*. The other partner holds up the rhyming card *rule*, and the group reads the words aloud.

ASSESS/CLOSE

Read and Use Long *u* Words in Sentences

Observe children as they build words in the Practice activity. Have children choose any two long *u* words that they built and use both in a sentence.

ADDITIONAL PHONICS RESOURCES

Phonics/ Phonemic Awareness Practice Book,
pages 147–150

PHONICS KIT
Hands-on Activities and Practice

McGraw-Hill School
TECHNOLOGY

Phonics CD-ROM
activities for practice with Blending and Segmenting

Meeting Individual Needs for Phonics

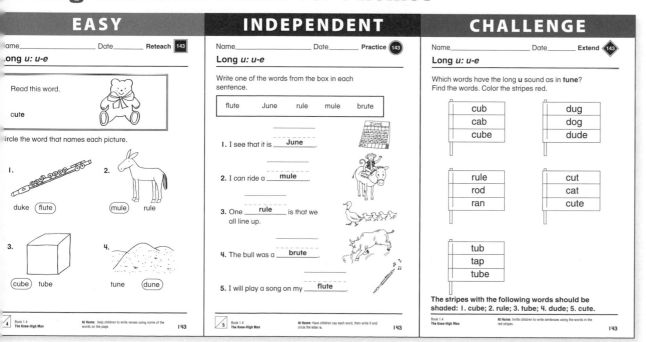

Reteach, 143   Practice, 143   Extend, 143

Daily Routines

DAY 1 **Segmenting** Distribute letter boxes. Say a long *u* word that follows the CVCe pattern aloud. Identify the pattern and have children write the letters in each box. (Use *cute, mule,* and *tube.*)

DAY 2 **Blending** Use letter cards to create the *-ule* phonogram. Place the letter *r* before the phonogram and model how to blend the r with the *-ule* sound. Repeat with the letter *m*.

DAY 3 **Fluency** Write on the chalkboard: *The mule is cute*. Ask children to blend sounds and read silently as you track print. Then, have them read aloud.

DAY 4 **Writing** Write the word *duke* on chart paper and define the word. Ask children to write a sentence about a duke and draw a picture to illustrate it.

DAY 5 **Letter Substitution** Using the letter and long *u* cards have pairs of children build the word *brute*. Then have them change letters to build *chute* and *flute*.

66J

OBJECTIVES

Children will read a poem with words containing long *u: u-e.*

Apply Long *u: u-e*

Duke the Ant

Duke the ant is quite a dude.
He is very polite and never rude.
Duke the ant is small and cute.
He plays music on his new flute.
Duke the ant is always in tune!
He gave a concert just last June.
Duke can make a tone that's pure.
Duke the bug is cool, for sure!

66　　　　67

Anthology pages 66–67

Read and Build Fluency

READ THE POEM　Tell children they will read a poem called *Duke the Ant.* Provide auditory modeling by having children listen as you read every two lines stressing the rhyming words. Read the exclamatory sentences with expression. Have children read with you.

REREAD FOR FLUENCY　Have pairs of children alter-

nate reading lines of the poem
PARTNERS aloud with expression.

READ A DECODABLE STORY　For additional practice reading and to develop fluency, have children read the story *Luke's Tune* from **Phonics Practice Reader, Vol. 2.**

Dictate and Spell

DICTATE WORDS　Segment the word *Duke* into its

three individual sounds. Repeat the word aloud
JOURNAL and use it in a sentence: *Duke is a cute ant.* Then have children say the word and write the letter or letters that represent each sound until they make the entire word. Repeat with *dude, rude, cute, flute, tune,* and *June* from the poem. Then repeat with long *u* words not from the poem, such as: *cube, fuse, mule, prune, rule,* and *tube.*

> **i Intervention** ▶ **Skills Intervention Guide,**
> **Book A,** for direct instruction and extra practice in
> Long *u: u-e*

Build Background

Concept: Self-Acceptance

Science

Evaluate Prior Knowledge

CONCEPT: SELF-ACCEPTANCE Display a picture of an elephant and a mouse. Ask which animal is big and which is small. Use the following activities to explore the concept of accepting being big and accepting being small.

CLASSIFY AND CATEGORIZE Have the class work together to make a story table telling why it is good to be big and why it is good to be small. Then have children take turns naming some animals that fit into each category.

Good to Be Big	Good to Be Small
strong (elephant)	fit anywhere (bug)
reach high (giraffe)	run fast (mouse)

A mouse runs fast

Develop Oral Language

CONNECT WORDS AND ACTIONS

ESL Have children describe what it would be like to be a big animal and a small animal. Give directions such as:

- Jump like a frog.
- Roar like a lion.
- Make a sound like a small animal.

Prompt children to say what animal they are or what they are doing by asking:

- Who is jumping?
- What are you doing?
- What animal makes that noise?

▶ **Kinesthetic/Linguistic**

DRAW AND LABEL A PICTURE Invite children to fold a sheet of paper in half. On one side, have them draw a big animal doing something that it can do only because it is big; on the other side, a small animal doing something that it can do only because it is small. Have them label each animal.

Anthology and Leveled Books

LANGUAGE SUPPORT

To build more background, see pages 154-157 in the **Language Support Book.**

DAILY Phonics ROUTINES

DAY 2 **Blending** Use letter cards to create the *-ule* phonogram. Place the letter *r* before the phonogram and model how to blend the *r* with the *-ule* sound. Repeat with the letter *m*.

Phonics CD-ROM

Children will:

• identify high-frequency words *carry, done, been, far,* and *clean.*

MATERIALS

• Teaching Chart 106

• Word Building Manipulative Cards *carry, done, been, far,* and *clean*

TEACHING TIP

The following chart indicates words from the upcoming story that children have learned to decode, as well as high-frequency words that have been taught in this lesson.

Decodable	High-Frequency
brute	carry
June	done
Mule	been
rule	far
	clean

SPELLING/VOCABULARY CONNECTIONS

The words *been, clean, done,* and *far* are Challenge Words. See page 95Q for Day 1 of the 5-Day Spelling Plan.

---

carry

done

been

far

clean

Vocabulary

High-Frequency Words

I Like Me

If I'm feeling bad or mad or sad,
There's a song I sing to make me glad.
Hummmmmmmm —
I like me. I clean myself.
I carry myself near and far.
I do things that I want done.
I buy myself things for fun.
I wish you could have been born as me,
And know how grand being me can be.
Then you could sing this song and see
why I like Me!

Teaching Chart 106

Auditory

LISTEN TO WORDS Without displaying it, read aloud "I Like Me" on **Teaching Chart 106**. Ask children why they think the song might work to cheer them up when they're feeling bad. Is there anything else they do to make them feel good about themselves?

RHYME HIGH-FREQUENCY WORDS Have children aurally identify each high-frequency word using the following activity:

• Say aloud one of the high-frequency words. Read a line of the poem where that word appears.

• Ask children to find words that rhyme with that word. Then have them use the high-frequency word and a rhyming word in a few short lines about something they can do. (Note: The lines don't have to rhyme.)

• Repeat this activity with each of the high-frequency words.

Visual

TEACH WORDS Display "I Like Me" on **Teaching Chart 106**. Read the poem, tracking the print with your finger. Next, point to and say the word *carry*. Have children say the word with you. Ask them to hold up the vocabulary card for *carry* and say the word. Repeat this procedure for *done, been, far,* and *clean.*

Hold up vocabulary cards for *carry, done, been, far,* and *clean* one at a time. Have volunteers read the words and then circle them on the chart.

Word Building Manipulative Cards

WRITE ME A STORY Divide the class into groups of five. Have each group use the high-frequency words to write sentences about liking themselves.

Activities

Word Wall

Common Traits   Ask children to look at the lesson's word wall words and find things that they have in common. For example, *carry* and *been* both have double letters, and *been* and *clean* both end with *n*. Have children point out the common traits on the word wall.

Raise the Roof   Ask children to stand up and "raise the roof" while they spell the word wall words. As they say each letter, have children move their open hands up toward the ceiling. Their hands should go a little higher as they say each letter.

Assess

Word Scramble   Write each word wall word on the chalkboard with the letters out of order. Have children unscramble the words and write them on a piece of paper. Then have children spell each word out loud.

LANGUAGE SUPPORT

To help children develop understanding and recognition of high-frequency words, see page 154 in the **Language Support Book**.

Meeting Individual Needs for Vocabulary

EASY	ON-LEVEL	ON-LEVEL	CHALLENGE
Reteach, 144	Practice, 144	Practice, 144a Take-Home Story	Extend, 144

68C

Comprehension

Prereading Strategies

PREVIEW AND PREDICT Point to the name of the author and read it aloud. Then ask children to point to the name of the illustrator as you read it aloud. Point to the word *adaptation* and explain that it means that the story is based on another work, in this case, a folktale. Then take a **picture walk** through the book, talking about the illustrations and the text format. Tell children that this is a play and that each character has lines to say. Have children note the character's name and lines on each page. Then, ask what the story might be about:

• How big is Sam?

• Why is he unhappy?

Ask children to make predictions about the story. Chart children's predictions and read them aloud.

SET PURPOSES Ask children what they want to find out as they read the story.

• What do the animals tell Sam?

• What does Sam do?

READ TOGETHER

Meet Ellen Dreyer

Ellen Dreyer has always loved writing. She has written many children's books. She gets her ideas from talking with children. Dreyer also teaches creative writing to children. She say it is important for writers to keep a noteboo and write down what they see and hear.

Meet Tim Raglin

Tim Raglin illustrates children's books, magazines, and advertisements. He spent a lot of time drawing as a boy, and later went to art school. Raglin likes to draw animals in human situations. He says, "If you like t draw, just keep practicing."

Meeting Individual Needs • Grouping Suggestions for Strategic Reading

EASY	ON-LEVEL	CHALLENGE
Shared Reading Track print as you read the story aloud. Invite children to read along with any familiar words or phrases. As you read, remind children how they can tell which character is speaking.	**Guided Instruction** Ask children to read the story with you. Monitor any difficulties that children may have while reading in order to determine which Comprehension questions to emphasize. After reading the story aloud with children, have them reread it alone. See the rereading suggestions on page 90.	**Independent Reading** Have children set purposes before they read. Remind them that as they read, visualizing the character who is speaking will help. Explain that in this play, the storyteller helps link the story ideas together. You may wish to have children read the story in small groups, each child taking the part of one character.

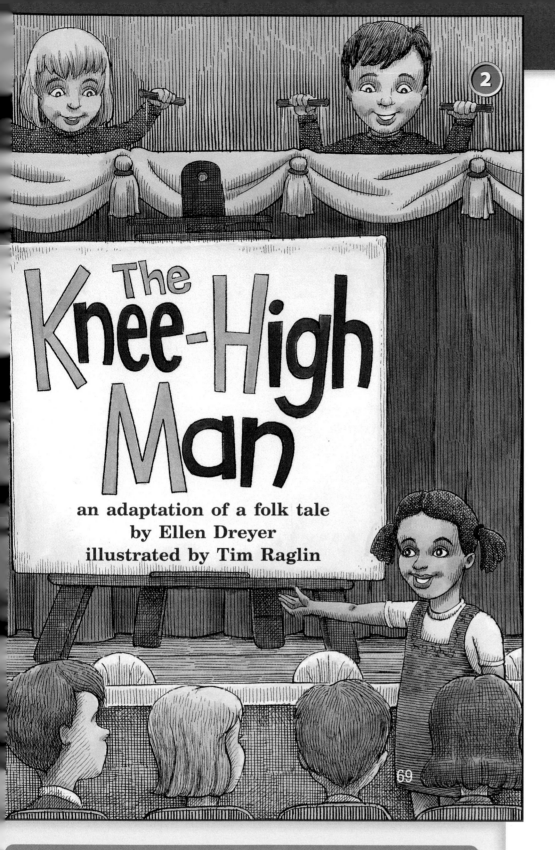

The Knee-High Man

an adaptation of a folk tale
by Ellen Dreyer
illustrated by Tim Raglin

69

Comprehension

☑ **Phonics** **Long *u: u-e***

☑ **Apply Cause and Effect**

STRATEGIC READING Explain to children that to help them understand the story, they can think about how one event causes another event to happen. Children will create a Story Comic Strip to focus on cause and effect.

① We are going to read *The Knee-High Man.* Let's look at the picture at the top of page 68. This is a picture of the author, Ellen Dreyer. Let's read about her. Now, let's read and see what the illustrator, Tim Raglin, says about drawing. *Concept of a Book: Author/Illustrator*

② Let's look at the picture on page 69. What do you see? (Answers will vary. Children should note the story title, the stage, the audience.) *Use Illustrations*

Play

Explain that in a play:

- the story is told in dialogue, or a conversation, that is spoken aloud by actors, who play characters on a stage.
- the focus is usually on one or more characters who solve a problem.

Activity After reading *The Knee-High Man*, ask children to identify the speaker. Explain that June is the narrator who speaks for each actor. Discuss how the puppets, or marionettes, take the place of the actors on the stage. Model how the narrator might have to change her voice to make the characters more identifiable.

LANGUAGE SUPPORT

A blackline master for making the Story Comic Strip can be found in the **Language Support Book**. You may want children to color in the pictures of Sam and his friends before they begin reading.

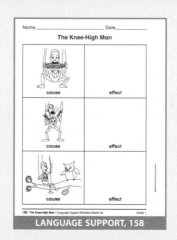

Name_____ Date_____
The Knee-High Man

cause	effect
cause	effect
cause	effect

158 The Knee-High Man • Language Support/Blackline Master 46   Grade 1

LANGUAGE SUPPORT, 158

Comprehension

3 This is the cast of characters in this play. How many people are there? (two) How many animals are there? (three) *Classify and Categorize*

PHONOLOGICAL AWARENESS
Listen to the word *storyteller*. How many syllables are in that word? (four) *Multisyllabic Words*

4 Point to that mark in the middle of the word *Knee-High*. This is a hyphen. It connects the two words used to describe what kind of man Sam is. *Concepts of Print*

3 The Players:

June
A Storyteller

Bob Bul

4 Sam
The Knee-High
Man

Kate Owl

Max Mul

70

 PREVENTION/INTERVENTION

PHONOLOGICAL AWARENESS
Say the word *book* aloud. Point out that this word has one syllable, or part. Then say the word *story*. Ask children how many parts they hear in this word. (two) Say *book* and *story* again, having children clap for each syllable they hear. Then say the word *storyteller* slowly. Have children clap out the syllables with you. Repeat this exercise with the words *biggest* and *wanted*. *Multisyllabic Words*

June: Some folks grow big. Some folks stay small. That's a rule of life. But Sam, the Knee-High Man, wanted to be big. He just had to find out how to do it.

71

Comprehension

5 Why do you think Sam is called the Knee-High Man? (because of his small size; he comes up to a normal person's knee) *Make Inferences*

6 **Phonics** LONG *u: u-e* . . . *That's a* . . . I'm not sure what this word is. Let's blend the sounds of the letters together to read it. r u l(e) rule *Graphophonic Cues*

7 Sam wanted to be big. Why would someone who is small want to be big? (Answers will vary.) Tell me something you were told you couldn't do until you were bigger. *Make Connections*

LANGUAGE SUPPORT

ESL Read the sentence *Some folks grow big.* Frame the word *grow* and talk about what it means. Ask children to role-play being a seed that is planted in the ground. Children begin by curling their bodies and then moving to show how the seed grows into a plant.

Then display a picture of a baby. Ask children to describe how the baby grows and changes.

Comprehension

8 **Phonics** **LONG** *u: u-e* *Max . . .*
Who can read the next word with me?
Remember to blend the sounds of the letters
together. M u l(e) Mule *Graphophonic
Cues*

Writer's Craft

DIALOGUE

Explain to children that a play is a story told
as characters talk to each other. The characters' conversation is called *dialogue*. Each
time a new character speaks, his or her
name is in front of the words.

Direct children to the example of the dialogue on page 73. (**Max:** What's up, Sam?
Sam: Max, you are so big!) Point out that
the characters' names are not said when
the dialogue is spoken aloud.

PARTNERS Ask partners to write their own two
lines of dialogue on one piece of
paper. Have each partner write his or her
own name and a greeting to the other.

8 Sam: Max Mule is sure to know how I can
get big like him. He will tell me how
to grow.

72

CULTURAL PERSPECTIVES

CORN VARIETIES Explain to children
that corn is an important basic food that
originated in this part of the world. The
Native Americans in North and Central
America cultivated many different types
of corn. Because of this, corn now comes
in many shapes, sizes, and colors.

RESEARCH AND INQUIRY Have children investigate the varieties of corn. Have
them cut out pictures in magazines and
seed catalogs of different types of corn
and make a display. ▶ **Visual**

interNET CONNECTION For more information
about vegetables, log on
to **www.mhschool.com/reading**.

Max: What's up, Sam?

Sam: Max, you are so big! The bugs carry
rope to get down from your back.
How can I get big like you?

73

Comprehension

9 Look at the dialogue between Max and Sam on page 73. Who is asking a question? (both characters) What lets you know that a question is being asked? (question mark) *Concepts of Print*

10 **CAUSE AND EFFECT** What does Sam want to know? (how to get big) Why does he ask Max Mule to help him? (because Max is big)

Minilesson

REVIEW/MAINTAIN

Blends *gr, fr, tr*

Read the sentences on page 72 and tell children to raise their hands when they hear a word that begins with the sound /gr/. (*grow*) Repeat with the sounds /fr/ and /tr/ using the words *from* and *try* on pages 73 and 75.

Activity Create a three-column chart on the chalkboard for *fr, gr,* and *tr* words. As children suggest other words that begin with these sounds, have them identify the column each belongs in. Then invite children to use a word from each column in a sentence.

Phonics CD-ROM Have children use the interactive phonics activities for reinforcement with blends.

Comprehension

CONCEPTS OF PRINT Point to the sentences that Max says. Begin with the third sentence, and count the commas. How many commas are there? (five) *Syntactic Cues*

74

Fluency

READING WITH EXPRESSION

PARTNERS Have children guess what type of voice Max Mule might have. Then discuss how he might sound as he gives advice to Sam.

- Have children practice reading Max's sentences aloud.

- Remind them to experiment with expression and voice.

- Then have them read the section to their partners.

PREVENTION/INTERVENTION

CONCEPTS OF PRINT Rewrite the sentences that Max says on chart paper. Invite volunteers to circle each comma. Remind children that a comma gives them a signal to pause when they are reading. Then have children point to the comma in Sam's response. Invite volunteers to read the response aloud, pausing at the comma. *Syntactic Cues*

74   *The Knee-High Man*

Max: This is what you do. Pick lots of corn **12** cobs. Clean them, eat them, and then run ten miles. Try that, Sam. In time, you will be big, just like me.

Sam: Thanks, Max. I sure will try. **11**

75

Comprehension

11 Do you think Sam likes Max's idea? Why or why not? (Answers will vary.)
Make Inferences

12 What is the first thing that Max says Sam must do? (pick lots of corn cobs) What is the next thing? (clean them and eat them) What is the last thing Sam must do? (run ten miles) *Sequence of Events*

13 What do you think will happen next? *Make Predictions*

Minilesson

REVIEW/MAINTAIN

Context Clues

Point out to children that we can use words and pictures to understand new words.

- Have children point to the word *cobs* on page 75. Discuss how other words in the sentence, such as *corn* and *eat,* can help them understand the meaning. Connect the words *corn* and *cobs.*

- Ask children to describe a corn cob. Have them use the illustration on page 76 to help.

Activity Invite children to make a list of other vegetables and then name their parts.

75

Comprehension

(14) June says that Sam *cleaned and then chomped on ten corn cobs.* Show me how you clean corn. Now show me how you eat corn. *Pantomime*

(15) How does Sam feel? Show me with your face. *Nonverbal Response*

June: So Sam cleaned and then chomped on ten corn cobs. He ran ten miles, too. When he was done, his tummy hurt an his legs hurt. But he did not grow one inch. He just got mad, as mad as can

(14) (1

Activity

Cross Curricular: Math

INCH BY INCH Display a ruler marked in inches and talk about units of measurement. Then display some corn cobs of different lengths or corn cobs cut from construction paper.

Activity Help children compare the lengths of the corn cobs. Demonstrate how to measure each one to the nearest inch and label each with the correct measurement. Invite children to order the corn cobs from shortest to longest.

▶ **Kinesthetic/Logical**

am: What have I done? I ate that much. I ran that far. And I am still small! **17**

77

Comprehension

16 **CAUSE AND EFFECT** When one thing happens in a story, it often causes something else to happen. What happened after Sam ate the corn cobs? (His tummy and his legs hurt.) Let's draw a picture on our Story Comic Strip to show what happened. *Graphic Organizer*

16

cause	effect

17 Look at the punctuation on this page. What type of sentence is the first thing Sam says? (a question) What type of sentence is the last thing Sam says? (an exclamation) Let's read these sentences with feeling like Sam would say them. *Concepts of Print*

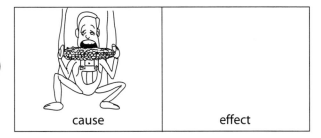
Minilesson
REVIEW/MAINTAIN
High-Frequency Words

Write each of the following high-frequency words on index cards: *he, I, and.* Distribute sets of cards to children.

Have pairs of children show each other the index cards in turn and practice reading them. Then have them find these words on pages 76–77.

Activity Give children a page from a newspaper or children's magazine. Ask them to circle any of these high-frequency words that they find.

Comprehension

18 What do you know about Sam so far? Do you think he will give up? (Answers will vary. Children should note that Sam wants something strongly and is trying hard to get it.) *Make Predictions*

p/i **CONCEPTS OF PRINT** Read the last sentence with me. Why do you think *Knee-High Man* starts with capital letters? (because Sam's title is part of his name and names begin with capital letters) *Syntactic Cues*

19 **Phonics** **LONG *u: u-e*** Who is narrating the story? Can you read her name? Let's blend the sounds of this person's name together. J u n(e) June *Graphophonic Cues*

19 June: But Sam did not give up. No not Sam, the Knee-High Ma

---

p/i **PREVENTION/INTERVENTION**

CONCEPTS OF PRINT Ask children to point to the first word of each statement June makes, and tell why the words begin with capital letters. (They begin a sentence.) Then ask why *Sam* and *the Knee-High Man* begin with capital letters. Direct children by asking:

- What is this character's name?
- Does he have a special title that is part of his name?

Point out to children that Sam's nam and special title begin with capital le ters because they are proper nouns. Then brainstorm a list of other prope nouns and invite volunteers to write words on the chalkboard, making su each one starts with a capital letter. *Syntactic Cues*

Sam: Bob Bull is the biggest one I know. He is sure to know how I can get big like him. I will go see him. He will tell me what to do.

79

Comprehension

20 Look at what Sam says. How many sentences do you see? (4) Does Sam ask any questions? (no) How can you tell? (No sentence ends with a question mark.) *Concepts of Print*

21 What big animal do you see on this page? (a bull) Is he bigger than Sam? (yes) *Use Illustrations*

LANGUAGE SUPPORT

ESL Ask children to predict what they think Sam will ask Bob Bull. Accept all responses, even gestures. Restate children's ideas using complete sentences. Always ask if what you have said meets with what the child has tried to communicate.

Comprehension

22 **CAUSE AND EFFECT** Let's look at our Story Comic Strips. What has Sam done so far? (asked Max Mule for advice and eaten lots of corn) Let's write what Sam is doing in our Story Comic Strips. *Graphic Organizer*

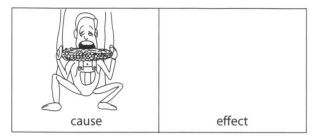

cause	effect

ⓈELF-MONITORING STRATEGY

SEARCH FOR CLUES Using pictures can help a reader understand the story and the characters.

MODEL I don't understand what Sam means when he says that frogs think the bull's horns are tree branches. But if I look at the picture, I see small frogs sitting on the horns. The bull is so big, the frogs must think he is a tree.

Sam: Bob Bull, you are so big. Frogs think your horns are tree branches. How can I get big like you?

22

80

Activity

Cross Curricular: Science

FROGS Invite children to find out about frogs. Explain that frogs are amphibians with long hind legs that help them jump. Frogs have thin, moist skin and are able to breathe through it. Have children investigate different kinds of frogs. Ask them to draw a frog and then label the parts of its body. ▶ **Visual/Linguistic**

RESEARCH AND INQUIRY Invite children to find out more about tree-peeper frogs.

interNET CONNECTION To find out more about amphibians, help children log on to **www.mhschool.com/reading**.

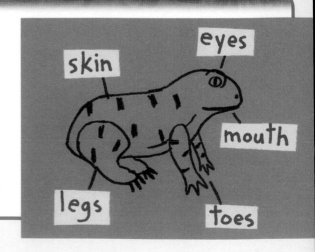

Bob: Well, Sam, this is what you do. Eat a lot of fine grass and yell and grunt a lot. Try that, Sam. In time, you will be a big old brute, just like me. **23**

81

Comprehension

23 **Phonics** **LONG** *u: u-e* There is a word on this page with the long *u* sound and silent *e*. Point to it. Now blend the sounds to read this word. Let's use what we know about *-ute*. b r u t(e) brute *Graphophonic Cues*

24 Let's look closely at the picture on this page. What does Bob Bull look like? (Answers will vary.) What is Bob Bull eating? (grass) Who is sitting on Bob Bull's horns? (two frogs) *Use Illustrations*

Comprehension

(25) What is Sam eating? (grass) Is there a large amount of grass or a small amount? (a large amount) *Use Illustrations*

June: Sam ate a peck of grass. He yelle and grunted till the sun set. Whe he was done, his tummy hurt and his throat hurt. But he did not grow one inch!

LANGUAGE SUPPORT

MULTIPLE-MEANING WORDS Tell children that some words, like *peck*, have more than one meaning. Reread the first sentence together. Then reread Bob's advice on page 81. Help children use context clues by asking:

• How much grass did Sam eat?

• What do you think the word *peck* might mean in this sentence?

Show that the word *peck* is used as a term of measurement. It means "a large amount" (or eight dry quarts). Then ask children to give other meanings for the word *peck*.

Sam: What bad, bad luck! I ate that grass. I yelled and grunted. And I am still small!

83

Comprehension

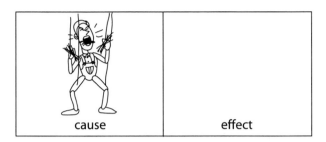

26 **CAUSE AND EFFECT** What did Sam do? (He ate a lot of grass and made loud noises.) **What happened?** (His tummy and throat hurt, but he is still small.) **Let's draw a picture on our Story Comic Strip to show what happened.** *Graphic Organizer*

cause	effect

TEACHING TIP

MANAGEMENT To help eliminate mistakes and frustration, ask children to make a few rough sketches of their Story Comic Strip pictures on scrap paper first. Children can choose which sketch they feel best represents the idea they wish to convey. Working from their sketches, children can then fill in the blank panels on their Story Comic Strips.

Comprehension

27 Who does Sam go to see next? (Kate Owl) *Sequence of Events*

28 So Sam hasn't given up yet. What does that tell you about him? (He's brave, he tries hard, he's determined.) *Analyze Character*

June: But Sam did not give up. No, not Sam, the Knee-High Man. He went to see Kate Owl.

Sam: Kate Owl is very wise. She will tell me how I can get bigger, for sure.

85

Comprehension

(29) Let's think about what we've already read. Every time Sam goes to see another friend, what does he ask? (how he can get big) So, what do you think Sam is going to ask Kate Owl? (Answers might vary.) *Make Predictions*

LANGUAGE SUPPORT

ESL In this selection there are several idiomatic expressions that may impede understanding for English learners. Take time to explain the following phrases. Suggestions for restatements follow

each in parentheses: page 72, *sure to know* (will tell him, will know); page 76, *as mad as can be* (He will be really mad.); page 78, *did not give up* (kept going, trying); page 85, *for sure* (She will know. I know she can tell me).

Comprehension

30 **CAUSE AND EFFECT** What has happened in the story so far? (Sam wants to be bigger. He has eaten corn and grass, but he is still small.) Whom is he asking for help now? (Kate Owl) Let's draw a picture on our Story Comic Strips. *Graphic Organizer*

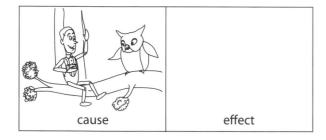

cause	effect

31 Sam has tried several different things in trying to grow bigger. Has anything changed in his size? Let's look at the picture on this page. How do you think Sam must feel? (Answers will vary.) *Make Inferences*

30 Sam: Kate, you are wise. Tell me how I can get bigger. I have been trying my best

Kate: Why do you want to be big, Sam?

32 Sam: If I am big, then I can win any fight.

86

Activity

Cross Curricular: Social Studies

PEACEFUL SOLUTIONS Read page 87 and talk about Sam's desire to win a fight. Brainstorm with children a list of problems or arguments they may have with their friends. Then make a list of peaceful ways to solve each problem. Help children focus by asking them what the outcome should be and then elicit ways to achieve that outcome. ▶ **Linguistic/Kinesthetic**

inter NET **CONNECTION** Help children log on to sites about well-known peace movements and organizations at *www.mhschool.com/reading*.

Peaceful Solutions
Apologize
Explain
Discuss the problem
Brainstorm solutions
Shake hands

Kate: Who has picked a fight with you?

Sam: No one.

Kate: Then you do not have to fight.
And you do not have to be big.

87

Comprehension

32 Point to the first question Kate asks Sam. How many commas are there? (one) Let's read the question together correctly. *Concepts of Print*

p/i **BLENDING WITH SHORT *i*** Tell children there are three words on this page that have the short *i* sound. Ask children to find the words. (*picked, with, big*) *Graphophonic Cues*

p/i PREVENTION/INTERVENTION

BLENDING WITH SHORT *i* Write the following words on a piece of chart paper: *inch, with, pick, chin, snip.* Cover the consonants of each word with a self-stick note, so that only the short *i* shows. Have children tell you what sound the short *i* makes. (/i/)

Then, starting with the first word, have a volunteer pull off one of the self-stick notes and blend the letters together. Have another child pull off any remaining notes and blend all the letters together to read the word. *Graphophonic Cues*

Comprehension

33 Ask children to describe what Sam is doing. (stretching tall and shading his eyes) Why is he doing this? (to see far away) *Use Illustrations*

Sam: But if I am big, I can see far away. I can see far, just like you.

88

Kate: Can't you go up a tree to look far
away?

Sam: Sure I can!

(34)

89

Comprehension

CONTRACTIONS Point to the first word that Kate says. What is the name of the mark you see in the middle of this word? (apostrophe) What does the apostrophe mean? (One or more letters have been taken out of the word.) Read the word with me. (*can't*) *Semantic Cues*

(34) What advice does Kate give Sam? (He doesn't have to fight anybody, and he can see far away just by climbing a tree.) Do you think Kate thinks Sam needs to be bigger? (no) *Critical Thinking*

PREVENTION/INTERVENTION

CONTRACTIONS Write the word *can't* on the chalkboard. Invite children to read it with you. Then write the words *can not* below it. Ask children which letters were removed from *can not* and replaced by the apostrophe in *can't*. (the letters *n, o*)

Ask children to use *can't* in a sentence. Then have them use *can not* in the same sentence. Make sure children understand that the meaning does not change. Repeat with the contractions *didn't* and *wasn't*. *Semantic Cues*

Minilesson

REVIEW/MAINTAIN

Main Idea

Explain to children that the main idea tells what the story is about. Work together to write three sentences that tell the main idea of *The Knee-High Man*. Guide results by asking the following questions:

- What was Sam's problem?
- How did he try to solve the problem?
- What did he learn?

Activity Have children summarize the story orally. Record the sentences that describe the main idea.

Comprehension

(35) CAUSE AND EFFECT Sam went up in the tree with Kate. What did he learn? (He was fine just as he is.) Let's write on our Story Comic Strip to show what happened. *Graphic Organizer*

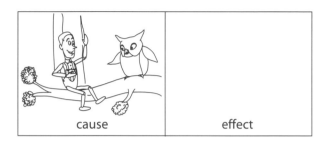

cause	effect

RETELL THE STORY Have groups of children retell the story, each taking the part of one of the characters. Have them use their Story Comic Strips to show how events caused other events to happen. Guide them to the conclusion by asking what Sam learned at the end of the story. *Graphic Organizer/Summarize*

STUDENT SELF-ASSESSMENT

Have children ask themselves the following questions to assess how they are reading:

- How did I use what I know about self-acceptance to help me understand the story?

- How did I use the pictures and words to help me understand what Sam learned?

- How did I use the pictures and the letters and sounds I know to help me read the words in the story?

TRANSFERRING THE STRATEGIES

- How can I use these strategies to help me read other stories?

Kate: You see, Sam. You do not have to **(35)** be bigger. You are just fine the way you are.

90

GROUP Children who need fluency practice can read aloud in groups, each taking a character part.

READING RATE When you evaluate reading rate, have children read aloud from the story for one minute. Place a stick-on note after the last word read. Count words read. To evaluate children's performance, see the Running Record in the **Fluency Assessment** book.

(i) Intervention For leveled fluency lessons, passages, and norms charts, see **Skills Intervention Guide**, Part 5, Fluency.

Sam: I think you are right, Kate.
Because if I were any bigger, I would
not be me. I would not be Sam,
the Knee-High Man!

91

Comprehension

Return to Predictions and Purposes

Reread children's predictions about the story. Ask if the story answered all of the questions they had before they read it. Discuss their predictions, noting which needed to be revised.

Have children discuss their Story Comic Strips. Did using the strips help children understand how one event led to another?

LITERARY RESPONSE

QUICK-WRITE Have children draw in their journals a picture of someone who is too tall, and give that person a name such as Toby, the Too-Tall Man.

ORAL RESPONSE Have children use their journal entries to discuss these questions:

• What did you draw?

• What advice would Sam have for someone who thinks he or she is too tall?

SENTENCE STRIPS Children can use strips 1–89 to retell the story:

> 1
> June: Some folks grow big.

> 2
> Some folks stay small.

Story Questions

Tell children that now they will read some questions about the story. Help children read the questions. Discuss possible answers.

Answers:

1. He told him to eat a lot of fine grass and yell and grunt a lot. *Literal/Details*

2. He only comes up to a person's knee. *Inferential/Character*

3. Answers will vary. Accept appropriate responses. *Inferential/Character*

4. Sam learned to accept himself the way he is. *Critical/Summarize*

5. Answers will vary. Accept appropriate responses. *Critical/Reading Across Texts*

Write a Journal Entry Help children read the directions in their anthologies. For a full writing process lesson related to writing that compares, see pages 95M–95N.

Story Questions & Activities

READ TOGETHER

1 What did Bob tell Sam to do?

2 Why is Sam called the Knee-High Man?

3 How did Kate help Sam?

4 Tell what you think Sam learned.

5 How is a play different from a story?

Draw Sam and Bob

Sam and Bob Bull are friends.
Write how they are the same.
Write how they are different.

Sam is small. Bob is big.

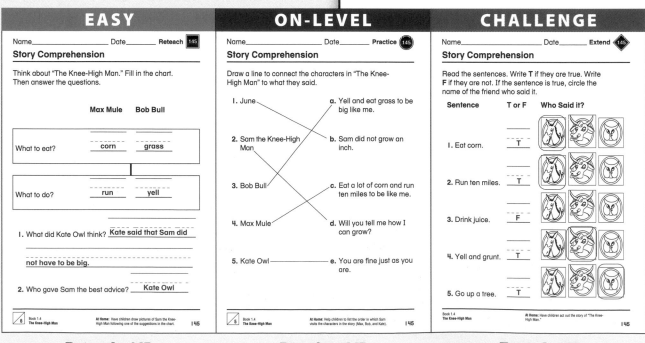

EASY	ON-LEVEL	CHALLENGE
Reteach, 145	Practice, 145	Extend, 145

Add to the Play

Work with your class.
Add two more animals to the play.
Make up things for them to say.
Then read the play aloud.

Find Out More

"The Knee-High Man" is a folktale.
It teaches a lesson.
Find another folktale that teaches
a lesson.

93

Story Activities

Add to the Play

Materials: chart paper

Read the directions aloud. Help children who have questions. Have the class discuss various animals they might add to the play. Are these animals small or big? What do the small animals say to the big animals? How do the big animals respond?

 You may wish to have children work **PARTNERS** as partners to come up with more lines for the play. Then, have the partners read their lines aloud with expression.

Find Out More

RESEARCH AND INQUIRY Again, read the directions aloud, and help children who have questions.

ONE

Point out that all cultures have folk tales and that such stories often teach a lesson. Explain that sometimes it's easier to teach something important by putting it in a story, rather than by just telling it to somebody. Then ask children if they have heard or read any folk tales that teach a lesson. Perhaps they can ask their parents or grandparents to tell them a tale that teaches a lesson. Have the children share the stories they have read or heard with the class.

interNET CONNECTION To learn more about folk tales, have children log on to **www.mhschool.com/reading**.

DAILY Phonics ROUTINES

DAY 3
Fluency Write on the chalkboard: *The mule is cute.* Ask children to blend sounds and read silently as you track print. Then, have them read aloud.

 **Phonics CD-ROM**

FORMAL ASSESSMENT

After page 93, see the Selection Assessment.

93

CHARTS

OBJECTIVES

Students will learn to use a chart to gather information.

PREPARE Tell children that they will read a chart, a kind of list that shows what some of the characters in the play said.

TEACH Display **Teaching Chart 107**. Have children read the sentences and the title of the chart. Read the lines together. Point to each animal and ask children to repeat what that character said to Sam.

PRACTICE Then help children read the questions below the chart. Have them answer the questions.

1. Eat corn and run ten miles.

2. Bull

ASSESS/CLOSE Have children tell how they would add their own advice for Sam to the chart.

STUDY **SKILLS**   READ TOGETHER

Who Said What? Chart

This chart shows what the animals said to Sam.

	Mule	eat corn run ten miles
	Bull	eat grass yell and grunt
	Owl	don't do anything

Look at the Chart

1 What did Mule say?

2 Who told Sam to yell?

Meeting Individual Needs

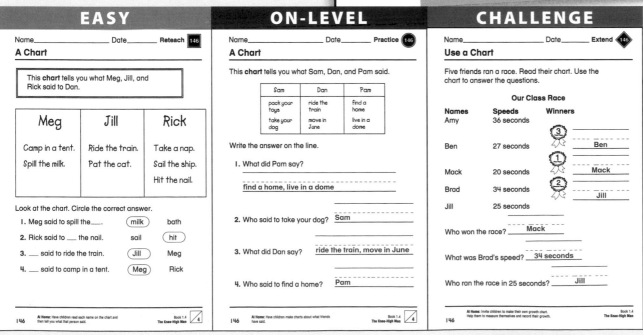

Reteach, 146   Practice, 146   Extend, 146

TEST POWER

What Is Polly Doing?

Polly put her toes out.

Polly put her legs out.

Polly put her fingers out.

Polly put her arms out.

Polly put her whole self out of bed.

The air was too cold.

So, Polly climbed back into her

warm bed.

Why did Polly climb back into her bed?

● The air was too cold.

○ She was sleepy.

Think about what the story tells you.

95

Test Power

THE PRINCETON REVIEW

Read the Page

Explain to children that you will be reading this story as a group. You will read the story, and they will follow in their books.

Request that children put pens, pencils, and markers away, since they will not be writing in their books.

Discuss the Question

Discuss with children what constitutes an answer to a "why" question. Have them re-read the story, find the place where Polly goes back to bed, and put their fingers on the reason why she does so.

Test-Tip

Always look back to the story to find the answer. The answer is always somewhere in the passage.

ITBS/TEST PREPARATION

TERRA NOVA/TEST PREPARATION

SAT 9/TEST PREPARATION

Leveled Books

Intervention ▶ **Skills**
Intervention Guide, for direct instruction and extra practice in vocabulary and comprehension

EASY

Fun Run

☑ **Phonics** Long *u: u-e*
☑ **Cause and Effect**
High-Frequency Words:
carry, been, clean, done, far

by Rachel Patrick
illustrated by Jane Sanders

Guided Reading

PREVIEW AND PREDICT Discuss the concept of cause and effect as you take a **picture walk** up to page 8. Encourage children to predict what will happen in the story. Write their predictions on the chalkboard.

SET PURPOSES Have children write or draw why they want to read *Fun Run*. For example: *I want to find out what happens when Will races.*

READ THE BOOK Use questions like the following to guide children's reading, or to discuss after they have read the story independently.

Pages 2–3: What does Will want to do? (help clean) *High-Frequency Words*

Pages 4–5: Let's read to find out what Will wants to play. Help me blend the sounds of the letters together to read the word.

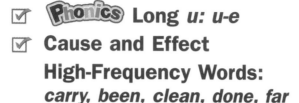

f l u t(e) flute *Phonics and Decoding*

Pages 6–7: Will's parents think he is too small to help clean or play the flute. How does that make him feel? (sad) *Cause and Effect*

Pages 8–9: Can you find a vocabulary word on these pages? (carry) *High-Frequency Words*

Pages 10–16: Why do you think Will won? (Answers will vary, including: he tried his best to have fun.) *Cause and Effect*

RETURN TO PREDICTIONS AND PURPOSES Discuss children's predictions. Do they feel that some of the wrong predictions might have made a better story? Why? Did they find out what they wanted?

LITERARY RESPONSE You can use the following questions to gauge children's responses to the story:

• Do you think Will is too little to help his mom clean or to play the flute? Why or why not?

• Will is good at running. What are you good at?

Also see the story questions and activity in *Fun Run*.

See the **Phonics** CD-ROM for practice with long *u: u-e.*

Answers to Story Questions

1. when he gets bigger
2. He feels good and proud.
3. Answers will vary.
4. Will wants to do what grown-ups do. They won't let him. He wants to try something new. He decides to join the track team, where he runs and wins a race. Everyone is happy in the end.
5. Like Sam, Will ends up happy just the way he is.

The Story Questions and Activity below appear in the Easy Book.

Story Questions and Activity
1. When can Will play the flute?
2. How does Will feel after he runs?
3. When might Will run again?
4. Tell the story in your own words.
5. How is Will like Sam in *The Knee-High Man*?

Make an Award
Draw a ribbon shape on paper.
Color it in.
Write "Number 1" on it.
Cut it out and tape it to your shirt.
Hooray!

from *Fun Run*

Leveled Books

A Bigger House for June

written by Anna Smyth
illustrated by Kathy Wilburn

INDEPENDENT

A Bigger House for June

- ☑ **Long** *u: u-e*
- ☑ **Cause and Effect**
  High-Frequency Words:
  carry, been, clean, done, far

Guided Reading

PREVIEW AND PREDICT Have children read the title aloud and predict what the story will be about. Then take a **picture walk** up to page 7, incorporating the high-frequency words and focusing children's attention on cause and effect.

SET PURPOSES Have children write or draw why they want to read *A Bigger House for June.* For example: *I want to find out why June gets a bigger house.*

READ THE BOOK Use the following prompts as children read together or to discuss after they read independently:

Pages 2–3: What does June like to do? (clean) *High-Frequency Words*

Pages 4–5: Let's reread these pages. Raise your hand when you hear a word with the long *u* sound. *(June, cube) Phonics and Decoding*

Pages 6–7: Find and read a word on this page that has the long *u* sound. *(mule) Phonics and Decoding*

Pages 8–11: Why doesn't Jake's tune make June glad? (She is jealous of his home.) *Make Inferences*

Pages 14–16: What has happened to make June change her mind about her house? (It now looks cute; it is the right size for all her small friends.) *Cause and Effect*

RETURN TO PREDICTIONS AND PURPOSES Review children's predictions and purposes. Were they surprised by what happened in the story? Did they find out what they wanted?

LITERARY RESPONSE The following questions will help focus children's responses:

- Would you tell a friend to read this story? Why or why not?

- Have you ever wanted something that someone else had? What happened?

Also see the story questions and activity in *A Bigger House for June.*

See the **CD-ROM** for practice with long *u: u-e.*

Answers to Story Questions
1. Jim, the mule
2. She doesn't like the shape and size.
3. Answers will vary.
4. no
5. *The Knee-High Man*

The Story Questions and Activity below appear in the Independent Book.

Story Questions and Activity
1. Which friend does June go to first?
2. Why doesn't June like her home?
3. What things does Jim carry on his back?
4. Do June's friends help her?
5. What's another story with a mule?

Draw a Home
Draw a picture of your home.
Write the name of your street near your home.
Put an **X** near your favorite room.
Share your picture with the class.

from A Bigger House for June

Leveled Books

CHALLENGE

Pete's Chicken

- ☑   Long *u: u-e*
- ☑ Cause and Effect

PETE'S CHICKEN

Harriet Ziefert · Laura Rader

Guided Reading

PREVIEW AND PREDICT Discuss illustrations up to page 20, making sure children understand the concept of cause and effect. Encourage children to predict what the story will be about. Have them write their ideas in their journals.

SET PURPOSES Have children write or draw why they want to read *Pete's Chicken*. For example: *I want to find out what Pete's chicken looks like.*

READ THE BOOK Use questions like the following to guide children's reading or to discuss after they have read the story independently. Page 1 of the book is the title page.

Pages 5–15: How does Pete feel about himself? (good) How can you tell? (He looks happy and says good things about himself.) *Make Inferences*

Pages 16–19: Let's reread these pages. Raise your hand when you hear a word with the long *u* sound. *(used)* How is that sound spelled? *(u-consonant-e) Phonics and Decoding*

Pages 20–27: Why does Pete feel bad? (No one likes his chicken.) *Cause and Effect*

Pages 28–31: Why doesn't Pete want a kiss from his mom? (Answers will vary.) *Make Inferences*

Pages 32–36: What makes Pete change his mind about his chicken? (He realizes it is special because only he could make it.) *Make Inferences/Cause and Effect*

RETURN TO PREDICTIONS AND PURPOSES Ask children to share their predictions and purposes. Then discuss which predictions were close and why. Which purposes were met?

LITERARY RESPONSE Use the following questions to engage children in a discussion about the story:

- Why do you think that Pete draws a chicken that doesn't look like most chickens?

- Have you ever felt like Pete? When?

- Which illustration did you like the best? Why?

Also see story questions and writing activity in *Pete's Chicken*.

See the  CD-ROM for practice with long *u: u-e.*

Answers to Story Questions

1. black, orange, blue, red, purple, yellow, green
2. because they thought Pete's chicken was a turkey
3. Answers will vary.
4. Pete is different. He draws a chicken of many colors. The class thought he drew a turkey. Pete took his chicken home. It was different. Just like Pete.
5. Answers will vary.

The Story Questions and Activity below appear in the Challenge Book.

Story Questions and Activity

1. What colors are in Pete's drawing?
2. Why do the children laugh at Pete?
3. What does the story tell you about being different?
4. Tell the story in your own words.
5. How is the story like *My Best Friend*?

Make Up an Animal
Think of an animal that no one has ever seen.

Draw a picture of it.

Write a few sentences describing it.

from *Pete's Chicken*

Bringing Groups Together

Anthology and Leveled Books

Connecting Texts

CLASS DISCUSSION	CHARACTER WEB
Lead a discussion of how the unit theme of Let's Find Out! applies to each of the stories. Have children construct a word web that describes what characters teach or what they learn from their own experiences or from others.	Have children create a web to compare the characters from their stories, their traits, and what they do.

The Knee-High Man
Sam decides he is big enough to do the things he wants to do.

Fun Run
Will feels good because he had fun running.

Self-Acceptance

A Bigger House for June
June feels good because her friends like her house.

Pete's Chicken
Pete feels better for having drawn the chicken.

Viewing/Representing

GROUP PRESENTATIONS Divide the class into groups, one for each of the four books read in the lesson. (For *The Knee-High Man*, combine children of different reading levels.) Have each group create over-sized comic strips that show the book's main events. Encourage them to use speech balloons where appropriate. Invite groups to display their comic strips.

AUDIENCE RESPONSE
Give children time to view each group's comic strip. Have them ask questions about what is happening in the frames and why.

Research and Inquiry

MORE ABOUT FEELINGS Have children share their experiences when they felt happy, sad, and angry. Use the following questions to initiate discussion:

- Can you remember a time when you wanted something and you couldn't have it?

- Can you remember a time when someone told you that you were too small to do something?

- Can you remember a time when you were excited about doing something for the first time?

inter NET CONNECTION Have children log onto **www.mhschool.com/reading** where they can access links to conflict resolution sites.

JOURNAL Children can write and draw what they learned in their journals.

OBJECTIVES

Children will:

- review long *u: u–e*.
- blend and read long *u: u-e* words.
- review consonants.

MATERIALS

- Letter and long *u* cards from the **Word Building Manipulative Cards**
- **Teaching Chart 108**
- index cards

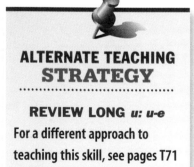

Skills Finder	
Long *u: u-e*	
Introduce	B4: 66I-J
Review	B4: 95E-F, 95G-H, 123G-H, 124I-J
Test	Book 4

ALTERNATE TEACHING STRATEGY

REVIEW LONG *u: u-e*
For a different approach to teaching this skill, see pages T71 and T72.

Review Long *u: u-e*

PREPARE

Listen for Long *u* Read the following sentence aloud and have children raise their hands whenever they hear a word with the long *u* sound:

- Duke is a cute mule with long brown ears.

TEACH

Review the Letters *u–e* as Symbols for /ū/

- Tell children that they will review long *u* spelled *u* consonant *e*.
- Write *u–e* on the chalkboard. Have children say /ū/ as you point to it.

BLENDING Model and Guide Practice with Long *u* words

- Display **Teaching Chart 108**. Tell children that there are five long *u: u–e* words hidden in the chart.
- Blend the first example for children, running your hand under the letters. Read the word *cute*. c u te   cute
- Repeat, having children read the word with you. Have a volunteer circle the word on the chart.

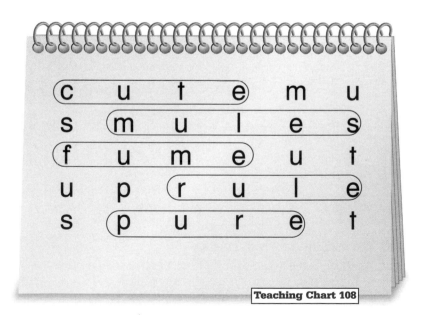

Teaching Chart 108

Use the Word in Context

- Use the word *cute* in a sentence. Example: *I have a cute, furry cat.*

Repeat the Procedure

- Have volunteers find and blend the remaining long *u: u–e* words in the chart and draw a circle around them.

PRACTICE

BLENDING
Build Long _u_ Words with Letter Cards

PARTNERS

Write the following letter clusters on index cards: _ure, ule, une, ute._ Place them in a bag. Place the letter cards for _p, s, t, d, J, t, m, r, c, l_ in a second bag. Have one child choose a letter cluster and blend the sounds aloud. Then have a second child choose consonants to place before the clusters until real words can be formed. Have pairs keep lists of the words they form. Encourage children to see how many word families they can create. Sort the words into five groups: _-ure, -ule, -une,_ and _-ute._ ▶ **Spatial/Kinesthetic**

ASSESS/CLOSE

Build and Read Long _u_ Words

To assess children's mastery of blending and reading long _u_ words, observe them as they form words in the Practice activity. Ask each child to read two words aloud from the list.

ADDITIONAL PHONICS RESOURCES

Phonics/Phonemic Awareness Practice Book, pages 147–150

PHONICS KIT
Hands-on Activities and Practice

McGraw-Hill School TECHNOLOGY

 CD-ROM

activities for practice with **Blending and Building**

DAILY _Phonics_ ROUTINES

DAY 4

Writing Write the word _duke_ on chart paper and give the meaning of the word. Ask children to write a sentence about a duke and draw a picture to illustrate it.

Phonics **CD-ROM**

SPELLING/PHONICS CONNECTIONS

Words with long _u_: _u-e:_ See the 5-Day Spelling Plan, pages 95Q–95R.

Intervention ▶ Skills

Intervention Guide, for direct instruction and extra practice in Long _u_: _u-e_

Meeting Individual Needs for Phonics

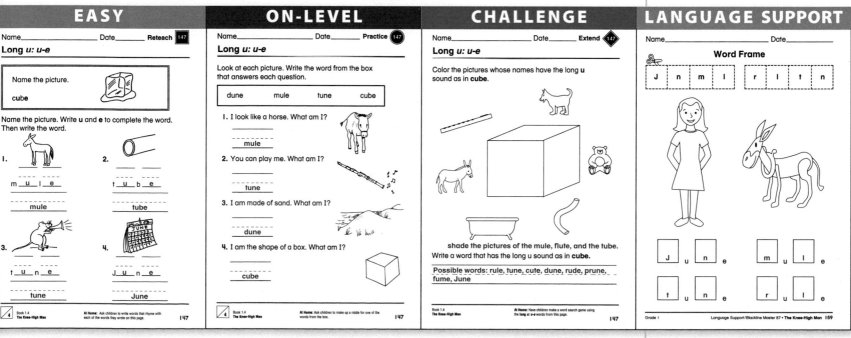

EASY	ON-LEVEL	CHALLENGE	LANGUAGE SUPPORT
Reteach, 147	Practice, 147	Extend, 147	Language Support, 159

OBJECTIVES

Children will:

- review long *u: u–e, o: o–e, i: i–e, a: a-e.*

- blend and read long *u, o, i,* and *a* words with silent *e.*

- cumulative review: consonants and blends.

....

MATERIALS

- letter and long vowel cards from the **Word Building Manipulative Cards**

- **Teaching Chart 109**

- **Phonics Practice Reader, Volume 2**

Skills Finder	
Long *u: u-e*	
▶ Introduce	B4: 66I-J
▶ Review	B4: 95E-F, 95G-H, 123G-H, 124I-J
▶ Test	Book 4

TEACHING TIP

LONG VOWELS Have children make up riddles for long *u, o, i,* and *a* words. Children can exchange and answer each other's riddles.

ALTERNATE TEACHING STRATEGY
....

PHONICS: LONG VOWELS *u, o, i, a*

For a different approach to teaching this skill, see pages **T64, T65, T69, T70, T71, and T72.**

Review *u-e, o-e, i-e, a-e*

PREPARE

Identify the Letters *u–e, o–e, i–e, a–e* as the Symbols for Long *u, o, i, a*

Remind children that the letter *u* when followed by a consonant and silent *e* stands for /ū/. Write *u–e* on the chalkboard, saying its sound aloud. Have children say the sound as you point to the letter *u*. Repeat for long *o, i,* and *a.*

Discriminate Among /ū/, /ō/, /ī/, and /ā/

Slowly say the following sentence: *Jake and June like to jump rope.* Have children raise a hand when they hear a word with /ū/. Repeat for long *a, o,* and *i.*

TEACH

BLENDING Model and Guide Practice in Matching Rhyming Words with Long *u, o, i, a*

- Display **Teaching Chart 109**. Explain that there are six pairs of rhyming words on the chart, but that they are all mixed up. Tell children that they will draw lines to connect the rhyming words.

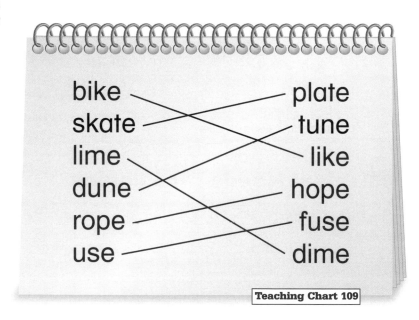

Teaching Chart 109

- Blend the first word on the chart with children. b i k e bike

- Then have volunteers blend and read aloud the words in the second column until they find the word that rhymes with *bike.*

- Have a volunteer read *bike* and *like* and draw a line to connect the two words.

Use the Word in Context

Have volunteers use the words in a sentence. For example: *I would like a red bike.*

Repeat the Procedure

Repeat the procedure until all the rhyming pairs have been connected.

PRACTICE

BLENDING
Build and Sort Long *u*, *o*, *i*, and *a* Words

GROUP

Have small groups use the letter cards and long vowel cards to build as many words as possible with long *u, o, i,* and *a*. Have groups choose two words for each vowel to put on a class bulletin board under *u, o, i,* or *a*. Have children then sort the words under each long vowel into groups of words that rhyme. ▶ **Linguistic/Kinesthetic**

f l u t e

ASSESS/CLOSE

Read Words with Long *u*, *o*, *i*, and *a*

Use your observations from the Practice activity to determine if children need more reinforcement with long *u, o, i,* and *a* words. Have children choose a long vowel word and draw and label a picture of it.

Read a Decodable Story

For additional practice reading words with long *u: u-e* and to develop fluency, direct children to read the story *A Fine Race* from the **Phonics Practice Reader, Volume 2.**

ADDITIONAL PHONICS RESOURCES

Phonics/Phonemic Awareness Practice Book,
pages 147–150

PHONICS KIT
Hands-on Activities and Practice

McGraw-Hill School
TECHNOLOGY
Phonics CD-ROM

activities for practice with
Blending and Building

DAILY **Phonics** ROUTINES

DAY 5
Letter Substitution
Using the letter and long vowel cards, have pairs of children build the word *brute*. Then have them change letters to build *chute* and *flute*.

Phonics CD-ROM

i **Intervention** **Skills**
Intervention Guide, for direct instruction and extra practice in Long *u: u-e*

Meeting Individual Needs for Phonics and Decoding

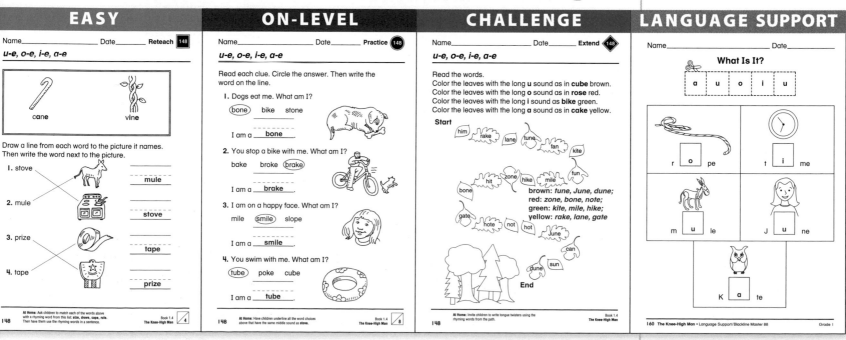

EASY	ON-LEVEL	CHALLENGE	LANGUAGE SUPPORT
Reteach, 148	Practice, 148	Extend, 148	Language Support, 160

95H

OBJECTIVES

Children will learn how to make inferences.

....

MATERIALS
• Teaching Chart 110

Skills Finder	
Make Inferences	
Introduce	B4: 95I-J
Review	B4: 123I-J, 133G-H
Test	Book 4
Maintain	B5: 27, 53, 171, 279

TEACHING TIP

MAKE INFERENCES
Making inferences is a subtle skill at which children may excel once they know what to look for. Use modeling to show children the kind of thinking they must do to make inferences.

SELF–SELECTED
Reading
....

Students may choose from the following titles.

ANTHOLOGY

• *The Knee-High Man*

LEVELED BOOKS

• *Fun Run*
• *A Bigger House for June*
• *Pete's Chicken*

Bibliography, pages T98–T99

Introduce **Make Inferences**

PREPARE

Introduce Make Inferences

Tell children that they will learn how to make inferences to help them understand characters and story events better. Explain that they can use clues in the text and illustrations, as well their own experiences, to make a good guess, or inference.

TEACH

Model Make Inferences

Display **Teaching Chart 110**. Allow children to comment on the pictures. Then read the first sentence aloud.

The man has a <u>map</u>.
He is <u>looking</u> at the map.
He has a <u>confused look</u> on his face.
What could this mean?

The girl is on the <u>bike</u>.
The boy <u>helps</u> the girl.
Her bike has <u>training wheels</u>.
What could this mean?

Teaching Chart 110

MODEL When I read, there are things that aren't always said, but that I can guess. I guess by looking at the pictures and reading what is on the page. When I guess it's called *making an inference*. In the first picture I see a man looking at a map. He looks confused. From the picture and the sentences, I can guess that the man is probably lost. It looks like he is trying to find out where he is supposed to go.

Help children make additional inferences about the first picture. Example: The man is wearing a shirt and tie. Maybe he is going to a new job. Have them use picture clues and draw on their own experiences to make their inferences. Write their ideas in a list on the chalkboard.

Make A List of Inferences

GROUP

Divide children into groups. Have them make inferences about the second picture on **Teaching Chart 110**. Have them use picture and text clues to make a list of inferences. Encourage children to draw on their own experiences as well. Have groups present their lists to the class. ▶ **Linguistic/Interpersonal**

she doesn't know how to push the pedals

she doesn't know how to steer

the boy is helping her

she will learn how to ride her bike

Make Other Inferences

Invite children to make inferences, based on the text and illustrations in other stories they have read. Create a new list for children's observations.

ALTERNATE TEACHING STRATEGY

MAKE INFERENCES

For a different approach to teaching this skill, see page T73.

ⓘ Intervention ▶ Skills

Intervention Guide, for direct instruction and extra practice in Making Inferences

Meeting Individual Needs for Comprehension

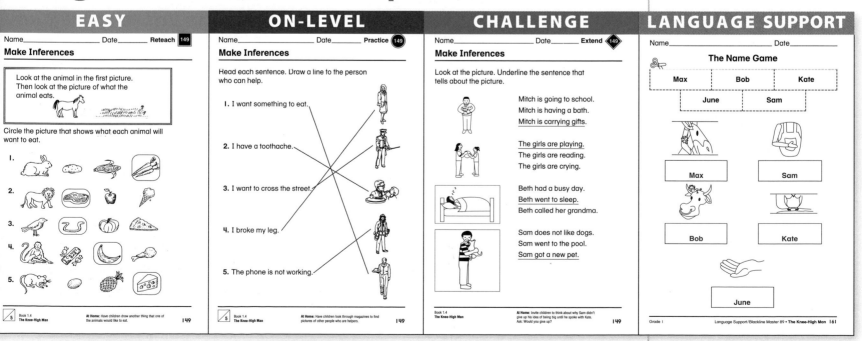

EASY	ON-LEVEL	CHALLENGE	LANGUAGE SUPPORT
Reteach, 149	Practice, 149	Extend, 149	Language Support, 161

TESTED
OBJECTIVES

Children will:

- learn to read words with inflectional endings *-er* and *-est*, including when the final consonant is doubled.

- understand the concept of root words and suffixes.

MATERIALS

- Teaching Chart 111

Skills Finder
Inflectional Endings
-er, -est

Introduce	B4: 95K-L
Review	B4: 123K-L, 133K-L
Test	Book 4

TEACHING TIP

INFLECTIONAL ENDING

-er Point out that not all the words that end in *-er* are adjectives. Often words with the *-er* ending mean a person or a thing that does a certain action. For example: *driver, baker, runner, player.*

PHONICS TEACHING TIP Tell children that the letters *er* stand for the sound /ər/. Write *er* on the board. Point to the letters, saying the sound /ər/, and have children repeat after you. Then write the word *bigger.* Blend the sounds of the letters together to read the word. Have children repeat after you.

Review Inflectional Endings -er, -est

PREPARE

Make Comparisons
On the chalkboard, draw three simple stick figures and write *big, bigger,* and *biggest* under the appropriate drawings. Elicit the words *big, bigger,* and *biggest* from children to describe the drawings.

TEACH

Identify Root Words and Endings
Read the sentences on **Teaching Chart 111**. Point out the words *big, bigger,* and *biggest.* Model how understanding inflectional endings can help children read.

Bob is <u>big</u>.

Ken is <u>bigger</u>.

Max is the <u>biggest</u>.

Teaching Chart 111

MODEL I can see in the three pictures that one boy is big, one is bigger, and one is the biggest. When I read the sentence *Ken is bigger,* I recognize the word *big.* I see that the last two letters of the word are *-er.* This is a suffix. I know that sometimes when these letters are at the end of a word, it means *more.* So Ken is "more big", or *bigger* than Bob. I also notice that the *-g* is doubled when the suffix *-er* is added.

Repeat the procedure for the word *biggest.* Invite volunteers to underline the root word in each.

Identify -er and -est Words

GROUP

Write the following words on the chalkboard: *wetter, fastest, taller, saddest,* and *slower.* Have children identify the root word in each. Then create a three-column chart that shows the root words along with the inflectional endings. Call on children to identify the missing comparative word and write it in the proper column. Discuss whether or not the final letter is doubled.

Root Word	-er	-est
wet	wetter	wettest
fast	faster	fastest
tall	taller	tallest
sad	sadder	saddest
slow	slower	slowest

ASSESS/CLOSE

Illustrate Comparatives

Have partners choose one of the sets of words from the Practice activity. Invite them to show objects or people to illustrate the three words in the set, and then label each picture.

ALTERNATE TEACHING STRATEGY

INFLECTIONAL ENDINGS
-er, -est

For a different approach to teaching this skill, see page T74.

i **Intervention** **Skills**

Intervention Guide, for direct instruction and extra practice in Inflectional Endings *-er* and *-est*

Meeting Individual Needs for Vocabulary

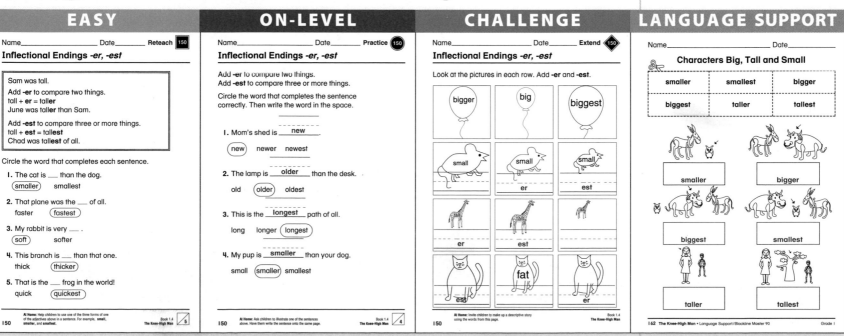

EASY	ON-LEVEL	CHALLENGE	LANGUAGE SUPPORT
Reteach, 150	Practice, 150	Extend, 150	Language Support, 162

95L

Handwriting CD-ROM

GRAMMAR/SPELLING CONNECTIONS

See the 5-Day Grammar and Usage Plan on *Go* and *Do*, pages 95O–95P.

See the 5-Day Spelling Plan on Words with Long *u: u-e (silent e rule)*, pages 95Q–95R.

TEACHING TIP

Technology
Introduce children to the "Print" icon on the toolbar. Encourage them to print out their stories and illustrate them as a display piece.

Handwriting
Remind children to write neatly, and keep all words on the line. All capital letters should be the same size, as should all lowercase letters. If children need extra practice forming their letters, you may wish to use pages T78–T91.

Writing That Compares

Prewrite

WRITE A LETTER Present this writing assignment: Pretend you are Kate Owl. Write a letter to Sam explaining how you and Sam are alike and different. Include clear details that describe both of you.

BRAINSTORM IDEAS Have children brainstorm ways that Sam and Kate are alike and different. Have them discuss how Sam and Kate look, act, and talk.

STRATEGY: PLAY A PARTNER GAME Have children list how Sam and Kate are alike and different. Use this game to help children:

- One partner plays the part of Sam, and the other partner plays the part of Kate. Have "Sam" describe himself.

- For each detail "Sam" gives about himself, "Kate" tells something that is alike or different about herself.

- Have children switch roles. Guide them to find more details about Sam and Kate and to elaborate on them.

- Have partners list their ideas as they role-play.

Draft

USE THE LIST In their letters, have children write complete sentences describing Sam and Kate. They should imagine how Sam and Kate look and act, and include these details in their sentences. Encourage them to write as if Sam is a real friend.

Revise

TAKING TIME OUT Ask children to put their work aside and think about Sam again. Discuss some more ways to describe Sam. Make a board list of their ideas.

PARTNERS Have children trade letters with a partner. Have one partner pretend to be Sam and read their partner's letter. Can they recognize the similarities and differences between themselves (as Sam) and Kate?

Edit/Proofread

CHECK FOR ERRORS Children should reread their letters for spelling, grammar, punctuation, paragraphs, and letter format.

Publish

TURN THE LETTERS INTO A BOOK Help children turn their letters into a class book. Have them decide what will go on each page. Then have them illustrate their letters.

Kate Owl
Big Oak Tree
The Forest
November 9, 2003

Dear Sam,
    It was nice to talk to you in the forest today. But I forgot to tell you something. I want to tell you some things that are the same and different about us.
    You are a person and I am an animal. But we both like to see things that are far away.
    You have skin and I have feathers. But we are both small. We are both small enough to sit in a tree.
    You are a boy and I am a girl. But we are both friends. I like to help my friends. I helped you remember that you are special just the way you are.

Sincerely,
Kate Owl

Presentation Ideas

MAKE PUPPETS Have children make a stick puppet of Sam and a stick puppet of Kate. ▶**Viewing/Representing**

PUT ON A PUPPET SHOW Have volunteers use their stick puppets to put on a puppet show about Sam and Kate. Have children use puppets to describe how Sam and Kate are the same and different.
▶**Speaking/Listening**

Consider students' creative efforts, possibly adding a plus (+) for originality, wit and imagination.

Scoring Rubric

Excellent	Good	Fair	Unsatisfactory
4: The writer	**3:** The writer	**2:** The writer	**1:** The writer
• presents an original, thorough comparison between Sam and Kate.	• presents a comparison between Sam and Kate.	• attempts to present a thorough comparison between Sam and Kate.	• may not grasp the task to compare.
• includes details from the story to support comparisons.	• attempts to include details from the story to support comparisons.	• may not include details from the story to support comparisons.	• may offer details that do not relate to Sam and Kate.
• writes in full sentences, and may use sophisticated vocabulary.	• writes in clear, full sentences.	• may not always use full sentences.	• may not write in full sentences, or may present disorganized ideas.

0: The writer leaves the page blank or fails to respond to the writing task. The writer does not address the topic or simply paraphrases the prompt. The response is illegible or incoherent.

Meeting Individual Needs for Writing

EASY

Draw a Scene Have children draw scenes featuring Sam the Knee-High Man in familiar settings: at a grocery store, in school, at the playground, and so on. Have them write one or two sentences about Sam's experiences in each place.

ON-LEVEL

Write a Thank-You Note Have children reread the letter they wrote. Have them pretend to be Sam, and write a thank-you note. They can tell her they like the letter she wrote to them, and they learned a lot about how they are the same and different. Children should use proper letter format when they write.

CHALLENGE

Make a Journal Entry Have children imagine a person named Pat the Mile-High Woman. Ask them to write a story about how she wishes she were smaller, and how she finds out that she is just right the way she is.

Listening and Speaking

LISTENING STRATEGIES

Encourage children to listen closely during the puppet show so they can describe the ways that Sam and Kate are alike and different.

SPEAKING STRATEGIES

Encourage children to speak clearly and at a volume audible in a small-group setting. Remind them that the voice and words they use in school may be different from the voice and words they use at home.

LANGUAGE SUPPORT

 ESL children may have difficulty verbalizing the ways in which Sam and Kate are alike and different. Have them work with a fluent partner who can role-play with them and help them put their thoughts into English.

 Invite children to PORTFOLIO include their letters to Sam or another writing project in their portfolios.

5 Day Grammar and Usage Plan

ESL Children acquiring English will need to hear the past tense of verbs used in context many times. Work together to complete the **Grammar Practice Book** pages emphasizing the past tense of *go* and *do*.

DAILY LANGUAGE ACTIVITIES

Write the Daily Language Activities on the chalkboard each day or use **Transparency 18**. Have children correct the sentences orally, using *go* or *do* in the past tense.

Day 1
1. Sam goes over the hill yesterday. went
2. Max and June go to the shack before. went
3. Sam go to see Bob Bull early. went

Day 2
1. Then Bob does what she asked. did
2. I do it last week. did
3. They do a lot of stuff early. did

Day 3
1. Sam goes to Max first. went
2. Max and Bob do their best. did
3. Last week Sam goes up the tree. went

Day 4
1. What does Sam do next? did
2. Finally, Sam goes to Kate Owl. went
3. Yesterday Kate does the math. did

Day 5
1. Sam does a good job this morning. did
2. Then Sam and Max go for a walk. went
3. Later they go to the cliff. went

Daily Language Transparency 18

DAY 1 — Introduce the Concept

Oral Warm-Up Ask children, "Where did you go yesterday after school?" Write their responses on the chalkboard, and circle the word *went* in each sentence.

Introduce *Go* Remind children that the past tense tells about an action that has already happened. Ask children how most past-tense verbs are formed. (add *-ed*) Explain that some verbs do not end with *-ed* in the past tense.

Go

- The verb *go* has a special form to tell about the past.
- Use *go* or *goes* to tell about something that happens in the present.
- Use *went* to tell about something that happened in the past.

Present the Daily Language Activity and have students correct orally.

 Assign the daily Writing Prompt on page 66E.

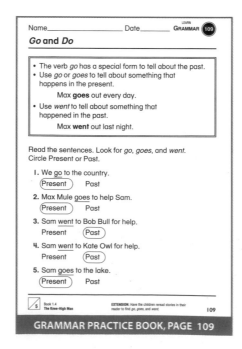

GRAMMAR PRACTICE BOOK, PAGE 109

DAY 2 — Teach the Concept

Review *Go* Write this on the chalkboard: *Today I go to the zoo.* Then ask children to change the sentence to begin with *Yesterday.* (Yesterday, I went to the zoo.)

Introduce *Do* Write this on the chalkboard: *Today I do my best.* Then ask children to change the sentence to begin with *Yesterday.* (Yesterday I did my best.)

Do

- The verb *do* has a special form to tell about the past.
- Use *do* or *does* to tell about something that happens in the present.
- Use *did* to tell about something that happened in the past.

Present the Daily Language Activity. Then have children write two sentences, using *do* and *did*.

 Assign the daily Writing Prompt on page 66E.

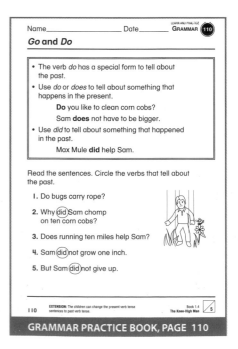

GRAMMAR PRACTICE BOOK, PAGE 110

Go and *Do*

Learn from the Literature Review *go* and *do* with children. Read the first and last sentences on page 85 of *The Knee-High Man*.

> **But Sam did not give up**
>
> **He went to see Kate Owl**

Emphasize *did* and *went* in the sentences. Then ask whether each sentence tells about the past or tells about now. (Both sentences tell about the past.)

Use *Go* and *Do* Present the Daily Language Activity and have children correct orally. Write the following sentences on the chalkboard: *Today I _____ to school. Yesterday we _____ to the park. Today I _____ some work. Yesterday they _____ a good job.* Ask children to fill in the sentences using the correct forms of *go* and *do*.

Present the Daily Language Activity and have children correct the sentences orally.

 Assign the daily Writing Prompt WRITING on page 66F.

Review *Go* and *Do* Write the following sentence on the chalkboard: *Kate and Sam go to the hill yesterday.* Ask children if the sentence is correct. (no) Why not? (The verb should be *went*.) Why? (because it happened in the past) Correct the sentence on the chalkboard, then present the Daily Language Activity for Day 4.

Mechanics and Usage Before children begin the daily Writing Prompt on page 66F, review proper nouns. Display and discuss:

> **Proper Nouns**
>
> The special name of a person or place begins with a capital letter.

 Assign the daily Writing Prompt WRITING on page 66F.

Assess Use the Daily Language Activity and page 113 of the **Grammar Practice Book** for assessment.

Reteach Write *Today* and *Yesterday* on the chalkboard. Then write the following sentences on paper strips: *The boys go to the store. We went to the store. She goes to the store. I do a good job. Pam does a good job. Nick and Jill did a good job.* Read the sentences aloud and ask whether each tells about the past or the present. Have children take turns placing the sentences under the appropriate column on the board.

Use page 114 of the **Grammar Practice Book** for additional reteaching.

Assign the daily Writing Prompt WRITING on page 66F.

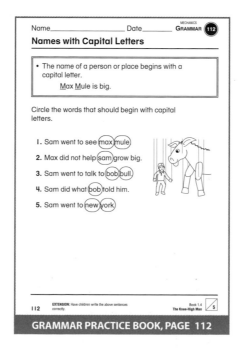

Name _____ Date _____ PRACTICE AND WRITE **GRAMMAR** 111

Go and *Do*

- The verb *go* has a special form to tell about the past.
- Use *went* to tell about something that happened in the past.
  Sam *went* to see Bob the Bull.
- The verb *do* has a special form to tell about the past.
- Use *did* to tell about something that happened in the past.
  Why *did* Sam want to be big?

Read the sentences. Write the verbs that tell about the past.

1. How **did** Kate Owl help Sam? (do did)

2. Who **did** Sam have to fight? (do did)

3. He **went** to see Kate Owl. (go went)

4. Why **did** Sam want to be big? (do did)

5. Sam **went** up a tree to look. (go went)

Book 1.4 *The Knee-High Man*   EXTENSION: The children can compose sentences about something that happened in the past.   111

GRAMMAR PRACTICE BOOK, PAGE 111

Name _____ Date _____ MECHANICS **GRAMMAR** 112

Names with Capital Letters

- The name of a person or place begins with a capital letter.
  Max Mule is big.

Circle the words that should begin with capital letters.

1. Sam went to see (max) (mule)

2. Max did not help (sam) grow big.

3. Sam went to talk to (bob) (bull)

4. Sam did what (bob) told him.

5. Sam went to (new) (york)

112   EXTENSION: Have children write the above sentences correctly.   *The Knee-High Man* 5

GRAMMAR PRACTICE BOOK, PAGE 112

Name _____ Date _____ TEST **GRAMMAR** 113

Test

Draw a line under each verb that tells about the present. Circle each verb that tells about the past.

1. Sam (went) up the tree.

2. Sam does not get help.

3. Kate and Owl (did) help.

4. Kate and Owl do the work.

5. Sam goes to the tree.

6. Sam (went) to get help.

7. Why do you go there?

8. Why (did) Sam go up a tree?

9. Sam goes to see Bob the Bull.

10. Sam (went) to see Bob the Bull.

10 Book 1.4 *The Knee-High Man*   113

GRAMMAR PRACTICE BOOK, PAGE 113

5 Day Spelling Plan

ESL The long *u* sound may be difficult for those children whose native language is not English. Say the following sentence, having children clap their hands when they hear the long *u*: *I can play the flute and tuba.*

DICTATION SENTENCES

Spelling Words

1. I do not like this rule.
2. What a cute cat you have!
3. The mule can work.
4. Look at that tube.
5. She likes this tune.
6. Do you have a flute?

Challenge Words

7. Where have you been?
8. She can clean the dish.
9. This job is done.
10. We went far away.

DAY 1 Pretest

Assess Prior Knowledge Use the Dictation Sentences at left and **Spelling Practice Book**, page 109 for the pretest. Allow children to correct their own papers. If children have trouble, have partners give each other a midweek test on Day 3.

Spelling Words		Challenge Words
1. r**ule**	4. tube	7. **been**
2. cute	5. tune	8. **clean**
3. mule	6. flute	9. **done**
		10. **far**

*Note: Words in **dark type** are from the story.*

Word Study On page 110 of the **Spelling Practice Book** are word study steps and an at-home activity.

DAY 2 Explore the Pattern

Sort and Spell Words Say and write the words *cut* and *cute*. Ask children what vowel sound they hear in each word. (short *u*, long *u*) Circle the *e* at the end of *tube* and remind children that the silent *e* helps make the vowel sound long. Tell them that the words in this lesson have long *u* spelled *u-consonant-e*. Underline the letters *ube* in *tube*.

Ask children to read aloud the six spelling words before sorting them according to the spelling pattern.

Words ending with			
-ule	**-ute**	**-une**	**-ube**
rule	cute	tune	tube
mule	flute		

Word Wall As children read other stories and texts, have them look for new words with long-vowel sounds that follow the silent *e* rule. Add them to a classroom word wall, underlining the vowel and the silent *e*.

Name_____ Date_____ PRETEST SPELLING **109**

Words with Long u: u-e

Pretest Directions
Fold back the paper along the dotted line. Use the blanks to write each word as it is read aloud. When you finish the test, unfold the paper. Use the list at the right to correct any spelling mistakes. Practice the words you missed for the Posttest.

1. _____ 1. rule
2. _____ 2. cute
3. _____ 3. mule
4. _____ 4. tube
5. _____ 5. tune
6. _____ 6. flute

To Parents
Here are the results of your child's weekly spelling Pretest. You can help your child study for the Posttest by following these simple steps for each word on the list:
1. Read the word to your child.
2. Have your child write the word, saying each letter as it is written.
3. Say each letter of the word as your child checks the spelling.
4. If a mistake has been made, have your child read each letter of the correctly spelled word aloud, and then repeat steps 1–3.

Challenge Words
_____ been
_____ clean
_____ done
_____ far

Book 1.4
The Knee-High Man 109

SPELLING PRACTICE BOOK, PAGE 109

WORD STUDY STEPS AND ACTIVITY, PAGE 110

Name_____ Date_____ EXPLORE THE PATTERN SPELLING **111**

Words with Long u: u-e

Look at the spelling words in the box.

rule	cute	mule	tube	tune	flute

Write the words that end with **ule**.

1. _____rule_____ 2. _____mule_____

Write the words that end with **ute**.

3. _____cute_____ 4. _____flute_____

Write the word that ends with **une**.

5. _____tune_____

Write the two letters that are found in every spelling word.

6. _____u_____ 7. _____e_____

Make a new word by changing the **r** of **rule** to **m**.

8. _____mule_____

Book 1.4
The Knee-High Man 111

SPELLING PRACTICE BOOK, PAGE 111

Words with Long *u: u-e*

Word Meaning: Add -s Remind children that we add *-s* to a noun to show that it names more than one. Ask children to add *-s* to the following spelling words and write sentences using the words: *rule, mule, tube, tune, flute.*

Identify Spelling Patterns Write this sentence on the chalkboard: *That mule is cute and clean.* Have a volunteer read it aloud. Ask children to tell which words have the spelling patterns *-ule* or *-ute* and which word is the Challenge Word. Repeat with the spelling patterns *-une* and *-ube*, using these sentences: *He was done with the tube. That tune has been played before.*

Then provide sentences with blanks for the Challenge Words and have students write and complete the sentences.

Proofread Sentences Write these sentences on the chalkboard, including the misspelled words. Ask children to proofread, circling incorrect spellings and writing the correct spellings. There are two errors in each sentence.

> **That is a (cut) (mul).** (cute, mule)
>
> **Shall I play a (tun) on my (flut)?** (tune, flute)

Have children create additional sentences with errors for partners to correct.

Have children use as many
WRITING Spelling Words as possible in the daily Writing Prompt on page 66F. Remind children to proofread their writing for errors in spelling, grammar, and punctuation.

Assess Children's Knowledge Use page 114 of the **Spelling Practice Book** or the Dictation Sentences on page 95Q for the posttest.

Personal Word List If children have trouble with any words in the lesson, have them add to their personal list of troublesome words in their journals. Have children draw a picture to illustrate each word.

Children should refer to their word lists during later writing activities.

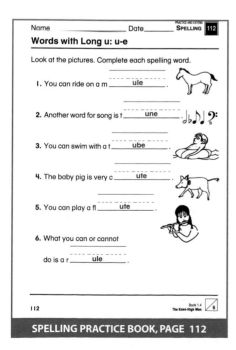

SPELLING PRACTICE BOOK, PAGE 112

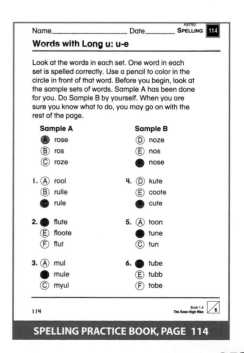

SPELLING PRACTICE BOOK, PAGE 113

SPELLING PRACTICE BOOK, PAGE 114

Reaching All Learners

Concept
• Trees/Plants

Comprehension
• Make Inferences

Phonics
• Long *a: ai, ay*

Vocabulary
• how
• light
• little
• live
• pretty

Anthology

Johnny Appleseed

Selection Summary In this biography of John Chapman, known as Johnny Appleseed, children will read about one man who shows people how to plant and cultivate apple seeds so that they can enjoy the fruit and beauty of the trees.

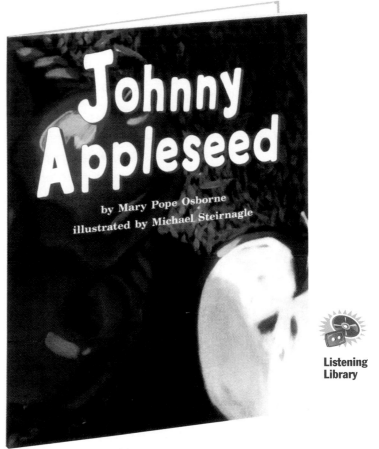

Johnny Appleseed
by Mary Pope Osborne
illustrated by Michael Steirnagle

Listening Library

INSTRUCTIONAL pages 98–123

Rhyme applies to Phonics

About the Author When Mary Pope Osborne was little, she lived with her family on different army bases. As an adult, she lived in Europe and traveled across Asia. Her travel experiences gave Ms. Osborne ideas for her writing.

About the Illustrator Michael Steirnagle has illustrated children's books as well as advertisements. He often uses his two children, Matthew and Stacy, and his dog, Ralph, in his pictures.

Same Concept, Skills and Vocabulary!

Leveled Books

EASY
Lesson on pages 123A and 123D

`DECODABLE`

INDEPENDENT
Lesson on pages 123B and 123D

🏠 *Take-Home version available*

`DECODABLE`

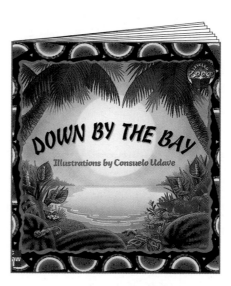

CHALLENGE
Lesson on pages 123C and 123D

Leveled Practice

EASY
Reteach, 151–158 Blackline masters with reteaching opportunities for each assessed skill

INDEPENDENT/ON-LEVEL
Practice, 151–158 Workbook with Take-Home Stories and practice opportunities for each assessed skill and story comprehension

CHALLENGE
Extend, 151–158 Blackline masters that offer challenge activities for each assessed skill

Quizzes Prepared by 📖 **Accelerated Reader**

Social Studies ... Family Farming, *106*

Science .... Terrific Trees!, *96D*
Plant a Seed, *102*

Math .... Estimation, *110*

Art .... Color Theory, *104*

Music .... Sing a Song of Science, *96D*

Language Arts .. Read Aloud, *96G*

Cultural
Perspectives ..... Apples, *100*

Research
and Inquiry ...... Find Out More, *121*

Internet
Activities .... www.mhschool.com/reading

CENTER Activities

Each of these activities takes 15–20 minutes.

Phonics

Words with Long *a*

MATERIALS
- Index cards
- Crayons

PARTNERS

Objective: Read and illustrate words with the long *a: ay, ai* sound.

◆ Display picturable *ay, ai* words.

◆ Have children choose five words and write each on a card.

◆ On the back of each card, children draw a picture of the word.

◆ Then partners use their cards for flashcard practice.

Writing

Apple Words

MATERIALS
- Apples
- White and red construction paper

PARTNERS

Objective: Work with partners to generate a list of apple words.

◆ Display apples in a bowl.

◆ Have children cut a large apple from the red paper and glue it onto white paper.

◆ Partners write words that describe apples on their paper apples.

Reading and Listening

Independent/Self-Selected Reading

ONE

Objective: Listen and use illustrations to understand a story.

Fill the Center with books and corresponding audiocassettes or CD-ROMS children have read or listened to this week. You can also include books from the Theme Bibliography on pages T98 and T99.

Leveled Readers

◆ *Fall is Fun!* by Ron Archer
◆ *The Land* by Wendy Pearl
◆ *Down by the Bay* by Consuelo Udave

◆ Theme Big Book *Fish Faces* by Norbert Wu
◆ *Johnny Appleseed* by Mary Pope Osborne
◆ "To the Top" by Sandra Liatos
◆ Phonics Practice Reader, Vol. 2

Working with Words

Sentence Search

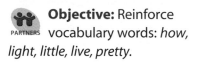 **Objective:** Reinforce vocabulary words: *how, light, little, live, pretty.*

◆ Have children write each word.

◆ Partners find the sentence in *Johnny Appleseed* with each word.

◆ Children write each sentence and draw an apple around the word.

MATERIALS
- *Johnny Appleseed* in the Student Anthology
- Paper
- Pencil
- Red crayons

 live | He did not (live) the way they did.

Music

Sing a Song of Science

Objective: Develop aural skills.

◆ Children can work in small groups to make up gestures for the song.

◆ Invite groups to perform their pantomimes for the rest of the class.

MATERIALS
- A song about Johnny Appleseed, apples, seeds, trees, or plants

Science

Terrific Trees!

Objective: Write and illustrate sentences about trees.

◆ Make nonfiction books about trees available.

◆ Children can look through the books for an interesting "tree fact."

◆ Children draw a picture of a tree and write a sentence that tells about it.

◆ Encourage children to include information that tells why trees are important to the Earth.

MATERIALS
- Nonfiction picture books
- Drawing paper
- Crayons

Animals make their homes in trees.

Johnny Appleseed

READING AND LANGUAGE ARTS	DAY 1 *Focus on Reading and Skills*	DAY 2 *Read the Literature*
● **Phonics Daily Routines**	Daily **Routine:** Segmenting, 96J **CD-ROM**	Daily **Routine:** Fluency, 98A  **CD-ROM**

● **Phonological Awareness**
 	
 ● **Phonics** *Long a*
 	
 ● **Comprehension**
 	
 ● **Vocabulary**
 	
 ● **Study Skills**
 	
 ● **Listening, Speaking, Viewing, Representing**
	Read Aloud, 96G
	 "The Great Big Enormous Turnip"
	
	 ☑ **Develop Phonological Awareness,** 96H
	
	 ☑ **Introduce** *a: ay, ai,* 96I–96J
	 Reteach, Practice, Extend, 151
	 Phonics/Phonemic Awareness Practice Book, 151–154
	
	  Apply Long *a: ay, ai,* 96/97
	 "The Gift"
	
	 ⓘ Intervention Program
		Build Background, 98A
		 Develop Oral Language
		
		 Vocabulary, 98B–98C
		
		 how *light* *little*
		 live *pretty*
		
		 Teaching Chart 112
		 Word Building Manipulative Cards
		 Reteach, Practice, Extend, 152
		
		  Read the Selection, 98–119
		 Guided Instruction
		 ☑ Long *a: ai, ay*
		 ☑ Make Inferences
		
		 Genre: Legend, 99
		
		 Cultural Perspectives, 100
		
		 ⓘ Intervention Program

● **Curriculum Connections**	Language Arts, 96G	Science, 96D, 98A
● **Writing**	**Writing Prompt:** Write a story about something Johnny Appleseed might always say.	**Writing Prompt:** Close your eyes and picture an apple. Write about what you see. **Journal Writing** Quick-Write, 119
● **Grammar**	**Introduce the Concept:** *See* and *Say,* 123O Daily Language Activity: Use the correct form of *see* and *say* in sentences. **Grammar Practice Book,** 115	**Teach the Concept:** *See* and *Say,* 123O Daily Language Activity: Use the correct form of *see* and *say* in sentences. **Grammar Practice Book,** 116
● **Spelling** *Long a*	**Pretest: Words with Long** *a: ai, ay,* 123Q **Spelling Practice Book,** 115–116	**Teach the Patterns: Words with Long** *a: ai, ay,* 123Q **Spelling Practice Book,** 117

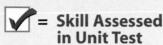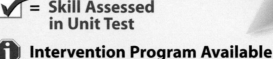

Meeting Individual Needs

 = **Skill Assessed in Unit Test**

 Intervention Program Available

DAY 3 *Read the Literature*

DAY 4 *Build Skills*

DAY 5 *Build Skills*

Daily  Routine:
Segmenting, 121
 **CD-ROM**

Daily Phonics Routine:
Writing, 123F
Phonics **CD-ROM**

Daily Phonics Routine:
Blending, 123H
Phonics **CD-ROM**

Reread for Fluency, 118

Story Questions, 120
 Reteach, Practice, Extend, 153

Story Activities, 121

Study Skill, 122
 ☑ **Charts**
 Teaching Chart 113
 Reteach, Practice, Extend, 154

 **Read the Leveled Books,**
 Guided Reading
 ☑ **Words with Long** *a: ai, ay*
 ☑ **Make Inferences**
 ☑ **High-Frequency Words**

 Intervention Program

 Read the Leveled Books and Self-Selected Books

 ☑ **Review Long** *a: ay, ai,* 123E–123F
 Teaching Chart 114
 Reteach, Practice, Extend, 155
 Language Support, 168
 Phonics/Phonemic Awareness
 Practice Book, 151–154

 ☑ **Review** *ai, ay; u-e, o-e,* 123G–123H
 Teaching Chart 115
 Reteach, Practice, Extend, 156
 Language Support, 169
 Phonics/Phonemic Awareness
 Practice Book, 151–154

 Minilessons, 101, 105, 107, 109, 115, 117

 Intervention Program

 **Read Self-Selected Books**

 ☑ **Review Make Inferences,** 123I–123J
 Teaching Chart 116
 Reteach, Practice, Extend, 157
 Language Support, 170

 ☑ **Review Inflectional Endings** *-er, est,*
 123K–123L
 Teaching Chart 117
 Reteach, Practice, Extend, 158
 Language Support, 171

 Listening, Speaking, Viewing,
 Representing, 123N

 Minilessons, 101, 105, 107, 109, 115, 117

 Intervention Program

Activity Art, 104
 Music, 96D

Activity Social Studies, 106

Activity Math, 110

 Writing Prompt: Write a story about what two children say to each other after they see Johnny Appleseed.

Journal Writing, 123D

Writing Prompt: Pretend you traveled with Johnny Appleseed. Write a letter to a friend telling about something you saw.

Writing that Compares, 123M
 Prewrite, Draft
Meeting Individual Needs for Writing, 123N

Writing Prompt: Pretend you are dreaming about Johnny Appleseed. Write about what you see in your dream.

Writing that Compares, 123M
 Revise, Edit/Proofread, Publish

Review and Practice: *See and Say,* 123P
 Daily Language Activity: Use the correct form of *see* and *say* in sentences.

Grammar Practice Book, 117

Review and Practice: *See and Say,* 123P
 Daily Language Activity: Use the correct form of *see* and *say* in sentences.

Grammar Practice Book, 118

Assess and Reteach: *See and Say,* 123P
 Daily Language Activity: Use the correct form of *see* and *say* in sentences.

Grammar Practice Book, 119–120

Practice and Extend: Words with Long *a: ai, ay,* 123R

Spelling Practice Book, 118

Proofread and Write: Words with Long *a: ai, ay,* 123R

Spelling Practice Book, 119

Assess and Reteach: Words with Long *a: ai, ay,* 123R

Spelling Practice Book, 120

Read Aloud

The Great Big Enormous Turnip
a Russian folktale by Alexei Tolstoi

Once upon a time an old man planted a little turnip and said: "Grow, grow, little turnip, grow strong!"

And the turnip grew up sweet and strong and big and enormous.

Then, one day, the old man went to pull it up. He pulled and pulled again, but he could not pull it up. He pulled and pulled again, but he could not pull it up.

He called the old woman.
The old woman pulled the old man,

The old man pulled the turnip.
And they pulled and pulled again, but they could not pull it up.

So the old woman called her granddaughter.
The granddaughter pulled the old woman,
The old woman pulled the old man,
The old man pulled the turnip.

Continued on page T4

Oral Comprehension

LISTENING AND SPEAKING Motivate children to make inferences by reading this Russian folktale by Alexei Tolstoi. Ask children to picture the action as you read the story. When you are done, ask: Do you think the roots of the turnip were strong? What makes you think so?

Activity Have children work in small groups to illustrate the situation described in "The Great Big Enormous Turnip." On a large piece of poster board, have each group draw the people and animals working together to pull out the turnip. Group members should take turns adding an animal or person to the chain. ▶ **Visual**

GENRE STUDY: FOLKTALE Remind children that a folktale is a story that is passed down through generations in a particular culture. Parents would tell their children the folktale, who would then tell their own children, and so on. The storyteller would add actions and gestures to make the story seem more real and interesting. Ask children to identify parts of this folktale that could be acted out.

Develop Phonological Awareness

Blend Sounds

Phonemic Awareness

Teach   Tell children you will say some sounds. They will clap each sound with you, and then blend the sounds to say the word. Demonstrate by saying /b/-/ā/ as you clap for each of the two sounds. Then say: *When we blend these two sounds together, what word do we get?* (bay)

Practice   Have children clap each sound and blend the sounds together to say the word. Use the following words: *bait, clay, day, faint, grain, gray, hail, jay, maid, play,* and *quail.*

Segment Sounds

Phonemic Awareness

name:
/n/-/ā/-/m/

MATERIALS
• Phonics Picture Cards

Teach   Display the Phonics Picture Cards for *cane* and *coat.* Tell children the word *cane* has three sounds: /k/-/ā/-/n/ and the word *coat* has three sounds /k/-/ō/-/t/. Tell children these words have the same beginning sound. Tell children to listen carefully as you say each word.

Practice   Have children segment the sounds in the following pairs of words and have them identify the sound that is the same in both words. Use these words: *name/nod; bay/jay; rail/well; main/bait; raise/paid.*

Substitute Sounds

Phonemic Awareness

MATERIALS
• puppet

Teach   Tell children the puppet will say some words. Have the puppet say: *bat . . . bait. What sound is different in the two words?* (the middle sound) Have children repeat the two words after the puppet: *bat, bait.*

Practice   Have children practice substituting middle sounds with the following words: *run/rain; grin/grain; sill/sail; pin/pain; wit/wait.*

 INFORMAL **ASSESSMENT**   Observe children as they blend sounds, segment sounds, and substitute middle sounds. If children have difficulty, see Alternate Teaching Strategies on page T75.

96H

 OBJECTIVES

Children will:

- identify long *a: ay, ai* words.
- blend and read long *a: ay, ai* words.
- review consonants and blends.

MATERIALS

- letter and vowel digraph cards and word building boxes from the **Word Building Manipulative Cards**

Skills Finder	
Long *a: ay, ai*	
▶ Introduce	B4: 96I-J
▶ Review	B4: 123E-F, 123G-H; B5: 191G-H, 225G-H
▶ Test	Book 4

SPELLING/PHONICS CONNECTIONS

Words with long *a: ai, ay:* See the 5-Day Spelling Plan, pages 123Q–123R.

TEACHING TIP

LONG *a* Point out to children that sometimes a sound can have more than one spelling. In this lesson, they will learn that long *a* can be spelled *ay* or *ai*. Remind children that they already learned that long *a* can be spelled *a-e*. Explain to children that only *ay* can appear at the very end of a word, as in *way*. The letters *ai* cannot appear at the end of a word.

Introduce Long *a: ay, ai*

TEACH

Identify the Letters *ay, ai* as Symbols for the Sound /ā/

Tell children they will learn to read words with the letters *ai* and *ay* that have the long *a* sound.

- Display the *ay* and *ai* letter cards and say /ā/.

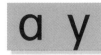

- Point to the *ay* card and have children repeat the sound after you. Do the same with the *ai* card.

BLENDING
Model and Guide Practice with Long *a: ay, ai* Words

- Place the *w* letter card before the *ay* card.
- Point to the letters as you blend the sounds to read *way*.
- Have children read the word with you as you blend the sounds together.
- Repeat, using the *ai* letter card and adding a *t* at the end to show the word *wait*.

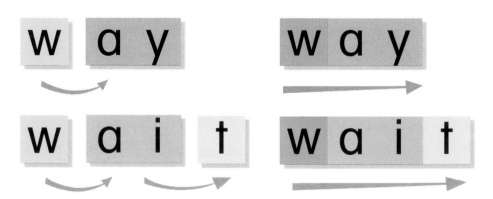

Use the Words in Context

Use the words in context to reinforce their meanings. Example: *Do you know the way to the park? I will wait for you there.* Then have children make up their own sentences using *way* and *wait*.

Repeat the Procedure

Use the following words to continue modeling and guided practice with long *a: ay, ai*.

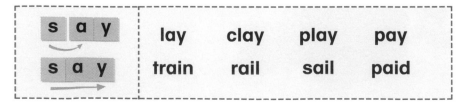

say	lay	clay	play	pay
say	train	rail	sail	paid

PRACTICE

LETTER SUBSTITUTION
Build Long *a: ay, ai* Words with Letter Cards

GROUP

Start with the letter card for *ay* and build the word *pay*. Ask children to repeat each sound after you. Replace the *ay* card with an *ai* card and add the *d* letter card to show *paid*. Ask children to identify the new sound at the end of the word. (/d/) Build and read the word *paid* together. Use both words in context and have children build and read these words: *stay, play, gray, maid, pain,* and *sail.* ▶ **Linguistic/Kinesthetic**

ASSESS/CLOSE

Read and Write Long *a* Words in Context

To assess children's ability to blend and read long *a: ai, ay* words, observe them as they build and read the words from the Practice activity. Tell children to write a sentence using two words—one with *ai* and one with *ay*.

ADDITIONAL PHONICS RESOURCES

Phonics/Phonemic Awareness Practice Book, pages 151–154

PHONICS KIT
Hands-on Activities and Practice

McGraw-Hill School
TECHNOLOGY

Phonics CD-ROM
activities for practice with Blending and Segmenting

Daily Routines

DAY 1
Letter Substitution Using the CVVC flip chart, have children build *pail*. Ask volunteers to change the first or last letter to build new words, reading each new word as they build it.

DAY 2
Fluency Write some sentences on the chalkboard and have children identify the long *a: ai, ay* words. Examples: *Wait* for the *rain* to go *away*. You *may play* with the *pail*.

DAY 3
Segmenting Give children blank word building boxes and say long *a: ay* words. Have children listen to the sounds in the word and write the letter(s) for each sound in the appropriate box.

DAY 4
Writing Have children write long *a: ai* or *ay* words to complete rhymes. Examples: If it starts to *rain*, let's take the ____. (*train*) If you *stay*, we can ____. (*play*)

DAY 5
Blending Write the spelling of each sound in *brain* as you say it. Have children repeat after you as they blend the sounds. Repeat with *mail, tray, bay,* and *clay.*

Meeting Individual Needs for Phonics

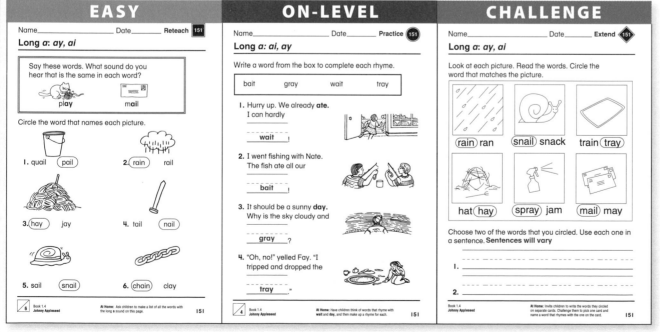

Reteach, 151   Practice, 151   Extend, 151

 **OBJECTIVES**

Children will read a poem with words containing long *a: ai* and *ay*.

Apply **Long *a: ai, ay***

The Gift

I got a present in the mail.
It was sent from my pal Gail.
Gail mailed me a box of chalk.
I made five trees out on the walk.
I added apples and two blue jays,
And a big fat sun,
With lots of rays.

96   97

Anthology pages 96–97

Read and Build Fluency

READ THE POEM Tell children they will read a poem called *The Gift*. Provide auditory modeling by stopping at periods and pausing at commas. Have children listen for long *a* words as you read aloud. Encourage children to read along with you.

REREAD FOR FLUENCY Have pairs of children reread the poem. Have them echo each other as they take turns reading.

READ A DECODABLE STORY For additional practice reading and to develop fluency, ask children to read *Dan and Gail's Plants* from **Phonics Practice Reader, Vol. 2.**

Dictate and Spell

DICTATE WORDS Segment the word *mail* into its three individual sounds. Repeat the word aloud and use it in a sentence: *She got a present in the mail.* Point out that the long *a* sound in *mail* is made with the letters *ai.* Then have children say the word as they write the letter or letters that represent each sound in the word. Repeat with *Gail, mailed, jays,* and *rays* from the poem. Then repeat with: *braid, chain, day, gray, hail, main, pain, spray, vain,* and *way.*

 **Intervention** Skills Intervention Guide, for direct instruction and extra practice in Long *a: ai, ay*

Build Background

science

Concept: Trees/Plants

Evaluate Prior Knowledge

CONCEPT: TREES/PLANTS Ask children to share what they know about trees. For example, talk about trees that lose their leaves in the fall versus trees that stay green all year. Ask children if they can name different kinds of trees. (maple, oak, pine, apple, cherry) Use the following activity to give children more information about trees.

MAKE A WORD WEB FOR TREES Ask children to create a word web to record the characteristics of a tree. For example: A tree starts from a seed. Some trees have leaves, others have needles. All trees have branches and roots. ▶ **Linguistic**

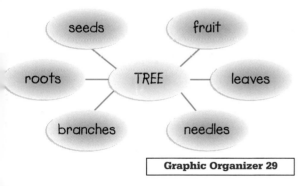

seeds
fruit
roots
TREE
leaves
branches
needles

Graphic Organizer 29

PLANT A GARDEN Encourage children to draw a picture of a garden. Suggest that children refer to the tree web when drawing the trees in their garden. They might also add flowers and plants. Have each child write a sentence to describe his or her picture.

ONE
WRITING

Develop Oral Language

CONNECT WORDS AND ACTIONS Have

ESL children follow simple instructions to act out planting their gardens. Examples:

• Show how to plant seeds.

• Water the flowers.

Ask children to say what they are doing in the garden by asking:

• What are you doing?

• Why are you bending down?

▶ **Kinesthetic/Linguistic**

Anthology and Leveled Books

DAILY **Phonics** ROUTINES

DAY 2 **Fluency** Write some sentences on the chalkboard and have children identify the long *a: ai, ay* words. Examples: *Wait* for the *rain* to go *away*. You *may play* with the *pail*.

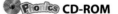
Phonics CD-ROM

LANGUAGE SUPPORT

To build more background, see pages 163–166 in the **Language Support Book**.

OBJECTIVES

Children will:
- identify high-frequency words *pretty, how, little, live,* and *light.*

MATERIALS
- Teaching Chart 112
- Word Building Manipulative Cards *pretty, how, little, live, light*

TEACHING TIP
The following chart indicates words from the upcoming story that children have learned to decode, as well as high-frequency words that have been taught in this lesson. As children read, observe any difficulties they may have.

Decodable		High-Frequency
day	rain	how
gray	sail	light
hail	say	little
jay	stay	live
may	wait	pretty
quail	way	

SPELLING/VOCABULARY CONNECTIONS

The words *how, light, live,* and *pretty* are Challenge Words. See page 123Q for Day 1 of the 5-Day Spelling Plan.

---

pretty

how

little

live

light

Vocabulary
High-Frequency Words

A Pretty Rose

A (pretty) rose
Will live for just a (little) in the (light)
And in the rain.
But (how) very long
It will (live) in my sight,
It will live in my nose,
It will live in my brain.

Teaching Chart 112

Auditory

LISTEN TO WORDS Without displaying it, read aloud "A Pretty Rose" on **Teaching Chart 112**. Ask children what they think the poem means. Is it only about a rose, or can it be about other things, too?

LISTEN TO THE "MUSIC" OF HIGH-FREQUENCY WORDS Tell children that not every poem rhymes or has a regular rhythm. Point out that sometimes the words still sound like music.

- Read the first two lines of the poem. *Pretty* doesn't rhyme with *little,* but when you listen to them, they have some sounds in common that make them go together nicely.

- Say the words *live, little,* and *light.* What makes these words sound interesting together?

Visual

TEACH WORDS Display "A Pretty Rose" on **Teaching Chart 112**. Read the poem, tracking the print with your finger. Next, point to and say the word *pretty.* Have children say the word with you. Ask them to hold up the vocabulary card for *pretty* and say the word. Repeat this procedure for *how, little, live,* and *light.*

Hold up vocabulary cards for *pretty, how, little, live,* and *light* one at a time. Have volunteers read the words and then circle them on the chart.

Word Building Manipulative Cards

WRITE POEMS Have small groups write each of the high-frequency words. Then tell them to write a poem using them. The poem doesn't have to rhyme, but it should sound "musical."

Word Wall

Tongue Twisters
Slowly point to each of the word wall words, keeping the words that start with the letter *l* together. Have children say the words in that order slowly, then faster and faster. Then rearrange the order of the words and try it again.

Jumping Jack Spelling
Encourage children to do a jumping jack as they spell each letter of a word wall word. Then have them do a knee bend as they say the whole word.

LANGUAGE SUPPORT

To help children develop understanding and recognition of high-frequency words, see page 163 in the **Language Support Book**.

Assess

Picture These Words
Divide a piece of paper into six sections. In the first section, ask children to write their name. In the remaining sections, have them write each of the word wall words and draw a simple illustration that goes with each word.

Meeting Individual Needs for Vocabulary

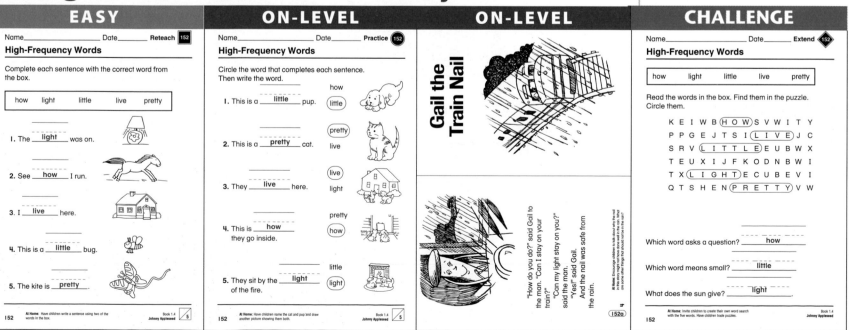

Reteach, 152

Practice, 152

Practice, 152a
Take-Home Story

Extend, 152

98C

Comprehension

Prereading Strategies

PREVIEW AND PREDICT Point to and read aloud the book title and the names of the author and illustrator. Take a **picture walk** to discuss what children see, stopping at pages 102–103. Using words from the story, talk about each illustration.

- Where do you think this story takes place?
- What clues about the main character does the picture on pages 98–99 give?
- Do you think the story is going to be real or make-believe?
- What is the story most likely about?

Children can record their predictions about the story and the characters in a predictions chart.

SET PURPOSES Ask children what they want to find out as they read the story. For example:

- Where does the man go?
- Why does he plant apple seeds?
- What happens to him?

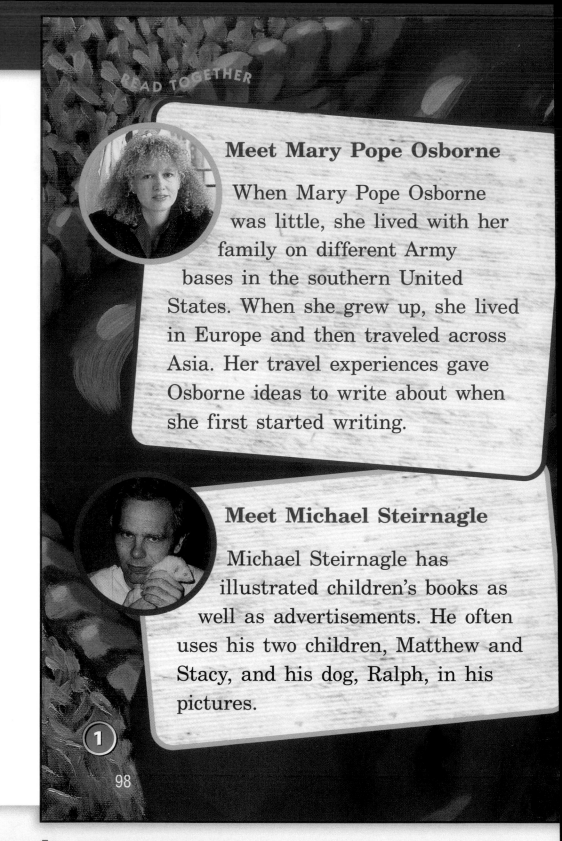

Meet Mary Pope Osborne

When Mary Pope Osborne was little, she lived with her family on different Army bases in the southern United States. When she grew up, she lived in Europe and then traveled across Asia. Her travel experiences gave Osborne ideas to write about when she first started writing.

Meet Michael Steirnagle

Michael Steirnagle has illustrated children's books as well as advertisements. He often uses his two children, Matthew and Stacy, and his dog, Ralph, in his pictures.

98

Meeting Individual Needs • Grouping Suggestions for Strategic Reading

EASY	ON-LEVEL	CHALLENGE
Shared Reading Read the story aloud as you track print and model directionality. Invite children to join in on repetitive words and phrases. Model the strategy of noticing characters' facial expressions and body language as well as picture details that enable you to make inferences about story events.	**Guided Instruction** Ask children to read the story with you. Monitor any difficulties in reading that children have, in order to determine which prompts from the Comprehension section to emphasize. After reading the story with children, have them reread it, using the rereading options on page 118.	**Independent Reading** Have children set purposes before they read. Remind them that they can make inferences about the story by noticing the characters' expressions, how they are dressed, and what's going on in the picture. After reading, have children retell the story. Children can use the questions on page 120 for a group discussion.

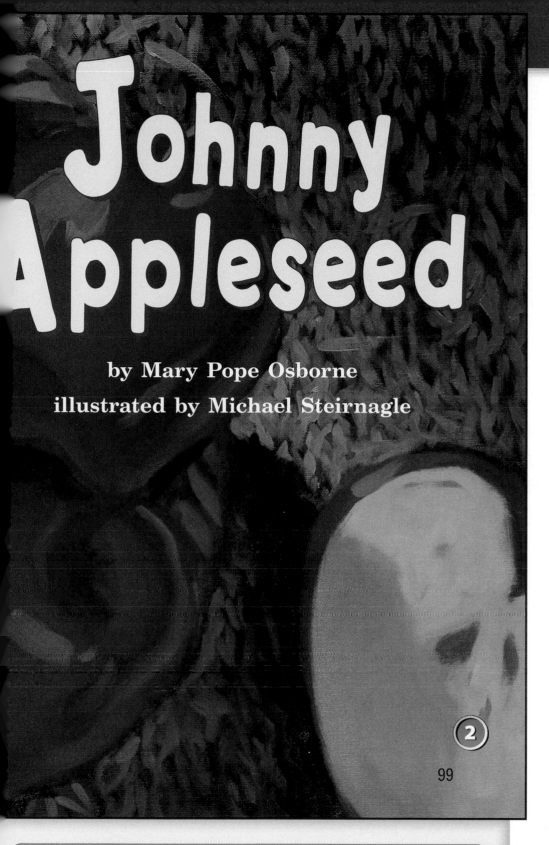

Johnny Appleseed

by Mary Pope Osborne

illustrated by Michael Steirnagle

②

99

Comprehension

☑ **Phonics** **Long *a: ai, ay***

☑ **Apply Make Inferences**

STRATEGIC READING Tell children that if they pay careful attention to details in the pictures that may not be mentioned in the words, it will help them understand more about the story. Explain that as they learn about Johnny Appleseed, they will make and use a tree chart to keep track of the information.

① We are going to read *Johnny Appleseed* by Mary Pope Osborne. Let's read about her. What might have led her to want to write the story of this man's life? Now let's read about Michael Steirnagle. Do you think he likes to draw trees? Why? *Concept of a Book: Author/Illustrator*

② **MAKE INFERENCES** Listen to the title of the story. What do you think the man in the story is famous for? (planting apple seeds)

Genre

Legend

Explain that a legend:

- tells about a person, who may or may not have really existed.
- tells that the person's strengths and positive traits are probably exaggerated.
- is usually handed down from long ago, and there is no way to check if it is true.

Activity After reading *Johnny Appleseed,* have children tell about some events that happened in Johnny's adult life. What situations did the author include that might not have been real? Discuss why you think this story is about a real man or about a man who may not have existed.

LANGUAGE SUPPORT

A blackline master for the tree chart can be found in the **Language Support Book**. Whenever Johnny Appleseed helps someone new in the story, children can draw a picture of them inside one of the apples. As children make inferences about Johnny Appleseed, they can write their ideas in the tree trunk.

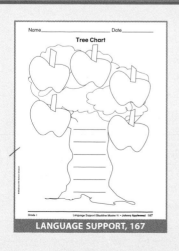

Name_____ Date_____
Tree Chart

Grade I   Language Support/Blackline Master 1 • Johnny Appleseed 167

LANGUAGE SUPPORT, 167

Comprehension

3 **MAKE INFERENCES** Why do you think John Chapman was called Johnny Appleseed? (to show what he did) **Who knows what a nickname is?** (a special name that tells something about you)

4 What do you think is the main idea of this story? (Johnny Appleseed's life)
Main Idea

100

CULTURAL PERSPECTIVES

APPLES Point out that apples are used to make apple pie, an all-American food.

RESEARCH AND INQUIRY Have small groups choose another country and find out about a fruit that is popular there.

• What is the name of the fruit?

• What food is it used to make?

Have each group draw a picture of the fruit that they researched and write one sentence about their findings.
▶ **Visual/Linguistic**

inter NET **CONNECTION** Children can learn more about different fruits by visiting **www.mhschool.com/reading**.

Mangos are grown in Brazil.

Comprehension

SHORT *e*, *i*, *a* Read the last three sentences on page 101. Then find one short *e* word, three short *i* words, and five short *a* words. (*dressed; in, tin, his; rags, and sacks, had, hat*) Model the sound of each letter and have children repeat after you. *Graphophonic Cues*

⑤ MAKE INFERENCES Why do you think Johnny Appleseed dressed the way he did? (It was what he had; he felt comfortable.)

His name was John Chapman. ③
But he was called Johnny Appleseed. ④
This is his tale.

He dressed in rags and old sacks. ⑤
He had no shoes. A tin pot was his hat.

101

Minilesson

REVIEW/MAINTAIN

Context Clues

Remind children that they can find clues in both words and pictures to figure out the meaning of an unfamiliar word.

- Point to the word *tin* in the last sentence, and then read the sentence aloud.
- Ask children if there is another word in the sentence that can help them understand the meaning of *tin*. (*pot*)
- Ask if anyone knows what most pots are made of. (*metal*)
- Guide children to see that *tin* is a kind of metal that pots are made of. Have them confirm their guess by looking at the picture on page 100.

Activity Have children use the same steps to figure out the meaning of the word *rags*.

p/i PREVENTION/INTERVENTION

SHORT *e*, *i*, *a* Children who are having trouble identifying the letters to be used for short vowel sounds will benefit from repeated exercises. Write a list of words with missing short vowels *e*, *i*, and *a*. Have children build the word with letter cards, placing one of the three vowels in the blank space. Ask children to read their words aloud and name the missing letter. Some words may lend themselves to more than one vowel. Examples: *sack/sick, quit, shed, mask, left/lift, west, stiff/staff, band/bend,* and *slant*. *Graphophonic Cues*

Comprehension

6 **MAKE INFERENCES** How do you suppose Johnny got so many apple seeds? (Possible responses: He ate apples and kept the seeds. He bought them. They were given to him.)

7 **MAKE INFERENCES** What is Johnny doing in the picture? (planting seeds) Let's put the information in our tree charts. *Graphic Organizer*

planting seeds

8 Why is Johnny planting apple seeds? (He wants apple trees to grow.) *Draw Conclusions*

6 Johnny knew a lot about plants and [how] to grow them. He had lots of

8 apple seeds.

102

Activity

Cross Curricular: Science

PLANT A SEED Ask if anyone has grown plants from seeds before. Lead a discussion about how plants grow: the seed is planted in soil, then water and sunlight help the seed grow roots and leaves. Ask children to identify plants they eat. (vegetables, fruits, nuts, seeds)

Activity Give each child a seed and a cup that has potting soil and a tiny hole in the bottom for drainage. Children will then gently press the seeds into the soil and lightly cover them with soil. Place cups in a sunny place and keep moist.
▶ **Kinesthetic**

Comprehension

9 **LONG *a: ay*** Let's read the first sentence. "One . . . hmm, what is the next word? Let's blend the sounds together and see. d ay day *Graphophonic Cues*

10 **PRONOUNS** Who is the "he" in all these sentences? (Johnny) How do you know? (He's named on the previous page.) *Make Inferences*

11 Johnny wanted people to plant apple trees. What are some ways he might help people do that? (Possible answers: He will give them seeds. He will show them how to plant and take care of the trees.) Do you think he will succeed? *Make Predictions*

One day, he packed his seeds and left home. He had a plan. He wanted to help the people who were going west. He wanted to help them plant apple trees.

9
10
11

103

Comprehension

(12) **Phonics** **LONG *a: ai*** Let's look at the second word here. (*sailed*) I'm going to blend the sounds of the letters together to read it. s ai l ed sailed *Graphophonic Cues*

(13) Do you see the mark after *Quick* and *seeds* in line 2? Who knows what it means? (to say the sentence with feeling) What is the name of this mark? (exclamation mark) There are other marks before the word *Quick!* and at the end of *Plant my apple seeds!* Does anyone know what these marks mean? (someone is saying something) What are these marks called? (quotation marks) *Concepts of Print*

(12) He sailed down the river on a raft.
(13) "Quick! Plant my apple seeds!" he said to those who were on the banks.

(14)

104

Activity

Cross Curricular: Art

COLOR THEORY Show children a color wheel and explain how many colors can be created from red, yellow, and blue—primary colors. Using paint, show how to make green by mixing blue and yellow. Make purple from red and blue. Mix the purple and green together to make black.

Have children make pink by mixing a small amount of red with a lot of white.

Activity Children can use sponges to sponge-paint pink apple blossoms on black tree trunks. They may wish to mix green and paint grass and leaves on their trees.
▶ **Visual/Kinesthetic**

"They will give you pretty, pink buds in May! In the fall, you can make pies and jam!" (15)

105

Comprehension

(14) **MAKE INFERENCES** What are the people on the river banks doing? (waving good-bye to Johnny) Do you think he helped them? How? (Yes, he gave them seeds for apples.) What kind of person do you think Johnny is? (helpful, kind) Let's include a drawing of the people in our tree chart. *Graphophonic Cues*

(15) Why do you think the people won't have pies and jam until fall? (There won't be apples until the trees grow.) *Critical Thinking*

(p/i) **CONCEPTS OF PRINT** Why is the word *May* written with a capital *M*? (name of month) *Syntactic Cues*

Minilesson

REVIEW/MAINTAIN

Vowels

You can use a calendar and the names of the months to review short and long vowels.

- Review the short and long vowel sounds and make a column for each on a chart.

- Display a calendar and read the names of the months slowly.

- Ask children to raise hands if they hear a short or long *a, e, i, o,* or *u*.

Activity Children can work in small groups to practice long and short vowel sounds. Ask them to practice saying the months aloud.

Phonics CD-ROM Have children use the interactive phonics activities for vowel review.

(p/i) **PREVENTION/INTERVENTION**

CONCEPTS OF PRINT Review capitalization with children: the first letter of a sentence or a proper name is capitalized. Say some proper nouns and common nouns and ask children to raise their hands when they hear a word that always starts with a capital letter. Examples could include names of children in the class, days of the week, months of the year, cities, and countries. *Syntactic Cues*

Comprehension

16 What is happening here? Why does Johnny want the people to plant the seeds? (so that more apple trees will grow) *Analyze Character and Plot*

17 Why are the farmers using mules instead of tractors to plant their crops? (The story takes place before tractors were invented.) *Critical Thinking*

As Johnny went west, he passed women in sun hats and men with mules.

16 "Take them and plant them!" he said.

17 And he gave them seeds.

106

Activity

Cross Curricular: Social Studies

FAMILY FARMING Explain that long ago many families raised their own food and sold any extra to buy other things. Families had fruit orchards or dairy farms. Have children draw a picture showing what they would have grown if they had lived in that time period.

RESEARCH AND INQUIRY Give children books and magazines about family farming in the 19th and early 20th centuries. ▶ **Linguistic/Visual**

interNET CONNECTION For more information on farming help children log on to **www.mhschool.com/reading.**

"Where is your home?" they asked him. He just smiled and went on his way. (18)

107

ESL Illustrations are key to helping children acquiring English understand the text. As you finish reading a sentence or a page, point to the illustrations to clarify what you have just read.

You may wish to point to a map or globe to make sure that children acquiring English understand the phrase "went west."

Comprehension

(18) **MAKE INFERENCES** Why did Johnny Appleseed just smile and go on his way? (He didn't really have a home. He just traveled from place to place.) **Why do you think the author chose to write "He just smiled and went on his way"?** (Possible answer: She wanted to show that Johnny Appleseed was a little bit mysterious; maybe he didn't always plan where he was going next; the author wanted readers to wonder what would happen next and want to read more.) *Find Author's Purpose*

Minilesson

REVIEW/MAINTAIN

Setting

Remind children that they can tell the time of the day or the season by looking at the pictures and reading the words.

- Ask children to tell what season they think it is. How do they know?
- Remind children that they can use the pictures and words to tell where a story is taking place.
- Have children suggest where and when the story takes place. (Examples: farmland, the country, long ago, daytime.)

Activity Have children draw pictures that illustrate a season. Ask them to include "clues," such as snow or trees with leaves. Display the pictures and invite other children to guess the season.

Comprehension

19 **Phonics** **LONG** *a: ai* Do you see two words with the long *a* sound in the first sentence? What are they? Let's blend the sounds together to read each one. r ai n rain h ai l hail *Graphophonic Cues*

20 **Phonics** **LONG** *a: ay* Let's read the second sentence. Which word has a long *a* sound? *(stayed)* Write the word on the board and underline the letters that make the long *a* sound. *(ay)*

p/i **WORDS WITH LONG** *a: a-e* Can you find a long *a* word on this page that does not have *ai* or *ay*? *(caves)* Let's practice saying this word and blending the sounds. Repeat after me. *Graphophonic Cues*

SELF-MONITORING STRATEGY

SEARCH FOR CLUES Go back through the story and look for clues to help you remember what has happened so far.

- Why did Johnny leave home?
- What did he take with him?
- Where did he go?
- What did he find along the way?

19 In rain and hail, mist and fog, he kept **20** on. He stayed in sheds with hens and chicks. He camped in caves with bats.

108

p/i **PREVENTION/INTERVENTION**

WORDS WITH LONG *a: a-e* Read the last sentence on page 108. Explain that *caves* is a long *a: a-e* word, even though it ends in *s* rather than *e*. The *s* shows more than one cave. The root word is *cave*.

Review the long *a: a-e* rule by showing children pairs of word cards and mod-eling as you read the words aloud. Identify which words show long *a: a-e*. Examples: *cap, cape, man, mane, rat, and rate*. Remind children that the *e* at the end is silent, and it makes the *a* say its name. *Graphophonic Cues*

But he was not sad.
He always had a big smile.
"What a pretty day this is,"
he would say. "Life is very good!"

109

Comprehension

21 Let's look at page 108. Where is Johnny? (in a cave) Think about what Johnny has done in the story so far. What do you think he will do next? (visit more places, plant more seeds) *Make Predictions*

22 **MAKE INFERENCES** Look at the picture of Johnny on page 108 and compare it to the one on page 109. How is Johnny's expression different? (He seems sad and lonely on one page, and smiling and happy in the other.) **Why do you think that is?** (On page 108, it's dark and he is in a cave with bats. But on page 109, it's a sunny, pretty day.) *Compare and Contrast*

Minilesson

REVIEW/MAINTAIN

Character

Remind children that they can tell about a character in a story by looking at the pictures and reading the words.

- Ask children to describe the kind of person Johnny Appleseed is.
- Have them indicate words and pictures in the story that led them to make these statements.
- Ask if they would like to have known Johnny Appleseed, and ask them to tell why.

Activity Ask children to think of someone they like and describe him or her.

LANGUAGE SUPPORT

ESL Page 108 may be difficult to understand for children acquiring English. Restate the first sentence: "In rain and hail, mist and fog, he kept on" using more familiar vocabulary, such as: "Johnny Appleseed walked when it was raining, snowing, and cloudy down to the ground. He kept going."

109

Comprehension

23 Why do you think Johnny might just fling seeds one day and dig holes another day? (Possible responses: He dug holes where he could; he flung seeds only when it was windy.) *Critical Thinking*

23 Some days, he stopped to dig holes and dropped in the seeds. But some days, he just flung them to the wind.

110

TEACHING TIP

EXPAND VOCABULARY Help children understand the differences between the words *some, all* and *none* by doing simple math activities with the counters. Example: Use 10 counters and two cups. Put some counters in each cup. Ask children to tell what they see, using the word *some*. Put all the counters in one cup and show both cups. (all) Now empty both cups and ask children how many counters there are. (none)

Activity

Cross Curricular: Math

ESTIMATION Put sticks of chalk or pencils in a cup and ask children to guess if there are "more than or fewer than five."

Activity Give pairs of children 10 counters and a small paper cup. The counters are apple seeds and the cups are holes. Children take turns deciding how many

"seeds" to "put in a hole" and how many to "fling to the wind" (put on the desk top). The partner guesses how many are in each place, then children count to check.

▶ **Logical**

> "Do not take them," he would tell the blue jays. "Wait for the trees to grow. **(24)** As they get bigger, you can live in **(25)** their branches."

111

Comprehension

(24) **MAKE INFERENCES** What is Johnny doing on this page? (talking to the bird) How is he helping the birds? (He's telling them to wait and not eat the seeds, so they'll have a home.) Let's draw a picture of the birds in one of the apples on our tree chart. *Graphic Organizer*

(25) What is the main idea this picture illustrates? (Johnny doesn't want the birds to eat the seeds; he wants the seeds to grow into apple trees.) *Main Idea*

(p/i) **TRACKING PRINT** How many sentences do you see on this page? (three) How can you tell? *Syntactic Cues*

(p/i) PREVENTION/INTERVENTION

TRACKING PRINT Ask children to put a self-stick note on the first word of each sentence. (*Do, Wait, As*) Ask children to read with you as you read the page aloud.

Pause briefly at the commas, longer after a period. Reread, and have children raise their hands each time you begin a sentence. *Syntactic Cues*

Comprehension

(26) MAKE INFERENCES Let's read these two pages and look at the illustrations. What does Johnny do to show that he's a good man? (He helped animals.) Let's put that information in our chart. *Graphic Organizer*

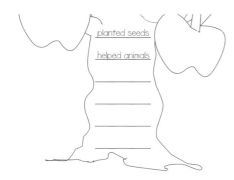

planted seeds

helped animals

(27) Phonics LONG *a: ai, ay* Point to and read aloud the word on this page that shows long *a: ai.* (*quail*) Now point to and read aloud the word that shows long *a: ay.* (*gray*) *Graphophonic Cues*

(p/i) CONCEPTS OF PRINT Why does the word *quail's* end in an apostrophe and the letter *s*? (shows the wing belongs to the quail) *Semantic Cues*

(26) Johnny was a good man.
(27) One time, he mended a quail's wing.
(28) Then he saved a gray wolf from a trap.

112

Fluency

READING WITH EXPRESSION

(ONE) Try echo reading one-on-one with a child who has demonstrated difficulty with fluent reading.

• Read one sentence of the text aloud with appropriate intonation and phrasing.

• Then ask a volunteer to imitate this oral reading model.

• Continue and repeat until the child can imitate more than one sentence at a time.

(p/i) PREVENTION/INTERVENTION

CONCEPTS OF PRINT Have children use the possessive to talk about items in the classroom and to whom or to what they belong. Point to and identify, for example: *Jack's shirt, Maria's desk, the teacher's hair, the book's cover.* Write *Jack's shirt* on the board. Ask children to tell why you added the apostrophe and letter *s* at the end. (to show something belongs to a person, animal, or thing) Invite children to identify and use the possessive in sentences. *Semantic Cues*

One day, he found an old horse. **29**
He fed him and gave him a bath.

113

Comprehension

28 Tell the order in which the things pictured on page 112 happened. What clues are in the words? (He mended the wing, then he saved the wolf.) *Sequence of Events*

29 **MAKE INFERENCES** How do you think the horse felt after Johnny gave him a bath and fed him? Why do you think this? (The horse probably felt better. Maybe it hadn't had food or a bath in a while.) Let's include all the animals we've seen Johnny help in our tree chart. *Graphic Organizer*

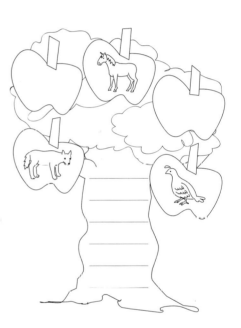

Comprehension

 Were you surprised that Johnny kept the wolf and the horse as pets? Why or why not? (Possible answers: Yes, because Johnny usually traveled alone; because a wolf is a wild animal.) Do you think a person in your neighborhood would travel with a wolf or horse? What animals might you travel with? (Answers will vary.) *Confirm Predictions/Compare and Contrast*

GROUP READING

Model tracking print and rereading to achieve fluency.

- Point to and read aloud each word in the first sentence, running your hand beneath the word as you read it.

- Pause briefly at a comma, longer at the end of a sentence.

- Have children repeat this process with you, pointing to each word as they read.

- Repeat the group reading. Encourage children to listen to each other and offer positive comments.

Now with his pets, he went to place after place. He visited mills and shops.

114

"I bring little seeds to grow into big

31 trees!" he said with a big smile. His

32 eyes flashed with light as he explained
how to plant them.

115

Comprehension

31 **MAKE INFERENCES** How do you think Johnny was feeling if he was smiling and his eyes flashed with light? (He was excited.) **What was he excited about?** (planting seeds that would grow into trees)

32 **USE PICTURE CLUES** Where are the people in the picture on these pages? (in a store) **Why do you think Johnny is visiting them?** (Possible answers: he may be asking them to sell seeds; he may be buying food and supplies) *Make Predictions*

Minilesson

REVIEW/MAINTAIN

Cause and Effect

Remind children that they can figure what is happening in a story by thinking about how the characters relate to one another.

- Have children talk about the people in the picture.
- Ask: Who is talking? Who is listening?
- Encourage children to notice the effect Johnny's words seem to be having on the people listening.
- What do the people do after listening to Johnny?

Activity Tell children that one person's words or actions may cause something to happen. Play "Simon Says" or "Mother May I." Point out the cause (what Simon or Mother says) and the effect (children move).

LANGUAGE SUPPORT

ESL Try to assess what your children acquiring English understand by pausing frequently to ask quick comprehension questions. The illustrations often do not provide the information needed visually to understand the text. For

example, on page 115, ESL children may not understand what "flashed with light" means. You can make this understandable by quickly opening your eyes wide as you read the phrase.

115

Comprehension

33 What is happening in the picture on these pages? (Johnny is having dinner with a family.) Do you think the family feels comfortable having Johnny in their home? Why or why not? (Yes, because they're talking and smiling.) *Use Illustrations*

34 Why do you think some people did not trust Johnny? (He was different.) Why would this make people not like him? (They were afraid of him and his different ways.) *Critical Thinking*

Some people did not trust Johnny. **33**
He did not live the way they did. **34**
But most people liked him.
They would ask him into their homes.

116

Visual Literacy

VIEWING AND REPRESENTING

Pretend that you are a neighbor of the family and have stopped by to visit.

- Where would you be standing or sitting in the room?

- What would you have to eat?

- Talk about how the artist makes the room on pages 116–117 seem cozy and friendly. (He uses warm colors; the people sit closely around a table; they are smiling.)

LANGUAGE SUPPORT

ESL Children acquiring English may need support to understand the first two sentences on page 116. You may wish to pause after reading to check if children understood. Check by asking them to tell you what the sentences meant. If necessary, restate the two sentences this way: "Sometimes Johnny didn't make friends. He was different from people, so they didn't understand him." Use vocabulary and experiences that your students will understand.

He would tell them about his trip west. **35**
They would give him some ham and
cake. Then he would rest.

117

Comprehension

35 Johnny tells the family about his
travels. Do you think Johnny will also
tell the family about how to plant apple
seeds? (Probably, because he's shared this
information with all the other people he's
met.) **Make Predictions**

117

Comprehension

(36) MAKE INFERENCES Let's reread the last sentence on page 119. What do you think it means that Johnny had *given a gift that would live on?* (The trees will keep growing and will produce more apples, which will produce more trees.) **Let's include that in our tree chart.** *Graphic Organizer*

planted seeds
helped animals

gave the gift
of many trees

RETELL THE STORY Have children sit in a circle to retell the story. They can use the ideas and pictures in their tree charts to help them remember what they have learned. *Summarize*

STUDENT SELF-ASSESSMENT

Have children listen to the questions and think about how they would answer them.

- How did I use the pictures in the story as clues to things the words did not tell me?
- How did I use what I already know about animals, plants, and people to understand the story?
- How did I use letters and sounds I already know to help me read the words in the story?

TRANSFERRING THE STRATEGIES

- How can I use these strategies to help me read other stories?

When the sun came up, he was on his way. He waved and flung his seeds to the wind.

 118

REREADING FOR *Fluency*

GROUP Children who need fluency practice can read aloud as they listen to the story being read.

READING RATE When you evaluate reading rate, have children read aloud from the story for one minute. Place a stick-on note after the last word read. Count words read. To evaluate children's performance, see

the Running Record in the **Fluency Assessment** book.

i Intervention For leveled fluency lessons, passages, and norms charts, see **Skills Intervention Guide**, Part 5, Fluency.

When Johnny died, he was missed a lot. But his trees got bigger and bigger. He had given a gift that would live on. **36**

119

Comprehension

Return to Predictions and Purposes

Reread and discuss children's predictions about the story. Ask how their predictions turned out, and if their questions got answered.

Have children talk about using the word web. Did it help them remember things about the people and events in the story?

INFORMAL ASSESSMENT

HOW TO ASSESS

Phonics LONG *a: ai, ay* Have children turn to pages 108–109 and read all the long *a: ai, ay* words. *(rain, hail, stayed, always, day, say)*

MAKE INFERENCES Ask children to describe the feelings of Johnny Appleseed and other characters in the story.

FOLLOW UP

Phonics LONG *a: ai, ay* Continue to model blending the sounds and distinguishing *ai* and *ay* words for children who are having difficulty.

MAKE INFERENCES Invite children who are having difficulty making inferences to use the story illustrations to help them.

LITERARY RESPONSE

QUICK-WRITE Have children list in their journals some parts of the story they found interesting. Have them write a question about the story. They can use the word web or ask for help with difficult words.

ORAL RESPONSE Have children use their journal entries to discuss these questions:

- What was Johnny's gift?
- Why did he make this journey?
- Why do you think people missed him after he died?

SENTENCE STRIPS Children can use strips 1–68 to retell the story.

> 1
> His name was John Chapman.

> 2
> But he was called Johnny Appleseed.

119

Story Questions

Tell children that now they will read some questions about the story. Help children read the questions. Discuss possible answers.

Answers:

1. He went west. *Literal*

2. He gave them apple seeds to plant. *Make Inferences*

3. because he thought life was very good *Inferential/Character*

4. Answers will vary. Accept appropriate summaries. *Critical/Summarize*

5. Answers will vary. Accept appropriate examples. *Critical/Reading Across Texts*

Make a Poster Help children read the directions in their anthologies. Have them discuss different foods that are made with apples. Examples: apple pie, applesauce, apple juice.

For a full writing process lesson on writing that compares, see pages 123M–123N.

Story Questions & Activities

READ TOGETHER

1. Where did Johnny go?

2. How did Johnny help people?

3. Why did Johnny always smile?

4. Tell about Johnny's life in your own words.

5. What other book have you read about a real person?

Make a Poster

Think about how Johnny's seeds change the land.
Draw the land before his visit.
Then draw the land after his visit.
Label the drawings **Before** and **After**.

Before   After

Meeting Individual Needs

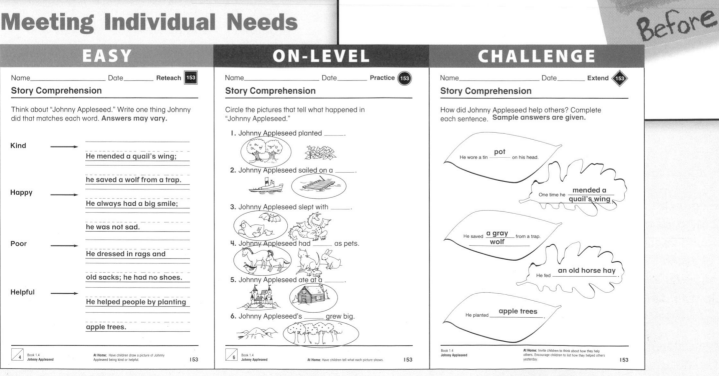

EASY	ON-LEVEL	CHALLENGE
Reteach, 153	Practice, 153	Extend, 153

120 *Johnny Appleseed*

Have an Apple Party!

There are many kinds of apples.
Bring in your favorite kind of apple.
Look at all the apples.
Taste them.
Talk about how they are alike
and different.

Find Out More

Find out about another good American.
Tell what the person did for our country.

121

Story Activities

Have an Apple Party!

Materials: different varieties of apples

ONE Read the directions aloud. Help children who have questions. Have the children discuss the kinds of apples they know.

It might be a good idea if you bring in samples of unusual varieties of apples.

Find Out More

RESEARCH AND INQUIRY Again, read the directions aloud and help children who have questions.

PARTNERS

Show children the biography section of the library and explain that biographies tell true stories about people. Help each pair choose one.

inter NET CONNECTION Have children log on to **www.mhschool.com/reading**, where they can access sites about famous Americans.

FORMAL ASSESSMENT

See the Selection Assessment Test for book 1.4.

DAY 3 **Segmenting** Give children word building boxes and say long *a: ay* words. Have children listen to the sounds in the word and write the letter(s) for each sound in the appropriate box.

 **Phonics** CD-ROM

Study Skills

CHARTS

✓OBJECTIVES

Children will read a chart to learn how an apple tree grows.

Remind children that they have just read a story about a man who plants apple trees. Tell them that now they will read a chart, a kind of picture with words, to learn more about apple trees.

Display **Teaching Chart 113.** Have children read the phrases and the title of the chart with you. Then invite children to explain each phrase. Help children read the questions below the chart, encouraging them to identify the phrases that answer each question.

STUDY SKILLS

READ TOGETHER

Apple Tree Chart

This chart tells how an apple tree grows.

Plant the Seed

Water the Seed

Let It Grow

Pick Apples

Look at the Chart

1 What do you do first to grow an apple tree?

2 What helps the apple tree grow?

Meeting Individual Needs

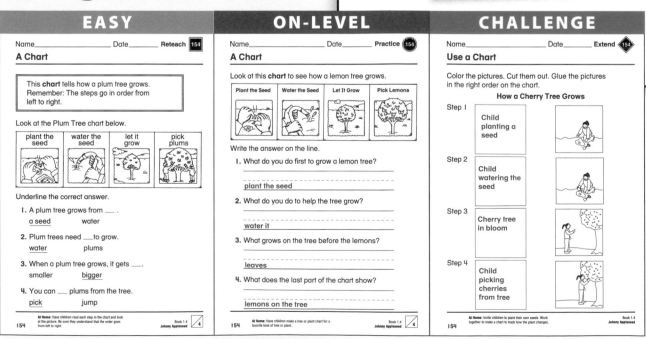

Reteach, 154   Practice, 154   Extend, 154

TEST POWER

A Trip to the Barn

It was early in the evening.
Farmer Joe wanted corn for dinner.
He had put the corn in the big red barn.
Farmer Joe put on his boots and walked
out to the barn.
He picked out three ears of corn.
"One, two, three," Farmer Joe counted.
"I can't wait to eat dinner," he said happily.
Then, Farmer Joe took the corn
back to the house.

What will Farmer
Joe do with the corn?

● Eat it
○ Feed it to the pigs

Read the story again to help answer the question.

123

Test Power

THE PRINCETON REVIEW

Read the Page

Explain to children that you will be reading this story as a group. You will read the story, and they will follow in their books.

Request that children put pens, pencils, and markers away, since they will not be writing in their books.

Discuss the Question

Have children reread the last line of the story. Ask them what Farmer Joe is doing at the end of the story. Then ask them what he will probably do with the corn.

Test-Tip

The answer to the question is always in the story—all you have to do is read carefully to find it.

ITBS Test Preparation and **Practice** Grade 1

TERRANOVA Test Preparation and **Practice** Grade 1

Stanford-9 Test Preparation and **Practice** Grade 1

ITBS/TEST PREPARATION   TERRA NOVA/TEST PREPARATION   SAT 9/TEST PREPARATION

Leveled Books

EASY

Fall Is Fun!

☑  **Phonics** Long *a: ai, ay*
☑ **Make Inferences**
High-Frequency Words:
how, light, little, live, pretty

ⓘ Intervention ▶ Skills
Intervention Guide, for direct instruction and extra practice in vocabulary and comprehension

---

Answers to Story Questions

1. It is cleaned and then put into bags. Some of the fruit goes into cans.
2. pumpkin pie
3. Answers will vary: at the super-market or grocery store.
4. pick fruit, cut grains, go for a hike
5. Answers may vary: *Johnny Appleseed.*

The Story Questions and Activity below appear in the Easy Book.

Story Questions and Activity

1. Where does fruit go after it is picked?
2. What kind of pie will the pump-kins make?
3. Where can you buy fruit in cans?
4. What are the three things to do in the fall?
5. What other story that you read had apples in it?

What Kind of Apples?

Go to the store with an adult.
Write down the names of the three apples.
Draw a picture of the apple under its name.

Guided Reading

PREVIEW AND PREDICT Take a **picture walk** up to page 5. Invite children to predict what else will happen on the farm. Chart their ideas.

SET PURPOSES Ask children to write or draw what they hope to learn in *Fall Is Fun!* For example: *I want to know what happens to the pumpkins.*

READ THE BOOK You can use questions like the following to help guide children as you read the story together or after they have read it independently.

Pages 2–3: What word does the girl use to describe where she lives? *(pretty)* What happens as the days get shorter? (There is less light.) *High-Frequency Words*

Pages 4–5: Raise your hands when you hear a word with the long *a* sound. *(grain, days)* What two different ways is the long *a* sound spelled in these words? *(ai, ay)* *Phonics and Decoding*

Pages 6–7: What other kinds of things do you think a baker might bake? *Make Inferences*

Pages 8–11: Look at the word *m-a-y.* Model: I don't know how to read this word. But I know that *m* makes the /m/ sound, and the letters *ay* can make the long *a* sound. If I blend the two sounds together, I get m ͝ ay, may. *Phonics and Decoding*

Pages 12–13: What happens after the fruit is picked? (It's cleaned, drained, and put into bags or cans.) *Make Inferences*

Pages 14–16: How do you think the chil-dren in these pictures feel? Why? (Answers will vary.) *Make Inferences*

RETURN TO PREDICTIONS AND PURPOSES Have children compare their predictions with what actually happened on the farm.

LITERARY RESPONSES If you could visit a farm, what would you enjoy doing the most?

Also see the story questions and writing activity in *Fall Is Fun!*

See the **Phonics** CD-ROM for practice using long *a: ai, ay* words.

Leveled Books

INDEPENDENT

The Land

☑ **Phonics** Long *a: ai, ay*

☑ **Make Inferences**

High-Frequency Words:
how, light, little, live, pretty

written by Wendy Pearl
illustrated by Alexandra Wallner

Guided Reading

PREVIEW AND PREDICT As you take a **picture walk** through page 5, help children use inference skills and high-frequency vocabulary to predict what will happen.

SET PURPOSES Children can write or draw what they want to learn by reading *The Land.* For example: *I want to learn what kind of plants will grow on the land.*

READ THE BOOK Use questions like the following while children are reading or after they have read independently:

Pages 2–3: When is this part of the story happening—now or a long time ago? How can you tell? (long ago; the children's dress) *Make Inferences*

Pages 4–5: Let's look for words with the long *a* sound spelled *ai.* (frail, rain) *Phonics and Decoding*

Pages 6–7: Where did the plants come from? (the seeds that were in the wind, the animals) *Make Inferences*

Page 9: Read the second sentence. What word helps you to know what *light* means? (sun) *High-Frequency Words*

Pages 12–13: What happened to the smaller plants that needed a lot of sun? (They died.) *Make Inferences*

Page 16: Is this part of the story happening now, or long ago? (now) How can you tell? (children's dress) *Make Inferences*

RETURN TO PREDICTIONS AND PURPOSES Ask children to read their predictions and purposes aloud. Were they close in predicting what would happen?

LITERARY RESPONSES Discuss with children the following questions:

• How does the land in this story change?

• Have you ever seen a place change? How did it change?

Also see the story questions and activity in *The Land.*

See the **Phonics CD-ROM** for practice using long *a: ai, ay* words.

Answers to Story Questions
1. playing
2. The wind blew it.
3. Answers will vary.
4. Ray and Gail played on the land. They moved away. Seeds landed on the land and grew into plants and trees. Time went by, and bigger trees grew and took over the land. Now children hike on the land.
5. Both stories have trees in them.

The Story Questions and Activity below appear in the Independent Book.

Story Questions and Activity
1. What are Ray and Gail doing on the land?
2. How did the seed get to the land?
3. Where did Ray and Gail move to?
4. Tell the story in your own words.
5. How are this story and *Johnny Appleseed* alike?

Go on a Hike
Find woods near your home.
Ask an adult to take you there.
Look around.
What kinds of things do you see?
Draw a picture about your hike.

from *The Land*

Leveled Books

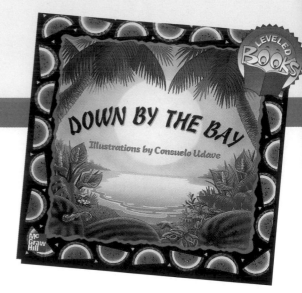

Down by the Bay

☑  **Phonics** Long *a: ai, ay*
☑ **Make Inferences**

Answers to Story Questions

1. row a boat
2. make-believe
3. Answers will vary.
4. The story is about animals doing strange things down by the bay.
5. Both stories are about animals that someone thinks they see.

The Story Questions and Activity below appear in the Challenge Book.

Story Questions and Activity

1. What does the goat do?
2. Is this story real or make-believe?
3. What other funny animals might you see down by the bay?
4. What is this story about?
5. How is this story like *Walking Through the Jungle*?

Make a Rhyme

Make up a funny rhyme about an animal.

Draw a picture to go with the rhyme.

Share your picture with your class.

from *Down by the Bay*

Guided Reading

PREVIEW AND PREDICT Take a **picture walk** up to page 10. Invite children to predict what other animals they might meet in the story. Have them record their ideas.

READ THE BOOK Use the following questions to guide children's reading or to ask after they have read the story independently.

Pages 4–5: What's the first word on this page that has the long *a* sound? *(bay)* What's the other word with the long *a* sound? *(say)* Which letters in both words make the long *a* sound? *(ay) Phonics and Decoding*

Pages 7–10: Why can't the narrator go back to his home? (because of what the mother will say) *Plot*

Pages 20–21: Where did the dragon get the watermelons? (The dragon picked them down by the bay.) *Make Inferences*

Pages 26–27: What are the animals doing? (riding in a watermelon boat) *Use Illustrations*

RETURN TO PREDICTIONS AND PURPOSES Ask children to read aloud their predictions. Were any of their animals in the story? Were they surprised by the ending?

LITERARY RESPONSE Have children discuss questions like the following:

- Which illustration did you like the best?
- Why? What part did you think was the funniest?

If you could add another verse to this song, what would it be?

Also see the story questions and activity in *Down by the Bay*.

See the **Phonics** CD-ROM for practice using long *a: ai, ay* words.

Bringing Groups Together

Anthology and Leveled Books

Connecting Texts

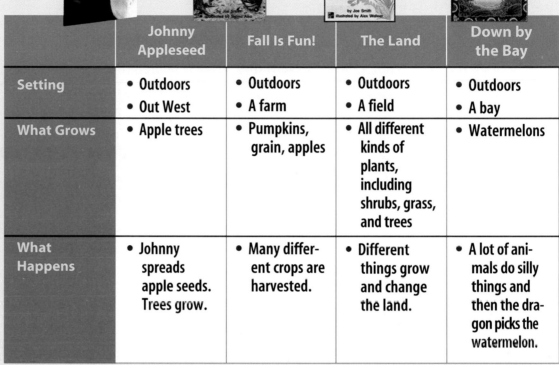

SETTING CHARTS

Write the story titles on a chart. Discuss the different settings in the books, including what grows and what happens in each setting. Write the children's ideas in the charts. Afterwards, have children discuss what is the same and what is different about the books.

	Johnny Appleseed	Fall Is Fun!	The Land	Down by the Bay
Setting	• Outdoors • Out West	• Outdoors • A farm	• Outdoors • A field	• Outdoors • A bay
What Grows	• Apple trees	• Pumpkins, grain, apples	• All different kinds of plants, including shrubs, grass, and trees	• Watermelons
What Happens	• Johnny spreads apple seeds. Trees grow.	• Many different crops are harvested.	• Different things grow and change the land.	• A lot of animals do silly things and then the dragon picks the watermelon.

Viewing/Representing

GROUP PRESENTATIONS Divide the class into groups, one for each of the four books read in the lesson. (For *Johnny Appleseed,* combine children of different reading levels.) Provide the groups with old magazines, posterboard, art materials, seeds, twigs, and other natural objects. Have children make collages to represent their books. Afterwards, have each group display and explain their collages.

AUDIENCE RESPONSE

Encourage children to discuss and compare the contents of the various collages.

Research and Inquiry

MORE ABOUT PLANTS Have children ask themselves: What else would I like to know about plants and how they grow? Then help them to do the following:

• Look at books to find out more about plants.

• Take a nature walk and observe different plants close up.

• Grow plants in the classroom.

interNET CONNECTION Have children log on to **www.mhschool.com/reading** for links to pages about plants.

JOURNAL

Children can write or draw what they learned in their journals.

OBJECTIVES

Children will:

- review long *a: ay* and *ai*.
- blend and read words with long *a: ay* and *ai*.
- review consonants and blends.

MATERIALS

- **Teaching Chart 114**
- letter and vowel digraph cards from the **Word Building Manipulative Cards**

Skills Finder

Long *a: ay, ai*

Introduce	B4: 96I-J
Review	B4: 123E-F, 123G-H, 124I-J; B5: 225G-H
Test	Book 4

ALTERNATE TEACHING STRATEGY

REVIEW LONG *a*

For a different approach to teaching this skill, see pages T75 and T76.

Review Long *a: ay, ai*

PREPARE

Listen for Long *a: ay, ai* — Read the following sentence aloud and ask children to clap when they hear a word with the long *a* sound spelled *ay* or *ai*.

- A <u>ray</u> of light showed on the <u>rail</u>.

TEACH

Review the Letters *ay, ai* as Spellings for Long *a* —
- Tell children that they will review the letters *ay* and *ai* and the sound they make. Say /ā/. Ask children to repeat after you and write the letter combinations that stand for /ā/ as they say it.

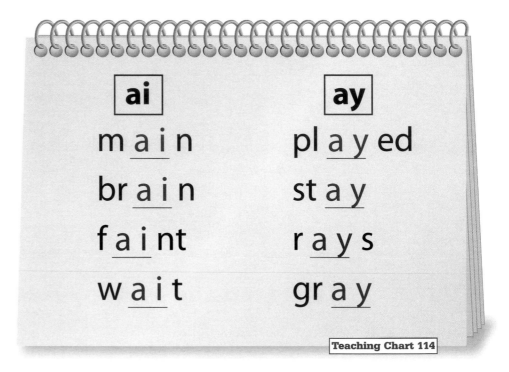

Teaching Chart 114

BLENDING Model and Guide Practice with Long *a* Words
- Display **Teaching Chart 114**. Point to the *ai* and *ay* at the top of the two columns.
- Write the letters *ai* in *main* and *ay* in *played*. Track the letters with your hand and ask children to blend and read each word with you.
- Repeat, and ask children to read words independently.

Use the Word in Context
- Invite volunteers to use each word in a sentence. Example: *What is the main idea of the paragraph? We played a game.*

Repeat the Procedure
- Continue, asking volunteers to fill in the missing letters to complete the /ā/ words on the chart.

PRACTICE

BLENDING
Build and Sort Long *a: ay, ai* Words with Letter Cards

PARTNERS

Children work in pairs. Give one child in each pair the *ay* letter card and give the other child the *ai* letter card. Ask them to choose other letter cards and build two words with their cards. Then have them exchange *ay* and *ai* cards and repeat the activity. Have them keep a list of the words they make. Then have children sort the words into two groups: *ay* and *ai*.

ASSESS/CLOSE

Read and Use Long *a: ai, ay* Words in Sentences

To assess children's mastery of blending and reading long *a: ai, ay* words, check the words they build in the Practice activity. Ask them to read some of the words from their lists and use each in a sentence.

ADDITIONAL PHONICS RESOURCES

Phonics/Phonemic Awareness Practice Book, pages 151–154

PHONICS KIT
Hands-on Activities and Practice

McGraw-Hill School
TECHNOLOGY

Phonics CD-ROM

activities for practice with **Blending and Building**

DAILY **Phonics** ROUTINES

DAY 4
Writing Have children write long *a: ay* or *ai* words to complete rhymes. Examples: If it starts to rain, let's take the _____ (train). If you stay, we can _____ (play).

Phonics CD-ROM

SPELLING/PHONICS CONNECTIONS

Words with long *a: ay, ai:* See the 5-Day Spelling Plan, pages 123Q–123R.

i **Intervention** Skills Intervention Guide, for direct instruction and extra practice in Long *a: ai, ay*

Meeting Individual Needs for Phonics

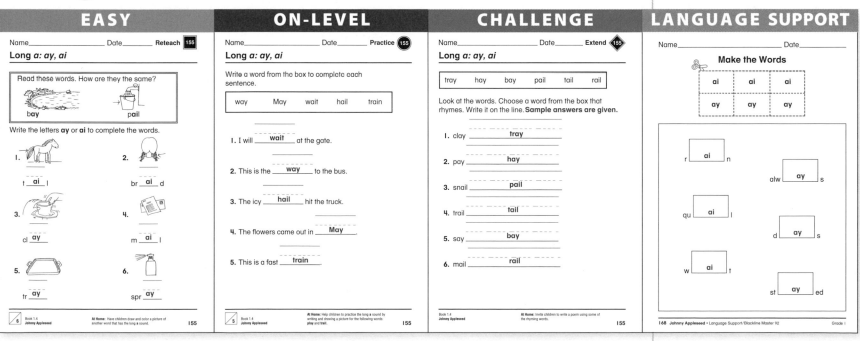

EASY	ON-LEVEL	CHALLENGE	LANGUAGE SUPPORT

Reteach, 155   Practice, 155   Extend, 155   Language Support, 168

123F

OBJECTIVES

Children will:

- review long *a: ai* and *ay*.
- blend and read long *a: ai* and *ay* words.
- review long *u: u-e* and long *o: o-e* words.
- cumulative review: blends.

MATERIALS

- **Teaching Chart 115**
- word building boxes from the **Word Building Manipulative Cards**
- **Phonics Practice Reader, Volume 2**

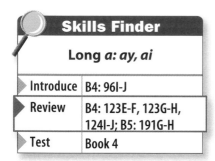

Skills Finder	
Long *a: ay, ai*	
Introduce	B4: 96I-J
Review	B4: 123E-F, 123G-H, 124I-J; B5: 191G-H
Test	Book 4

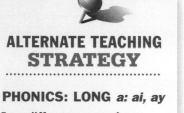

ALTERNATE TEACHING STRATEGY

PHONICS: LONG *a: ai, ay*
For a different approach to teaching this skill, see pages T75 and T76.

Review *ai, ay; u-e, o-e*

PREPARE

Identify the Letters *ai* and *ay* as Symbols for /ā/

Identify the letters *ai* and *ay* as symbols for /ā/. Remind children that the letters *ai* and *ay* stand for the sound /ā/. Write the letters *ai* and *ay* on the chalkboard and say their sounds aloud.

Discriminate Among *ai, ay; u-e*, and *o-e* Words

Write the following words on the chalkboard: *main, rope, cute, tray.* Ask volunteers to read the words and identify the long vowel sound in each word.

TEACH

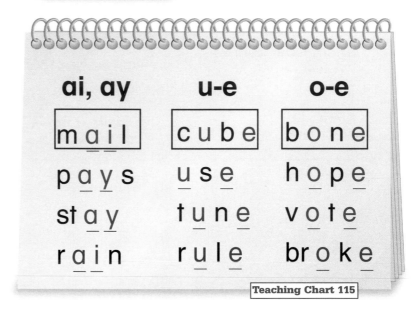

Teaching Chart 115

BLENDING Model and Guide Practice with Long *a: ai, ay, u-e,* and *o-e* Words

- Display **Teaching Chart 115**. Point to the *ai, ay, u-e,* and *o-e* at the top of the three columns.
- Point to the first example on the chart and ask children which letters at the top of the column will make a word.
- Write the letters *ai* in the blanks and have children repeat after you as you blend the sounds and read the word *mail*.

Use the Word in Context

- Have children use the word in a sentence to reinforce its meaning. Example: *Please mail this letter.*

Repeat the Procedure

- Continue until the chart is complete, asking volunteers to fill in the blanks with *ai, ay, u-e,* or *o-e* to make words.

PRACTICE

BLENDING
Build ai, ay; u-e, o-e Words

GROUP

Have children work in small groups. Ask them to build *ai, ay, u-e,* and *o-e* words using word building boxes. Have each group read their words and choose one word for each vowel combination to write on chart paper.

▶ **Linguistic/Visual**

ASSESS/CLOSE

Write a Story Using ai, ay, u-e, and o-e Words

Some children may need more reinforcement with *ai, ay, u-e,* and *o-e* words. Have them write a short story (two to four sentences) using words displayed on the chart that the class created in the Practice activity.

Read a Decodable Story

For additional practice reading words with long *a: ai, ay* and to develop fluency, direct children to read the story *The Duke's Jester* from the **Phonics Practice Reader, Volume 2.**

ADDITIONAL PHONICS RESOURCES

Phonics/Phonemic Awareness Practice Book, pages 151–154

PHONICS KIT
Hands-on Activities and Practice

McGraw-Hill School
TECHNOLOGY
Phonics CD-ROM

activities for practice with
Blending and Building

DAILY Phonics ROUTINES

DAY 5
Blending Write the spelling of each sound in *brain* as you say it. Have children repeat after you. Ask children to blend the sounds to read the word. Repeat with *mail, tray, bay, clay.*

Phonics CD-ROM

Intervention ▶ Skills
Intervention Guide, for direct instruction and extra practice in Long *a: ai, ay*

Meeting Individual Needs for Phonics

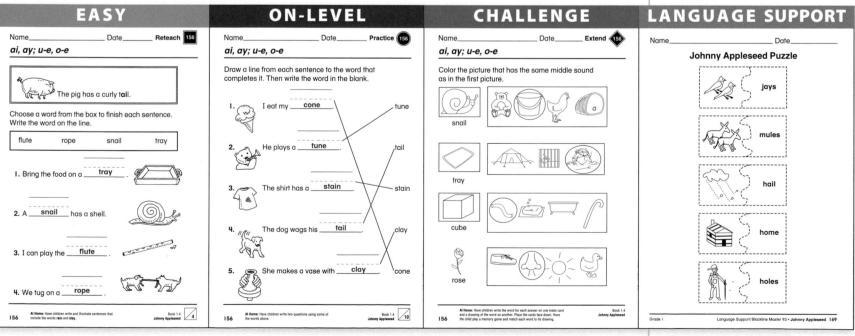

EASY	**ON-LEVEL**	**CHALLENGE**	**LANGUAGE SUPPORT**

Reteach, 156   Practice, 156   Extend, 156   Language Support, 169

Review Make Inferences

OBJECTIVES

Children will make inferences based on words, pictures, and what they already know.

MATERIALS
• Teaching Chart 116

Skills Finder

Make Inferences

Introduce	B4: 95I-J
Review	B4: 123I-J, 133G-H
Test	Book 4
Maintain	B5: 27, 53, 171, 279

TEACHING TIP

MANAGEMENT Find a few picture books without any text. Have children divide into groups to look at the pictures. Ask them to tell the story by discussing the pictures.

SELF-SELECTED Reading

Children may choose from the following titles.

ANTHOLOGY

• *Johnny Appleseed*

LEVELED BOOKS

• *Fall is Fun!*

• *The Land*

• *Down by the Bay*

ly, pages T98–T99

Johnny Appleseed

PREPARE

Introduce the Concept Tell children they can figure out things in a story by thinking about what they see in the pictures and about the words they read. They can also use what they already know to help them understand a story better. Explain that when readers use these clues they are making inferences.

TEACH

Make Inferences Using Words and Pictures Display **Teaching Chart 116**. Encourage children to look carefully at the pictures and think about the words as they read them.

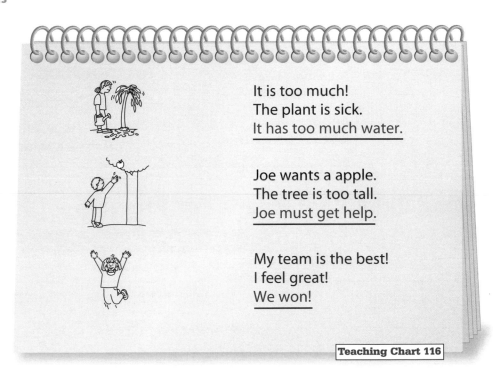

It is too much!
The plant is sick.
It has too much water.

Joe wants a apple.
The tree is too tall.
Joe must get help.

My team is the best!
I feel great!
We won!

Teaching Chart 116

MODEL I can tell how the girl with the watering can is feeling by looking at her expression. She looks sad. I think she is sad because the plant does not look healthy. I see water around the plant, and I read the words *It is too much!* So I can figure out that the plant has been given too much water.

Ask children to help figure out the other pictures on the chart using picture and word clues. Have volunteers write a sentence with the class's inference for each example on **Teaching Chart 116**. Sample answers are given.

Make Inferences Using Words and Pictures

PARTNERS

Provide pairs of children with books and magazines and have them select a picture. Encourage partners to discuss what they can tell about the picture by looking at people's expressions and/or what they are doing with their bodies. They can think about their own experiences as well. Then have each pair write a few sentences that tell about their picture. Invite volunteers to share their sentences with the rest of the class. Encourage them to explain what clues they used to decide what the picture was about.

▶ **Visual/Linguistic**

ASSESS/CLOSE

Create Pictures and Captions

Form small groups. Ask children to draw a picture that tells a story—a picture in which something is happening. Then have groups trade pictures, and let each group create a caption for another group's picture. Discuss with the groups how correct their inferences were.

ALTERNATE TEACHING STRATEGY

MAKE INFERENCES

For a different approach to teaching this skill, see page T73.

ℹ Intervention ▸ Skills Intervention Guide, for direct instruction and extra practice in Making Inferences

---

Meeting Individual Needs for Comprehension

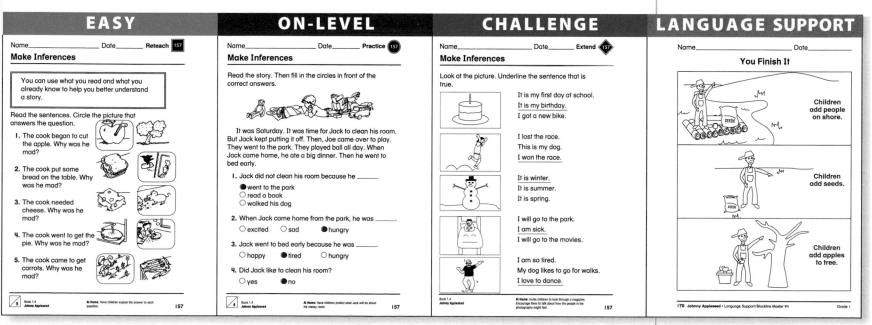

Reteach, 157   Practice, 157   Extend, 157   Language Support, 170

OBJECTIVES

Children will read words with the comparative suffixes *-er* and *-est*.

MATERIALS
- Teaching Chart 117
- index cards

Skills Finder

Inflectional Endings *-er*, *-est*

Introduce	B4: 95K-L
Review	B4: 123K-L, 133K-L
Test	Book 4

TEACHING TIP

INFLECTIONAL END-INGS Point out to the class that the *-er* ending is used when comparing two objects, while *-est* words are used when comparing three or more. Ask questions to illustrate this: *Who has the bigger chair, Ted or the teacher? Who is the tallest person in the room?*

Review Inflectional Endings -er, -est

PREPARE

Review the Concept   Write the word *fast* on the chalkboard. Ask a volunteer to clap his or her hands. Tell the class that the volunteer is clapping fast. Then have another volunteer clap faster. Elicit that the second volunteer is clapping faster. Then begin clapping even faster. Ask children to describe how you are clapping compared to the others. (fastest)

TEACH

Identify Root Words   Track the first sentence on **Teaching Chart 117** as you read it with children: *Whose hair is longer?* Point to the word *longer* and ask children if they recognize the root word. *(long)* Then model the skill.

Whose hair is longer?   Which boy is the tallest?

Which bird is shorter?   Who has the cleanest shirt?

Teaching Chart 117

MODEL I know the root word *long.* I can see the last two letters of the word are *-er.* I know that sometimes when these two letters appear together at the end of a word it means "more." The word is *longer,* which means "more long."

Repeat for the other three sentences. Invite volunteers to underline the root words and circle the suffixes, and to point to the pictures that answer the questions.

thick | er

clean | est

Meeting Individual Needs for Vocabulary

EASY	ON-LEVEL	CHALLENGE	LANGUAGE SUPPORT

EASY

Name_____ Date_____ Reteach **158**

Inflectional Endings -er, -est

Add **-er** to compare two things.
warm + **er** = warm**er**
This lake is warm**er** than that one.

Add **-est** to compare three or more things.
warm + **est** = warm**est**
This is the warm**est** lake in the world.

Circle the words that compare two things. Underline the words that compare three or more things.

1. Dave's cab is (newer) than my truck.

2. This is the longest kite in the park.

3. My hair is (shorter) than yours.

4. These grapes are the freshest of all.

5. Kate is (faster) than Jan.

6. I saw the oldest map in the world.

At Home: Invite children to illustrate two of the comparisons made with -er and -est words above.
158   Book 1.4 Johnny Appleseed   6

Reteach, 158

ON-LEVEL

Name_____ Date_____ Practice **158**

Inflectional Endings -er, -est

Add **-er** to compare two things.
Add **-est** to compare three or more things.

Read the word after each sentence. Then add **-er** or **-est** and write the word to complete the sentence.

1. Gail plays the game ___faster___ than me.   fast

2. Kate's braid is the ___thickest___ of all.   thick

3. My train is ___longer___ than yours.   long

Now draw a line from each sentence to the word that completes it.

4. That is the _____ flag pole.   softest

5. This plum is _____ than that one.   fresher

6. Kate's bed is the _____ of all.   tallest

At Home: Work with children to illustrate one of these sentences.
158   Book 1.4 Johnny Appleseed   6

Practice, 158

CHALLENGE

Name_____ Date_____ Extend **158**

Inflectional Endings -er, -est

Look at the pictures. Write a sentence about each one. Use words from the box.
Sample sentences are given.

| bigger | biggest | taller | tallest | faster | fastest |

1. Max is taller than Ben.

2. The first duck is the biggest.

3. She is the fastest rider.

At Home: Invite children to compare two items or people. For example: My dog runs faster than me.
158   Book 1.4 The Knee-High Man

Extend, 158

LANGUAGE SUPPORT

Name_____ Date_____

Look Around

old	older	oldest
pink	pinker	pinkest
big	bigger	biggest
little	littler	littlest

Grade 1   Language Support/Blackline Master 95 • Johnny Appleseed 171

Language Support, 171

Handwriting CD-ROM

GRAMMAR/SPELLING
CONNECTIONS

See the 5-Day Grammar and Usage Plan on *See* and *Say*, pages 123O–123P.

See the 5-Day Spelling Plan on Words with Long *a: ai, ay*, pages 123Q–123R.

TEACHING **TIP**

Technology

Show children how to access the print function on the file menu. Help them choose the number of copies they want to make of their letter. Then they can print a copy of the letter for each "settler".

Writing That Compares

Prewrite

WRITE A LETTER Present this writing assignment: Pretend you are Johnny Appleseed. Write a letter to a settler friend telling him or her about two ways to prepare food with apples. Describe the foods and tell how they are alike and different.

BRAINSTORM IDEAS Have children brainstorm ideas about foods that are made with apples. Encourage them to choose two foods.

STRATEGY: VISUALIZE AND DRAW Have children draw two foods made with apples. Suggest the following:

- Think about how apples are used to make this food.
- Think about how these foods look, taste, and smell.

Draft

USE THE DRAWING In their letters, have children write full sentences that refer to what they visualized and drew. Have them elaborate on the things they drew and tell how those things are alike and different. Letters should include a heading with the writer's address, the date, a greeting, and a closing signature.

Revise

CREATING A CHECKLIST Ask children if they remembered to put in all the details that explain how the foods are alike and different. Suggest they create a checklist showing:

- how each food looks
- how each food smells
- how each food tastes

GROUP Have children pretend they're settlers. Have them read each other's letters and talk about which foods they like.

Edit/Proofread

CHECK FOR ERRORS Children should reread their letters for spelling, grammar, punctuation, paragraphs, and letter format.

Publish

SHARE LETTERS Children can "mail" their letters to one another. Encourage the recipients to tell the writers which food they like better.

Johnny Appleseed
Somewhere in the West
USA
May 5, 20__

Dear Bob,

Here are some apples. I like to make applesauce and apple pie with them. Which do you like better?

Applesauce is sweet. I eat it cold with a spoon. You don't even have to bake it.

Apple pie is sweet, too. It is hot when you take it out of the oven. But you can also eat it cold with a fork.

Apple pie is a lot like applesauce. They are both sweet. Applesauce is cold, and you eat it with a spoon. But you can eat apple pie with a fork when it is hot or cold.

Your Friend,
Johnny Appleseed

Presentation Ideas

MAKE AN APPLE PIE Have children paint a white paper plate with light brown paint. Have them spread some glue over the paint and sprinkle cinnamon over it. Finally, have them glue cotton balls to the plate, for the whipped cream on top. ▶
Viewing/Representing

TALK ABOUT APPLES Have children imagine that they met a Martian who has never seen or tasted food made with apples

before. Encourage them to describe the food to their new acquaintance.
▶ **Speaking/Listening**

Consider children's creative efforts, possibly adding a plus (+) for originality, wit, and imagination.

Scoring Rubric

Excellent	Good	Fair	Unsatisfactory
4: The writer • clearly writes in full sentences and uses vivid descriptions. • gives several strong details that compare and contrast two foods made with apples. • goes beyond the material in the story.	**3:** The writer • writes in full sentences and uses vivid descriptions. • gives some good details that compare and contrast two foods made with apples. • effectively uses much of the material in the story.	**2:** The writer • may not always use full sentences, or may not attempt to describe. • gives only one or two details that compare and contrast two foods made with apples. • may not effectively use material from the story.	**1:** The writer • may not always use full sentences. • may not grasp the task to compare. • may not respond to material from the story.

0: The writer leaves the page blank or fails to respond to the writing task. The writer does not address the topic or simply paraphrases the prompt. The response is illegible or incoherent.

Meeting Individual Needs for Writing

EASY

Draw Contrasting Scenes Ask children to draw a picture of two children eating two different foods made with apples. Have them write a few simple sentences under the pictures telling what the children are eating.

ON-LEVEL

Write a Cookbook Recipe Have children write a simple cookbook recipe for people who want to make food with apples. The recipe should tell people how to use apples to prepare a type of food.

CHALLENGE

Make a Journal Entry Have children make up an adventure that Johnny Appleseed has while he's walking through the West giving out his apple seeds. Apples, apple trees, or apple seeds should be featured prominently in the adventure.

Viewing and Speaking

VIEWING STRATEGIES
Have children close their eyes and visualize what an apple pie looks like. How is it shaped? What color is it? What is it made of?

SPEAKING STRATEGIES
Encourage children to speak slowly and clearly. Martians don't understand English very well!

LANGUAGE SUPPORT

ESL Review all stories and poems about apples from this lesson. Focus on the foods made from apples and what apple trees look like. Work with children to compose a group letter, following the lesson plan for Writing That Compares. Encourage children to share the letter with the whole class.

PORTFOLIO Invite children to include the letters they wrote as Johnny Appleseed in their portfolios.

5 Day Grammar and Usage Plan

ESL Point to an object in the classroom and say, "I see a chair. I see a desk." Then ask, "What did I see?" Guide children to respond, "You saw a chair. You saw a desk."

DAILY LANGUAGE ACTIVITIES

Write the Daily Language Activities on the chalkboard each day or use **Transparency 4**. Have children correct the sentences orally, using the past tense of *see* or *say*.

Day 1

1. Johnny sees the tree yesterday. saw
2. Before, he sees a bird. saw
3. Johnny sees the town later. saw

Day 2

1. Last week Johnny says, "Plant this." said
2. Later, he says, "I have a plan." said
3. After, he says, "Life is good!" said

Day 3

1. Last night they see the river. saw
2. The men say they took the seeds. said
3. Finally Johnny sees the sun. saw

Day 4

1. Yesterday I say hello to Johnny. said
2. We see him early. saw
3. Last night Johnny says, "Seeds grow into trees." said

Day 5

1. Last year Johnny sees an old horse. saw
2. Later, Johnny says good-bye. said
3. I see Johnny this morning. saw

Language Transparency 4

Johnny Appleseed

DAY 1 — Introduce the Concept

Oral Warm-Up Ask children, "Yesterday, what did you see?" Write children's responses on the chalkboard and circle the word *saw* in each sentence.

Introduce *See* Remind children that a verb is a word that shows action. Discuss with children:

See

- The verb *see* has a special form to tell about the past.
- Use *see* or *sees* to tell about something that happens in the present.
- Use *saw* to tell about something that happened in the past.

Present the Daily Language Activity and have children correct the sentences orally. Then have them write their own sentences using *see* and *saw*.

 WRITING Assign the daily Writing Prompt on page 96E.

Name_____ Date_____ **LEARN GRAMMAR 115**

See and Say

- The verb *see* has a special form to tell about the past.
- Use *see* or *sees* to tell about the present.
  Johnny Appleseed **sees** pink buds.
- Use *saw* to tell about the past.
  He **saw** people going west.

Write the underlined verb so that it tells about the past.

1. Johnny sees the trees. _____ saw
2. He sees the people. _____ saw
3. They see his smile. _____ saw
4. Johnny sees the buds. _____ saw
5. Then he sees apples. _____ saw

Book 1.4
Johnny Appleseed 115

GRAMMAR PRACTICE BOOK, PAGE 115

DAY 2 — Teach the Concept

Review *See* Write on the chalkboard: *Meg sees a cat.* Then ask children to change the sentence to begin with *Yesterday.* (*Yesterday Meg saw a cat.*)

Introduce *Say* Read aloud the following sentence: *Today Pam says yes.* Then ask children to change the sentence to begin with *Yesterday.* (*Yesterday Pam said yes.*)

Say

- The verb *say* has a special form to tell about the past.
- Use *say* or *says* to tell about something that happens in the present.
- Use *said* to tell about something that happened in the past.

Present the Daily Language Activity. Then have children write their own sentences, using *say* and *said*.

 WRITING Assign the daily Writing Prompt on page 96E.

Name_____ Date_____ **LEARN AND PRACTICE GRAMMAR 116**

See and Say

- The verb *say* has a special form to tell about the past.
- Use *say* and *says* to tell about the present.
- Use *said* to tell about something that happened in the past.
  I **say** something.   He **said** something.

Write the underlined verb so that it tells about the past.

1. Johnny says the ham was good. _____ said
2. He says he would rest. _____ said
3. He says the sun was up. _____ said
4. He says, "I'm Johnny." _____ said
5. They say, "Hello, Johnny." _____ said

116
Book 1.4
Johnny Appleseed 5

GRAMMAR PRACTICE BOOK, PAGE 116

See and Say

DAY 3 — Review and Practice

Learn from the Literature Review *see* and *say* with children. Read the following sentence from page 104 of *Johnny Appleseed*:

> **"Quick! Plant my apple seeds," he said to those who were on the banks.**

Emphasize the word *said*. Ask children whether the sentence tells about the past or tells about the present. (tells about the past)

Use *See* and *Say* Present the Daily Language Activity and have children correct orally.

Ask children to write sentences using *see* and *say*. Then have children exchange papers with partners and rewrite the sentences, beginning them with *Yesterday*. For example: *I see a van. Yesterday I saw a van.*

 Assign the daily Writing Prompt on page 96F.

DAY 4 — Review and Practice

Review *See* and *Say* Write the following sentence on the chalkboard: *Yesterday Johnny sees an apple tree.* Ask children if the sentence is correct. (no) Why not? (The verb should be *saw*.) Why? (because it happened in the past) Correct the sentence on the chalkboard, then present the Daily Language Activity for Day 4.

Mechanics and Usage Before children begin the daily Writing Prompt on page 96F, review commas. Display and discuss:

Commas

- Use a comma between the day and year in a date.
- Use a comma between the name of a city and a state.
- Use a comma after the greeting in a letter.
- Use a comma after the closing in a letter.

 Assign the daily Writing Prompt on page 96F.

DAY 5 — Assess and Reteach

Assess Use the Daily Language Activity and page 120 of the **Grammar Practice Book** for assessment.

Reteach Write *Today* and *Yesterday* on the chalkboard. Then write the following sentences on paper strips: *I saw a big dog. She sees the movie. The boys saw the bike. We say yes. He gave a speech. Nick said nothing.* Read the sentences aloud and ask whether each tells about the past or the present. Have children take turns placing the sentences under the appropriate column on the board.

Have children create a classroom word wall with sentences using *say* and *see*.

Use page 121 of the **Grammar Practice Book** for additional reteaching.

 Assign the daily Writing Prompt on page 96F.

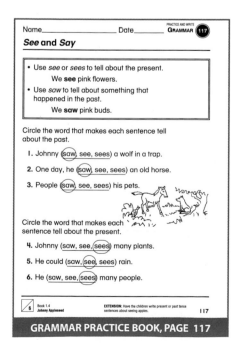

GRAMMAR PRACTICE BOOK, PAGE 117

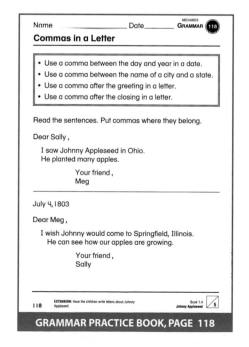

GRAMMAR PRACTICE BOOK, PAGE 118

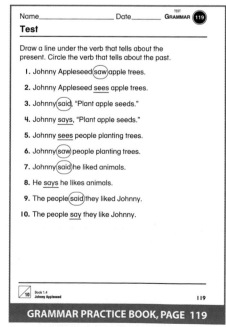

GRAMMAR PRACTICE BOOK, PAGE 119

5Day Spelling Plan

DICTATION SENTENCES

Spelling Words

1. I have a hat for the rain.
2. Can you wait for me?
3. Is this the way to go?
4. Do you know what day it is?
5. What could you say?
6. That cat has a small tail.

Challenge Words

7. How big you are!
8. The sun gives us light.
9. Where do you live?
10. What a pretty dress that is!

DAY 1 — Pretest

Assess Prior Knowledge Use the Dictation Sentences at left and **Spelling Practice Book** page 115 for the pretest. Allow children to correct their own papers. If children have trouble, have partners give each other a midweek test on Day 3.

Spelling Words		Challenge Words
1. **rain**	4. **day**	7. **how**
2. **wait**	5. say	8. **light**
3. **way**	6. tail	9. **live**
		10. **pretty**

*Note: Words in **dark type** are from the story.*

Word Study On page 116 of the **Spelling Practice Book** are word study steps and an at-home activity.

DAY 2 — Explore the Pattern

Sort and Spell Words Say the words *way* and *rain*. Ask children what vowel sound they hear in each word. (long *a*) Write the words on the chalkboard and circle the letters that spell long *a*.

Words with long *a* spelled	
ay	*ai*
way	rain
day	wait
say	tail

Word Wall As children read other stories and texts, have them look for new words with long *a* spelled *ay* or *ai*. Add them to a classroom word wall, underlining the *ay* or *ai* in each word.

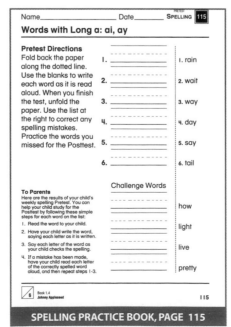

SPELLING PRACTICE BOOK, PAGE 115

WORD STUDY STEPS AND ACTIVITY, PAGE 116

SPELLING PRACTICE BOOK, PAGE 117

Words with Long *a: ai, ay*

DAY 3 Practice and Extend

Word Meaning: Synonyms Remind children that synonyms are words that mean the same, or nearly the same, thing. For example, *big* and *large* are synonyms. Ask children to think of a synonym for *say*. *(tell)* Then remind children that synonyms for some words are given in the Glossary. Have children look up the words *bag, jars,* and *rocket* in the Glossary and find their synonyms. Have children match the following synonyms:

rock	**also**
little	**stone**
too	**small**

(rock/stone; little/small; too/also)

Identify Spelling Patterns Write this sentence on the chalkboard: *How long will we wait for the rain?* Have a volunteer read it aloud. Ask children to tell which words have the spelling pattern *ai* and which is the Challenge Word. Repeat with the spelling pattern *ay* using these sentences: *This is the way to live. The cat had a pretty tail.* Then have children write sentences using the Challenge Words.

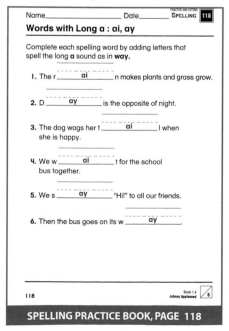

SPELLING PRACTICE BOOK, PAGE 118

DAY 4 Proofread and Write

Proofread Sentences Write these sentences on the chalkboard, including the misspelled words. Ask children to proofread, circling incorrect spellings and writing the correct spellings. There are two errors in each sentence.

> Did you (sae) you like the (rane)? (say, rain)
>
> I cannot (wate) for that (dai). (wait, day)
>
> That cat's (tayl) is (wai) too big. (tail, way)

Have students create additional sentences with errors for partners to correct.

 WRITING Have students use as many Spelling Words as possible in the daily Writing Prompt on page 96F. Remind students to proofread their writing for errors in spelling, grammar, and punctuation.

SPELLING PRACTICE BOOK, PAGE 119

DAY 5 Assess and Reteach

Assess Children's Knowledge Use page 120 of the **Spelling Practice Book** or the Dictation Sentences on page 123Q for the posttest.

Personal Word List If children have trouble with any words in the lesson, have them add them to a personal list of troublesome words in their journals. Have children write a sentence using as many of the Spelling Words as they can.

Children should refer to their word lists during later writing activities.

SPELLING PRACTICE BOOK, PAGE 120

Cumulative Review with Expository Text

Time to Review

Anthology

Ring! Ring! Ring! Put Out the Fire!

Selection Summary Children will be reading about firefighters and the work they do. They will learn about fire trucks, ladders, hoses, and water pumps.

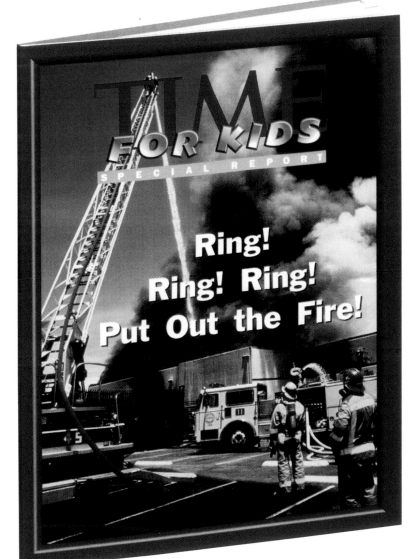

Rhyme applies to Phonics

Listening Library

INSTRUCTIONAL pages 126–133

Time to Reread

Reread Leveled Books

EASY
Lesson on pages 133A and 133D
`DECODABLE`

INDEPENDENT
Lesson on pages 133B and 133D

■ *Take-Home version available*
`DECODABLE`

CHALLENGE
Lesson on pages 133C and 133D

Leveled Practice

EASY
Reteach, 159-166 Blackline masters with reteaching opportunities for each assessed skill

INDEPENDENT/ON-LEVEL
Practice, 159-166 Workbook with Take-Home Stories and practice opportunities for each assessed skill and story comprehension

CHALLENGE
Extend, 159-166 Blackline masters that offer challenge activities for each assessed skill

Quizzes Prepared by Accelerated Reader®

Center Activities

Social Studies ...	**Community Workers,** *124D*
Language Arts ..	**Read Aloud,** *124G*
Art	**Fire Prevention Posters,** *124D*
	Make a Fire Safety Badge, *131*
Writing	**A Speech,** *130*
Research and Inquiry	**Find Out More,** *131*
Internet Activities	**www.mhschool.com/reading**

Center Activities

Each of these activities takes 15-20 minutes.

Phonics

Sort Long Vowel Words

PARTNERS **Objective:** Identify and sort picture cards according to their vowel sounds.

◆ Give partners copies of the cards and have them write *a, i, o,* and *u* across the top of a piece of paper.

◆ Partners put the cards in the appropriate columns and make up sentences with the words.

MATERIALS
- Phonics Picture Cards (*cane, nine, rope, cube*)
- Large sheets of paper

Writing

Fire Rules

GROUP **Objective:** Write and illustrate rules of fire safety.

◆ Have small groups discuss what should be done during a fire drill.

◆ Children can write and illustrate a sentence about a rule the class should follow during a fire drill.

◆ Display the drawings near the classroom door.

MATERIALS
- Drawing paper
- Crayons

Reading and Listening

Independent/Self-Selected Reading

ONE **Objective:** Listen and use illustrations to understand a story.

Fill the Center with books and corresponding audiocassettes or CD-ROMs children have read or listened to this week. You can also include books from the Theme Bibliography on pages T98 and T99.

Leveled Books

◆ *A Pet for Max* by Cynthia Benjamin
◆ *Spot's Trick* by Judy Nayer
◆ *Fun Run* by Rachel Patrick
◆ *Fall is Fun!* by Ron Archer
◆ *The Big Secret* by Tim Kane

◆ *Show and Tell Rose* by Josie Lee
◆ *A Bigger House for June* by Anna Smyth
◆ *The Land* by Wendy Pearl
◆ *Who Took the Farmer's Hat?* by Joan L. Nodset
◆ *My Best Friend* by Pat Hutchins
◆ *Pete's Chicken* by Harriet Ziefert
◆ *Down by the Bay* by Consuelo Udave
◆ "Ring! Ring! Ring! Put Out the Fire!" by *Time for Kids*
◆ "To the Top" by Sandra Liatsos

Working with Words

Color Coded Words

 PARTNERS

Objective: Reinforce vocabulary words: *always, work, clean, done, how.*

MATERIALS
- **Construction paper**
- **Pencil**

- Have children find each word in the story.

- Then partners make up a sentence related to fire safety with each word.

- Partners can write and illustrate their sentences.

Always remember to let a grown-up light the fire.

Art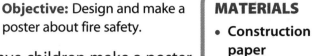

Fire Prevention Posters

ONE

Objective: Design and make a poster about fire safety.

MATERIALS
- **Construction paper**
- **Various art materials**

- Have children make a poster that communicates information about fire prevention and safety.

- Invite volunteers to share their posters.

- Display the completed posters.

Social Studies

Community Helpers

 PARTNERS

Objective: Write and illustrate sentences about community workers.

MATERIALS
- **Butcher paper**
- **Drawing paper**
- **Crayons**

- Hang a sheet of butcher paper with the title "Community Helpers."

- Write "firefighters" as the first item.

- Have partners brainstorm and write the names of other community helpers they know.

- Children choose one job and write and illustrate a sentence that tells about it.

A police officer keeps us safe.

READING AND LANGUAGE ARTS	DAY **1** *Focus on Reading and Skills*	 DAY **2** *Read the Literature*
● **Phonics Daily Routines**	Daily **Routine: Segmenting,** 124J **CD-ROM**	Daily **Phonics Routine: Blending,** 126A 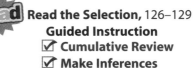 **CD-ROM**

● **Phonological Awareness**
 	
 ● **Phonics** *Review*
 	
 ● **Comprehension**
 	
 ● **Vocabulary**
 	
 ● **Study Skills**
 	
 ● **Listening, Speaking, Viewing, Representing**
	Read Aloud, 124G
	 "The Brave Ones"
	
	 ☑ **Develop Phonological Awareness,** 124H
	
	 ☑ **Review** *ai, ay; u-e, o-e, i-e, a-e,* 124I–124J
	 Reteach, Practice, Extend, 159
	 Phonics/Phonemic Awareness Practice Book, 155–158
	
	  Review, 124/125
	 "Fire Pup"
	
	  Intervention Program
		Build Background, 126A
		 Develop Oral Language
		
		 Vocabulary, 126B–126C
		
		 always work clean
		 done how
		
		 Teaching Chart 119
		 Word Building Manipulative Cards
		 Reteach, Practice, Extend, 160
		
		  Read the Selection, 126–129
		 Guided Instruction
		 ☑ **Cumulative Review**
		 ☑ **Make Inferences**
		
		 Genre: Narrative Nonfiction, 127

● **Curriculum Connections**	Language Arts, 124G	**Link** Social Studies, 124D, 126A
● **Writing**	**Writing Prompt:** Write some rules about fires.	**Writing Prompt:** Write about the differences between a fire truck and a bus. Why can't a bus help put out a fire? **Journal Writing** Quick-Write, 129
● **Grammar**	**Introduce the Concept: Contractions with** *Not,* 133O Daily Language Activity: Write contractions correctly. **Grammar Practice Book,** 121	**Teach the Concept: Contractions with** *Not,* 133O Daily Language Activity: Write contractions correctly. **Grammar Practice Book,** 122
● **Spelling** *Words from Social Studies*	**Pretest: Words from Social Studies,** 133Q **Spelling Practice Book,** 121, 122	**Explore the Pattern: Words from Social Studies,** 133Q **Spelling Practice Book,** 123

Meeting Individual Needs

 = **Skill Assessed in Unit Test**

 Intervention Program Available

 **Read the Literature**	 **Build Skills**	 **Build Skills**
 **Daily Phonics Routine:** Fluency, 131 Phonics CD-ROM	**Daily Phonics Routine:** Writing, 133F Phonics CD-ROM	**Daily Phonics Routine:** Letter Substitution, 133H Phonics CD-ROM

DAY 3 — Read the Literature

Reread for Fluency, 128

Story Questions, 130
   Reteach, Practice, Extend, 161

Story Activities, 131

Study Skill, 132
   ☑ **Charts**
   Teaching Chart 120
   Reteach, Practice, Extend, 162

Test Power, 133

 **Read the Leveled Books, Guided Reading**
   ☑ **Cumulative Review**
   ☑ **Comprehension**

 Intervention Program

DAY 4 — Build Skills

 **Read the Leveled Books and Self-Selected Books**

☑ **Review Cause and Effect,** 133E–133F
   Teaching Chart 121
   Reteach, Practice, Extend, 163
   Language Support, 177

☑ **Review Make Inferences,** 133G–133H
   Teaching Chart 122
   Reteach, Practice, Extend, 164
   Language Support, 178

 Intervention Program

DAY 5 — Build Skills

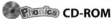 **Read Self-Selected Books**

☑ **Review Inflectional Endings -s, -es,** 133I–133J
   Teaching Chart 123
   Reteach, Practice, Extend, 165
   Language Support, 179

☑ **Review Inflectional Endings -er, -est,** 133K–133L
   Teaching Chart 124
   Reteach, Practice, Extend, 166
   Language Support, 180

Listening, Speaking, Viewing, Representing, 133N

Intervention Program

Activity Art, 124D, 131

Writing Prompt: Write about some things we wouldn't be able to do without fire.

Journal Writing, 133D

Writing Prompt: Write a funny story about a firefighter who can't slide down the pole in the firehouse.

Writing that Compares, 133M
   Prewrite, Draft

Meeting Individual Needs for Writing, 133N

Writing Prompt: Write a letter to an aunt or uncle who isn't careful about fire. Tell them what you think.

Writing that Compares, 133M
   Revise, Edit/Proofread, Publish

Review and Practice: Contractions with Not, 133P
   Daily Language Activity: Write contractions correctly.

Grammar Practice Book, 123

Review and Practice: Contractions with Not, 133P
   Daily Language Activity: Write contractions correctly.

Grammar Practice Book, 124

Assess and Reteach: Contractions with Not, 133P
   Daily Language Activity: Write contractions correctly.

Grammar Practice Book, 125, 126

Practice and Extend: Words from Social Studies, 133R

Spelling Practice Book, 124

Practice and Write: Words from Social Studies, 133R

Spelling Practice Book, 125

Assess Words from Social Studies, 133R

Spelling Practice Book, 126

124F

Read Aloud

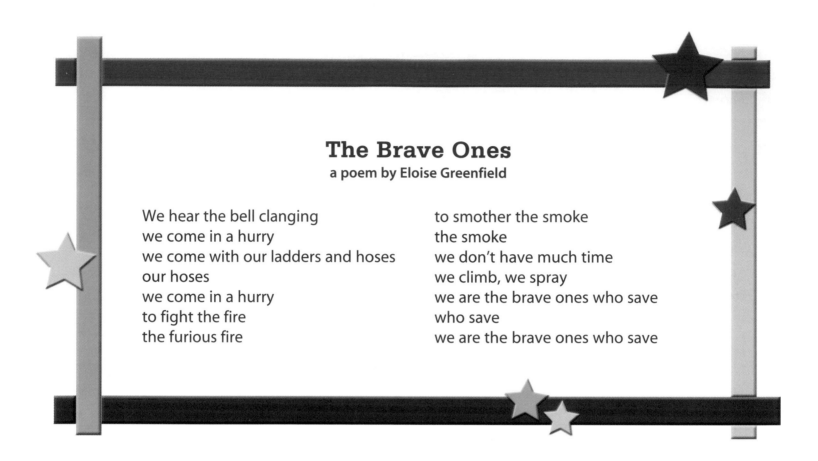

The Brave Ones
a poem by Eloise Greenfield

We hear the bell clanging
we come in a hurry
we come with our ladders and hoses
our hoses
we come in a hurry
to fight the fire
the furious fire

to smother the smoke
the smoke
we don't have much time
we climb, we spray
we are the brave ones who save
who save
we are the brave ones who save

Oral Comprehension

LISTENING AND SPEAKING Motivate children to think about why a poet repeats words and phrases by reading this poem about firefighters. Ask children to listen for words, word pairs, and sentences that are repeated as you read the poem. When you are done, ask, "What are some words that are repeated during the poem?" Then point out repeated word pairs and phrases such as *we come in a hurry, the smoke,* and *we are the brave ones who save.* Ask children why the poet might have repeated those words.

Activity Ask children to act out the situation described in "The Brave Ones." When you ring a bell, volunteers will pretend to be firefighters responding to the fire. Ask children to mime driving to the fire, climbing, and spraying water. ▶ **Kinesthetic/Auditory**

GENRE STUDY: POEM Remind children that, in a poem, the way the words are arranged is as important as the words themselves. Point out that this poem has short lines. Also point out that although the poem begins with a capital letter, there is no punctuation throughout. Demonstrate how the short lines make the reader want to read faster. Explain that the poet probably wrote it this way to reflect how firefighters move quickly to put out fires.

Develop Phonological Awareness

Blend Sounds

MATERIALS
- puppet

Teach   Tell children the puppet will speak very slowly. If the puppet says /r/-/ī/-/d/, you know the word is *ride*. Tell children they will listen to the puppet's sounds and blend them together to say the words. Have the puppet say: */f/-/ū/-/m/. What word did I say?* (*fume*)

Practice   Use the following words to have children blend sounds and say words: *bite, cute, five, globe, home, joke, mule, nose, ripe, smile.*

Segment Sounds

MATERIALS
- Phonics Picture Posters

Teach   Tell children you will say the word that names a picture, and they will repeat it, sound by sound. Hold up the picture of the kite and say: *I hear three sounds in the word* kite. (/k/-/ī/-/t/) Have children repeat the sounds with you: *kite: /k/-/ī/-/t/.*

Practice   Have children practice segmenting the sounds in the picture names of the following Phonics Picture Posters: *cane, nine, rope, cube, train, whale, ship, duck, fish,* and *nest.*

Delete Sounds

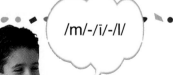

/m/-/ī/-/l/

Teach   Tell children that you will say a word, and they will repeat the word without the beginning sound. Say: *If I take the /s/ sound away from the word* smile, *I make the word* mile. *Say the words with me:* smile, mile.

Practice   Have children make words from the following list by first saying the whole word, then saying the word without its beginning sound: *gripe, pride, slime, spine, swipe, spoke, stone, grain,* and *snail.*

INFORMAL ASSESSMENT   Observe children as they blend sounds, segment sounds, and delete initial phonemes. If children have difficulty, see Alternate Teaching Strategies on pages T64, T69, T71, and T75.

OBJECTIVES

Children will:

- review long u: *u-e*; *o*: *o-e*; *i*: *i-e*; *a*: *a-e*; *a*: *ai*, *ay* words.

- blend and read long u: *u-e*; *o*: *o-e*; *i*: *i-e*; *a*: *a-e*; *a*: *ai*, *ay* words.

- review consonants.

MATERIALS

- **Teaching Chart 118**

- letter cards and word building boxes from the **Word Building Manipulative Cards**

- index cards

Skills Finder	
Long *a: ay, ai*	
Introduce	B4: 96I-J
Review	B4: 123E-F, 123G-H B5: 191G-H, 225G-H
Test	Book 4

SPELLING/PHONICS CONNECTIONS

Words with long u: *u-e*; *o*: *o-e*; *i*: *i-e*; *a*: *a-e*; *a*: *ai*, *ay*: See the 5-Day Spelling Plan, pages 133Q–133R.

ALTERNATE TEACHING STRATEGY

PHONICS: LONG *u, o, i, a*

For a different approach to teaching these skills, see pages T64, T68, T69, T71, T75, and T76.

Review *ai, ay; u-e, o-e, i-e, a-e*

PREPARE

Identify the Patterns *u-e, o-e, i-e, a-e*, and *ai, ay* as Symbols for /ū/, /ō/, /ī/, and /ā/.

Remind children that they have learned to read words with the vowel-consonant-silent *e* pattern for long *u, o, i,* and *a,* and that *ai* and *ay* make the long *a* sound.

- Display the letter cards for the long vowels. Ask children to make each sound as you point to the card.

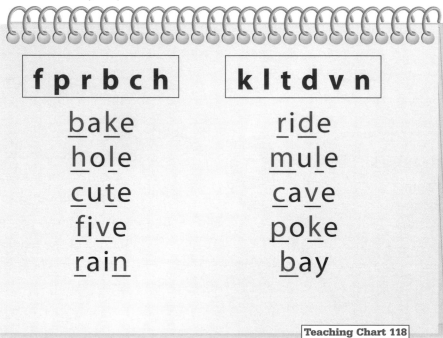

Teaching Chart 118

TEACH

BLENDING
Model and Guide Practice with *u-e, o-e, i-e, a-e, ai, ay*

- Display **Teaching Chart 118**. Run your hand under the letters *a-e* in the first item and say the sound /ā/.

- Write the letter *k* in the blank space between the letters *a-e*. Write the letter *b* in the first blank space. Blend all the sounds together to say the word *bake*. b‿ak(e) bake Explain to children that they can build words by choosing a letter from the second letter bank to fit between the letters *u-e, o-e, i-e,* and *a-e,* and then choosing a letter from the first letter bank to complete the word.

Use the Words in Context

Have children use the word in a sentence to reinforce its meaning. Example: *I like to bake cakes.*

Repeat the Procedure

Repeat the procedure with the remaining words on the chart.

PRACTICE

LETTER SUBSTITUTION
Build Long *u: u-e; o: o-e; i: i-e; a: a-e; a: ai, ay* Words

PARTNERS

Build the word *rate,* asking children to repeat after you. Change the word to *late* by replacing the *r* with *l*. Next, ask pairs of children to build and write the following words: *pure; cure; time; lime; main; may; rode; code.* ▶ **Linguistic/Kinesthetic**

ASSESS/CLOSE

Build and Read Long *u: u-e; o: o-e; i: i-e; a: a-e; a: ai, ay* Words

To assess children's ability to blend and read CVCe and double-vowel pattern words, observe them as they build words in the Practice activity. Ask children to read the words they have written.

ADDITIONAL PHONICS RESOURCES

Phonics/Phonemic Awareness Practice Book pages 155–158

PHONICS KIT Hands-on Activities and Practice

McGraw-Hill School **TECHNOLOGY**

Phonics CD-ROM activities for practice with **Blending and Segmenting**

Meeting Individual Needs for Phonics

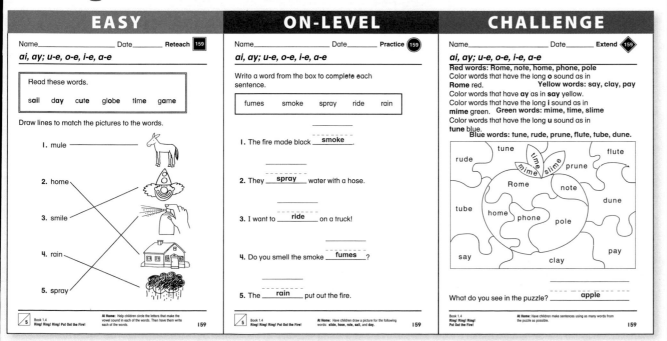

Reteach, 159   Practice, 159   Extend, 159

Daily Routines

DAY 1 **Segmenting** Distribute word building boxes. Say a CVCe pattern word aloud. Have children write the spelling of each sound in the appropriate box. (Use *bake, nine, rope, fuse.*)

DAY 2 **Blending** Write the spelling of each sound in *fire* as you say it. Have children repeat after you, blending the sounds to read the word. Repeat with *tire* and *wire.*

DAY 3 **Fluency** Write a list of long *u: u-e; o: o-e; i: i-e; a: a-e; a: ai, ay* words. Point to each word, asking children to blend the sounds silently. Ask a volunteer to read each word.

DAY 4 **Writing** Have children choose two CVCe pattern or double-vowel pattern words and create a rhyming couplet with the words. Children can illustrate their rhymes.

DAY 5 **Letter Substitution** Using letter and long-vowel cards, have pairs of children build *rule.* Taking turns, one child is to change a letter to build a new word, asking the partner to read it.

^{TESTED}
OBJECTIVES

Children will read a poem with words containing long *a: ai, ay,* long *i: i-e,* and *long o: o-e.*

Apply *ai, ay;*
u-e, o-e, i-e, a-e

Fire Pup

I'm a little fire pup. My name is Spot.
You can ask for me when things get
very hot.

If you see a fire and if you need
a water hose,
I'll use my fast fire truck and bring you
one of those.

Is there a trail of smoke or a bit
of flame?
Anytime day or night, just yell out
my name!

124

125

Anthology pages 124–125

Read and Build Fluency

READ THE POEM Tell children they will read a poem called *Fire Pup.* Model changing inflection and expression when you read the question and the exclamation. Encourage children to read with you.

REREAD FOR FLUENCY Have groups of three children reread the poem, taking turns reading each stanza.

READ A DECODABLE STORY For additional practice reading and to develop fluency, have children read one of this week's **Phonics Practice Reader, Vol. 2** stories.

Dictate and Spell

DICTATE WORDS Segment the word *fire* into its three individual sounds. Repeat the word aloud and use it in a sentence: *Use a water hose to put out a fire.* Then have children say the word and write the letter or letters that represent each sound until they make the entire word. Repeat with *hose, those, trail, smoke,* and *day* from the poem. Then repeat with words such as: *bite, five, smile, time, globe, hope, hole, home, gray, jays,* and *rain.*

i **Intervention** **Skills Intervention Guide,**
Book A, for direct instruction and extra practice in
Long *a: ai, ay;* Long *i: i-e;* Long *o: o-e*

Build Background

Concept: Fire

Link

ocial Studies

CONCEPT: FIRE Ask children to share what they know about fire. Have them talk about any experiences they may have had, such as building a fire at a campground or in a fireplace; or seeing firefighters put out a fire. Use the following activities if children need more information about fire.

MAKE A WORD WEB FOR FIRE Work with children to create a word web to record various words associated with fire.

▶ **Linguistic**

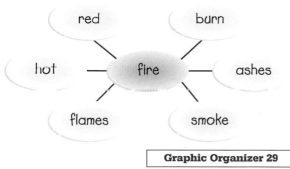

red   burn

hot   fire   ashes

flames   smoke

Graphic Organizer 29

DRAW FIRE Have children draw a scene in which there is fire, for example at a campground or in a fireplace. Encourage children to think of places where they have seen fires. Have them refer to the word web and write a sentence describing fire.

ONE   WRITING

Develop Oral Language

CONNECT WORDS AND ACTIONS Write

ESL the following words on the board: *pop, hiss, crackle, roar*. Say these words aloud as you point to them. Explain to children that flames of a fire often make these sounds.

Then divide children into four groups and give each group one of the fire sounds. Tell children they will play a game called "Dancing Flames." As you call out each sound, the appropriate group will say the sound. ▶ **Auditory**

The flames are hot.

Anthology and Leveled Books

LANGUAGE SUPPORT

For additional teaching support to help build more background, see pages 172–175 in the Language Support Book.

DAILY Phonics ROUTINES

DAY 2 **Blending** Write the spelling of each sound in the word *fire* as you say it. Have children repeat after you, blending the sounds to read the word. Repeat with *tire* and *wire*.

Phonics CD-ROM

clean

always

work

done

how

OBJECTIVES

Children will:

- identify high-frequency words *clean, always, work, done,* and *how.*

MATERIALS

- Teaching Chart 119
- Word Building Manipulative Cards *clean, always, work, done, how*

TEACHING TIP

The following chart indicates words from the upcoming story that children have learned to decode, as well as high-frequency words that have been taught in previous lessons.

Decodable		High-Frequency	
hose	ride	how	clean
day	slide	always	done
fire(s)	smoke	work	
fumes	sprays		
stay	used		
	pole		

SPELLING/VOCABULARY CONNECTIONS

The words *clean, always, work, done* are Challenge Words. See page 133Q for Day 1 of the 5-Day Spelling Plan.

Vocabulary

High-Frequency Words

Fire! Fire!

Fire! Fire! Ring! Ring! Ring!

Get the fire truck. Ding! Ding! Ding!

There is (work) that must be (done)

We (always) run, run, run!

The fire is hot and the smoke is thick.

This is (how) we get there quick.

Out of the way! Here comes the hose.

Today we can't (clean) The flames rose and rose.

Pump that pump! Spray that spray!

Make the fire go away!

Teaching Chart 119

Auditory

LISTEN TO WORDS Without displaying it, read aloud "Fire! Fire!" on **Teaching Chart 119.** Ask children if they were able to hear the noise and yelling at the fire. It wasn't always clear who was yelling, was it? Have any of them ever seen a fire truck in action at a fire? What did the firefighters do? Was the scene noisy?

RING FOR HIGH-FREQUENCY WORDS Have children aurally identify each high-frequency word using the following activity:

- Say aloud each high-frequency word, and have children repeat it.
- Tell children that they should make believe the poem is on fire. To put out the fire, they can say "Ring!" every time you come to one of the high-frequency words, and then say the word. Read the poem again, pausing at each high-frequency word.

Visual

TEACH WORDS Display "Fire! Fire!" on **Teaching Chart 119.** Read the poem, tracking the print with your finger. Next, point to and say the word *clean.* Have them say the word with you. Ask them to hold up the vocabulary card for *clean* and say the word. Repeat this procedure for *always, work, done,* and *how.*

Hold up vocabulary cards for *clean, always, work, done,* and *how* one at a time. Have volunteers read the words and then circle them on the chart.

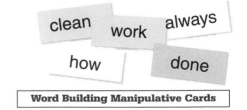

Word Building Manipulative Cards

MATCH WORDS Supply two sets of cards. One partner displays a vocabulary card; the other reads the word, and displays a matching card.

Activities

Word Wall

Fill in the Blanks Write the following sentence on the chalkboard.

_____ do you _____ get your _____ _____ and the house _____ while I am in school? (How, always, work, done, clean)

Tell children that word wall words complete the sentence. Ask volunteers to identify the words that fill in each of the blanks. Then encourage them to read the complete sentence aloud.

Color the Words Give children crayons and paper. Call out a word wall word and have children write the word using a color of their choice. Continue until children have had the chance to write each word.

Assess

Complete the Sentence Ask children to write the sentence from the first word wall activity on the board, but this time fill in the blanks with the correctly spelled word wall words.

LANGUAGE SUPPORT

To help children develop understanding and recognition of high frequency words, see page 172 in the **Language Support Book.**

Meeting Individual Needs for Vocabulary

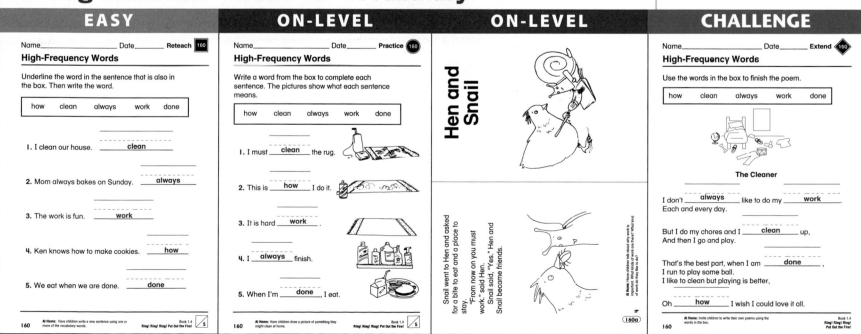

EASY

Reteach, 160

ON-LEVEL

Practice, 160

ON-LEVEL

Practice, 160a
Take-Home Story

CHALLENGE

Extend, 160

126C

Comprehension

Prereading Strategies

PREVIEW AND PREDICT Ask children to look at the picture on the title page. Discuss how the photograph might give clues about the story.

- What might this story be about?
- Where might it take place?
- Will the story be real or make-believe? How can you tell? (The story will be real, because the people and the scenes look like something you might see happen.)

Next, take a **picture walk** through the story. Have children pay attention to the details of the photographs, such as what the fire trucks look like and what the firefighters are wearing. Have children make predictions about the story. Chart their predictions and read them aloud.

SET PURPOSES Ask children what they want to find out as they read the story. For example:

- What kind of work do firefighters do?
- Why do firefighters need to rush?

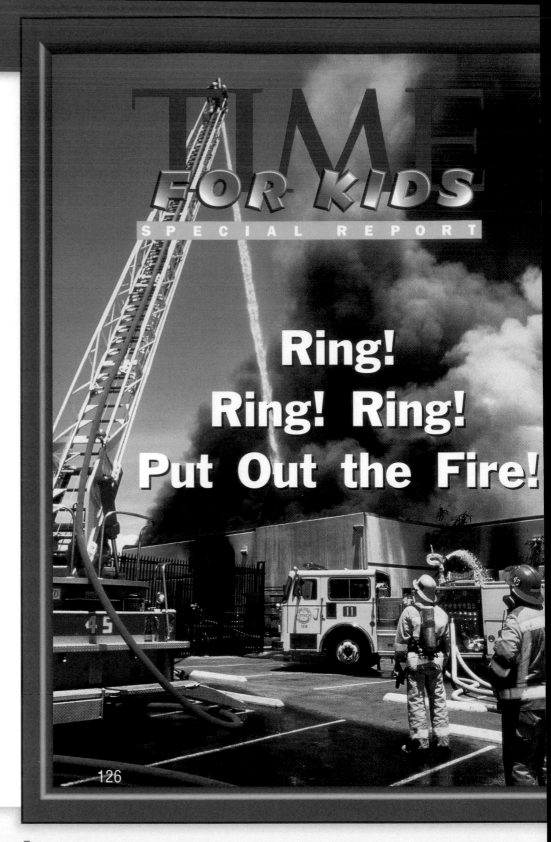

Meeting Individual Needs • Grouping Suggestions for Strategic Reading

EASY	ON-LEVEL	CHALLENGE
Shared Reading Read the story aloud as you track print and model directionality. Invite children to chime in when they see words they know. As you read each page, discuss the photographs.	**Guided Instruction** Ask children to read the story with you. Monitor any difficulties that children may have to determine which numbered prompts to use. Model strategies using the Comprehension prompts as you read the story together. After reading the story with children, have children reread it. See the rereading suggestions on page 128.	**Independent Reading** Have children set purposes before they read. Remind children that as they read, noticing words they know can help them understand the story. Children can also use the questions on page 130 for a group discussion.

How do firefighters do their work? They must ride in a big, red fire truck to get to the fire. The big, red fire truck has lots of things that are used to put out fires. The ladder helps the firefighter get to the hot flames. The engine pumps water through the long fire hose. The fire hose sprays it on the fire.

1

2

127

Comprehension

 ☑ **Phonics** *ai, ay; u-e, o-e, i-e, a-e*

☑ **Apply Make Inferences**

STRATEGIC READING Tell children they will use cutouts to help them understand what they learn from the story. The cutouts will also help them connect the story to the real world.

1 **MAKE INFERENCES** What do you see in the photographs on page 127? (a fire truck, a fire hose pumping water, a firefighter on a ladder) What do these photographs tell us about the work firefighters do? (They ride in a truck. They use ladders and hoses.) Now let's cut out our story cutouts ladder and hose and paste them on the truck. *Story Props*

2 **Phonics** *ai, ay; u-e, o-e, i-e, a-e*
Let's read long *i* words on this page. Remember that the *e* is silent. *(ride, fire)* Now let's read the long *a* words. *(flames, spray)* What is different about these words? (The long *a* is spelled with silent *e* in *flames* and with *ay* in *sprays.*) Can you find a long *o* word? *(hose)* *Graphophonic Cues*

Genre

Narrative Nonfiction

Explain that narrative nonfiction:

- gives facts about a topic in a story format, with real characters and their actions as the plot.

- may include photographs, illustrations, and other graphics, such as charts.

Activity After reading *Ring! Ring! Ring! Put Out the Fire!,* discuss how the story used photographs to present information. Ask children if they have ever seen a place like the one shown. Ask why they think the setting looks realistic.

LANGUAGE SUPPORT

A blackline master of story cutouts can be found in the **Language Support Book**.

LANGUAGE SUPPORT, 176

127

Comprehension

③ MAKE INFERENCES Now let's look at the right-hand photograph on this page. What is the firefighter wearing over his face? (a mask) Why do firefighters need to wear masks? (Responses may vary; for example, to protect themselves, to keep the smoke away, to stay safe.) Let's cut out the clothing items from the story cutouts and paste them on the firefighter. *Story Props*

④ **Phonics** *u-e* Let's read the last sentence on this page: "*The firefighters have masks to stay safe and keep out smoke and…*" hmm, I'm not sure what this word is. Let's blend the sounds together and read it.
f u m(e) s fumes *Graphophonic Cues*

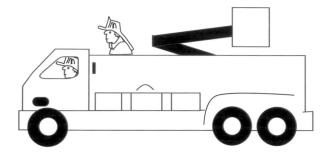

ORGANIZE INFORMATION Ask volunteers to tell what they learned about firefighters and the work they do. Then have children summarize their ideas in a statement about firefighters. *Summarize*

MICHAEL HART/FPG

There is always work that has to be done. The fire trucks have to be clean and ready to go. The firefighters have masks to stay safe and keep out smoke and fumes.

FIND OUT MORE
Visit our website:
www.mhschool.com/reading

*inter***NET**
CONNECTION

128

REREADING FOR *Fluency*

PARTNERS Children who need fluency practice can read with a partner. Ask children to read aloud, alternating sentences. Remind children to track print as they read and to be aware of punctuation marks.

READING RATE When you evaluate reading rate, have children read aloud from the story for one minute. Place a stick-on note after the last word read.

To evaluate children's performance, see the Running Record in the **Fluency Assessment** book.

① Intervention For leveled fluency lessons, passages, and norms charts, see **Skills Intervention Guide**, Part 5, Fluency.

LADDER

Boston LADDER 15

Boston

LEFT: SPENCER GRANT/PHOTO EDIT; FAR LEFT: GWYN KIBBLE/STOCK BOSTON

⑤

Ring! Ring! Ring! Ring! Ring! The fire bell rings, and the firefighters run! They slide down the long pole and put on fire gear. They rush, rush, rush to put out the fire. They can put out the biggest fires. They are very fast! Don't you think they are brave? Would you want to put out big fires one day?

A story from the editors of *TIME FOR KIDS.*

129

Comprehension

⑤ **MAKE INFERENCES** How do you think the firefighters know there is a fire? (They hear the fire bell ringing.) Do you think the firefighters need to work slowly or quickly? (They need to work quickly.) Why do you think they need to work quickly? (Answers will vary.)

Return to Predictions and Purposes

Reread children's predictions about the story. Discuss these predictions, noting which need to be revised. Then ask the children if the story answered the questions they had before they read.

INFORMAL ASSESSMENT

HOW TO ASSESS

Phonics *ai, ay; u-e, o-e, i-e, a-e*
Write the following words on the chalkboard and ask children to read them aloud: *rain, day, fumes, pole, slide, safe.*

MAKE INFERENCES Ask children how they think firefighters feel about the work they do.

FOLLOW UP

Phonics *ai, ay; u-e, o-e, i-e, a-e*
Continue to model the blending of sounds in long vowel words for children who are having difficulty.

MAKE INFERENCES Children who are having difficulty can look at the pictures in the story and use the story cutouts to make more inferences about firefighters.

LITERARY RESPONSE

QUICK-WRITE Have children write a short letter to a firefighter about what they do.

ORAL RESPONSE Have children use their letters for discussion:
• Why is it important for firefighters to wear special uniforms and hats?
• Why do fire trucks have sirens?

RESEARCH AND INQUIRY Have children find out other facts about firefighters to share with the class.

*inter*NET **CONNECTION** For more information or activities on occupations that help people, go to **www.mhschool.com/reading.**

SENTENCE STRIPS Children can use strips 1–27 to retell the selection.

> 1
> How do firefighters do their work?

> 2
> They must ride in a big,

Story Questions

Help children read the questions. Discuss possible answers:

Answers:

1. The engine pumps water through the fire hose. *Literal*

2. The fire truck's sirens will blow and bells will ring. *Inferential/Make Inferences*

3. Firefighters lift heavy equipment and sometimes they carry people and animals to rescue them. *Inferential/Make Inferences*

4. Firefighters put out fires and keep the trucks and hoses clean and safe. *Critical/Summarize*

5. Firefighters wear masks and heavy gear; vets do not. Firefighters use ladders and hoses; vets use medical equipment. *Critical/Reading Across Texts*

Compare Two Jobs Ask children to cite specific details as they describe the job of the firefighter, comparing the job of another person they know about. For a full lesson on writing that compares, see pages 133M–133N.

Story Questions & Activities

READ TOGETHER

1. What pumps water through the fire hose?

2. How can you tell if a fire truck is going to a fire?

3. Why must firefighters be strong?

4. Tell about the work a firefighter does.

5. What are some differences between the work of a firefighter and the work of a vet?

Compare Two Jobs

Think about a firefighter and a nurse. How are their jobs the same?

Meeting Individual Needs

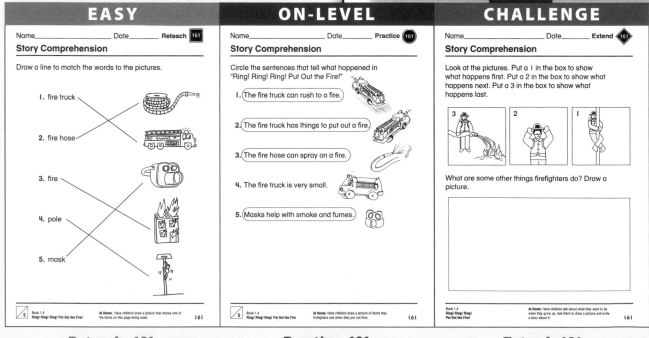

EASY

Name_____ Date_____ **Reteach** 161
Story Comprehension

Draw a line to match the words to the pictures.

1. fire truck
2. fire hose
3. fire
4. pole
5. mask

Book 1.4
Ring! Ring! Ring! Put Out the Fire!
At Home: Have children draw a picture that shows one of the items on this page being used. 161

Reteach, 161

ON-LEVEL

Name_____ Date_____ **Practice** 161
Story Comprehension

Circle the sentences that tell what happened in "Ring! Ring! Ring! Put Out the Fire!"

1. (The fire truck can rush to a fire.)
2. (The fire truck has things to put out a fire.)
3. (The fire hose can spray on a fire.)
4. The fire truck is very small.
5. (Masks help with smoke and fumes.)

Book 1.4
Ring! Ring! Ring! Put Out the Fire
At Home: Have children draw a picture of items that firefighters use when they put out fires. 161

Practice, 161

CHALLENGE

Name_____ Date_____ **Extend** 161
Story Comprehension

Look at the pictures. Put a 1 in the box to show what happens first. Put a 2 in the box to show what happens next. Put a 3 in the box to show what happens last.

What are some other things firefighters do? Draw a picture.

Book 1.4
Ring! Ring! Ring! Put Out the Fire!
At Home: Have children talk about what they want to be when they grow up. Ask them to draw a picture and write a story about it. 161

Extend, 161

Make a Fire Safety Badge

Make yourself a fire
safety badge.
Color it and cut it out.
Wear it on your shirt.

I know how
to keep safe
from fire.

I know how to
keep safe from fire.

I know how to keep
safe from fire.

Find Out More

Find out the best
way to exit from
school and your
home in case
of a fire.

131

DAY 3 **Fluency** Write a list of
long *u: u-e; o: o-e; i: i-e;
a: a-e; a: ai, ay* words. Point to
each word, asking children to
blend the sounds silently. Ask a
volunteer to read each word.

Phonics CD-ROM

Story Activities

Make a Fire Safety Badge

Materials: cutouts of safety badges (made of
oaktag or poster board), paints and paint-
brushes, or felt-tipped markers

Read the directions aloud. Help children who
have questions. First, ask children if they have
ever seen firefighters at work. Invite children
to talk about what they saw. Was a building
in their neighborhood on fire? Did the children hear sirens and bells? What were the
firefighters wearing?

ONE Have children design and color their
own fire safety badges. When they are
finished, children can wear them on their shirts.

Find Out More

RESEARCH AND INQUIRY Divide
children into pairs and ask them to
PARTNERS find out more about fire safety. Have
partners find out the best way to exit from
the school and their homes in case of a fire.
Have each pair report its findings.

 **interNET CONNECTION** To access Web sites on
firefighters go to
www.mhschool.com/reading.

FORMAL ASSESSMENT

See the Selection and Unit Assessment
Tests for Book 1.4.

131

Study Skills

CHARTS

OBJECTIVES

Children will learn to read a tally chart to count votes.

Remind children that they have just read a story about the job of a firefighter. Tell them that now they will think about different kinds of jobs, and talk about what some children want to do when they grow up.

Display **Teaching Chart 120**. Have children read the title of the tally chart. Then invite children to describe what they notice about the chart, such as the illustrations and the column with the number of votes. Together read the words using picture clues. Point to each face and ask children to name the job. Have them explain what each person does. Then help children read the questions below the tally chart, encouraging them to identify the labels that answer each question.

STUDY SKILLS

READ TOGETHER

Vote and Tally

Children voted on what they want to be when they grow up. This tally shows their votes.

When I Grow Up

Job	Number of children
firefighter	IIII
baker	II
vet	IIII
teacher	IIII I

Look at the Tally

❶ How many children want to be vets?

❷ Which job did the most children want to do?

Meeting Individual Needs

EASY

Name_____ Date_____ Reteach 162

A Chart

A vote and tally **chart** helps you figure out the results of an election.

Child	Number of Votes
Jill	IIIIIIIII
Will	IIIIIII
Jim	IIII
Kim	IIIIII

Choose the correct answer and write it on the line.

1. How many votes did Jim get? **four**
   four   six

2. How many votes did Jill get? **nine**
   seven   nine

3. Who had the fewest votes? **Jim**
   Jill   Jim

4. Which child had six votes? **Kim**
   Kim   Will

At Home: Have children read the tally sheet aloud and determine who won the election.
162   Book 1.4 / 4
Ring! Ring! Ring! Put Out the Fire!

ON-LEVEL

Name_____ Date_____ Practice 162

A Chart

Jon's class voted about where to go on a picnic. They chose from four places. This **chart** tells you how many votes each place got.

Place	Number of Votes
Mill Pond Park	IIIIIIIIII
Fish Creek	IIIIIIII
Sand Beach	IIIII
Stone Hills	IIIIII

1. How many votes did Fish Creek get? **seven**

2. How many votes did Stone Hills get? **six**

3. Which place got the most votes? **Mill Pond Park**

4. Which place got the least votes? **Sand Beach**

At Home: Ask children to add the total number of votes to determine how many students were in the class.
162   Book 1.4 / 4
Ring! Ring! Ring! Put Out the Fire!

CHALLENGE

Name_____ Date_____ Extend 162

Use a Chart

What does a firefighter need? Read the list.
Use ✓ check marks to fill in the chart.

Answers may vary.

What Does a Firefighter Need?	A Firefighter Needs . . .	A Firefighter Does Not Need . . .
hose	✓	
cat		✓
fire truck	✓	
iron		✓
fire hat	✓	
horse		✓
sneakers		✓
boots	✓	
lamp		✓
ladder	✓	

Use / tally marks to answer.
How many things does a firefighter need? ⊬⊬
How many things does a firefighter not need? ⊬⊬

At Home: Invite children to add to the list any other items that a firefighter might need.
162   Book 1.4
Ring! Ring! Ring! Put Out the Fire!

Reteach, 162   **Practice, 162**   **Extend, 162**

TEST POWER

The Fireplace

The man came in from outside.
He shook the snow off his boots.
He had a bundle of wood in his arms.
He put some wood on the fire.
Then, he put the fire screen in front.
The fire in the fireplace was warm.
It warmed the man's toes.
The man sat down in his chair.
He rocked forward and backward.
His cat came and sat on his lap.
Then, they took a little nap together.

What time of year is it
in this story?
○ Summer
● Winter

Read both answer choices. Which one fits the story?

133

Test Power

Read the Page

Explain to children that you will be reading this story as a group. You will read the story, and they will follow in their books.

Request that children put pens, pencils, and markers away, since they will not be writing in their books.

Discuss the Question

Discuss with children the kinds of things that might indicate the season. If it's very warm, it is probably summer. If it's snowing, it is probably winter.

Test-Tip

Sometimes you can use the answer choices to help you locate the answer in the passage. Look at each choice and see which one is better.

ITBS/TEST PREPARATION

TERRA NOVA/TEST PREPARATION

SAT 9/TEST PREPARATION

Self-Selected Reading
Leveled Books

☑  **Phonics**

- Review long *u: u-e,* long *o: o-e,* long *i: i-e,* long *a: a-e,* long *a: ai, ay.*

☑ **Comprehension**

- Review cause and effect.
- Review make inferences.

Answers will vary. Have children cite examples from the story to support their answers.

EASY

Story Questions for Selected Reading

1. Who is the main character in the story?
2. Which illustrations did you like best? Why?
3. How was the story problem solved?
4. If you could be a character in the story, who would you be? Why?
5. Did you like the story? Why or why not?

Draw a Picture

Draw a picture for the selected story.

EASY

UNIT SKILLS REVIEW

☑  **Phonics**

☑ **Comprehension**

Help children self-select an Easy Book to read and apply phonics and comprehension skills.

Guided Reading

PREVIEW AND PREDICT Discuss the illustrations in the beginning of the book. As you take the **picture walk**, have children predict what the story will be about. List their ideas.

SET PURPOSES Have children write or draw why they want to read the book. Have them share their purposes.

READ THE BOOK Use the following items to guide children's reading, or to discuss after they have read the story independently. Model blending and other phonics and decoding strategies for children who need help.

Let's look at the pictures. Where does this story take place? *Use Illustrations*

Can you find a word in the story with the long *a* sound spelled *ai, ay,* or *a-e*? Let's say the word aloud. *Phonics and Decoding*

What happens at the end of the story? *Summarize*

RETURN TO PREDICTIONS AND PURPOSES Discuss children's predictions. Ask which were close to the book contents and why. Have children review their purposes for reading. Did they find out what they wanted to know?

LITERARY RESPONSE Have children discuss questions such as the following:

- Which part of the book was most interesting?
- What might be another good title for the book?

 **Phonics CD-ROM**

Self-Selected Reading
Leveled Books

INDEPENDENT

UNIT SKILLS REVIEW

☑

☑ **Comprehension**

Help children self-select an Independent Book to read and apply phonics and comprehension skills.

Guided Reading

PREVIEW AND PREDICT Discuss the illustrations in the beginning of the book. As you take the **picture walk**, have children predict what the story will be about. List their ideas.

SET PURPOSES Have children write or draw why they want to read the book. Have them share their purposes.

READ THE BOOK Use the following items to guide children's reading, or to discuss after they have read the story independently. Model blending and other phonics and decoding strategies for children who need help.

Can you find a word in the story with the long *a* sound spelled *ai, ay,* or *a-e* ? Let's say the word aloud. *Phonics and Decoding*

Do you think this story is real or make-believe? *Distinguish Between Fantasy and Reality*

Think about the story. Has something similar happened to you? *Make Inferences*

RETURN TO PREDICTIONS AND PURPOSES Discuss children's predictions. Ask which were close to the book's contents and why. Have children review their purposes for reading. Did they find out what they wanted to know?

LITERARY RESPONSE Have children discuss questions such as the following:

- Which part of the book was most interesting?
- What might be another good title for the book?

 CD-ROM

- Review long *u: u-e*, long *o: o-e*, long *i: i-e*, long *a: a-e*, long *a: ai, ay*.

☑ **Comprehension**

- Review cause and effect.
- Review make inferences.

Answers will vary. Have children cite examples from the story to support their answers.

INDEPENDENT

Story Questions for Selected Reading

1. Where does this story take place?
2. Did the story teach you anything new? What?
3. Did you like the ending? Why or why not?
4. What caused the main event to happen?
5. How is the main character like you? How is he or she different?

Draw a Picture

Draw a picture for the selected story.

Self-Selected Reading
Leveled Books

- Review long *u: u-e*, long *o: o-e*, long *i: i-e*, long *a: a-e*, long *a: ai*, *ay*.

☑ **Comprehension**

- Review cause and effect.

- Review make inferences.
  Answers will vary. Have children cite examples from the story to support their answers.

CHALLENGE

Story Questions for Selected Reading

1. If you could change something about the story, what would it be?

2. Did you learn anything new from the story?

3. If you could talk to the author, what questions would you ask?

4. Did anything surprise you about the story? What was it?

5. Could this story be made into a TV show? Why or why not?

Draw a Picture

Draw a picture for the selected story.

CHALLENGE

UNIT SKILLS REVIEW

☑

☑ **Comprehension**

Help children self-select a Challenge Book to read and apply phonics and comprehension skills.

Guided Reading

PREVIEW AND PREDICT Discuss the illustrations in the beginning of the book. As you take the **picture walk**, have children predict what the story will be about. List their ideas.

SET PURPOSES Have children write or draw why they want to read the book. Have them share their purposes.

READ THE BOOK Use the following items to guide children's reading, or to discuss after they have read the story independently. Model blending and other phonics and decoding strategies for children who need help.

What happens at the end of the story? *Summarize*

Do you think this story is real or make-believe? Why? *Distinguish Between Fantasy and Reality*

Think about the story. Has something similar happened in your own life? *Make Inferences*

RETURN TO PREDICTIONS AND PURPOSES Discuss children's predictions. Ask which were close to the book's contents and why. Have children review their purposes for reading. Did they find out what they wanted to know?

LITERARY RESPONSE Have children discuss questions such as the following:

- Which part of the book was most interesting?

- What might be another good title for the book?

 **CD-ROM**

Bringing Groups Together

Anthology and Leveled Books

Connecting Texts

CLASS DISCUSSION	CHARACTER WEB
Lead a discussion of how the unit theme Let's Find Out! applies to each of the stories: • What did the characters in each story find out? • Is there anything new you would like to find out? Explain what it is.	Have children create a web for several Leveled Books or Anthology selections they have read. Have them compare the main characters from the stories. Who are they? What did they find out? A sample web is shown here.

Spot's Trick
Spot finds out how to do a trick.

Fall Is Fun
A girl finds out what happens in the fall.

Let's Find Out!

The Big Secret
Dan finds out what the big secret is.

Who Took the Farmer's Hat?
The farmer finds out what happened to his hat.

Viewing/Representing

GROUP PRESENTATIONS Ask children to choose their favorite book. Divide them into groups, one for each of the four books. Have children create a skit for one scene from the story. Have a narrator introduce each scene.

AUDIENCE RESPONSE Have children explain what they found interesting about each performance. Suggest that children respond by telling the "actors" what they liked about each skit.

Research and Inquiry

MORE ABOUT FINDING OUT! Tell children that they are going to be reporters to find out more about one another. Ask: Is there something new you would like to find out about your classmates? Divide children into pairs and have them interview one another. Suggest that they take notes to remember the information. Children might use the following questions: How old are you? Where were you born? Where do you live? Who do you live with?

interNET CONNECTION Have children log on to *www.mhschool.com/reading* to access Web sites about well-known people.

 Children can write and draw what they learned in their journals.

JOURNAL

OBJECTIVES

Children will review cause and effect.

....

MATERIALS

• Teaching Chart 121

Skills Finder

Cause & Effect

Introduce	B4: 37I-J
Review	B4: 65I-J, 133E-F
Test	Book 4
Maintain	B5: 17, 251, 267

TEACHING TIP

CAUSE AND EFFECT

During the course of the day, if any cause-and-effect instances occur, point them out immediately. (Examples: The bell rings so the class is over; it's raining outside so everyone stays inside for recess.)

Review Cause and Effect

PREPARE

Review the Concept
Tell children that when certain things happen, they often cause other things to happen. This is called *cause and effect*. Ask: If you stand out in the rain, what will happen? (You will get wet.) That is the effect. What was the cause? (standing in the rain)

TEACH

Identify Causes and Their Effects
Display **Teaching Chart 121**. Ask volunteers to read the sentences about the puppy. Discuss with children cause and effect in the sentences; then, if necessary, model the skill.

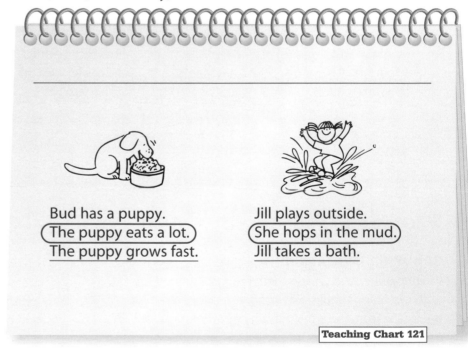

Bud has a puppy.
(The puppy eats a lot.)
The puppy grows fast.

Jill plays outside.
(She hops in the mud.)
Jill takes a bath.

Teaching Chart 121

MODEL From these sentences, I know that the puppy eats a lot and grows fast. Why does the puppy grow fast? It eats a lot. This must be the cause. What happens because it eats a lot? It grows fast. This must be the effect.

Have volunteers circle the sentence that tells the cause, and underline the sentence that tells the effect. Repeat the procedure for the second set of sentences.

Use Cause and Effect Examples

Put two columns on the chalkboard, labeled CAUSE and EFFECT, with an arrow between them. Read the following sets of sentences aloud. Have children discuss which sentence is the cause and which is the effect. As children answer, write the sentences in the correct columns.

▶ **Linguistic**

CAUSE ⟶	EFFECT
I like milk.	I pour milk in my mug.
The cat is afraid of the dog.	The cat runs away from the dog.
I sit in the tub.	I get clean.
It is dark.	I cannot see.
I sing a song for my mom and dad.	My mom and dad clap.

ASSESS/CLOSE

Create Cause/Effect Examples

Have children work in small groups to try to come up with examples of cause and effect. Then have volunteers share their examples orally with the class. Write some of their examples on the chalkboard.

DAY 4

Writing Have children choose two CVC*e* pattern or double-vowel pattern words and create a rhyming couplet with the words. Children can illustrate their rhymes.

ALTERNATE TEACHING STRATEGY

CAUSE AND EFFECT

For a different approach to teaching this skill, see page T67.

i Intervention ▶ Skills Intervention Guide, for direct instruction and extra practice in Cause and Effect

Meeting Individual Needs for Comprehension

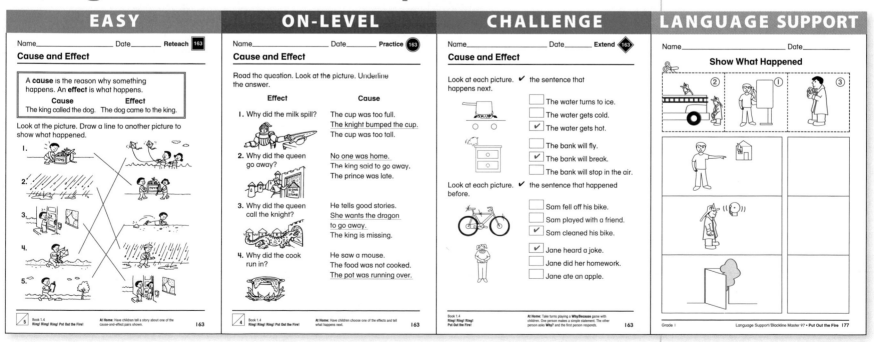

EASY	ON-LEVEL	CHALLENGE	LANGUAGE SUPPORT
Reteach, 163	Practice, 163	Extend, 163	Language Support, 177

Children will review making inferences.

MATERIALS
• Teaching Chart 122

Skills Finder

Make Inferences

Introduce	B4: 95I-J
Review	B4: 123I-J, 133G-H
Test	Book 4
Maintain	B5: 27, 53, 171, 199, 279

TEACHING TIP

MAKING INFERENCES
Some children may be timid about "guessing" for fear that they will be wrong. Encourage them to take part by telling them that there really isn't any such thing as a right or wrong guess. Some guesses are better than others, but all guesses are just what they're called—guesses.

Review Make Inferences

PREPARE

Review the Concept   Remind children that sometimes we can look at a picture or read words and make a guess about something. Explain that when readers do this it's called "making an inference." Tell children they can make inferences about events or characters in a story in order to understand a story better.

TEACH

Make Inferences About the Weather   Display **Teaching Chart 122**. Point to the first picture and read the sentences.

Bob wants to go outside.
He puts on his <u>coat</u> and <u>boots</u>.
He puts on his <u>hat</u> and <u>gloves</u>.

Peg wears a <u>party hat</u>.
Her mom <u>bakes a cake</u>.
Her dad <u>brings a gift</u>.

Jack wants to <u>play a game</u>.
He has a <u>bat</u> and <u>ball</u>.
He wears a <u>cap</u>.

Teaching Chart 122

MODEL In the first picture, I see a boy looking out the window. The sentence says he wants to go outside. The next sentence says he is putting on his coat and boots. Then it says he is putting on his hat and gloves. Even though I can't see out the window, and the sentences don't tell me, I can guess that it is very cold outside, and maybe icy or snowing.

Read and discuss each example with children. In all three examples, ask volunteers to underline the words or phrases that help them make their inference.

PRACTICE

Make More Inferences

GROUP

Separate the class into three groups, one group for each set of pictures on **Teaching Chart 122**. Ask each group to make other inferences about the set of pictures. Prompt them by asking questions. (Examples: Does Bob like cold weather? Where do you think Bob was going? Why is the girl wearing a party hat? Why do you think her dad is bringing her a present?) ▶ **Linguistic**

ASSESS/CLOSE

Make Inferences Using Pictures

Have small groups create their own two-picture stories. The first picture could have someone (a person or animal) preparing or waiting for an event. The second picture should show what happens after that. (Remind children that facial expressions can help make the meaning of their pictures clear.) Then have groups challenge each other to make inferences about the pictures. The class can then create sentences to describe the events in the pictures.

DAY 5 **Letter Substitution**
Using letter and long-vowel cards, have pairs of children build *rule*. Taking turns, one child is to change a letter to build a new word, asking the partner to read it.

ALTERNATE TEACHING STRATEGY

MAKE INFERENCES

For a different approach to teaching this skill, see page T73.

i **Intervention** ▶ **Skills**
Intervention Guide, for direct instruction and extra practice in Making Inferences

---

Meeting Individual Needs for Comprehension

EASY	ON-LEVEL	CHALLENGE	LANGUAGE SUPPORT

EASY

Name_____ Date_____ Reteach 164
Make Inferences

> You can use what you read and what you already know to answer questions about stories.

Read each story and look at the pictures. Circle the word or the picture clue that answers each question about the story.

Mom and Dad gave Tara a present.
Tara sees a toy animal.
The animal has a great big body.
The nose is very long.
The ears are big.
The tail is not very long.
Tara said, "This is great!"

1. How old is Tara?
   (6) 7 8

2. Whose birthday is it?
   Mom's Dad's (Tara's)

3. What kind of toy animal is the present?
   donkey (elephant) rabbit

4. Does Tara like the present?
   (yes) no

164 At Home: Have children ask another question about the story. Book 1.4 Ring! Ring! Ring! Put Out the Fire!

ON-LEVEL

Name_____ Date_____ Practice 164
Make Inferences

Read the sentences. Circle the word that tells how the person might feel. Then write the word on the line.

1. Jill wants a new toy.
   Her mom says no.
   Jill is _____.
   (sad) happy excited   **sad**

2. Ann loves animals.
   Dad brings her a hamster.
   Ann is _____.
   sad mad (happy)   **happy**

3. Ray wants a snack.
   He asks for an apple.
   Ray is _____.
   silly (hungry) happy   **hungry**

4. Dad looks at the clock.
   He yawns.
   Dad is _____.
   sad happy (sleepy)   **sleepy**

164 At Home: Have children cut out pictures of a person from a magazine and then tell something about the person. Book 1.4 Ring! Ring! Ring! Put Out the Fire!

CHALLENGE

Name_____ Date_____ Extend 164
Make Inferences

Look at the chart. Read the words. Make the ☐ red if it is a word that tells about a firefighter.

brave	June	trained
strong	good	while
busy	lake	hard-working
when	fast	helpful

Shade in these spaces: brave, strong, trained, good, helpful, busy, hard-working, fast

164 At Home: Invite children to think about other brave or helpful people. Who are they? Ask children to make drawings of them. Book 1.4 Ring! Ring! Ring! Put Out the Fire!

LANGUAGE SUPPORT

Name_____ Date_____
Look For Clues

There is a fire.	The fire is out.
The smoke is bad.	Get the ladder.

The fire is out. | The smoke is bad.

There is a fire. | Get the ladder.

178 Put Out the Fire • Language Support/Blackline Master 98 Grade 1

Reteach, 164　　**Practice, 164**　　**Extend, 164**　　**Language Support, 178**

OBJECTIVES

Children will:

- read words with the inflectional endings -s and -es.
- understand the concept of root words and suffixes.

MATERIALS

- Teaching Chart 123
- index cards

Skills Finder

Inflectional Endings -s, -es

Introduce	B1: 31K-L
Review	B4: 37K-L, 133I-J
Test	Book 4

TEACHING TIP

INFLECTIONAL ENDINGS Point out that the endings -s and -es don't always signal a plural noun. They can also be added to verbs, as in *taps* and *wishes*.

Review Inflectional Endings -s, -es

PREPARE

Review the Concept

Write the word *truck* on the chalkboard. Draw a simple truck on the board, or hold up a picture of a truck. Say: *Here is a truck.* Draw two or more trucks, or show children a scene in which there are many trucks. Say: *Here are many trucks.* Then repeat the procedure using *bench.* Explain that adding the suffix -s or -es to a word shows there is more than one.

TEACH

Identify Root Words

Track the sentence on **Teaching Chart 123** as you read it with children: *The flames are very hot.* Then point to *flames* and model for children how understanding inflectional endings can help them read.

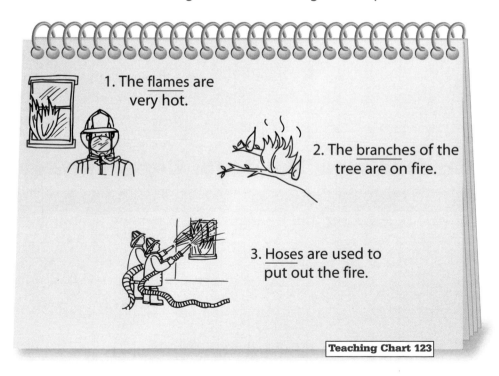

1. The flames are very hot.

2. The branches of the tree are on fire.

3. Hoses are used to put out the fire.

Teaching Chart 123

MODEL I can use what I already know to help me read words I don't recognize. I know the root word *flame.* I can see that the last letter of the words is -s. I know that sometimes when this letter appears at the end of a word, it means that there is more than one. The word is *flames.*

Repeat for the other two sentences. Have children come up and underline the root word and circle the suffix in each sentence.

PRACTICE

Add -s and -es

GROUP

Distribute index cards to children. Then write *flames, branches,* and *hoses* on the chalkboard. Have children read each word, identifying the part of the word they know first. Then ask children to write each word on an index card so that the suffix *-s* or *-es* appears after a dotted line. Have pairs practice reading the words. ▶ **Kinesthetic/Linguistic**

flame : s   branch : es   hose : s

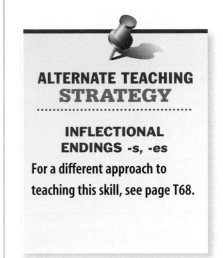

ALTERNATE TEACHING STRATEGY

INFLECTIONAL ENDINGS -s, -es

For a different approach to teaching this skill, see page T68.

ASSESS/CLOSE

Identify -s, es Words

Invite children to use their word cards from the previous activity. Say some sentences aloud, repeating the word on the card after the sentence is read. Tell children to hold up the card for that word. Point out that they may only need to show part of the word by folding the card back along the dotted line, or they may need to show the whole word. Use the following sentences:

• Don't get too close to the flames. (flames)

• The branches of the tree are broken. (branches)

• Let's water the grass with the hose. (hose)

ⓘ Intervention ▶ Skills Intervention Guide, for direct instruction and extra practice in Inflectional Endings -s and -es

Meeting Individual Needs for Vocabulary

EASY	ON-LEVEL	CHALLENGE	LANGUAGE SUPPORT

EASY

Name_____ Date_____ Reteach **165**

Inflectional Endings -ed, -s, -es

Add **-ed** to tell what happened in the past.
Last week, Jay wash**ed** his cars.

Add **-s** or **-es** to tell what one person or thing is doing now.
Today Jay wax**es** his cars.

Circle **-ed** words that tell what happened in the past. Underline **-s** or **-es** words that tell what happens now.

1. Tom (fixed) the van.
2. The ship (sailed) away.
3. Beth mends her pants.
4. Jane (wiped) the glass.
5. Dad tosses the salad.
6. Mom plays with the cat.
7. The firefighter sprays the flames.
8. Max (fetched) the stick.

Book 1.4
Ring! Ring! Ring! Put Out the Fire!   At Home: Help children to make a list of the verbs from this page that includes all three forms of the word such as fold, folds, folded.   165

Reteach, 165

ON-LEVEL

Name_____ Date_____ Practice **165**

Inflectional Endings -ed, -s, -es

Add **-s** or **-es** to tell what one person or thing does **now.** Add **-ed** to tell what happened in the **past.**

Look at the underlined word in each sentence. Then look at the word after the sentence. Add **-s, -es,** or **-ed** to the underlined word and write the new word.

1. Dad braid Dale's hair.   past   braided
2. Lane grill the fish.   now   grills
3. Nash and I plant grapes.   past   planted
4. Gram wish for a soft quilt.   now   wishes
5. Jen chain up her bike.   past   chained
6. Pat miss the bus.   now   misses

Book 1.4
Ring! Ring! Ring! Put Out the Fire!   At Home: Choose two sentences and act them out with children.   165

Practice, 165

CHALLENGE

Name_____ Date_____ Extend ◆**165**

Inflectional Endings -s, -es

Choose the right word. Write it in the blank.

A firefighter can put out a (fire fires) ____fire____.

My mom (smile smiles) ____smiles____ at me.

How many (grape grapes) ____grapes____ can you hold?

The (fume fumes) ____fumes____ made me sick.

There were (flame flames) ____flames____ in the fireplace.

The firefighter (chop chops) ____chops____ down the door.

Book 1.4
Ring! Ring! Ring! Put Out the Fire!   At Home: On individual index cards, write -es, -s, and these base words: flame, muffin, fire, can, fume, and grape. Turn the word cards face down on a table. Have the child pick a card and point to the correct ending.   165

Extend, 165

LANGUAGE SUPPORT

Name_____ Date_____

Word Math

✂ [saved | branches | firefighters | dripped]

drip + p + ed =   [dripped]

branch + es =   [branches]

save - e + ed =   [saved]

firefighter + s=   [firefighters]

Grade 1   Language Support/Blackline Master 99 • Put Out the Fire **179**

Language Support, 179

Review Inflectional Endings -er, -est

TESTED OBJECTIVES

Children will read words that end in the suffixes *-er* and *-est*.

....

MATERIALS

• Teaching Chart 124

• index cards

Skills Finder

Inflectional Endings -er, -est

Introduce	B4: 95K-L
Review	B4: 123K-L, 133K-L
Test	Book 4

TEACHING TIP

INFLECTIONAL END-INGS You might want to point out to children that the *-er* ending is used to compare two objects, while *-est* words are used to compare three or more objects. You can ask questions to illustrate this: *Who has the bigger desk, Sarah or the teacher? Which window in the room is the widest?*

PREPARE

Review the Concept Write the word *big* on the chalkboard. Display a picture of a big animal, such as a dog. Say: *This is a big animal.* Then show a picture of a larger animal, such as a lion. Write *bigger* on the board and say: *This animal is bigger.* Continue the process with an even larger animal, such as an elephant, to illustrate the word *biggest.* Explain that sometimes the final consonant is doubled when suffixes such as *-er* or *-est* are added.

TEACH

Identify Base Words Track the sentences on **Teaching Chart 124** as you read them aloud. Ask: *Which fire is the smallest?* Point to the word *smaller* and ask children if they recognize the root word. (*small*)

Jane made a fire. Brad made a smaller fire. Nick made the smallest fire.

Teaching Chart 124

MODEL I can use what I know to help me read difficult words. I know the root word *small.* I can see the last two letters of the word are *-er.* I know that sometimes when these two letters appear together at the end of a word it means "more." The word is *smaller,* which means more small.

Invite a volunteer to point out the root word in *smallest.* Then underline the root word *small* in both phrases.

Read Words with -er, -est

PARTNERS

Give each pair of children an index card with an *-er* or *-est* word, such as *hottest, safer, faster, longer, bravest*. Have each pair practice saying the word aloud. Then have the children say what the root word is. Ask each pair to create a sentence with the word. Lastly, have volunteers read their sentences aloud to the rest of the class.

▶ **Linguistic**

hottest

Use the Words in Context

Now invite pairs of children to make up stories using two of the words from the above activity. Have volunteers tell their stories aloud. They may also wish to act them out. Call on other children to identify the root words.

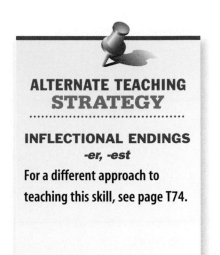

ALTERNATE TEACHING STRATEGY

INFLECTIONAL ENDINGS
-er, -est

For a different approach to teaching this skill, see page T74.

Intervention ▶ **Skills**

Intervention Guide, for direct instruction and extra practice in Inflectional Endings *-er* and *-est*

Meeting Individual Needs for Vocabulary

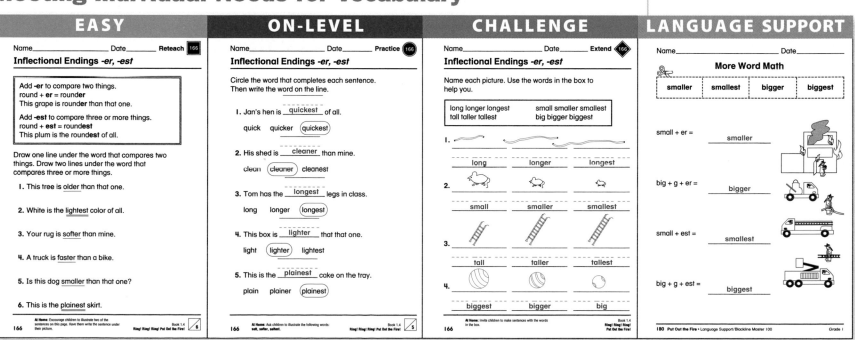

EASY	ON-LEVEL	CHALLENGE	LANGUAGE SUPPORT
Reteach, 166	Practice, 166	Extend, 166	Language Support, 180

133L

Handwriting CD-ROM

GRAMMAR/SPELLING CONNECTIONS

See the 5-Day Grammar and Usage Plan on More Contractions with *Not,* pages 133O–133P.

See the 5-Day Spelling Plan on Cumulative Review, pages 133Q–133R.

TEACHING TIP

Technology

Many word-processing programs and printers allow different colors of type within the same document. If the machines at your school have this capability, encourage children to select a specific color of type for each of the subjects that they are comparing.

Writing That Compares

Prewrite

WRITE A SPEECH Present this writing assignment: Pretend someone has asked you whether he or she should become a firefighter or a police officer. Write a speech comparing how the two jobs are alike and different. Give details about each job and why both are important.

BRAINSTORM IDEAS Have children brainstorm about what it means to be firefighters and police officers. Also have children discuss what a firefighter and a police officer wear and the vehicles they drive.

STRATEGY: TALK WITH A PARTNER Have children practice giving impromptu speeches to partners. As they give their speeches, have the listeners make notes for comments and questions afterwards. Suggest the following:

• What do a firefighter and police officer do that is the same and different?

• Did you understand everything the speaker said?

• Do you think the speaker left out anything important?

Draft

WRITE THE SPEECH Guide children to recall the main points from their partner exercise, and use them to begin drafting full sentences. Remind them to describe the ways the jobs are alike and different in detail.

Revise

ELABORATING Guide children to assess their drafts to make sure that they have included details in their writing that compares. Remind them that providing details is a good way to explain how two things are alike and different.

Have children work in small groups to read their speeches aloud.

Edit/Proofread

CHECK FOR ERRORS Children should reread their speeches for spelling, grammar, and punctuation.

Publish

SHARE THE SPEECHES Children can present their speeches to the whole class. Have classmates tell what they liked best about each presenter's speech.

Two Important Jobs

Firefighters and police officers have important jobs. They both are brave and help people. They also both wear uniforms.

A firefighter wears a helmet, a heavy coat, and boots with his uniform. The firefighter rides on a truck that has a ladder and a siren.

A police officer wears a hat and a badge with his uniform. The police officer rides in a special car that also has a siren.

Firefighters and police officers wear different uniforms. A firefighter rides in a truck, but a police officer rides in a car. But a firefighter and a police officer both help people.

Pamela Green

Presentation Ideas

MAKE A CAREER CHART Have children make a chart that shows a picture of a firefighter and a picture of a police officer. Ask them to include objects that belong to each person in their drawing.

▶ **Viewing/Representing**

ACT OUT A TV NEWS REPORT Ask volunteers to put on a play about an emergency. Pick a child to be the television news reporter.

The reporter should interview the firefighters and police officers at the scene.

▶ **Speaking/Listening**

Consider children's creative efforts, possibly adding a plus (+) for originality, wit, and imagination.

Scoring Rubric			
Excellent	**Good**	**Fair**	**Unsatisfactory**
4: The writer • presents full sentences. • effectively organizes ideas and clearly compares points. • provides many vivid details drawn from real life.	**3:** The writer • presents full sentences. • presents well-organized ideas and clear comparisons. • provides some details drawn from real life.	**2:** The writer • may not always use full sentences. • may show trouble with organizing ideas. • provides few or vague details.	**1:** The writer • may not grasp the task to compare. • may not use full sentences. • may present vague or irrelevant ideas and details.

0: The writer leaves the page blank or fails to respond to the writing task. The writer does not address the topic or simply paraphrases the prompt. The response is illegible or incoherent.

Meeting Individual Needs for Writing

EASY	ON-LEVEL	CHALLENGE
Draw a Fire Scene Have children pretend that they are present at the scene of a fire. Have them draw what they see. Then have them write a few sentences describing their drawings.	**Write About Fighting a Fire** Ask children to pretend they are firefighters and the alarm rings. Have them describe the events that occur when they are going to fight the fire, using as many details as possible.	**Make a Journal Entry** Have children think about the house they live in. Have them write a paragraph explaining how their family would evacuate the house in the event of a fire. Have them include possible escape routes and where the family would meet once they were outside and safe.

Listening and Speaking

LISTENING STRATEGIES
Encourage children to listen carefully to what the firefighters and police officers say so they can decide which job they think is more interesting.

SPEAKING STRATEGIES
Remind children to speak clearly when they tell which job they think is more interesting, so that their fellow speakers and the rest of the class can understand them. Encourage them to use as many details from their own speech and the TV news report as they can.

LANGUAGE SUPPORT

ESL Children acquiring English may have difficulty imagining themselves as speechmakers. Have them work with a fluent partner, who can help them put their thoughts into English.

PORTFOLIO Invite children to include their speeches about firefighters and police officers in their portfolios.

5 Day Grammar and Usage Plan

LANGUAGE SUPPORT

ESL Write *was not, were not, do not,* and *did not* on the chalkboard. Then erase the *o* in each word, add an apostrophe, and form the contractions *wasn't, weren't, don't,* and *didn't.* Have children repeat each word as you pronounce it.

DAILY LANGUAGE ACTIVITIES

Write the Daily Language Activities on the chalkboard each day or use **Transparency 20.** Have students correct the sentences orally.

Day 1
1. The men werent there yet. weren't
2. The ladder wasnt short. wasn't
3. We werent here. weren't

Day 2
1. Jim didnt start the fire. didn' t
2. Dont put that out! Don't
3. The hoses werent in the truck. weren't

Day 3
1. The fire wasnt going out. wasn't
2. The trucks werent clean. weren't
3. The men didnt have their masks. didn't

Day 4
1. I dont want to go. don't
2. The smoke wasnt thick. wasn't
3. Pam and Tom werent sad. weren't

Day 5
1. The men werent quick. weren't
2. The bell wasnt loud. wasn't
3. Dont go out there! Don't

Daily Language Transparency 20

1330 *Ring! Ring! Ring! Put Out the Fire!*

DAY 1 — Introduce the Concept

Oral Warm-Up Read these two sentences aloud: *I did not go to school. I didn't go to school.* Ask children if these sentences mean the same thing.

Introduce Contractions Review with children that using a contraction is like saying two words at once.

Contractions

- A **contraction** is a short form of two words.

- An **apostrophe** (') takes the place of the letters that are left out.

Write the following on the chalkboard: *was + not = wasn't; were + not = weren't.*

Present the Daily Language Activity and have students correct orally. Then have students write their own sentences using *wasn't* and *weren't.*

 WRITING Assign the daily Writing Prompt on page 124E.

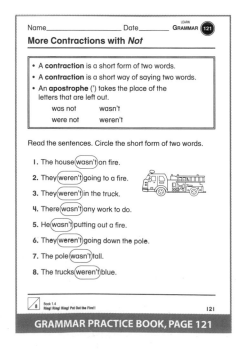

GRAMMAR PRACTICE BOOK, PAGE 121

DAY 2 — Teach the Concept

Review Contractions Remind children that a contraction is a short form of two words. Ask children to change the underlined words into contractions in the following sentences: *It was not a big cat. We were not sad.*

Introduce More Contractions Explain to children that they can make contractions out of other words. Write the following on the chalkboard: *do + not = don't; did + not = didn't.*

Present the Daily Language Activity and have children correct orally. Then have children write their own sentences, using *don't* and *didn't.*

 WRITING Assign the daily Writing Prompt on page 124E.

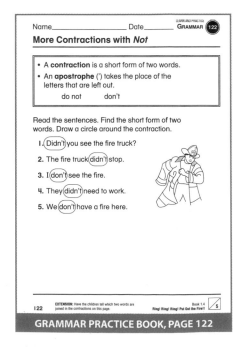

GRAMMAR PRACTICE BOOK, PAGE 122

Contractions with *Not*

Learn from the Literature Review contractions with *not*. Read aloud the second-to-last sentence on page 129 of *Put Out the Fire!*

Don't you think they are brave?

Ask children which word is a contraction. (*Don't*) Then ask what two words make up the contraction. (*Do not*)

Use Contractions with *Not* Present the Daily Language Activity and have children correct orally.

Write these sentences on the board: *I was happy. Mom and Dad were coming. They did have a ball. They do like cake.* Have children add *not* to each sentence and then make contractions.

WRITING Assign the daily Writing Prompt on page 124F.

Review Contractions Write *wasn't, weren't, didn't,* and *don't* on the chalkboard. Have children take turns saying which two words make up each contraction. Have them use the words orally in a sentence. Then present the Daily Language Activity for Day 4.

Mechanics and Usage Review the use of apostrophes in contractions with *not*.

Apostrophes

- Use an **apostrophe** in place of an *o* in contractions with *not*.

Expand the Concept: Double Negatives You can challenge children further by presenting double negatives in lessons on contractions. Write: *I didn't not go to the park. I did go to the park.* Explain that these statements have the same meaning.

WRITING Assign the daily Writing Prompt on page 124F.

Assess Use the Daily Language Activity and page 125 of the **Grammar Practice Book** for assessment.

Reteach Have children write from dictation the four contractions studied this week. Then have them write a simple sentence for each contraction. If they'd like, they can write the contraction in a different color pencil. Have children create a word wall with two columns: in the first column, a list of words (*was, were, do,* and *did*) followed by *not*; in the second column, a list of contractions.

WRITING Assign the daily Writing Prompt on page 124F.

Name_____ Date_____ **GRAMMAR 123** PRACTICE AND WRITE

More Contractions with *Not*

- A **contraction** is a short form of two words.
- An **apostrophe** (') takes the place of the letters that are left out.

was not	wasn't
were not	weren't
do not	don't
did not	didn't

Read the sentences. Circle the two words that make the contraction in each sentence.

1. The firefighters don't always need masks.
   (do not)   was not   did not
2. The firefighters weren't on their way.
   (were not)   was not   do not
3. They didn't rush away.
   (did not)   was not   do not
4. They didn't go down the pole.
   (did not)   was not   did not
5. That wasn't the ladder.
   (was not)   did not   do not

GRAMMAR PRACTICE BOOK, PAGE 123

Name_____ Date_____ **GRAMMAR 124** MECHANICS

More Contractions with *Not*

- A **contraction** is a short form of two words.
- Use an **apostrophe** (') in place of o in a contraction with *not*.

| was not | wasn't |

On the lines, write the contractions for the words in ( ).

1. (Do not) **Don't** stop, the firefighters are on the way.
2. (Does not) **Doesn't** the fireman work fast?
3. The fireman (was not) **wasn't** in the fire truck.
4. They (were not) **weren't** in the fire truck.
5. The firefighters (were not) **weren't** working.

GRAMMAR PRACTICE BOOK, PAGE 124

Name_____ Date_____ **GRAMMAR 125** TEST

Test

Write the contraction for the underlined words.

1. The house was not on fire.
   _____ **wasn't**
2. The men did not rush.
   _____ **didn't**
3. Do not go near the fire.
   _____ **Don't**
4. They were not at home.
   _____ **weren't**
5. She did not see the truck.
   _____ **didn't**

GRAMMAR PRACTICE BOOK, PAGE 125

133P

5 Day Spelling Plan

LANGUAGE SUPPORT

ESL Contractions do not exist in many other languages. ESL children will need lots of practice listening to contractions in speech. Work with children to make a chart of contractions they understand and can use. Hang it in the classroom for children to use as a reference. Add contractions to the chart as children learn more.

DICTATION SENTENCES

Spelling Words

1. Here comes the fire <u>truck</u>.
2. I see the <u>smoke</u>.
3. I have the <u>bell</u>.
4. The man went down the <u>pole</u>.
5. Can I make it <u>ring</u>?
6. She is very <u>brave</u>.

Challenge Words

7. We will <u>clean</u> the truck.
8. I <u>always</u> wait for my dad.
9. He can work at <u>home</u>.
10. Are you <u>done</u>?

DAY 1 — Pretest

Assess Prior Knowledge Use the Dictation Sentences at left and **Spelling Practice Book** page 121 for the pretest. Allow children to correct their own papers. If children have trouble, have partners give each other a midweek test on Day 3.

Spelling Words		Challenge Words
1. **truck**	4. **pole**	7. **clean**
2. **smoke**	5. **ring**	8. **always**
3. **bell**	6. **brave**	9. **work**
		10. **done**

*Note: Words in **dark type** are from the story.*

Word Study On page 122 of the **Spelling Practice Book** are word study steps and an at-home activity.

DAY 2 — Explore the Pattern

Sort and Spell Words Say *sock* and *smoke*. Ask children what vowel sound they hear in each word. Discuss with children how each vowel (*a, e, i, o,* and *u*) can have a short sound and a long sound.

Ask children to read aloud the six Spelling Words before sorting them into words with short-vowel sounds and words with long-vowel sounds.

Short Vowels	Long Vowels
truck	smoke
bell	pole
ring	brave

Word Wall As children read other stories and texts, have them look for new words with short- or long- vowel sounds. Add them to a classroom word wall, underlining the letters in the word that make the long- or short- vowel sound.

SPELLING PRACTICE BOOK, PAGE 121

WORD STUDY STEPS AND ACTIVITY, PAGE 122

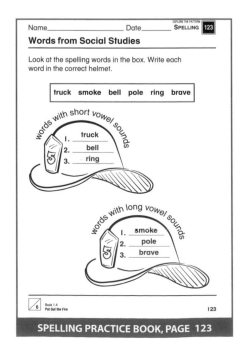

SPELLING PRACTICE BOOK, PAGE 123

Words from Social Studies

DAY 3 — Practice and Extend

Word Meaning: Definitions Have children match each definition below with a Spelling Word.

> **Sound a bell makes** (ring)
>
> **Not afraid** (brave)
>
> **Something that comes from fire** (smoke)
>
> **Bigger than a car** (truck)
>
> **Something to slide down** (pole)
>
> **Something that makes a ringing sound** (bell)

Identify Spelling Patterns Write the following on the board: *We always keep the truck clean. You can ring the bell when the work is done.* Have volunteers read aloud and tell which are the Spelling Words and Challenge Words. Then have children use Spelling and Challenge Words in a sentence.

DAY 4 — Proofread and Write

Proofread Sentences Write these sentences on the chalkboard, including the misspelled words. Ask children to proofread, circling incorrect spellings and writing the correct spellings. There are two spelling errors in each sentence.

> The braev man sat on the truk. (brave, truck)
>
> The bel rang, and we saw smok (bell, smoke)
>
> Rign the bell and go down the pol. (ring, pole)

 WRITING Have children use as many Spelling Words as possible in the daily Writing Prompt on page 124F. Remind children to proofread their writing for errors in spelling, grammar, and punctuation.

DAY 5 — Assess

Assess Children's Knowledge Use page 126 of the **Spelling Practice Book** or the Dictation Sentences on page 133Q for the posttest.

JOURNAL **Personal Word List** If children have trouble with any words in the lesson, have them add to their personal list of troublesome words in their journals. Have children draw pictures of each Spelling Word and label it.

Children should refer to their word lists during later writing activities.

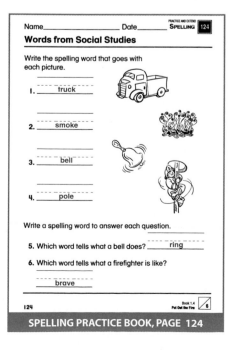

Name_____ Date_____ PRACTICE AND EXTEND SPELLING 124
Words from Social Studies

Write the spelling word that goes with each picture.

1. truck
2. smoke
3. bell
4. pole

Write a spelling word to answer each question.

5. Which word tells what a bell does? ring
6. Which word tells what a firefighter is like? brave

124 Book 1.4 Put Out the Fire 6

SPELLING PRACTICE BOOK, PAGE 124

Name_____ Date_____ PROOFREAD AND WRITE SPELLING 125
Words from Social Studies

Finding Mistakes
Read the story. There are six spelling mistakes. Circle the mistakes. Write the words correctly on the lines.

The fire bel goes "Ringe!" The firefighters slide down the pol. They jump into the fire fruc. They rush to put out a fire. They get there very fast. When they see smok, they rush in to help. Firefighters are very braav.

1. bell   2. ring   3. pole
4. truck   5. smoke   6. brave

Writing Activity
Write a story about someone who was brave. Use two spelling words in your story.

6 Book 1.4 Put Out the Fire 125

SPELLING PRACTICE BOOK, PAGE 125

Name_____ Date_____ POSTTEST SPELLING 126
Words from Social Studies

Look at the words in each set. One word in each set is spelled correctly. Use a pencil to color in the circle in front of that word. Before you begin, look at the sample sets of words. Sample A has been done for you. Do Sample B by yourself. When you are sure you know what to do, you may go on with the rest of the page.

Sample A
- Ⓐ those
- Ⓑ thoze
- Ⓒ thos

Sample B
- Ⓓ wai
- Ⓔ wae
- ● way

1. Ⓐ ringe
   Ⓑ rin
   ● ring

2. Ⓓ braf
   ● brave
   Ⓕ brav

3. Ⓐ truc
   Ⓑ truk
   ● truck

4. Ⓓ poole
   Ⓔ pol
   ● pole

5. ● bell
   Ⓑ bel
   Ⓒ bbel

6. Ⓓ smok
   ● smoke
   Ⓕ smool

126 Book 1.4 Put Out the Fire 6

SPELLING PRACTICE BOOK, PAGE 126

Wrap Up the Theme

Let's Find Out!
Looking for answers is an adventure.

REVIEW THE THEME Remind children that all the selections in this unit relate to the theme Let's Find Out! What were some of the answers that the characters found? Were children surprised by any of the adventures or answers? Ask children to name other stories or movies they know that also fit the theme Let's Find Out!

READ THE POEM Read "Who Lived in a Shoe" by Beatrix Potter aloud to children. After reading, discuss how the poem connects to the theme Let's Find Out! What story is the poet writing about? What is the poet trying to figure out? Reread the poem, having children chime in with you.

LISTENING LIBRARY The poem is available on **audiocassette** and on **compact disc.**

MAKE CONNECTIONS Have children work in small groups to brainstorm a list of ways that the stories, poems, and the *Time for Kids* magazine article relate to the theme Let's Find Out!

Groups can then compare their lists as they share them with the class.

134

LOOKING AT GENRE

Have children review *Yasmin's Ducks* and *The Knee-High Man*. What makes *Yasmin's Ducks* an informational science story? What makes *The Knee-High Man* a play?

Help children list the key characteristics of each literary form or genre. Encourage children to give other examples of informational stories and plays.

INFORMATIONAL SCIENCE STORY *Yasmin's Ducks*	PLAY *The Knee-High Man*
• Characters and story plot are made up. • Story gives true facts about a science topic (*ducks*).	• Has parts for different characters. • Story is told in dialogue. • You could act it out with others.

Who Lived in a Shoe?

You know that old woman
Who lived in a shoe?
She had so many children
She didn't know what to do?

I think if she lived in
A little shoe-house
That little old lady was
Surely a mouse!

by Beatrix Potter

135

Research and Inquiry

Complete the Theme Project Have children work in teams to complete their group project. Remind children that the information that they have gathered on their place to explore can be presented in any creative way. For example, they might enjoy making an illustrated map of their place. Encourage children to share tasks so that each member of the team can contribute to the project.

Make a Classroom Presentation Have teams take turns presenting their projects. Be sure to include time for questions from the audience.

Draw Conclusions Have children draw conclusions about what they learned from researching, preparing, and sharing their projects. Was the Resource chart they made helpful? Was using the Internet helpful? What other resources did they use? What conclusions have children reached about their topic? Finally, ask children if the project has changed their opinion about the place they want to explore. What conclusions can they draw from this?

Ask More Questions What additional questions do children now have about their place to explore? Do children have questions about other places? You might encourage the teams to continue their research and prepare another presentation.

LEARNING ABOUT POETRY

Literary Devices: Rhyme Read the poem aloud, having children listen for words that rhyme. Reread the poem, having children echo the last word in each line. Have volunteers give pairs of rhyming words from the poem. *(shoe, do; house, mouse)*

Response Activity. Have children draw a picture based on the poem. Encourage them to think about how big a real shoe is, and how many mice could fit in it.

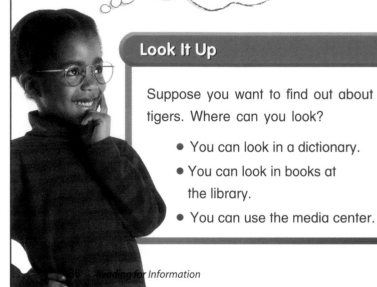

Reading for Information

READ TOGETHER

Reading to Find Answers

Asking questions and looking up answers is called research. We can look for answers in different places.

Where do tigers live?
What do tigers eat?

Look It Up

Suppose you want to find out about tigers. Where can you look?

- You can look in a dictionary.
- You can look in books at the library.
- You can use the media center.

Reading for Information

Use a Dictionary

You can look up *tiger* in a dictionary. Start by finding words that begin with the letter *t*. Then look for words that begin with the letters *ti*. Keep hunting until you find *tiger*.

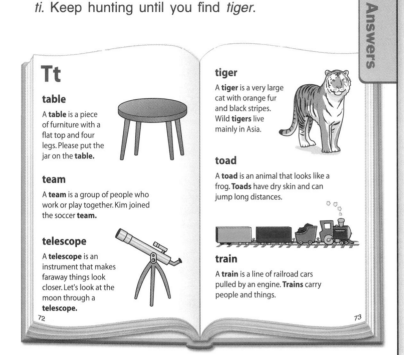

Tt

table
A **table** is a piece of furniture with a flat top and four legs. Please put the jar on the **table**.

team
A **team** is a group of people who work or play together. Kim joined the soccer **team**.

telescope
A **telescope** is an instrument that makes faraway things look closer. Let's look at the moon through a **telescope**.

72

tiger
A **tiger** is a very large cat with orange fur and black stripes. Wild **tigers** live mainly in Asia.

toad
A **toad** is an animal that looks like a frog. **Toads** have dry skin and can jump long distances.

train
A **train** is a line of railroad cars pulled by an engine. **Trains** carry people and things.

73

Reading to Find Answers 137

Reading to Find Answers

Anthology pages 136-137

Reading to Find Answers

OBJECTIVES Children will:

- generate questions about a chosen topic.
- use a dictionary, a nonfiction book, and the media center as sources of information.
- use alphabetical order to locate information.

INTRODUCE Ask children to **preview** pages 136–139 by looking carefully at the pictures. Then **set purposes.** **Say:** In these pages we will be learning about asking questions and looking up the answers. The little girl on page 136 is asking herself questions about tigers.

- What other questions about tigers could you ask?
- These pages show three places where you could look for answers. What are they?

Read pages 136–139 aloud with children. Then **model** the

steps in doing research, starting with the use of the alphabet to look up something in the dictionary. **Say:**

- Let's say I want to learn more about *turtles*. First, I need to think of some questions. Are there different kinds of turtles? Where do they live? What do they eat? How big do they get? How long do they live? To find the answers, I need to start my research.
- I begin by looking in a dictionary. Every dictionary is arranged in alphabetical order, from *a* to *z*. I see that *turtle* begins with a *t*, so I go to the *Tt* part of the dictionary. To help me find the entry for *turtle* among all the other entries beginning with *t*, I use the alphabet again. This time I look at its first *two* letters, which are *tu*. Using *tu* as a guide, I quickly find *tub, tugboat, tulip, tunnel, turkey,* and **turtle**.
- Using the first letter(s) of a word to find it in a dictionary is called sorting by first letter, or alphabetizing.

Use the Library

Look for books that give facts about tigers. Books that give facts are called nonfiction. Storybooks are called fiction.

Tigers can live almost anywhere. All they need is food, water, and shade. They do not like to be out in the open.
Tiger cubs live with their mothers. When they grow up, tigers tend to travel alone.
34
35

Use the Media Center

You can use the classroom media center to find information. Use the Internet or a CD-ROM to look up facts about tigers.

Tigers
Where Tigers Live
What Tigers Eat
How Tigers Sound
Fun Tiger Facts

Questions

1. What should you do before you start your research?
2. Where can you look for answers?

138 *Reading for Information*

Reading to Find Answers 139

Anthology pages 138-139

Sorting by first letter will also help me find a book about turtles in the library, where nonfiction books are arranged alphabetically by subject. Sorting by first letter will help me in the media center, too, where I can use alphabetical order to find information on a CD-ROM.

PRACTICE Say:

- Let's say I want to learn about ants. What should I do before I start my research? (Think of the questions I want answers to.)
- Where can I find answers? (a dictionary, a nonfiction library book, and the media center)

ANSWERS TO QUESTIONS

1. Think of questions you want to ask.
2. a dictionary, a nonfiction book, or the media center

TRANSFER THE STRATEGY Explain to children that knowing how to sort by first letter will help them find information in telephone books and address books. Ask them to use their newfound skill in looking up their family's name and number in the telephone book.

Activity

Divide the class into small groups. Give each group a simple animal topic, such as *bears, seals, worms, swans, goats, frogs,* or *crows*. Have children generate a few main questions they want to learn about their animals. Have children do their research using a dictionary, nonfiction books, and the media center. Have groups share their research with the class.

138/139

Writing That Compares

CONNECT TO LITERATURE Remind children that, in "The Shopping List," each person tried to help Mike remember the missing item from his list. Have a class discussion about how each person helped, and the suggestions they made to Mike. Ask children what suggestions they would have made to help him.

Dear Mrs. Nevins,

A long time ago, people went many places. They went to school and to work. People also liked to visit each other. They walked or rode a horse and wagon.

We travel differently today. People long ago rode a horse and wagon or walked. We ride in a car or on a bus. But people today also go to school and work. We like to visit our friends, too.

Sincerely,
Yannek Liederman

Prewrite

PURPOSE & AUDIENCE Children will write a letter that compares to a parent or teacher. Explain to children that the purpose of the letter will be to compare two activities or outings.

STRATEGY: BRAINSTORM Have children brainstorm ideas about activities or outings they could take part in. Make a list on the chalkboard of children's remarks for reflection later.

Use **Writing Process Transparency 1A** to model a Writing That Compares organizer.

WRITING THAT COMPARES FEATURES

A good comparison:

• uses words that compare.

• tells how things are alike.

• tells how things are different.

PREWRITE TRANSPARENCY

What I Want to Do:
Let's Visit the Zoo or the Aquarium

How the Zoo and the Aquarium Are Alike	How the Zoo and the Aquarium Are Different
• There are many different animals to see in both places.	• The aquarium has animals that live in the water.
• You can see animals up close in both places.	• The zoo has animals that live on land.
• You can learn more about animals at the aquarium and at the zoo.	• The animals live inside at the aquarium.
	• The animals live outside at the zoo.

McGraw-Hill School Division

Book 1.4: Writing That Compares / Prewriting 1A

Writing That Compares

Draft

STRATEGY: DEVELOP A MAIN IDEA/PARAGRAPH Have children write a sentence that states their suggestions for an activity or outing. Point out that this is the main idea of their writing. Then have children review the list of details that they made. Explain that these details support the main idea.

Tell children that a group of sentences that tells about one main idea is called a **paragraph**. A paragraph contains one main idea and supporting details that tell about it.

Have children continue writing their draft by writing sentences that give details about how their activities or outings are alike and different. Guide them to write freely, without self-editing for punctuation or spelling.

Use **Writing Process Transparency 1B** to model a first draft.

WORD CHOICE Have children review *alike, same, different, more, also, but, too,* and *both.* For example, *We both play the same games, but we read different books.* They can save the exercise in their writing portfolios.

DRAFT TRANSPARENCY

Woods Elementary
543 High Street
Long City, Idaho 99999
April 7, 20___
Dear Ms. adams
I want to visit the aquarium or the zoo on monday. we could learn about animals.

    The aquarium has animals that live in the water. The zoo has animals that live on land. But we could see the animals up close at both places.

    the animals live inside at the aquarium. The animals live outside at the zoo. We can learn more about animals at both places. I cant wait for our trip!
sincerely,
Nora Ruiz

McGraw-Hill School Division

Book 1.4: Writing That Compares / Drafting 1B

Revise

Have a class discussion on how to make children's letters more effective. Ask children to comment on what they think their audience would find interesting about their comparisons. Challenge them to come up with more similarities and differences to include in their writing.

STRATEGY: ELABORATION Have children examine their work for changes that will enhance their writing that compares. Use the following questions to inspire the revision process:

- Do my words clearly describe each activity or outing?

- Does my letter sound like how I naturally talk?

- What else could I say to show how these two activities or outings are alike and different? Do I need to add more details?

Use **Writing Process Transparency 1C** for classroom discussion on the revision process. Ask children to comment on how revisions may have improved this writing sample.

TEACHING TIP

TEACHER CONFERENCE
Reinforce the importance of writing paragraphs correctly. (They should be indented and have a main idea and supporting details.) Ask children to consider these questions while revising:

- Does each paragraph have a clear main idea and supporting details?
- Did you indent the beginning of each paragraph?
- Do you need to share more details to explain how the two things are alike and different?
- Are your ideas written in an organized way?

REVISE TRANSPARENCY

Woods Elementary
543 High Street
Long City, Idaho 99999
April 7, 20___

Dear Ms. adams

I want to visit the aquarium or the zoo on monday. we could learn about animals.

The aquarium has animals that live in the water. ^like fish and turtles The zoo has animals that live on land. ^like lions and bears But we could see the animals up close at both places.

the animals live inside at the aquarium. The animals live outside at the zoo. We can learn more about animals at both places. I cant wait for our trip!

sincerely,

Nora Ruiz

McGraw-Hill School Division

Book 1.4: Writing That Compares / Revising 1C

Edit/Proofread

After children finish revising their texts, have them proofread for final corrections and additions.

GRAMMAR/SPELLING CONNECTIONS

See the 5-Day Grammar and Usage Plan on verbs, on pages 370–37P, 650–65P, 950–95P, and 1230–123P, 1330–133P.

See the 5-Day Spelling Plans, pages 37Q–37R, 65Q–65R, 95Q–95R, 123Q–123R, and 133Q–133R.

GRAMMAR, MECHANICS, USAGE

- Begin sentences with a capital letter and end them with a period.
- Begin names of people or special places with a capital letter.
- Use an apostrophe in place of the *o* when *not* is joined with another word.
- Begin the names of days and months with a capital letter.

Publish

SEND THE LETTERS Help children correctly address and stamp their letters for mailing. They can decorate the envelopes.

Use **Writing Process Transparency 1D** as a proofreading model and **Writing Process Transparency 1E** as a model to discuss publishing ideas for their writing.

PROOFREAD TRANSPARENCY

Woods Elementary
543 High Street
Long City, Idaho 99999
April 7, 20___

Dear Ms. adams,

¶I want to visit the aquarium or the zoo on monday. we could learn about animals.

The aquarium has animals that live in the water. The zoo has animals that live on land. But we could see the animals up close at both places.

the animals live inside at the aquarium. The animals live outside at the zoo. We can learn more about animals at both places. I cant wait for our trip!

sincerely,
Nora Ruiz

McGraw-Hill School Division

Book 1.4: Writing That Compares / Proofreading 1D

PUBLISH TRANSPARENCY

Woods Elementary
543 High Street
Long City, Idaho 99999
April 7, 20___

Dear Ms. Adams,

I want to visit the aquarium or the zoo on Monday. We could learn about animals.

The aquarium has animals that live in the water, like fish and turtles. The zoo has animals that live on land, like lions and bears. We could see the animals up close at both places.

The animals live inside at the aquarium. The animals live outside at the zoo. We can learn more about animals at both places. I can't wait for our trip!

Sincerely,
Nora Ruiz

McGraw-Hill School Division

Book 1.4: Writing That Compares / Publishing 1E

Presentation Ideas

DISPLAY THE LETTERS Make a board display of the letters, and give children a chance to see others' work. Children may wish to read their letters aloud to classmates. ▶ **Representing/Speaking**

HAVE A CLASS DISCUSSION Ask children to comment on which letters tell the most about how the activities are different and how they are alike. ▶ **Viewing/Speaking**

Assessment

SCORING RUBRIC When using the rubric, consider children's creative efforts, possibly adding a plus (+) for originality, wit, and imagination.

Scoring Rubric: 6-Trait Writing

4 Excellent

- **Ideas & Content** crafts a thorough comparison, with a full set of supporting details and ideas; holds reader's attention throughout.

- **Organization** careful strategy moves the reader logically through the comparison; has a strong beginning and ending.

- **Voice** states a detailed and accurate comparison between two things; writer's deep understanding of how the things are alike and different makes the comparison interesting.

- **Word Choice** thoughtfully uses words to communicate clear descriptions and details; advanced vocabulary helps to create a convincing tone.

- **Sentence Fluency** fluid sentences flow naturally; a variety of beginnings, lengths, and patterns adds interest to the comparison.

- **Conventions** has skills in most writing conventions; proper use of the rules of English enhances clarity of the argument; editing is largely unnecessary.

3 Good

- **Ideas & Content** crafts a solid comparison, with supporting details and ideas that show an understanding of the topic; holds reader's interest.

- **Organization** presents a capable strategy; reader can follow the logic from beginning to end; ideas and details fit where they are placed.

- **Voice** shows who is behind the words; personal message matches the writing purpose and reaches out to make comparison.

- **Word Choice** uses a variety of words that fit the message; may experiment with new words or use familiar words in a fresh way.

- **Sentence Fluency** sentences make sense and are easy to follow and read aloud; lengths and patterns vary, and fit well together.

- **Conventions** uses a variety of conventions correctly; some editing may be needed; errors are few and do not interfere with understanding the argument.

2 Fair

- **Ideas & Content** has some control of the writing that compares, but may not offer adequate supporting details and ideas; may not keep the reader's attention.

- **Organization** tries to structure a comparison, but has trouble sequencing information; may lose control of topic after stating the main idea; beginning or ending may be missing or underdeveloped.

- **Voice** states a comparison between two things; writer may seem personally uninvolved with the writing and the audience.

- **Word Choice** gets the message across, but experiments with few new words; some words may not fit the topic or the audience.

- **Sentence Fluency** sentences are understandable, but may be incomplete or awkward; some of the writing is difficult to follow or read aloud.

- **Conventions** makes frequent mistakes which may interfere with a smooth reading of the text; extensive need for editing and revision.

1 Unsatisfactory

- **Ideas & Content** does not successfully present a comparison; it is hard to tell what is alike and different between the things being compared; ideas and details are not connected, and may not fit the comparison.

- **Organization** extreme lack of structure makes the text difficult to follow; points of the comparison may be disordered; no clear beginning and ending.

- **Voice** is not involved in showing how two things are alike and different; lacks a purpose and interaction with the reader.

- **Word Choice** does not use words that clearly compare two things; some words may take away from the meaning; words do not fit, or are overused.

- **Sentence Fluency** uses incomplete or confusing sentences; does not understand how words and sentences fit together; writing is hard to read aloud.

- **Conventions** has repeated errors in spelling, word choice, punctuation and usage; reader has a hard time getting through the text.

0: This piece is either blank, or fails to respond to the writing task. The topic is not addressed, or the child simply paraphrases the prompt. The response may be illegible or incoherent.

VOCABULARY

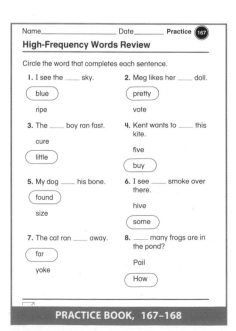 Have partners write all the vocabulary words from one selection on pieces of paper, and place the pieces in a bag. Taking turns, have each partner pull a word from the bag and make up a riddle for it. The other partner must try to answer the riddle.

Unit Review

The Shopping List

after	blue	who
always	were	

Yasmin's Ducks

work	buy	some
because	found	

The Knee-High Man

carry	clean	far
been	done	

Johnny Appleseed

how	little	pretty
light	live	

Ring! Ring! Ring! Put Out the Fire!

always	clean	how
work	done	

Name_____ Date_____ Practice **167**

High-Frequency Words Review

Circle the word that completes each sentence.

1. I see the ____ sky.
   - blue
   - ripe

2. Meg likes her ____ doll.
   - pretty
   - vote

3. The ____ boy ran fast.
   - cure
   - little

4. Kent wants to ____ this kite.
   - five
   - buy

5. My dog ____ his bone.
   - found
   - size

6. I see ____ smoke over there.
   - hive
   - some

7. The cat ran ____ away.
   - far
   - yoke

8. ____ many frogs are in the pond?
   - Pail
   - How

PRACTICE BOOK, 167–168

GRAMMAR

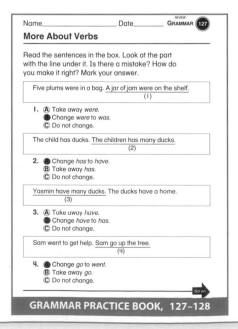 Write some sentences on the chalkboard leaving a blank space for the following verbs to be filled in by the children: *was, were, has, have, go, do* (past tense), *see, say* (past tense). Call on volunteers to come to the chalkboard to supply the correct form of each verb.

Unit Review

The Shopping List
Was and *Were*

Yasmin's Ducks
Has and *Have*

The Knee-High Man
Go and *Do*

Johnny Appleseed
See and *Say*

Ring! Ring! Ring! Put Out the Fire!
More Contractions with *Not*

Name_____ Date_____ REVIEW **GRAMMAR** **127**

More About Verbs

Read the sentences in the box. Look at the part with the line under it. Is there a mistake? How do you make it right? Mark your answer.

> Five plums were in a bag. A jar of jam were on the shelf.
> (1)

1. Ⓐ Take away *were*.
   ● Change *were* to *was*.
   Ⓒ Do not change.

> The child has ducks. The children has many ducks.
> (2)

2. ● Change *has* to *have*.
   Ⓑ Take away *has*.
   Ⓒ Do not change.

> Yasmin have many ducks. The ducks have a home.
> (3)

3. Ⓐ Take away *have*.
   ● Change *have* to *has*.
   Ⓒ Do not change.

> Sam went to get help. Sam go up the tree.
> (4)

4. ● Change *go* to *went*.
   Ⓑ Take away *go*.
   Ⓒ Do not change.

GRAMMAR PRACTICE BOOK, 127–128

SPELLING

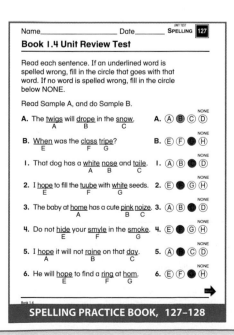

PARTNERS Assign spelling words from two different selections to partners. Have each partner write his or her words in scrambled form on a sheet of paper. Then have partners exchange papers and try to unscramble the spelling words as fast as they can.

Unit Review

Long i
smile
white
hide

Long a
rain
day
tail

Long o
home
hope
nose

Social Studies Words
truck
smoke
ring

Long u
rule
cute
tube

Name_____ Date_____ UNIT TEST SPELLING **127**

Book 1.4 Unit Review Test

Read each sentence. If an underlined word is spelled wrong, fill in the circle that goes with that word. If no word is spelled wrong, fill in the circle below NONE.

Read Sample A, and do Sample B.

A. The <u>twigs</u> will <u>drope</u> in the <u>snow</u>.
  A   B   C
A. Ⓐ ⬤ Ⓒ Ⓓ NONE

B. <u>When</u> was the <u>class</u> <u>tripe</u>?
  E   F   G
B. Ⓔ Ⓕ ⬤ Ⓗ NONE

1. That dog has a <u>white</u> <u>nose</u> and <u>taile</u>.
          A   B   C
1. Ⓐ Ⓑ ⬤ Ⓓ NONE

2. I <u>hope</u> to fill the <u>tuube</u> with <u>white</u> seeds.
       E   F   G
2. Ⓔ ⬤ Ⓖ Ⓗ NONE

3. The baby at <u>home</u> has a cute <u>pink</u> <u>noize</u>.
              A   B   C
3. Ⓐ Ⓑ ⬤ Ⓓ NONE

4. Do not <u>hide</u> your <u>smyle</u> in the <u>smoke</u>.
          E   F   G
4. Ⓔ ⬤ Ⓖ Ⓗ NONE

5. I <u>hope</u> it will not <u>raine</u> on that <u>day</u>.
       A   B   C
5. Ⓐ ⬤ Ⓒ Ⓓ NONE

6. He will <u>hope</u> to find a <u>ring</u> at <u>hom</u>.
           E   F   G
6. Ⓔ Ⓕ ⬤ Ⓗ NONE

Book 1.4 →

SPELLING PRACTICE BOOK, 127–128

✓ SKILLS & STRATEGIES

Phonics and Decoding
☑ Long *i: i-e*
☑ Long *o: o-e*
☑ Long *u: u-e*
☑ Long *a: ay, ai*

Comprehension
☑ Cause and Effect
☑ Make Inferences

Vocabulary Strategies
☑ Inflectional Endings -*s, -es*
☑ Inflectional Ending -*ed*
☑ Inflectional Endings -*er, -est*

Study Skills
☑ Charts

Writing
Writing That Compares

MCGRAW-HILL READING

Unit Test

Student Name: _____

Date: _____

Grade 1 • Book 4

McGraw-Hill

BOOK 4 ASSESSMENT

Assessment
Follow-Up

Use the results of the informal and formal assessment opportunities in the unit to help you make decisions about future instruction.

SKILLS AND STRATEGIES	Reteaching Blackline Masters	Alternate Teaching Strategies	Skills Intervention Guide ⓘ
Phonics and Decoding			
Long *i: i-e*	127, 131, 132, 140, 148, 159	T64, T65	✓
Long *o: o-e*	135, 139, 140, 148, 156, 159	T69, T70	✓
Long *u: u-e*	143, 147, 148, 156, 159	T71, T72	✓
Long *a: ay, ai*	151, 155, 156, 159	T75, T76	✓
Comprehension			
Cause and Effect	133, 141, 163	T67	✓
Make Inferences	149, 157, 164	T73	✓
Vocabulary Strategies			
Inflectional Endings *-s, -es*	134, 142, 165	T68	✓
Inflectional Endings *-er, -est*	150, 158, 166	T74	✓
Study Skills			
Charts	130, 138, 146, 154, 162	T66	✓

	Alternate Writing Project–Easy	Unit Writing Process Lesson
Writing		
Writing That Compares	37N, 65N, 95N, 123N, 133N	140A–140F

McGraw-Hill School
TECHNOLOGY

 CD-ROM provides extra phonics support.

 Research & Inquiry ideas. Visit **www.mhschool.com/reading.**

Glossary

Introduce children to the Glossary by inviting them to look through the pages, describing and discussing what they see there.

Explain that the Glossary will help them find out the meanings of words. Explain that the **Glossary** is a special kind of dictionary just for words from the selections in this book. You will probably want to give a simple definition of *dictionary*, such as: "a book that shows how words are spelled and what they mean."

Point out that words in a glossary, like words in a dictionary, are listed in **alphabetical order.** Explain that in this glossary, not all the letters of the alphabet are represented.

Point out the **entry words.** Ask children to note that each entry word is printed in heavy black type and that it appears on a line by itself. Also point out that each entry word is used in a sentence and is illustrated in a picture. Mention that there are two sentences for some of the words; in such cases, the second sentence includes a word that has the same meaning as the entry word. Also mention that each picture helps to make the meaning of the accompanying word clearer.

Give children time to study the Glossary and discover what information it includes.

Glossary

This glossary can help you to find out the meanings of words in this book that you may not know.

The words are listed in alphabetical order. There is a picture and a simple sentence for each word. You can use the picture and sentence to help you understand the meaning of each word.

Sample Entry

Main Entry   Sample Sentence

Plant
I love to **plant** seeds in the garden.

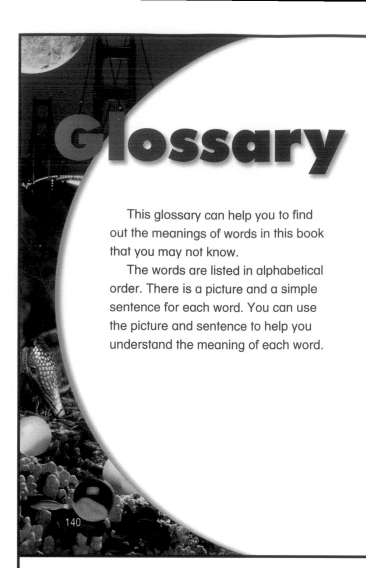

Sample Picture

Apple
An **apple** is a fruit.

Bag
Tim put the potatoes in the **bag**.
Another word for **bag** is *sack*.

Corn
I love to eat **corn** on the cob.

Ducks
Ducks are birds that swim in ponds.

Grapes

Grapes grow on a grapevine.

Hose

Water in the **hose** will help put out the fire.

144

Jars

The **jars** are filled with jelly.
Bottles is another word for **jars.**

Ladder

The **ladder** helps the fireman put out the fire.

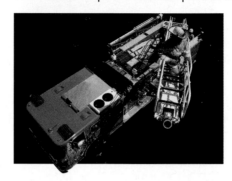

145

Plant

I love to **plant** seeds in the garden.

Pole

The **pole** helps firefighters get to the fire quickly.

146

Rocket

The **rocket** travels to outer space.
Another word for **rocket** is *spaceship*.

Smoke

The **smoke** is coming from the burning building.

147

G3

"The Brave Ones" from UNDER THE SUNDAY TREE by Eloise Greenfield. Text copyright © 1988 by Eloise Greenfield. Paintings copyright © 1988 by Amos Ferguson. Used by permission of HarperCollins Publishers.

"The Ducks and the Fox" from FABLES by Arnold Lobel. copyright © 1980 by Arnold Lobel. Used by permission of Harper & Row, Publishers.

"General Store" from TAXIS AND TOADSTOOLS by Rachel Field. Copyright © 1926 by the Century Company. Used by permission of Bantam Doubleday Dell Publishing Group.

"The Great Big Enormous Turnip" by Alexi Tolstoi from RUSSIAN TALES FOR CHILDREN. Used by permission of Associated Book Publishers (U.K.), Ltd.

"Timimoto" from ONCE UPON A TIME CHILDREN'S ANTHOLOGY GR. K. Copyright © 1988 by MacMillan Publishing Company.

ZB Font Method Copyright © 1996 Zaner-Bloser. Manuscript handwriting models. Used by permission.

Art/Illustration
Taia Morley, 96H; Richard Kolding, 8D, 38H; 66D (t), 66D (b)

Photography
All photographs are by the Macmillan/McGraw-Hill School Division (MMSD); Clara Aich for MMSD; Ken Karp for MMSD; Dave Mager for MMSD; Mike Provost for MMSD; and John Serafin for MMSD except as noted below.

Unit 5: 153A: bc.: Daniel Pagbourne Media/FPG

ACKNOWLEDGMENTS

The publisher gratefully acknowledges permission to reprint the following copyrighted material:

"To the Top" by Sandra Liatsos. Copyright © 1992 by Sandra Liatsos. Used by premission of Marian Reiner for the author.

"Who Lived in a Shoe?" by Beatrix Potter from SING A SONG OF POPCORN. Copyright © 1988 by Scholastic Inc. Reprinted by permission of Scholastic Inc.

Illustration
Steve Johnson, Lou Francher, 6–7; Michele Noiset, 8–9; Shirley Beckes, 10–33, 34tl; Daniel Del Valle, 34br, 62br, 120b; Rita Lascaro, 35tr, 36, 64, 94, 122; Ken Bowser, 37, 123; Nancy Davis, 38–39; Dominic Catalano, 40–61, 62tl; Bernard Adnet, 65, 133; Doreen Gay–Kassel, 66–67; Tim Raglin, 68–93; Eldon Doty, 95; Kathleen O'Malley, 96–97; Michael Steirnagle, 98–119, 120tl; Darcia Labrosse, 124–125; Nancy Tobin, 132; Yuri Salzman, 134–5; George Thompson, 142; Peter Fasolino, 144–145; Holly Jones, 146–147.

Photography
40: b. Nick Cantalano/Courtesy of Dominic Catalano. 68: t. Courtesy of Ms. Ellen Dryer. 98: b. Courtesy of Michael Steirnagle. 143: b. Image Bank/Alvis Upitis. t. Corbis/Philip Gould; 144: t. The Stock Market/(c) Bo Zaunders. 145: b. Corbis/George Hall. 146: b. FPG international/(c) Ron Rovtar. 147: t. Image Bank.

READING FOR INFORMATION
All illustrations and photographs are by Macmillan/McGraw-Hill (MMH) except as noted below:
Photography
136 bl: MMH. 139: CMCD/Photo Disc.

Backmatter Contents

General Store
Rachel Field

Someday I'm going to have a store
With a tinkly bell hung over the door,
With real glass cases and counters wide
And drawers all spilly with things inside.
There'll be a little of everything:
Bolts of calico; balls of string;
Jars of peppermint; tins of tea;
Pots and kettles and crockery;
Seeds in packets; scissors bright;
Kegs of sugar, brown and white;
Sarsaparilla for picnic lunches,
Bananas and rubber boots in bunches.
I'll fix the window and dust each shelf,
And take the money in all myself,
It will be my store and I will say:
"What can I do for you today?"

The Duck and the Fox
retold by Arnold Lobel

Two Duck sisters were waddling down the road to the pond for their morning swim.

"This is a good road," said the first sister, "but I think, just for a change, we should find another route. There are many other roads that lead to the pond."

"No," said the second sister, "I do not agree. I really do not want to try a new way. This road makes me feel comfortable. I am accustomed to it."

One morning the Ducks met a Fox sitting on a fence along the road.

"Good morning, ladies, " said the Fox. "On the way to the pond, I suppose?"

"Oh, yes," said the sisters, "we come along here every day."

"Interesting," said the Fox with a toothy smile.

When the sun came up the next morning, the first sister said, "We are sure to meet that Fox again if we go our usual way. I did not like his looks. Today is the day we must find another road!"

▶ "You are being just plain silly," said the second sister. "That Fox smiled at us. He seemed most gentlemanly."

The two Ducks waddled down the same road to the pond. There was the Fox, sitting on the fence. This time he carried a sack.

"Lovely ladies," said the Fox, "I was expecting you. I am glad you have not disappointed me."

Opening his sack, he jumped upon them.

The sisters quacked and screamed. They flapped and flopped their wings. They flew home and bolted their door.

The next morning, the two Ducks did not go out. They rested at home to quiet their nerves. On the following day they carefully searched for a new and different road. They found one, and it took them safely to the pond.

Moral: *At times, a change of routine can be most healthful.*

Timimoto

retold by Margaret H. Lippert

Once upon a time in Japan there lived an old man and an old woman. They were very lonely because they had no children. One day the old woman said to her husband, "I wish we had a child. I would like a little boy, even if he is no bigger than my finger."

That day as the old woman went to fetch water, she heard crying by the side of the path. She looked in the grass and there lay a tiny baby, only one inch long, wrapped in a red handkerchief.

The old woman was overjoyed. She took the baby home and showed him to her husband. "My wish has come true," she said. "Now we will never be lonely again." They named the baby Timimoto.

Timimoto grew up, but not very much. When he was five years old, he was as tall as his mother's thumb. At fifteen, he was only as tall as his mother's middle finger.

One morning Timimoto said, "I am going on a journey to see the world. Do not worry about me, for I will return safely." His parents were sad, but they did not want to stop him. They knew he would not be happy unless they let him go. "You will need a sword," said his mother. She took a sewing needle, slid it into a piece of straw, and tied it to his belt. "Use this to defend yourself against danger," she said.

His father got a rice bowl from the cupboard and carried it down to the river. He gave a chopstick to his son and said, "Now you have a boat and a paddle." Timimoto climbed into his boat and paddled happily down the river. His parents waved until he disappeared behind a bend.

Suddenly Timimoto felt something slap him across his back. Turning quickly, he saw a huge green frog behind his boat. The frog's long tongue lashed out at him again.

Timimoto ducked. He pushed the chopstick as hard as he could against the giant frog's jaw. The frog tumbled over in the water and dived out of sight. Timimoto turned his boat and paddled across the river.

Near the other shore the wind blew stronger. The waves got higher and higher. One wave broke over the bowl and almost turned it upside-down. Timimoto paddled as hard as he could toward the shore. It was getting late, and he did not want to spend the night on the water.

Just ahead he saw a dock. Beyond the dock was a town. He tied up his little boat and climbed onto the dock. The dock was crowded with people rushing to town. Timimoto walked along the dock with them, taking care to stay out of the way of their huge feet.

At the end of the dock, Timimoto could see a road crowded with carts, all going to town. To keep from being run over, Timimoto climbed up onto the wheel of a cart and rode there. When the cart stopped he hopped down. "Thank you," he called up to the driver.

The driver looked all around, then he looked down by his feet. "Ho, little one, you must be new in town," he said. "Don't you know that a terrible giant comes out when the sun sets?" The driver hurried away, and Timimoto saw that all the people were going into their houses.

Soon the streets were empty. The sun went down. Timimoto heard the earth rumble. He looked up and saw a huge giant with red eyes and sharp teeth standing over him. Strong fingers closed around him and lifted him into the air.

"AH-AH! A tender little morsel!" roared the giant. He popped Timimoto into his mouth. Timimoto drew his sword and stabbed the giant's tongue. "AGGGGH!" screamed the giant, and Timimoto leaped from his open mouth to the ground.

The giant ran screaming into the forest. Timimoto heard cheering all around him. People poured from their houses into the street. "You have defeated the giant!" they shouted. All night long they feasted and danced in his honor. When the sun came up everyone went down to the dock. Timimoto untied his little boat, climbed in, and headed home.

▶ Continue reading here.

The Great Big Enormous Turnip

a Russian Folktale
retold by Alexei Tolstoi

Once upon a time an old man planted a little turnip and said: "Grow, grow, little turnip, grow strong!"

And the turnip grew up sweet and strong and big and enormous.

Then, one day, the old man went to pull it up. He pulled and pulled again, but he could not pull it up.

He called the old woman.

The old woman pulled the old man,

The old man pulled the turnip.

And they pulled and pulled again, but they could not pull it up.

So the old woman called her granddaughter.

The granddaughter pulled the old woman,

The old woman pulled the old man,

The old man pulled the turnip.

▶ And they pulled and pulled again, but they could not pull it up.

The granddaughter called the black dog,

The black dog pulled the granddaughter,

The granddaughter pulled the old woman,

The old woman pulled the old man,

The old man pulled the turnip.

And they pulled and pulled again, but they could not pull it up.

The black dog called the cat,

The cat pulled the black dog,

The black dog pulled the granddaughter,

The granddaughter pulled the old woman,

The old woman pulled the old man,

The old man pulled the turnip.

And they pulled and pulled again, but they could not pull it up.

The cat called the mouse.

The mouse pulled the cat,

The cat pulled the dog,

The dog pulled the granddaughter,

The granddaughter pulled the old woman,

The old woman pulled the old man,

The old man pulled the turnip.

And they pulled and pulled again, and up came the turnip at last.

The Brave Ones

Eloise Greenfield

We hear the bell clanging
we come in a hurry
we come with our ladders and hoses
our hoses
we come in a hurry
to fight the fire
the furious fire
to smother the smoke
the smoke
we don't have much time
we climb, we spray
we are the brave ones who save
who save
we are the brave ones who save

Name_____ Date_____ Practice **127**

Long *i: i-e*

Use the words in the box to answer the riddles.

five	smile	time	bike	ripe

1. Six is after me. What am I? _____**five**_____

2. You do this with your lips. What am I? _____**smile**_____

3. A good plum is this way. What am I? _____**ripe**_____

4. A clock tells you about me. What am I? _____**time**_____

5. You can ride me. What am I? _____**bike**_____

5 Book 1.4
The Shopping List

At Home: Have children make up sentences using each of the words in the box.

127

Name_____ Date_____ Practice **128**

High-Frequency Words

Write the word from the box that completes each sentence.

after	always	blue	were	who

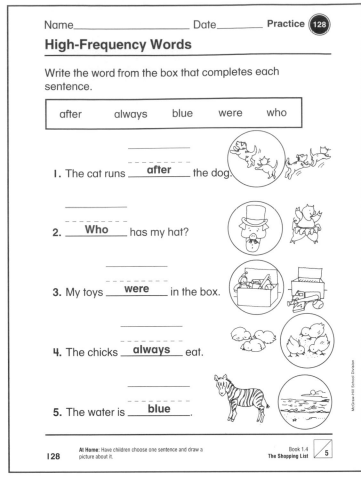

1. The cat runs ____**after**____ the dog.

2. ____**Who**____ has my hat?

3. My toys ____**were**____ in the box.

4. The chicks ____**always**____ eat.

5. The water is ____**blue**____.

128

At Home: Have children choose one sentence and draw a picture about it.

Book 1.4
The Shopping List 5

The Wish Fish

Then the man wished for a kite. So the fish tied the man and his wife to the kite. Soon they were up in the sky. "Now I have my wish!" said the fish. "They are gone."

At Home: Have children draw you a picture that illustrates the story.

128a 4

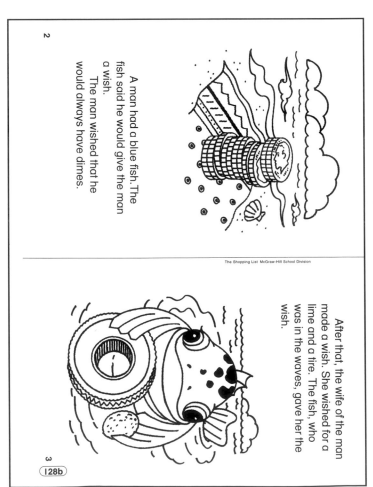

2

A man had a blue fish. The fish said he would give the man a wish.
The man wished that he would always have dimes.

The Shopping List McGraw-Hill School Division

After that, the wife of the man made a wish. She wished for a lime and a tire. The fish, who was in the waves, gave her the wish.

128b 3

The Shopping List • PRACTICE

Story Comprehension

Think about what happened in "The Shopping List."
Write **T** if the sentence is **true**. Write **F** if the
sentence is **false**.

1. __T__ Mike has a list.

2. __F__ His dad drives a bus.

3. __T__ Dad wants to know what Mike forgot.

4. __T__ Dad hunts and hunts.

5. __T__ Fran and Ann try to help Mike.

6. __T__ At last, Miss Lin gives up.

7. __F__ Mike gets sad and goes away.

8. __T__ Mom wants Mike to tell Dad it is time to eat.

8 Book 1.4
The Shopping List
At Home: Help children to write a shopping list for a meal
you are planning together.
129

A Chart

Look at the **chart**.

| What You Buy in a Hardware Store ||
Kitchen	Workshop
pot	pipe
cups	lock
forks	file
cake pan	nails
plates	pump
	clamp

Write the correct answer on the line.

1. Which things are for the workshop?

   pipe, lock, file, nails, pump, clamp

2. Which things are for the kitchen?

   pot, cups, forks, cake pan, plates

3. Name something you
   use to eat with.

   fork

4. What is something you
   might hit with a
   hammer?

   nails

130
At Home: Have children make lists of items in the kitchen
and another room at home.
Book 1.4
The Shopping List 4

Long *i*: *i-e*

Write the words in each group that have the same
middle sound as in hid**e**.

1. bike   nine   take
   bike   **nine**

2. lime   pine   cane
   lime   **pine**

3. late   slide   kite
                slide   **kite**

4. write   wide   wade
   write   **wide**

5. tire   ride   tale
   tire   **ride**

5 Book 1.4
The Shopping List
At Home: Ask children to choose a word with the long i
sound and use it in a sentence.
131

i-e, a-e

Circle the word that completes the sentence.
Then write it on the line.

1. They __bite__ the chunk.
   (bite)   fake   wade

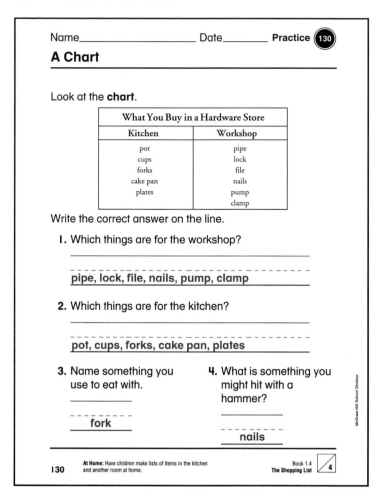

2. He locks the __gate__.
   shame   (gate)   tale

3. Fish swim in the __lake__.
   bake   late   (lake)

4. We see a bee __hive__.
   (hive)   rake   size

5. The clock __wakes__ me up.
   (wakes)   trade   line

132
At Home: Have children write sentences using other words
from this page that contain long a spelled a-e or long i
spelled i-e.
Book 1.4
The Shopping List 5

The Shopping List • PRACTICE

Name_____ Date_____ Practice (133)

Cause and Effect

Look at the picture. Underline the sentence that tells what will probably happen.

1 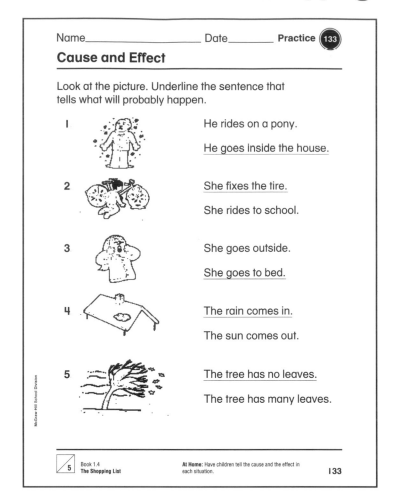 He rides on a pony.

He goes inside the house.

2 She fixes the tire.

She rides to school.

3 She goes outside.

She goes to bed.

4 The rain comes in.

The sun comes out.

5 The tree has no leaves.

The tree has many leaves.

5 Book 1.4
The Shopping List

At Home: Have children tell the cause and the effect in each situation.

133

Name_____ Date_____ Practice (134)

Inflectional Endings -s, -es

Add -s or -es to tell what only one person or thing does.

When a word ends in e or most consonants, add -s. When a word ends in sh, ch, x, or ss, add -es.

Circle the word that completes each sentence. Then write the word on the line.

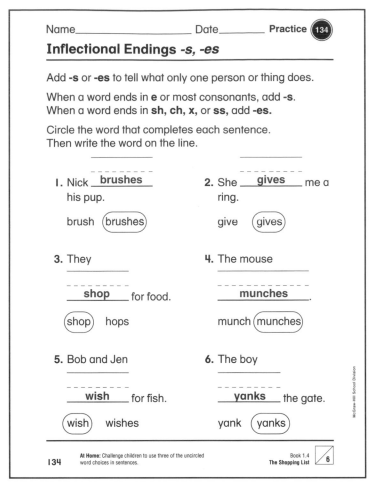

1. Nick __brushes__ his pup.

brush (brushes)

2. She __gives__ me a ring.

give (gives)

3. They _____ __shop__ for food.

(shop) hops

4. The mouse _____ __munches__.

munch (munches)

5. Bob and Jen _____ __wish__ for fish.

(wish) wishes

6. The boy _____ __yanks__ the gate.

yank (yanks)

134

At Home: Challenge children to use three of the uncircled word choices in sentences.

Book 1.4
The Shopping List 6

The Shopping List • RETEACH

Long *i*: *i-e*

Read the sentence.
Would you **like** to **bite** a **lime**?

Circle the word that completes the sentence.
Then write the word.

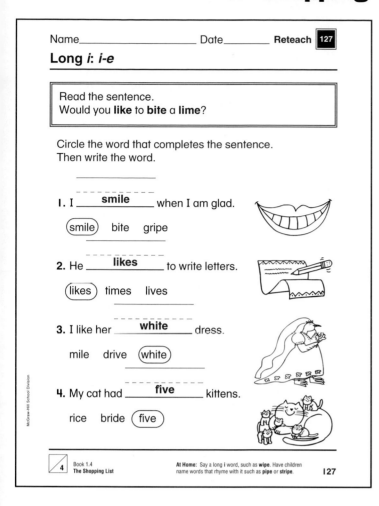

1. I ___**smile**___ when I am glad.
   (smile) bite gripe

2. He ___**likes**___ to write letters.
   (likes) times lives

3. I like her ___**white**___ dress.
   mile drive (white)

4. My cat had ___**five**___ kittens.
   rice bride (five)

At Home: Say a long **i** word, such as **wipe**. Have children name words that rhyme with it such as **pipe** or **stripe**.

High-Frequency Words

Write the word in each sentence that is taken from the box.

always	after	blue	were	who

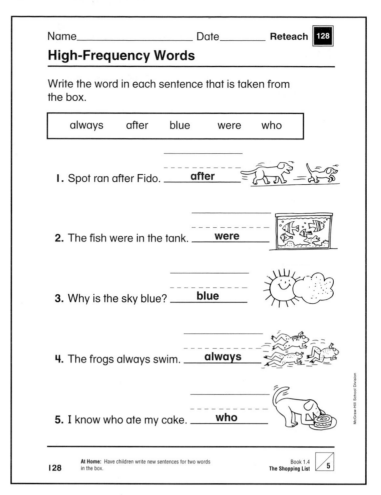

1. Spot ran after Fido. ___**after**___

2. The fish were in the tank. ___**were**___

3. Why is the sky blue? ___**blue**___

4. The frogs always swim. ___**always**___

5. I know who ate my cake. ___**who**___

At Home: Have children write new sentences for two words in the box.

Story Comprehension

Think about "The Shopping List." Fill in the chart below.

First: Mike goes to the store with a shopping list.

Then: Mike can't remember one thing he had to get.

Next: Miss Lin, Fran, and Ann try to help Mike.

Finally: Mike remembers what is not on the list.
Mom wants Dad to come home with Mike.

At Home: Help children make a list of things they might want to have at a party.

A Chart

This **chart** tells you which things are food and which are not.

FOOD		NONFOOD	
jam	cake	lamp	drum
ham	grapes	box	crib
milk	fish	tent	lock
lime	dill	mask	hat

Circle the word that completes each sentence.

1. A box (is (is not)) a food.

2. Milk is a ((food) nonfood).

3. Two nonfoods are the tent and the (jam (mask)).

4. Two foods are ham and (tent (fish)).

At Home: Ask children to name three more foods and three more nonfoods that could be found in a supermarket or grocery store.

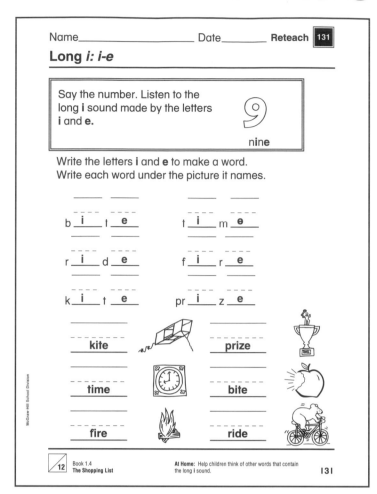

Name_____ Date_____ Reteach **131**

Long *i*: *i-e*

Say the number. Listen to the long **i** sound made by the letters **i** and **e**.

9

nine

Write the letters **i** and **e** to make a word.
Write each word under the picture it names.

b <u>i</u> t <u>e</u>   t <u>i</u> m <u>e</u>

r <u>i</u> d <u>e</u>   f <u>i</u> r <u>e</u>

k <u>i</u> t <u>e</u>   pr <u>i</u> z <u>e</u>

kite   prize

time   bite

fire   ride

12 Book 1.4
The Shopping List

At Home: Help children think of other words that contain the long **i** sound.

131

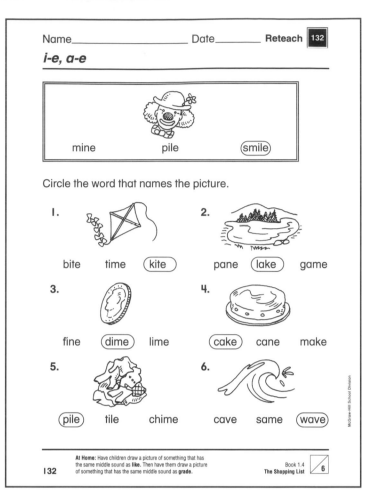

Name_____ Date_____ Reteach **132**

i-e, *a-e*

mine   pile   (smile)

Circle the word that names the picture.

1.   bite   time   (kite)

2.   pane   (lake)   game

3.   fine   (dime)   lime

4.   (cake)   cane   make

5.   (pile)   tile   chime

6.   cave   same   (wave)

At Home: Have children draw a picture of something that has the same middle sound as **like.** Then have them draw a picture 132 of something that has the same middle sound as **grade.**

Book 1.4
The Shopping List 6

Name_____ Date_____ Reteach **133**

Cause and Effect

The **cause** tells why something happened.
The **effect** tells what happened.

Look at the first picture. Then, underline the picture that shows what happened next.

1.

2.

3.

4.

4 Book 1.4
The Shopping List

At Home: Have children tell a story about each of the picture sequences.

133

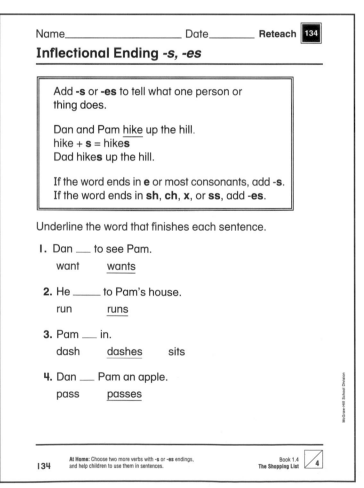

Name_____ Date_____ Reteach **134**

Inflectional Ending *-s*, *-es*

Add **-s** or **-es** to tell what one person or thing does.

Dan and Pam <u>hike</u> up the hill.
hike + **s** = hike**s**
Dad hike**s** up the hill.

If the word ends in **e** or most consonants, add **-s**.
If the word ends in **sh**, **ch**, **x**, or **ss**, add **-es**.

Underline the word that finishes each sentence.

1. Dan __ to see Pam.
   want   <u>wants</u>

2. He _____ to Pam's house.
   run   <u>runs</u>

3. Pam __ in.
   dash   <u>dashes</u>   sits

4. Dan __ Pam an apple.
   pass   <u>passes</u>

134   **At Home:** Choose two more verbs with **-s** or **-es** endings, and help children to use them in sentences.

Book 1.4
The Shopping List 4

The Shopping List • EXTEND

Long *i: i-e*

Read the words in the box. Find them in the puzzle.
Circle them.

like	white	ride	ripe	Mike	nine	smile

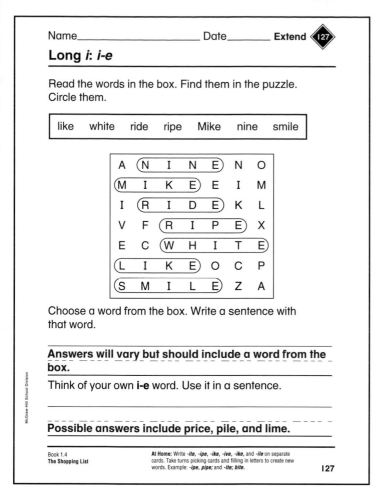

```
A  N  I  N  E  N  O
M  I  K  E  E  I  M
I  R  I  D  E  K  L
V  F  R  I  P  E  X
E  C  W  H  I  T  E
L  I  K  E  O  C  P
S  M  I  L  E  Z  A
```

Choose a word from the box. Write a sentence with
that word.

**Answers will vary but should include a word from the
box.**

Think of your own **i-e** word. Use it in a sentence.

Possible answers include price, pile, and lime.

Book 1.4
The Shopping List

At Home: Write -ite, -ipe, -ike, -ive, -ike, and -ile on separate
cards. Take turns picking cards and filling in letters to create new
words. Example: -ipe, pipe; and -ite; bite.

127

High-Frequency Words

after	always	blue	were	who

Write the word from the box that completes each
sentence. Then write a sentence using the word
that is left.

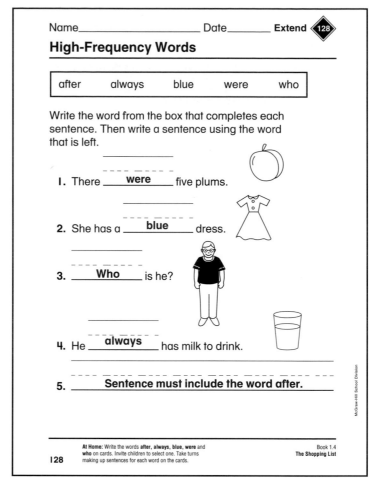

_____

1. There ___**were**___ five plums.

_____

2. She has a ___**blue**___ dress.

_____

3. ___**Who**___ is he?

_____

4. He ___**always**___ has milk to drink.

_____

5. ___**Sentence must include the word after.**___

128

At Home: Write the words after, always, blue, were and
who on cards. Invite children to select one. Take turns
making up sentences for each word on the cards.

Book 1.4
The Shopping List

Story Comprehension

What do you put on a shopping list? Look at the pictures.
Make a list of things to buy. Then add more things. Draw a
picture, too.

SHOPPING LIST

cake

milk

grapes

Book 1.4
The Shopping List

At Home: Invite children to identify the fruits and
vegetables and their colors. Make a shopping list
together.

129

Use a Chart

Fill in the chart.

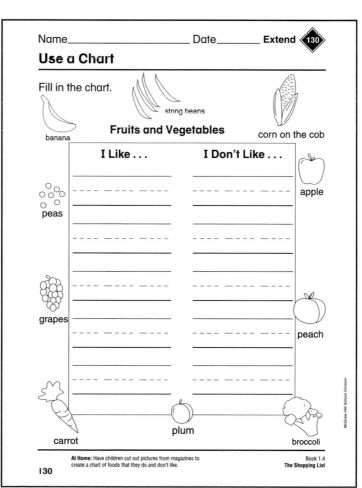

Fruits and Vegetables

I Like . . .	I Don't Like . . .

130

At Home: Have children cut out pictures from magazines to
create a chart of foods that they do and don't like.

Book 1.4
The Shopping List

T11

The Shopping List • EXTEND

Name_____ **Date**_____ **Extend** ◆131

Long *i: i-e*

Make a word. Put the letter **i** or **e** in each blank. Then write a word that rhymes with the word you made.
Sample answers are given.

Word	Rhyming Words

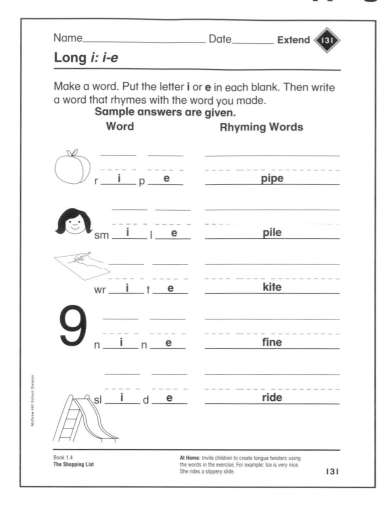

r __i__ p __e__   pipe

sm __i__ l __e__   pile

wr __i__ t __e__   kite

n __i__ n __e__   fine

sl __i__ d __e__   ride

Book 1.4
The Shopping List

At Home: Invite children to create tongue twisters using the words in the exercise. For example: Ice is very nice. She rides a slippery slide.

131

Name_____ **Date**_____ **Extend** ◆132

i-e, a-e

Play a word game with a friend. Move one space. Read the word. Then use the word in a sentence. Take turns. Get to the end!

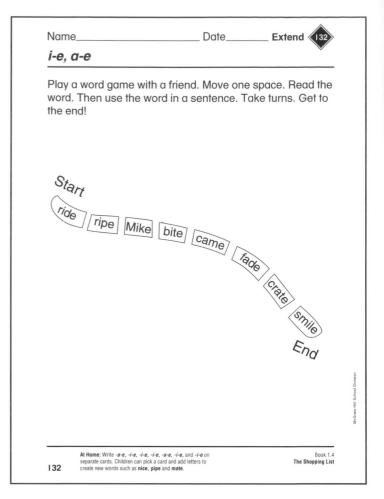

Start
ride · ripe · Mike · bite · came · fade · crate · smile
End

132

At Home: Write *-a-e, -i-e, -i-e, -a-e, -i-e,* and *-i-e* on separate cards. Children can pick a card and add letters to create new words such as **nice, pipe** and **mate**.

Book 1.4
The Shopping List

Name_____ **Date**_____ **Extend** ◆133

Cause and Effect

Draw a picture of what could happen next.

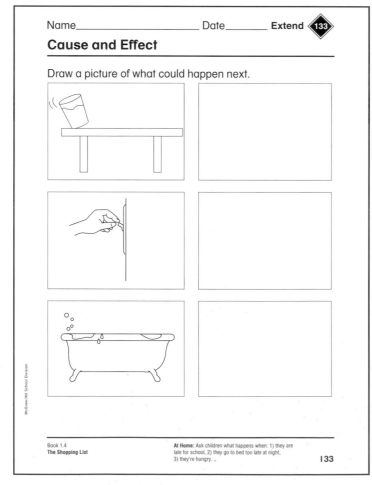

Book 1.4
The Shopping List

At Home: Ask children what happens when: 1) they are late for school, 2) they go to bed too late at night, 3) they're hungry.

133

Name_____ **Date**_____ **Extend** ◆134

Inflectional Endings *-s, -es*

Choose one of the two words. Use it in a sentence.
Circle the word you used.   **Sample answers are given.**

can   cans

_____

I will buy a can of soup.

grape   grapes

_____

Here are the red grapes.

muffin   muffins

_____

I like corn muffins.

plum   plums

_____

Plums taste good.

Look at the picture. Write a sentence about it. Use one of the words in the box.

duck   ducks

_____

The mother duck swims in the front.

At Home: Have children use words such as **bench/benches, doll/dolls, wing/wings,** and **frogs/frogs** in sentences.

134

Book 1.4
The Shopping List

The Shopping List • GRAMMAR

Was and *Were*

- The words *was* and *were* are verbs that tell about the past.
- The word *was* tells about one person, place, or thing.

    Mike **was** in his Dad's store

Read the sentences. Write *was* in each sentence.

1. Dad _____ was _____ happy.

2. Mike _____ was _____ in the store.

3. No one _____ was _____ home.

4. Miss Lin _____ was _____ with Mike.

5. The store _____ was _____ full of people.

5 Book 1.4
The Shopping List   EXTENSION: Ask students to use the words *was* and *were* to write sentences about what they did yesterday.   97

Was and *Were*

- The words *was* and *were* are verbs that tell about the past.
- The word *was* tells about one person, place, or thing.
- The word *were* tells about more than one person, place, or thing.

    Gran and Ann **were** in the store.

Read the sentence about each picture.
Circle the verb for more than one person, place, or thing.

1. Mom and Dad (were) happy.

2. The jam and rice (were) for supper.

3. Mike and Dad (were) smiling.

4. The five plums (were) in a bag.

5. Grapes (were) on the list.

98   EXTENSION: Have the children think of sentences about shopping for groceries. The sentences should be about more than one person, place, or thing.   Book 1.4
The Shopping List   5

Was and *Were*

- The words *was* and *were* are verbs that tell about the past.
- The word *was* tells about one person, place, or thing.

    Mike **was** smiling.

- The word *were* tells about more than one person, place, or thing.

    Fran and Ann **were** smiling.

Read the sentences. Write *was* for one person, place, or thing. Write *were* for more than one person, place, or thing.

1. Mike _____ was _____ in the store.

2. Fran _____ was _____ in the store.

3. Fran and Ann _____ were _____ there.

4. Tin cans and glass jars _____ were _____ on the shelves.

5. Fran and Ann _____ were _____ trying to help.

5 Book 1.4
The Shopping List   EXTENSION: Have the children change the sentences with one person, place, or thing to sentences with more than one.   99

Capital Letters

- The name of each day begins with a capital letter.
- The name of each month begins with a capital letter.
- The name of a holiday begins with a capital letter.

Read the sentences. Circle each word that should begin with a capital letter.

1. Ann Gomez was home on (thursday).

2. Last (april) was Mike's birthday.

3. Ann and Fran were at the (thanksgiving) dinner.

4. Miss Lin was celebrating (new year's day).

5. Mike was looking for birthday presents on (sunday).

6. It was cold last (november).

100   EXTENSION: Have the students write sentences that use names of days, months, and holidays.   Book 1.4
The Shopping List   6

The Shopping List • GRAMMAR

Test

Circle *was* or *were* to complete each sentence.

1. Mike _____**was**_____ glad to see Mom.
   (was)   were

2. Miss Lin and Dad _____**were**_____ helping.
   was   (were)

3. Ann and Fran _____**were**_____ helping.
   was   (were)

4. There _____**was**_____ something else to get.
   (was)   were

5. It _____**was**_____ not milk.
   (was)   were

More Practice With *Was* and *Were*

- The words *was* and *were* are verbs that tell about the past.
- The word *was* tells about one person, place, or thing.
- The word *were* tells about more than one person, place, or thing.

Read each sentence. Write *was* or *were* in the blank. Color the pictures. The sentences tell you how.

1. The grapes _____**were**_____ green. Color them purple.

2. The can _____**was**_____ tan. Color it red.

3. The boxes _____**were**_____ yellow. Color them blue.

4. The ducks _____**were**_____ white. Color them yellow.

T14 *Annotated Workbooks*

The Shopping List • SPELLING

Words with Long i : i-e

Pretest Directions
Fold back the paper along the dotted line. Use the blanks to write each word as it is read aloud. When you finish the test, unfold the paper. Use the list at the right to correct any spelling mistakes. Practice the words you missed for the Posttest.

1. _____   1. smile

2. _____   2. white

3. _____   3. wide

4. _____   4. while

5. _____   5. bite

6. _____   6. hide

To Parents
Here are the results of your child's weekly spelling Pretest. You can help your child study for the Posttest by following these simple steps for each word on the list:

1. Read the word to your child.

2. Have your child write the word, saying each letter as it is written.

3. Say each letter of the word as your child checks the spelling.

4. If a mistake has been made, have your child read each letter of the correctly spelled word aloud, and then repeat steps 1-3.

Challenge Words

_____ after

_____ blue

_____ were

_____ who

Words with Long *i*: *i-e*

Using the Word Study Steps

1. LOOK at the word.

2. SAY the word aloud.

3. STUDY the letters in the word.

4. WRITE the word.

5. CHECK the word. Did you spell the word right? If not, go back to step 1.

Spelling Tip
When there is a long vowel sound at the beginning or in the middle of a one-syllable word, it usually has two vowels.

wi**de**

X the Word
In each row, put an X on the word that does not belong.

1.	smile	pile	~~win~~
2.	white	~~pan~~	red
3.	wide	~~dig~~	tide
4.	hot	cold	~~while~~
5.	bite	~~back~~	kite
6.	~~like~~	hide	ride

To Parents or Helpers:
Using the Word Study Steps above as your child comes across any new words will help him or her spell well. Review the steps as you both go over this week's spelling words.
Go over the Spelling Tip with your child. Help your child write new one-syllable words that have a long vowel sound at the beginning or in the middle and have two vowels.
Help your child complete the spelling activity.

Words with Long i : i-e

Look at the spelling words in the box.

| smile | white | wide | while | bite | hide |

Write the two letters that are found in every spelling word.

1. ____i____   2. ____e____

Write the words that end with **ite**.

3. ___white___   4. ___bite___

Write the words that end with **ile**.

5. ___smile___   6. ___while___

Write the words that end with **ide**.

7. ___wide___   8. ___hide___

Words with Long I : I-e

Look at the pictures. Complete each spelling word by adding **ite, ile,** or **ide.**

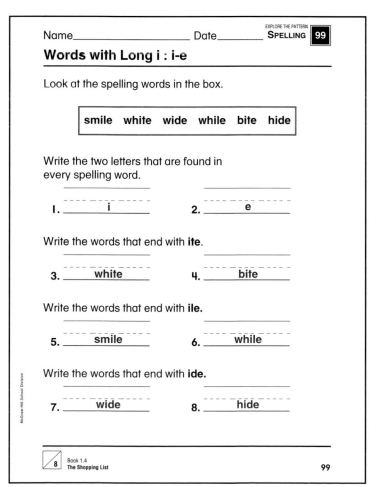

1. My pal Dina always has a big
_____
sm ___ile___ on her face.

2. Her teeth are wh ___ite___ .

3. Her grin is very w ___ide___ .

4. The dog will not
_____
b ___ite___ your hand.

5. He will wag his tail wh ___ile___ you pet him.

6. Sometimes he likes to
_____
h ___ide___ in his doghouse.

The Shopping List • SPELLING

Words with Long i : i-e

Finding Mistakes
Read the poem. There are six spelling mistakes.
Circle the mistakes. Write the words correctly on
the lines.

A tent that is (whide)
Is a good place to (hyd).
All the (whyle),
I sit and (smil).
I take a (bitte)
Of cake so (wite).

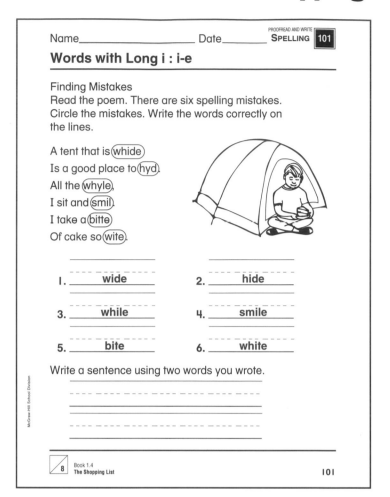

1. __wide__   2. __hide__

3. __while__   4. __smile__

5. __bite__   6. __white__

Write a sentence using two words you wrote.
_____

Words with Long i : i-e

Look at the words in each set. One word in each
set is spelled correctly. Use a pencil to color in the
circle in front of that word. Before you begin, look at
the sample sets of words. Sample A has been
done for you. Do Sample B by yourself. When you
are sure you know what to do, you may go on with
the rest of the page.

Sample A   **Sample B**
ⒶⒶ side   Ⓓ lak
Ⓑ sid   Ⓔ lacke
Ⓒ sidde   ● lake

1. Ⓐ byt   4. Ⓓ hyde
   Ⓑ biet   Ⓔ heid
   ● bite   ● hide

2. ● while   5. Ⓐ smyl
   Ⓔ wile   ● smile
   Ⓕ whyl   Ⓒ smil

3. Ⓐ wid   6. Ⓓ wite
   ● wide   ● white
   Ⓒ wyde   Ⓕ whyte

Yasmin's Ducks • PRACTICE

Long *o: o-e*

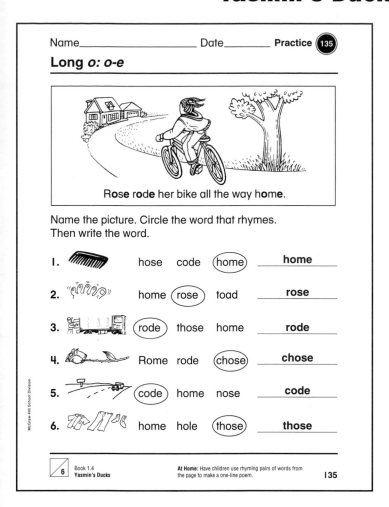

Rose r**o**de her bike all the way h**o**me.

Name the picture. Circle the word that rhymes.
Then write the word.

1. hose code (home) — **home**
2. home (rose) toad — **rose**
3. (rode) those home — **rode**
4. Rome rode (chose) — **chose**
5. (code) home nose — **code**
6. home hole (those) — **those**

McGraw-Hill School Division

Book 1.4
Yasmin's Ducks

At Home: Have children use rhyming pairs of words from the page to make a one-line poem.

135

High-Frequency Words

Write the words from the box to finish the sentences.

some	found	work	because	buy

1. Dad went to _____ **work** _____.

2. We _____ **found** _____ our cat.

3. I will _____ **buy** _____ it at the store.

4. Jane is sad _____ **because** _____ she lost her ball.

5. Pam wants _____ **some** _____ chips.

136

At Home: Have children draw a picture to go along with one of the sentences.

Book 1.4
Yasmin's Ducks

5

McGraw-Hill School Division

Jake Gets Work

Now Jake has found a job. He puts out fires. And he is good at it. Now Jake can buy things. He has a home in Rome!

At Home: Invite children to talk about what jobs they would like to have when they are older.

4

136a

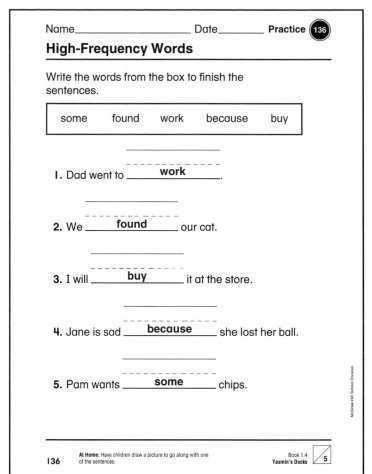

One day Jake went to work. But there was no work for him. Jake said. "I can go fast. I have a hose, I have to work. I want to buy some things."

2

NO WORK TODAY!

Yasmin's Ducks McGraw-Hill School Division

Jake went in his truck to Rome. "There must be work here because it is big," said Jake.

At the woods near Rome, Jake saw smoke. He drove close. It was a fire. He got his hose. He put out the fire.

3

136b

T17

Yasmin's Ducks • PRACTICE

Story Comprehension

Think about "Yasmin's Ducks." Finish each
sentence by circling the picture that tells the answer.

1. Yasmin likes to draw ___.

   a.   b.

2. Yasmin saw ducks in a ___.

   a.   b.

3. Ducks stay dry by ___.

   a.   b.

4. Ducks can dive in a ___.

   a.   b.

5. The ducks can't eat when the lake is ___.

   a.   b.

Book 1.4
Yasmin's Ducks   5   **At Home:** Have children tell what was their favorite part of
the story.   137

A Chart

Look at the tally **chart** below.

What Pets Do You Like Best?			
Mice	llllll	Rats	lllll
Cats	llllllll	Birds	llll
Dogs	llllll	Fish	lllll

This chart shows some children's favorite pets.
Count the marks next to each item. Then you will
know which pets the children like best.

Write the correct word to complete each sentence.

1. The favorite pet of most of the children is a ___**cat**___.

2. ___**Five**___ children like rats best.

3. Mice and dogs each have ___**six**___ tally marks.

4. Birds have ___**four**___ tally marks.

At Home: Help children to make a tally sheet to record
138   people's preferences about something that interests them.   Book 1.4
Yasmin's Ducks   4

Long *o*: *o-e*

Circle the picture in each box that has the long **o**
sound as in j**oke**. Then write the word from the list
that tells what the picture shows.

rose	rope	globe	cone

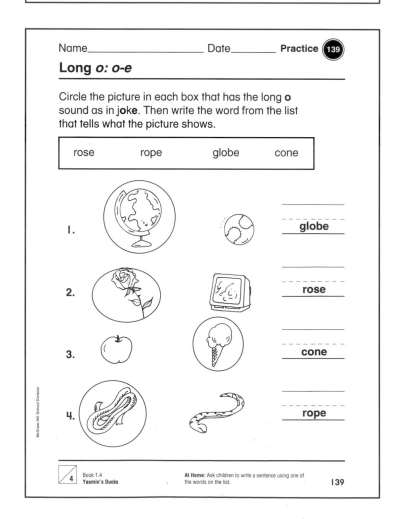

1.   **globe**

2.   **rose**

3.   **cone**

4.   **rope**

Book 1.4
Yasmin's Ducks   4   **At Home:** Ask children to write a sentence using one of
the words on the list.   139

---

o-e, i-e, a-e

Look at the picture. Complete each word by writing
a, i, or **o** in the blank.

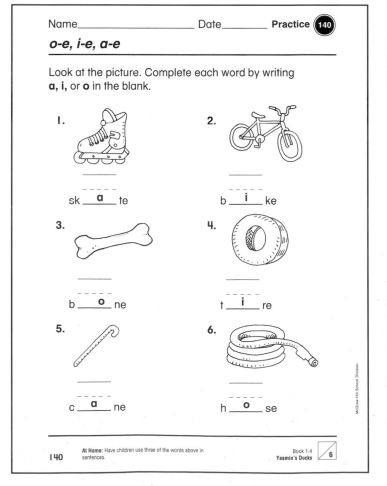

1.   sk __**a**__ te

2.   b __**i**__ ke

3.   b __**o**__ ne

4.   t __**i**__ re

5.   c __**a**__ ne

6.   h __**o**__ se

At Home: Have children use three of the words above in
140   sentences.   Book 1.4
Yasmin's Ducks   6

Cause and Effect

Look at each picture. It shows what happened.
Underline the sentence that tells why it happened.

Effect	**Cause**

1. Grandma lives near us.
   Grandma lives far away.
   Grandma came to see us.

2. Dad rides the bike.
   Dad will go away.
   Dad needs some help.

3. They are looking for a cat.
   The girl wants a new ball.
   Mother wants a green hat.

4. The dog wants the bone.
   The dog will go away.
   The dog hit its nose.

Inflectional Ending -ed

Add **-ed** to show what one or more people or things did in the past.

Add **-ed** to the word. Then write the new word on the line to tell what happened in the past.

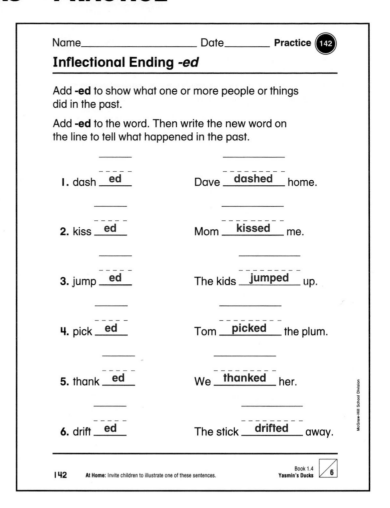

1. dash ___ed___   Dave ___dashed___ home.

2. kiss ___ed___   Mom ___kissed___ me.

3. jump ___ed___   The kids ___jumped___ up.

4. pick ___ed___   Tom ___picked___ the plum.

5. thank ___ed___   We ___thanked___ her.

6. drift ___ed___   The stick ___drifted___ away.

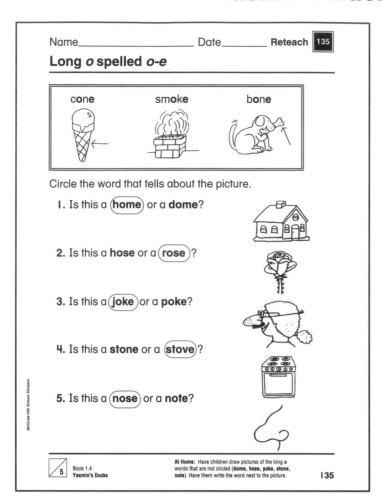

Name_____ Date_____ Reteach 135

Long o spelled o-e

cone   smoke   bone

Circle the word that tells about the picture.

1. Is this a (home) or a **dome**?

2. Is this a **hose** or a (rose)?

3. Is this a (joke) or a **poke**?

4. Is this a **stone** or a (stove)?

5. Is this a (nose) or a **note**?

5 | Book 1.4
Yasmin's Ducks

At Home: Have children draw pictures of the long o words that are not circled (**dome, hose, poke, stone, note**). Have them write the word next to the picture.

135

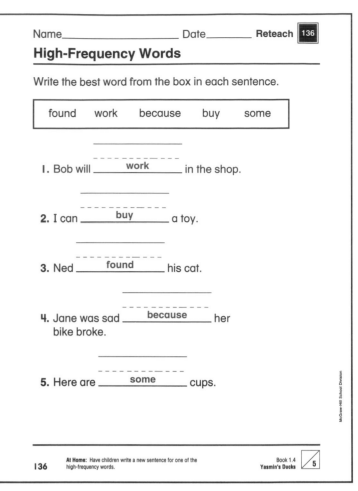

Name_____ Date_____ Reteach 136

High-Frequency Words

Write the best word from the box in each sentence.

| found | work | because | buy | some |

1. Bob will _____**work**_____ in the shop.

2. I can _____**buy**_____ a toy.

3. Ned _____**found**_____ his cat.

4. Jane was sad _____**because**_____ her bike broke.

5. Here are _____**some**_____ cups.

Name_____ Date_____ Reteach 137

Story Comprehension

Draw a line from the children to their pictures.

1. Tim

2. Kate

3. Mack

4. Yasmin

4 | Book 1.4
Yasmin's Ducks

At Home: Ask children to draw and label a picture of something they like.

137

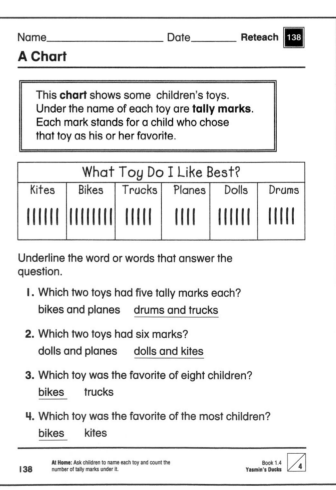

Name_____ Date_____ Reteach 138

A Chart

This **chart** shows some children's toys. Under the name of each toy are **tally marks**. Each mark stands for a child who chose that toy as his or her favorite.

What Toy Do I Like Best?					
Kites	Bikes	Trucks	Planes	Dolls	Drums

Underline the word or words that answer the question.

1. Which two toys had five tally marks each?
   bikes and planes   <u>drums and trucks</u>

2. Which two toys had six marks?
   dolls and planes   <u>dolls and kites</u>

3. Which toy was the favorite of eight children?
   <u>bikes</u>   trucks

4. Which toy was the favorite of the most children?
   <u>bikes</u>   kites

Yasmin's Ducks • RETEACH

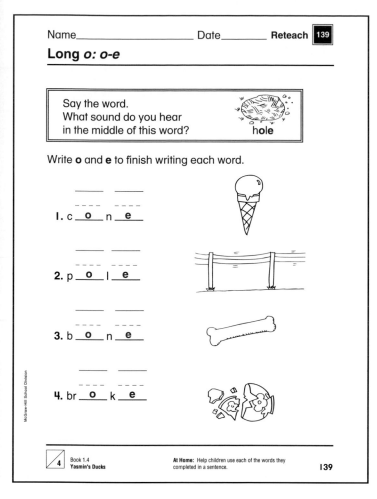

Name_____ Date_____ **Reteach** 139

Long *o: o-e*

Say the word.
What sound do you hear
in the middle of this word?
hole

Write **o** and **e** to finish writing each word.

1. c _o_ n _e_

2. p _o_ l _e_

3. b _o_ n _e_

4. br _o_ k _e_

Book 1.4
Yasmin's Ducks

At Home: Help children use each of the words they
completed in a sentence.

139

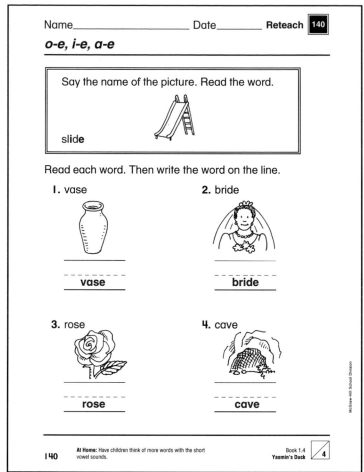

Name_____ Date_____ **Reteach** 140

o-e, i-e, a-e

Say the name of the picture. Read the word.

slide

Read each word. Then write the word on the line.

1. vase
vase

2. bride
bride

3. rose
rose

4. cave
cave

140

At Home: Have children think of more words with the short
vowel sounds.

Book 1.4
Yasmin's Duck

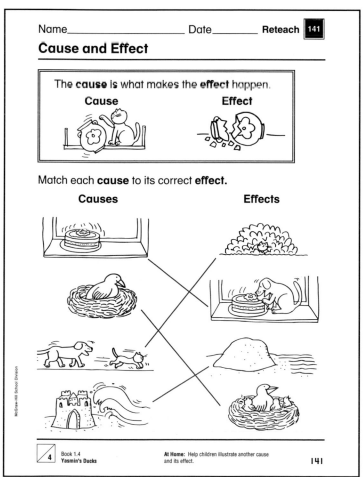

Name_____ Date_____ **Reteach** 141

Cause and Effect

The **cause** is what makes the **effect** happen.
Cause   **Effect**

Match each **cause** to its correct **effect**.

Causes   Effects

Book 1.4
Yasmin's Ducks

At Home: Help children illustrate another cause
and its effect.

141

Name_____ Date_____ **Reteach** 142

Inflectional Ending *-ed*

Add **-ed** to show what one or more people
or things did in the past.
pick + **ed** = pick**ed**
Pat pick**ed** the rose.

Underline the word in each sentence that has **-ed**.

1. The ducks <u>drifted</u> across the pond.

2. One duck <u>bumped</u> into a log.

3. Mike and Mack <u>quacked</u> like ducks.

4. They <u>wanted</u> to feed the birds.

5. The boys <u>tossed</u> bread into the pond.

6. The ducks <u>splashed</u> around in the water.

142

At Home: Help children to rewrite each sentence in the
present tense.

Book 1.4
Yasmin's Ducks

T21

Yasmin's Ducks • EXTEND

Long *o: o-e*

Fill in the letters **o** and **e** to complete the words listed below. Read the word. Write the word. Then write a word that rhymes.

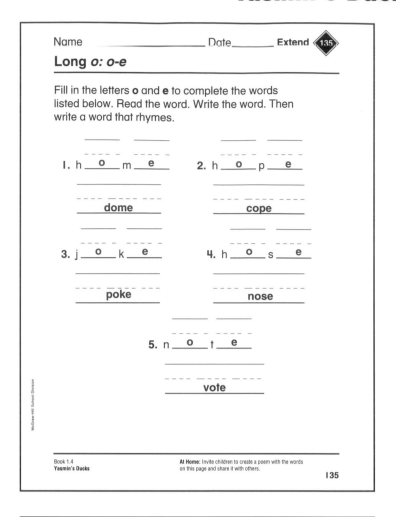

1. h __o__ m __e__

   dome

2. h __o__ p __e__

   cope

3. j __o__ k __e__

   poke

4. h __o__ s __e__

   nose

5. n __o__ t __e__

   vote

Book 1.4
Yasmin's Ducks

At Home: Invite children to create a poem with the words on this page and share it with others.

135

High-Frequency Words

| work | because | buy | found | some |

Look at the letters. Cross out the words **in** and **on**. Then read the words that are left.

~~ON~~~~IN~~WORK~~IN~~~~ON~~~~IN~~BECAUSE~~IN~~~~IN~~ BUY~~ON~~~~IN~~FOUND~~ON~~~~IN~~~~ON~~~~IN~~SOME

Choose two of the words. Write a sentence for each one. **Sentences will vary.**

1. _____

   _____

   _____

2. _____

   _____

   _____

At Home: Invite children to write a sentence about something they have found and then something they would like to buy.

136

Book 1.4
Yasmin's Ducks

Story Comprehension

Yasmin learned a lot from her book on ducks. What did you learn?

Read each sentence. Write **Yes** or **No.**

Oil and water mix.	**No**
Ducks have wings.	**Yes**
Ducks can't swim.	**No**
Ducks don't get wet.	**Yes**
A duck wipes oil on its body.	**Yes**
Kids do not get wet in rain.	**No**
Ducks go south in the fall for food.	**Yes**

Book 1.4
Yasmin's Ducks

At Home: Invite children to correct the incorrect facts. Have them rewrite the statements so that they are true.

137

Use a Chart

Take a class vote. Find what children like to draw.

What Do You Like to Draw?

Look at the chart. What do children like to draw best?

Answer should be based on the chart.

At Home: Ask children other questions about the chart they made, such as: How many children chose ducks to draw?

138

Book 1.4
Yasmin's Ducks

T22 *Annotated Workbooks*

Yasmin's Ducks • EXTEND

Long *o: o-e*

nose	rose	globe	home	stone

Read each riddle. Use a word in the box to solve it.
Write the word on the line.

You live in me.
You eat, sleep, and play in me.

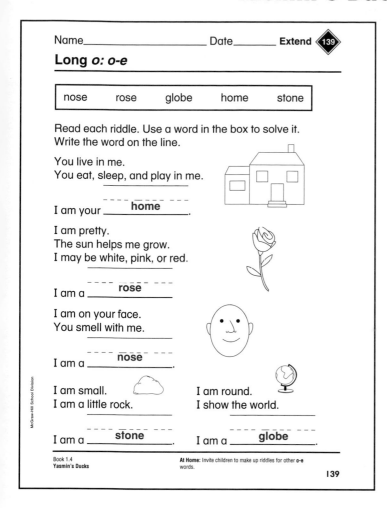

I am your _____**home**_____.

I am pretty.
The sun helps me grow.
I may be white, pink, or red.

I am a _____**rose**_____.

I am on your face.
You smell with me.

I am a _____**nose**_____.

I am small.
I am a little rock.

I am round.
I show the world.

I am a _____**stone**_____.   I am a _____**globe**_____.

Book 1.4
Yasmin's Ducks

At Home: Invite children to make up riddles for other *o-e* words.

139

---

o-e, i-e, a-e

Unscramble the words. Look at the pictures for clues.

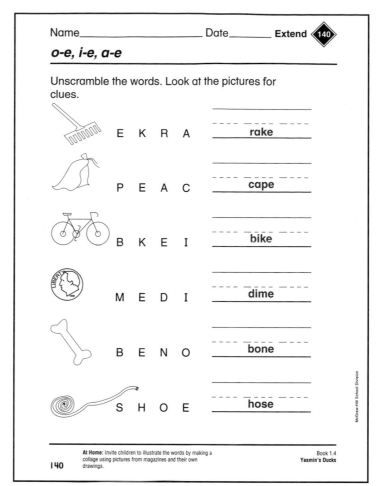

E K R A   _____**rake**_____

P E A C   _____**cape**_____

B K E I   _____**bike**_____

M E D I   _____**dime**_____

B E N O   _____**bone**_____

S H O E   _____**hose**_____

At Home: Invite children to illustrate the words by making a collage using pictures from magazines and their own drawings.

140   Book 1.4
Yasmin's Ducks

Cause and Effect

Draw what could happen next.

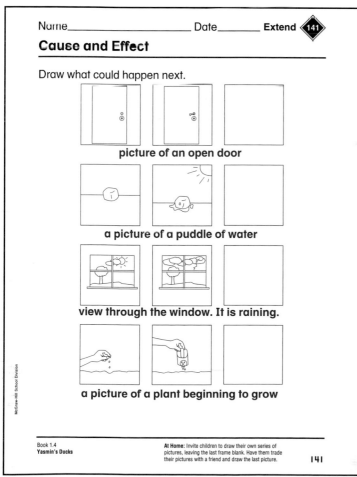

picture of an open door

a picture of a puddle of water

view through the window. It is raining.

a picture of a plant beginning to grow

Book 1.4
Yasmin's Ducks

At Home: Invite children to draw their own series of pictures, leaving the last frame blank. Have them trade their pictures with a friend and draw the last picture.

141

Inflectional Ending *-ed*

quacked	smiled	liked
waited	grabbed	added

Use words from the box to complete the story.
Answers may vary.

The small duck _____**quacked**_____ to her mother. The

small duck's mother _____**waited**_____ for her. We

_____**smiled**_____ at the ducks. Then we _____**added**_____

corn to their food. The ducks _____**liked**_____ the food.

They _____**grabbed**_____ it and ate it.

At Home: Invite children to write a story about what they did when they were little.

142   Book 1.4
Yasmin's Ducks

Yasmin's Ducks • GRAMMAR

Has and Have

> • The words *has* and *have* are verbs that tell about the present.
> • The word *has* tells about one person, place, or thing.
>
> Yasmin has the best ducks.
> Yasmin is one person.
> The verb is *has*.

Circle the verb for one person, place, or thing in each sentence.

1. Tim (has) pictures of fish.

2. Kate (has) trucks.

3. One truck (has) four wheels.

4. The duck (has) feathers.

5. The lake (has) ducks.

Has and Have

> • The words *has* and *have* are verbs that tell about the present.
> • The word *have* tells about more than one person, place, or thing.

Circle the verb that tells about more than one person, place, or thing.

1. The ducks (have) fun in the lake.

2. The child has ducks.

3. The children (have) many ducks.

4. Yasmin and Mack (have) water and oil.

5. The ducks (have) food.

6. The children (have) a good time.

7. The ducks (have) a home.

8. Yasmin has many ducks.

Has and Have

> • The words *has* and *have* are verbs that tell about the past.
> • The word *has* tells about one person, place, or thing.
> • The word *have* tells about more than one person, place, or thing.

Read each sentence. Then write *has* for one person, place, or thing. Write *have* for sentences with more than one person, place, or thing.

1. This duck _____has_____ fun with the children.

2. The duck _____has_____ plenty of food.

3. Yasmin _____has_____ a book about ducks.

4. Ducks _____have_____ oil on their feathers.

5. Yasmin and Tim _____have_____ ducks.

Correcting Sentences with Has and Have

> • Begin every sentence with a capital letter.
> • End every sentence with a period.
> • End every question with a question mark.

Write each sentence correctly.

1. the children have show and tell

   The children have show and tell.

2. Does Tim have pictures of fish

   Does Tim have pictures of fish?

3. mom has ducks too

   Mom has ducks too.

4. Kate has a picture of fire trucks

   Kate has a picture of fire trucks.

5. do Kate and Mack have pictures for show and tell

   Do Kate and Mack have pictures for show and tell?

Yasmin's Ducks • GRAMMAR

Test

Read each sentence. Circle the correct verb for each sentence.

1. Yasmin _____ a duck.

   (has)　　have　　do

2. Ducks _____ oil next to their tails.

   has　　(have)　　are

3. The duck _____ a friend.

   (has)　　have　　are

4. That duck _____ food.

   can　　(has)　　have

5. The ducks _____ fun.

   do　　has　　(have)

More Practice with *Has* and *Have*

- The words *has* and *have* are verbs that tell about the present.
- The word *has* tells about one person, place, or thing.
- The word *have* tells about more than one person, place, or thing.

Read each sentence aloud. Write the sentences to make them correct.

1. Yasmin have three ducks.

   Yasmin has three ducks.

2. Yasmin's ducks has fun.

   Yasmin's ducks have fun.

3. Pets has fun with us.

   Pets have fun with us.

4. Mack have a pup.

   Mack has a pup.

5. Ducks has a home.

   Ducks have a home.

Yasmin's Ducks • SPELLING

Name_____ Date_____

Words with Long o: o-e

Pretest Directions
Fold back the paper along the dotted line. Use the blanks to write each word as it is read aloud. When you finish the test, unfold the paper. Use the list at the right to correct any spelling mistakes. Practice the words you missed for the Posttest.

1. _____ 1. home
2. _____ 2. hope
3. _____ 3. hole
4. _____ 4. nose
5. _____ 5. rope
6. _____ 6. those

To Parents
Here are the results of your child's weekly spelling Pretest. You can help your child study for the Posttest by following these simple steps for each word on the list:

1. Read the word to your child.
2. Have your child write the word, saying each letter as it is written.
3. Say each letter of the word as your child checks the spelling.
4. If a mistake has been made, have your child read each letter of the correctly spelled word aloud, and then repeat steps 1-3.

Challenge Words

_____ work
_____ because
_____ buy
_____ some

Name_____ Date_____

Words with Long o : o-e

Using the Word Study Steps

1. LOOK at the word.
2. SAY the word aloud.
3. STUDY the letters in the word.
4. WRITE the word.
5. CHECK the word.
   Did you spell the word right? If not, go back to step 1.

> **Spelling Tip**
> Use beginnings and endings of words you can spell to help you spell new words.
> then + nose = those

Fill in the Blank
Write the spelling word that best fits each sentence.

1. I __hope__ you will come.
2. __Those__ pots are hot!
3. I like to jump __rope__.
4. I go __home__ on the bus.
5. I have a __hole__ in my sock.
6. My __nose__ is on my face.

To Parents or Helpers:
Using the Word Study Steps above as your child comes across any new words will help him or her spell well. Review the steps as you both go over this week's spelling words.
Go over the Spelling Tip with your child. Help your child write new words that use beginnings and endings of words he or she can spell.
Help your child complete the spelling activity.

Name_____ Date_____

Words with Long o: o-e

Look at the spelling words in the box.

| home hope hole nose rope those |

Write the words that end with **ope**.

1. __hope__   2. __rope__

Write the words that end with **ose**.

3. __nose__   4. __those__

Write the word that ends with **ome**.

5. __home__

Write the word that ends with **ole**.

6. __hole__

All of these words have an **o** and a final **e**.

7. Which letter says its name? __o__

8. Which letter is silent? __e__

Name_____ Date_____

Words with Long o: o-e

Look at the pictures. Write the spelling word to answer each question.

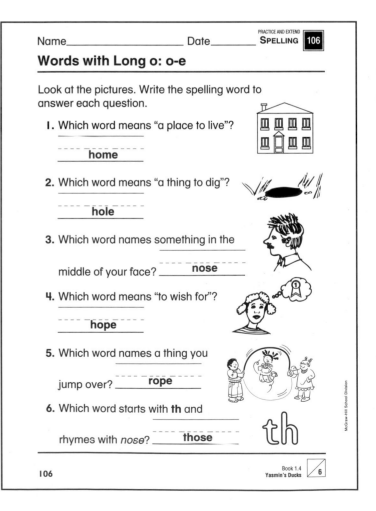

1. Which word means "a place to live"?
   __home__

2. Which word means "a thing to dig"?
   __hole__

3. Which word names something in the middle of your face? __nose__

4. Which word means "to wish for"?
   __hope__

5. Which word names a thing you jump over? __rope__

6. Which word starts with **th** and rhymes with *nose*? __those__

T26 Annotated Workbooks

Yasmin's Ducks • SPELLING

Words with Long o: o-e

Read the poem. There are six spelling mistakes.
Circle the mistakes. Write the words correctly on the lines.

Look at that (hol.)
It is (hom) to a mouse.
He packs it with (roep).
To make a house.
He adds thin sticks.
Can you see (thoze)?
I (hopp) we see him.
Look! There is his (noze).

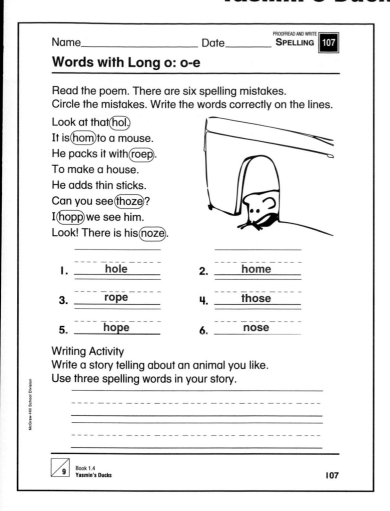

1. _____hole_____   2. _____home_____

3. _____rope_____   4. _____those_____

5. _____hope_____   6. _____nose_____

Writing Activity
Write a story telling about an animal you like.
Use three spelling words in your story.

_____
_____
_____

Words with Long o: o-e

Look at the words in each set. One word in each
set is spelled correctly. Use a pencil to color in the
circle in front of that word. Before you begin, look at
the sample sets of words. Sample A has been done
for you. Do Sample B by yourself. When you are
sure you know what to do, you may go on with the
rest of the page.

Sample A   **Sample B**

Ⓐ hose   Ⓓ bitte
Ⓑ hoze   ● bite
Ⓒ hoose   Ⓕ byt

1. ● home   4. Ⓓ hopp
   Ⓑ hom   ● hope
   Ⓒ hoem   Ⓕ hoope

2. Ⓓ nos   5. ● rope
   ● nose   Ⓑ rop
   Ⓕ noze   Ⓒ roope

3. Ⓐ whol   6. Ⓓ thoz
   Ⓑ hol   ● those
   ● hole   Ⓕ thos

T27

Practice 143

Name_____ Date_____ Practice (143)

Long *u*: *u-e*

Write one of the words from the box in each sentence.

| flute | June | rule | mule | brute |

1. I see that it is ___**June**___.

2. I can ride a ___**mule**___.

3. One ___**rule**___ is that we all line up.

4. The bull was a ___**brute**___.

5. I will play a song on my ___**flute**___.

5
Book 1.4
The Knee-High Man

At Home: Have children say each word, then write it and circle the letter **u**.

143

Practice 144

Name_____ Date_____ Practice (144)

High-Frequency Words

Choose a word from the box to finish each sentence.

| carry | been | clean | done | far |

1. We will | c | l | e | a | n | the van.

2. We are not | f | a | r | from my home.

3. Is the cake | d | o | n | e | yet?

4. I have | b | e | e | n | on a ship.

5. I can | c | a | r | r | y | the pot on my head.

June Rules

"Can I rule June?" asked Max. "No, I cannot!" He still had far to go. But not on June. She was in her shed.

At Home: Encourage children to talk about different kinds of transportation. What is good about each kind? What may be difficult?

144a

2

June was a mule. One day, Max went to her clean shed. "June will give me a ride," he said. "I will make her carry me." Max got his flute to play June a tune. But June did not want a tune!

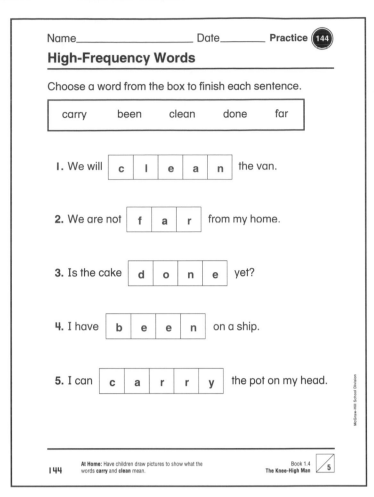

June had been sad. Max wanted to help her. He got a prune for June. But June did not want a prune.

The Knee-High Man • PRACTICE

Story Comprehension

Draw a line to connect the characters in "The Knee-High Man" to what they said.

1. June
2. Sam the Knee-High Man
3. Bob Bull
4. Max Mule
5. Kate Owl

a. Yell and eat grass to be big like me.

b. Sam did not grow an inch.

c. Eat a lot of corn and run ten miles to be like me.

d. Will you tell me how I can grow?

e. You are fine just as you are.

5 Book 1.4
The Knee-High Man

At Home: Help children to list the order in which Sam visits the characters in the story (Max, Bob, and Kate).

145

A Chart

This **chart** tells you what Sam, Dan, and Pam said.

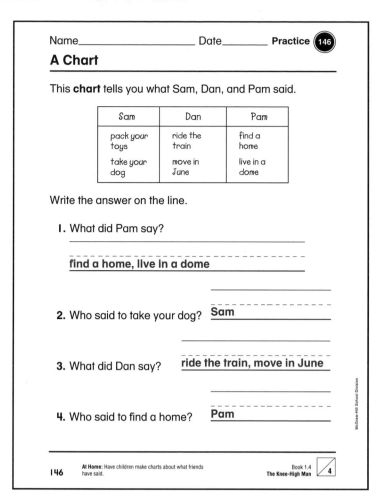

Sam	Dan	Pam
pack your toys	ride the train	find a home
take your dog	move in June	live in a dome

Write the answer on the line.

1. What did Pam say?

   find a home, live in a dome

2. Who said to take your dog? **Sam**

3. What did Dan say? **ride the train, move in June**

4. Who said to find a home? **Pam**

146 At Home: Have children make charts about what friends have said.

Book 1.4
The Knee-High Man 4

Long *u: u-e*

Look at each picture. Write the word from the box that answers each question.

| dune | mule | tune | cube |

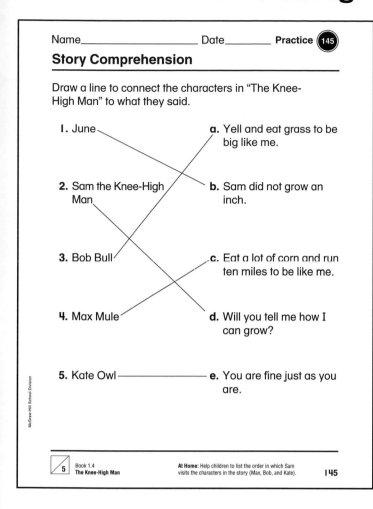

1. I look like a horse. What am I?

   mule

2. You can play me. What am I?

   tune

3. I am made of sand. What am I?

   dune

4. I am the shape of a box. What am I?

   cube

4 Book 1.4
The Knee-High Man

At Home: Ask children to make up a riddle for one of the words from the box.

147

u-e, o-e, i-e, a-e

Read each clue. Circle the answer. Then write the word on the line.

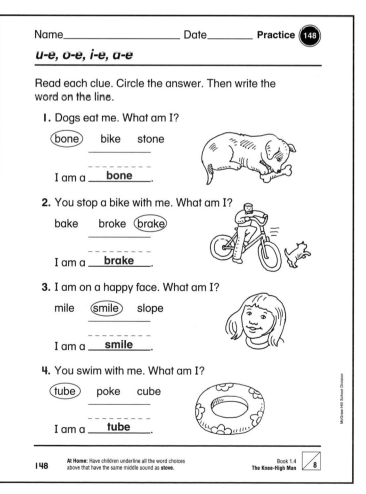

1. Dogs eat me. What am I?

   (bone)   bike   stone

   I am a ___**bone**___.

2. You stop a bike with me. What am I?

   bake   broke   (brake)

   I am a ___**brake**___.

3. I am on a happy face. What am I?

   mile   (smile)   slope

   I am a ___**smile**___.

4. You swim with me. What am I?

   (tube)   poke   cube

   I am a ___**tube**___.

148 At Home: Have children underline all the word choices above that have the same middle sound as **stove**.

Book 1.4
The Knee-High Man 8

Make Inferences

Name_____ Date_____ Practice 149

Read each sentence. Draw a line to the person who can help.

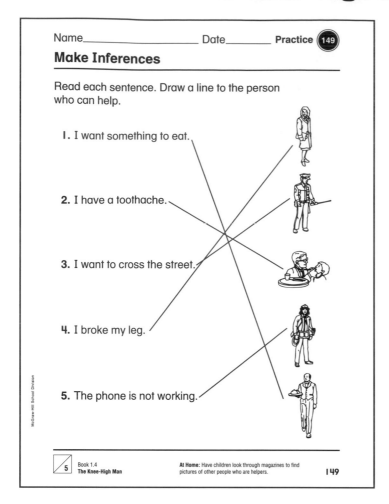

1. I want something to eat.

2. I have a toothache.

3. I want to cross the street.

4. I broke my leg.

5. The phone is not working.

Inflectional Endings -er, -est

Name_____ Date_____ Practice 150

Add **-er** to compare two things.
Add **-est** to compare three or more things.

Circle the word that completes the sentence correctly. Then write the word in the space.

1. Mom's shed is _____**new**_____.

   (new)   newer   newest

2. The lamp is _____**older**_____ than the desk.

   old   (older)   oldest

3. This is the _____**longest**_____ path of all.

   long   longer   (longest)

4. My pup is _____**smaller**_____ than your dog.

   small   (smaller)   smallest

The Knee-High Man • RETEACH

Long *u*: *u-e*

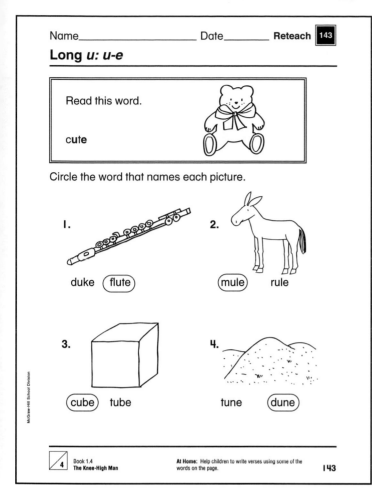

Read this word.

cute

Circle the word that names each picture.

1. duke (flute)

2. (mule) rule

3. (cube) tube

4. tune (dune)

High-Frequency Words

Write the correct word to complete each sentence.

done	clean	far	carry	been

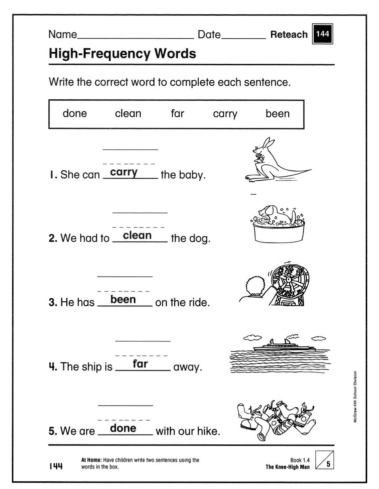

1. She can __carry__ the baby.

2. We had to __clean__ the dog.

3. He has __been__ on the ride.

4. The ship is __far__ away.

5. We are __done__ with our hike.

Story Comprehension

Think about "The Knee-High Man." Fill in the chart. Then answer the questions

	Max Mule	Bob Bull
What to eat?	corn	grass
What to do?	run	yell

1. What did Kate Owl think? __Kate said that Sam did__ __not have to be big.__

2. Who gave Sam the best advice? __Kate Owl__

A Chart

This **chart** tells you what Meg, Jill, and Rick said to Dan.

Meg	Jill	Rick
Camp in a tent.	Ride the train.	Take a nap.
Spill the milk.	Pat the cat.	Sail the ship.
		Hit the nail.

Look at the chart. Circle the correct answer.

1. Meg said to spill the___.   (milk)   bath

2. Rick said to ___ the nail.   sail   (hit)

3. ___ said to ride the train.   (Jill)   Meg

4. ___ said to camp in a tent.   (Meg)   Rick

The Knee-High Man • RETEACH

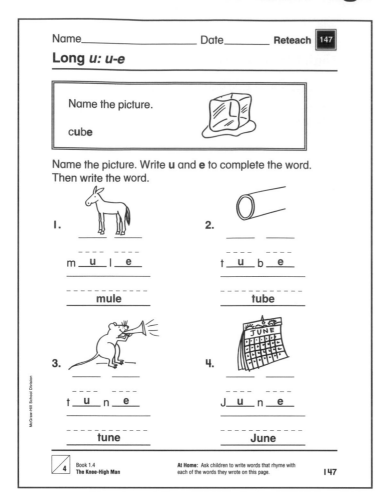

Name_____ Date_____ Reteach 147

Long u: u-e

Name the picture.

cube

Name the picture. Write **u** and **e** to complete the word.
Then write the word.

1. m __u__ l __e__

mule

2. t __u__ b __e__

tube

3. t __u__ n __e__

tune

4. J __u__ n __e__

June

4 | Book 1.4
The Knee-High Man

At Home: Ask children to write words that rhyme with
each of the words they wrote on this page.

147

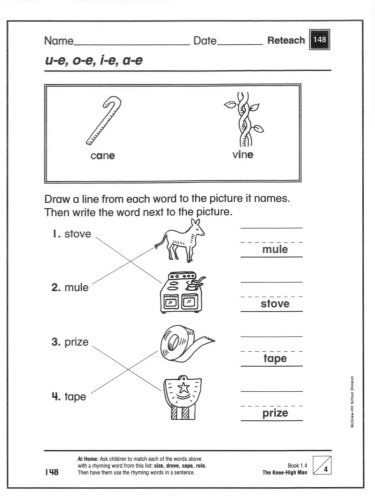

Name_____ Date_____ Reteach 148

u-e, o-e, i-e, a-e

cane   vine

Draw a line from each word to the picture it names.
Then write the word next to the picture.

1. stove

mule

2. mule

stove

3. prize

tape

4. tape

prize

At Home: Ask children to match each of the words above
with a rhyming word from this list: **size, drove, cape, rule.**
Then have them use the rhyming words in a sentence.

148 | Book 1.4
The Knee-High Man | 4

Name_____ Date_____ Reteach 149

Make Inferences

Look at the animal in the first picture.
Then look at the picture of what the
animal eats.

Circle the picture that shows what each animal will
want to eat.

1.

2.

3.

4.

5.

5 | Book 1.4
The Knee-High Man

At Home: Have children draw another thing that one of
the animals would like to eat.

149

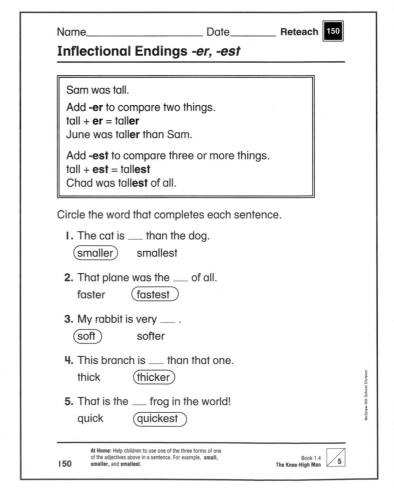

Name_____ Date_____ Reteach 150

Inflectional Endings -er, -est

Sam was tall.

Add **-er** to compare two things.
tall + **er** = tall**er**
June was tall**er** than Sam.

Add **-est** to compare three or more things.
tall + **est** = tall**est**
Chad was tall**est** of all.

Circle the word that completes each sentence.

1. The cat is ___ than the dog.
   (smaller)   smallest

2. That plane was the ___ of all.
   faster   (fastest)

3. My rabbit is very ___ .
   (soft)   softer

4. This branch is ___ than that one.
   thick   (thicker)

5. That is the ___ frog in the world!
   quick   (quickest)

At Home: Help children to use one of the three forms of one
of the adjectives above in a sentence. For example, **small,
smaller,** and **smallest.**

150 | Book 1.4
The Knee-High Man | 5

The Knee-High Man • EXTEND

Long *u: u-e*

Which words have the long **u** sound as in **tune**?
Find the words. Color the stripes red.

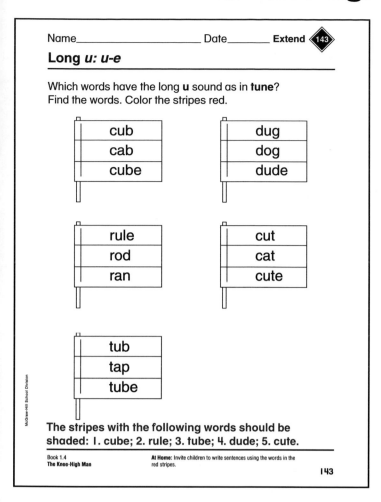

cub
cab
cube

dug
dog
dude

rule
rod
ran

cut
cat
cute

tub
tap
tube

The stripes with the following words should be shaded: 1. cube; 2. rule; 3. tube; 4. dude; 5. cute.

Book 1.4
The Knee-High Man

At Home: Invite children to write sentences using the words in the red stripes.

143

High-Frequency Words

carry	been	clean	done	far

Write the word from the box that completes each sentence.

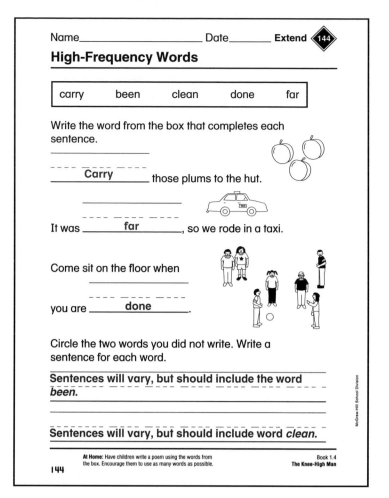

_____

Carry _____ those plums to the hut.

_____

It was _____ **far** _____, so we rode in a taxi.

Come sit on the floor when
_____

you are _____ **done** _____.

Circle the two words you did not write. Write a sentence for each word.

Sentences will vary, but should include the word *been*.

Sentences will vary, but should include word *clean*.

At Home: Have children write a poem using the words from the box. Encourage them to use as many words as possible.

144

Book 1.4
The Knee-High Man

Story Comprehension

Read the sentences. Write **T** if they are true. Write **F** if they are not. If the sentence is true, circle the name of the friend who said it.

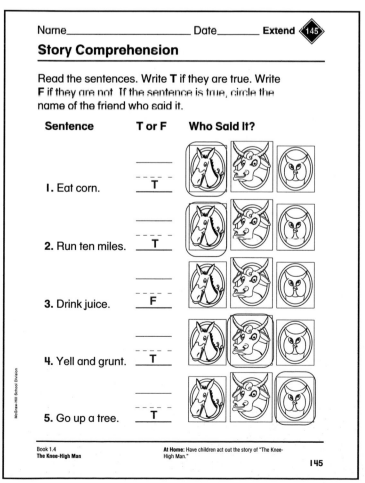

Sentence	T or F	Who Said It?
1. Eat corn.	T	
2. Run ten miles.	T	
3. Drink juice.	F	
4. Yell and grunt.	T	
5. Go up a tree.	T	

Book 1.4
The Knee-High Man

At Home: Have children act out the story of "The Knee-High Man."

145

Use a Chart

Five friends ran a race. Read their chart. Use the chart to answer the questions.

Our Class Race

Names	Speeds	Winners
Amy	36 seconds	
Ben	27 seconds	3 ___ **Ben**
Mack	20 seconds	1 ___ **Mack**
Brad	34 seconds	2
Jill	25 seconds	___ **Jill**

Who won the race? _____ **Mack** _____

What was Brad's speed? _____ **34 seconds** _____

Who ran the race in 25 seconds? _____ **Jill** _____

At Home: Invite children to make their own growth chart. Help them to measure themselves and record their growth.

146

Book 1.4
The Knee-High Man

The Knee-High Man • EXTEND

Long *u: u-e*

Color the pictures whose names have the long **u** sound as in **cube**.

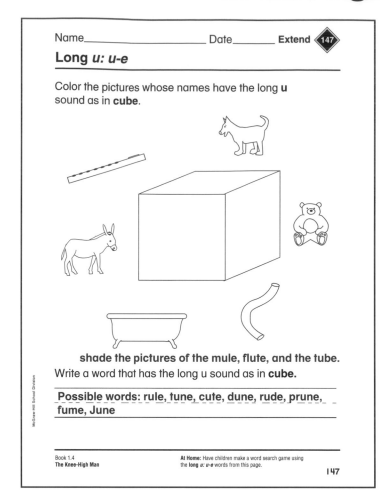

shade the pictures of the mule, flute, and the tube.

Write a word that has the long u sound as in **cube**.

_____

Possible words: rule, tune, cute, dune, rude, prune, fume, June
_____

At Home: Have children make a word search game using the **long** *u: u-e* words from this page.

147

---

u-e, o-e, i-e, a-e

Read the words.
Color the leaves with the long **u** sound as in **cube** brown.
Color the leaves with the long **o** sound as in **rose** red.
Color the leaves with the long **i** sound as **bike** green.
Color the leaves with the long **a** sound as in **cake** yellow.

Start

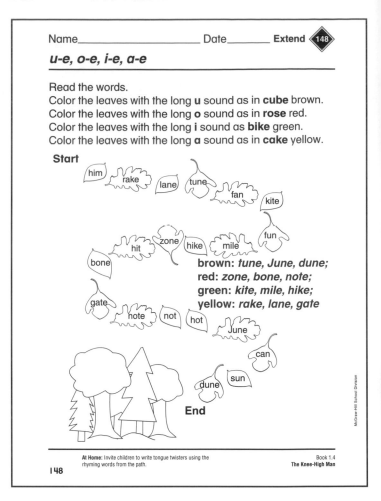

brown: *tune, June, dune;*
red: *zone, bone, note;*
green: *kite, mile, hike;*
yellow: *rake, lane, gate*

End

At Home: Invite children to write tongue twisters using the rhyming words from the path.

148

Make Inferences

Look at the picture. Underline the sentence that tells about the picture.

Mitch is going to school.
Mitch is having a bath.
Mitch is carrying gifts.

The girls are playing.
The girls are reading.
The girls are crying.

Beth had a busy day.
Beth went to sleep.
Beth called her grandma.

Sam does not like dogs.
Sam went to the pool.
Sam got a new pet.

At Home: Invite children to think about why Sam didn't give up his idea of being big until he spoke with Kate. Ask: Would you give up?

149

Inflectional Endings *-er, -est*

Look at the pictures in each row. Add **-er** and **-est**.

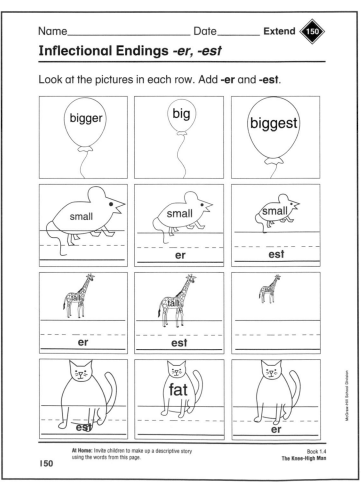

At Home: Invite children to make up a descriptive story using the words from this page.

150

The Knee-High Man • GRAMMAR

Go and Do

- The verb *go* has a special form to tell about the past.
- Use *go* or *goes* to tell about something that happens in the present.

    Max **goes** out every day.
- Use *went* to tell about something that happened in the past.

    Max **went** out last night.

Read the sentences. Look for *go*, *goes*, and *went*. Circle Present or Past.

1. We go to the country.
   (Present)   Past

2. Max Mule goes to help Sam.
   (Present)   Past

3. Sam went to Bob Bull for help.
   Present   (Past)

4. Sam went to Kate Owl for help.
   Present   (Past)

5. Sam goes to the lake.
   (Present)   Past

Book 1.4
The Knee-High Man   EXTENSION: Have the children reread stories in their reader to find *go*, *goes*, and *went*.   109

Go and Do

- The verb *do* has a special form to tell about the past.
- Use *do* or *does* to tell about something that happens in the present.

    Do you like to clean corn cobs?

    Sam **does** not have to be bigger.
- Use *did* to tell about something that happened in the past.

    Max Mule **did** help Sam.

Read the sentences. Circle the verbs that tell about the past.

1. Do bugs carry rope?

2. Why (did) Sam chomp on ten corn cobs?

3. Does running ten miles help Sam?

4. Sam (did) not grow one inch.

5. But Sam (did) not give up.

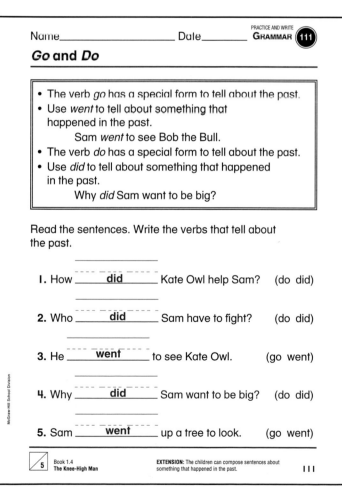

110   EXTENSION: The children can change the present verb tense sentences to past verb tense.   Book 1.4
The Knee-High Man   5

Go and Do

- The verb *go* has a special form to tell about the past.
- Use *went* to tell about something that happened in the past.

    Sam *went* to see Bob the Bull.
- The verb *do* has a special form to tell about the past.
- Use *did* to tell about something that happened in the past.

    Why *did* Sam want to be big?

Read the sentences. Write the verbs that tell about the past.

1. How ____**did**____ Kate Owl help Sam?   (do did)

2. Who ____**did**____ Sam have to fight?   (do did)

3. He ____**went**____ to see Kate Owl.   (go went)

4. Why ____**did**____ Sam want to be big?   (do did)

5. Sam ____**went**____ up a tree to look.   (go went)

Book 1.4
The Knee-High Man   EXTENSION: The children can compose sentences about something that happened in the past.   111

Names with Capital Letters

- The name of a person or place begins with a capital letter.

    Max Mule is big.

Circle the words that should begin with capital letters.

1. Sam went to see (max) (mule)

2. Max did not help (sam) grow big.

3. Sam went to talk to (bob) (bull).

4. Sam did what (bob) told him.

5. Sam went to (new) (york)

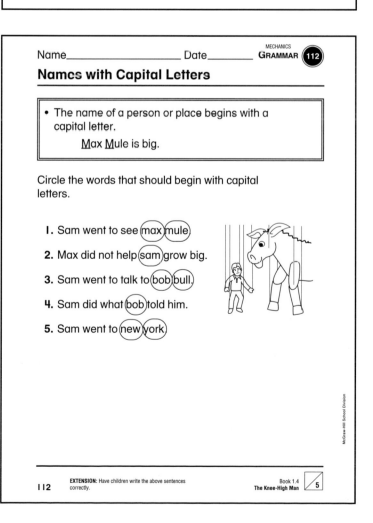

112   EXTENSION: Have children write the above sentences correctly.   Book 1.4
The Knee-High Man   5

T35

The Knee-High Man • GRAMMAR

Test

Draw a line under each verb that tells about the present. Circle each verb that tells about the past.

1. Sam (went) up the tree.

2. Sam <u>does</u> not get help.

3. Kate and Owl (did) help.

4. Kate and Owl <u>do</u> the work.

5. Sam <u>goes</u> to the tree.

6. Sam (went) to get help.

7. Why <u>do</u> you go there?

8. Why (did) Sam go up a tree?

9. Sam <u>goes</u> to see Bob the Bull.

10. Sam (went) to see Bob the Bull.

More Practice with *Go* and *Do*

- Use *go* or *goes* to tell about the present.
- Use *went* to tell about the past.
- Use *do* or *does* to tell about the present.
- Use *did* to tell about the past.

Look at Picture 1. Read the sentences next to it. Circle the sentences about the past.

1. (Sam went to get help.)

2. Sam does things to get big.

3. (Sam did not want to fight.)

4. (Sam went to Kate the Owl.)

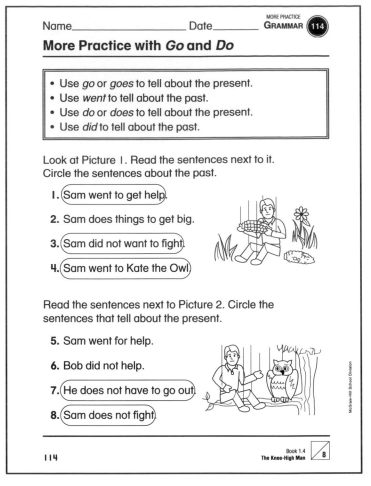

Read the sentences next to Picture 2. Circle the sentences that tell about the present.

5. Sam went for help.

6. Bob did not help.

7. (He does not have to go out.)

8. (Sam does not fight.)

The Knee-High Man • SPELLING

Name_____ Date_____

Words with Long *u*: *u-e*

Pretest Directions
Fold back the paper along the dotted line. Use the blanks to write each word as it is read aloud. When you finish the test, unfold the paper. Use the list at the right to correct any spelling mistakes. Practice the words you missed for the Posttest.

1. _____   1. rule
2. _____   2. cute
3. _____   3. mule
4. _____   4. tube
5. _____   5. tune
6. _____   6. flute

To Parents
Here are the results of your child's weekly spelling Pretest. You can help your child study for the Posttest by following these simple steps for each word on the list:

1. Read the word to your child.
2. Have your child write the word, saying each letter as it is written.
3. Say each letter of the word as your child checks the spelling.
4. If a mistake has been made, have your child read each letter of the correctly spelled word aloud, and then repeat steps 1-3.

Challenge Words
_____ been
_____ clean
_____ done
_____ far

Name_____ Date_____

Words with Long *u* : *u-e*

Using the Word Study Steps

1. LOOK at the word.
2. SAY the word aloud.
3. STUDY the letters in the word.
4. WRITE the word.
5. CHECK the word. Did you spell the word right? If not, go back to step 1.

Spelling Tip
When there is a long vowel sound at the beginning or in the middle of a one-syllable word, it usually has two vowels.
    tune   flute

Find and Circle
Where are the spelling words?

p	d	(r	u	l	e)	k	(c	u	t	e)
s	(m	u	l	e)	i	(t	u	b	e)	o
(t	u	n	e)	q	(f	l	u	t	e)	g

To Parents or Helpers:
Using the Word Study Steps above as your child comes across any new words will help him or her spell well. Review the steps as you both go over this week's spelling words.
Go over the Spelling Tip with your child. Help your child write new one-syllable words that have a long vowel sound at the beginning or in the middle that have two vowels.
Help your child find and circle the spelling words in the puzzle.

Name_____ Date_____

Words with Long *u*: *u-e*

Look at the spelling words in the box.

| rule | cute | mule | tube | tune | flute |

Write the words that end with **ule**.

1. ____rule____   2. ____mule____

Write the words that end with **ute**.

3. ____cute____   4. ____flute____

Write the word that ends with **une**.

5. ____tune____

Write the two letters that are found in every spelling word.

6. ____u____   7. ____e____

Make a new word by changing the **r** of **rule** to **m**.

8. ____mule____

Name_____ Date_____

Words with Long *u*: *u-e*

Look at the pictures. Complete each spelling word.

1. You can ride on a m____ule____ .

2. Another word for song is t____une____ .

3. You can swim with a t____ube____ .

4. The baby pig is very c____ute____ .

5. You can play a fl____ute____ .

6. What you can or cannot do is a r____ule____ .

T37

The Knee-High Man • SPELLING

Words with Long u: u-e

Finding Mistakes
Read the story. There are six spelling mistakes.
Circle the mistakes. Write the words correctly on the lines.

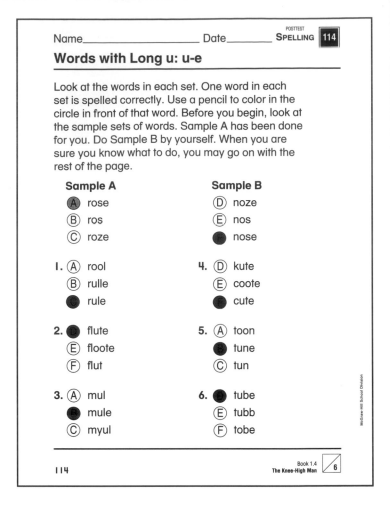

In June, Will and I go to a camp in the woods. We
ride on (muls) up and down the hills. We swim in the
lake with (toobs) We learn to play a (toon) on a (flut.)
We take care of (kute) hens, chicks, and ducks. We
obey all the (rools.) We want to go back soon.

1. **mules**   2. **tubes**   3. **tune**

4. **flute**   5. **cute**   6. **rules**

Writing Activity
Your school has rules. Write about a rule in your
school. Tell why it is a good rule.
Use two spelling words in your story.

_____

_____

_____

_____

Words with Long u: u-e

Look at the words in each set. One word in each
set is spelled correctly. Use a pencil to color in the
circle in front of that word. Before you begin, look at
the sample sets of words. Sample A has been done
for you. Do Sample B by yourself. When you are
sure you know what to do, you may go on with the
rest of the page.

Sample A   **Sample B**

(A) ● rose   (D) noze
(B) ros   (E) nos
(C) roze   (F) ● nose

1. (A) rool   4. (D) kute
   (B) rulle   (E) coote
   ● rule   (F) ● cute

2. ● flute   5. (A) toon
   (E) floote   ● tune
   (F) flut   (C) tun

3. (A) mul   6. (D) ● tube
   ● mule   (E) tubb
   (C) myul   (F) tobe

Practice 151

Name_____ Date_____ Practice 151

Long a: ai, ay

Write a word from the box to complete each rhyme.

| bait | gray | wait | tray |

1. Hurry up. We already **ate.**
   I can hardly
   wait !

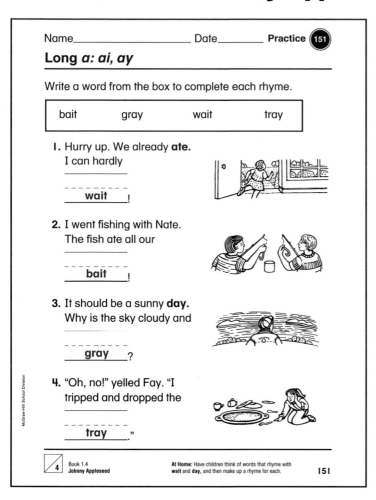

2. I went fishing with Nate.
   The fish ate all our
   bait !

3. It should be a sunny **day.**
   Why is the sky cloudy and
   gray ?

4. "Oh, no!" yelled Fay. "I
   tripped and dropped the
   tray ."

Book 1.4
Johnny Appleseed

At Home: Have children think of words that rhyme with
wait and day, and then make up a rhyme for each.

151

Practice 152

Name_____ Date_____ Practice 152

High-Frequency Words

Circle the word that completes each sentence.
Then write the word.

1. This is a ___**little**___ pup.   how (little)

2. This is a ___**pretty**___ cat.   (pretty) live

3. They ___**live**___ here.   (live) light

4. This is ___**how**___ they go inside.   pretty (how)

5. They sit by the ___**light**___ of the fire.   little (light)

152

At Home: Have children name the cat and pup and draw
another picture showing them both.

Book 1.4
Johnny Appleseed

Gail the Train Nail

"How do you do?" said Gail to the man. "Can I stay on your train?"
"Can my light stay on you?" said the man.
"Yes!" said Gail.
And the nail was safe from the rain.

At Home: Encourage children to talk about why the nail in this story might not have done well in the rain. What are some other things that should not be in the rain?

152a

One day the rain came. Gail the little nail did not like rain.
"I can not stay pretty in the rain," said Gail. "I do not have a place to live!"

Then a train came in the rain. The man in the train had a light.
"I need light for my train to go. But there is no place for my light to stay."

Johnny Appleseed McGraw-Hill School Division

2

3

152b

T39

Johnny Appleseed • PRACTICE

Name_____ Date_____ Practice **153**

Story Comprehension

Circle the pictures that tell what happened in "Johnny Appleseed."

1. Johnny Appleseed planted _____.

2. Johnny Appleseed sailed on a _____.

3. Johnny Appleseed slept with _____.

4. Johnny Appleseed had _____ as pets.

5. Johnny Appleseed ate at a _____.

6. Johnny Appleseed's _____ grew big.

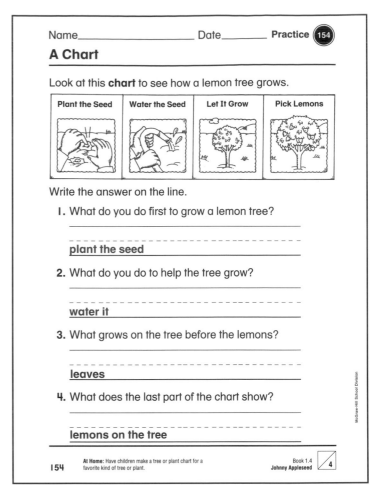

Name_____ Date_____ Practice **154**

A Chart

Look at this **chart** to see how a lemon tree grows.

Plant the Seed	Water the Seed	Let It Grow	Pick Lemons

Write the answer on the line.

1. What do you do first to grow a lemon tree?

   _____
   plant the seed

2. What do you do to help the tree grow?

   _____
   water it

3. What grows on the tree before the lemons?

   _____
   leaves

4. What does the last part of the chart show?

   _____
   lemons on the tree

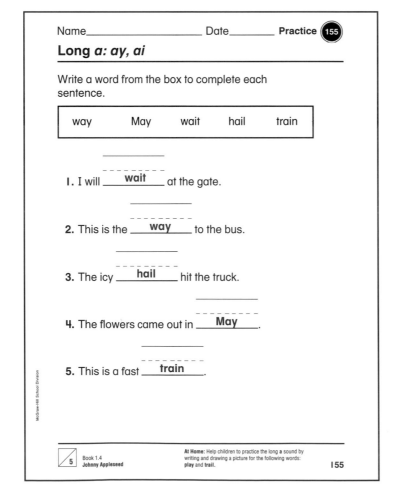

Name_____ Date_____ Practice **155**

Long *a: ay, ai*

Write a word from the box to complete each sentence.

way	May	wait	hail	train

1. I will ____**wait**____ at the gate.

2. This is the ____**way**____ to the bus.

3. The icy ____**hail**____ hit the truck.

4. The flowers came out in ____**May**____.

5. This is a fast ____**train**____.

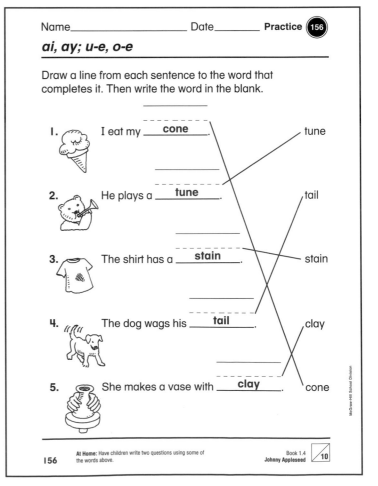

Name_____ Date_____ Practice **156**

ai, ay; u-e, o-e

Draw a line from each sentence to the word that completes it. Then write the word in the blank.

1. I eat my ____**cone**____.   tune

2. He plays a ____**tune**____.   tail

3. The shirt has a ____**stain**____.   stain

4. The dog wags his ____**tail**____.   clay

5. She makes a vase with ____**clay**____.   cone

T40 *Annotated Workbooks*

Johnny Appleseed • PRACTICE

Make Inferences

Read the story. Then fill in the circles in front of the correct answers.

It was Saturday. It was time for Jack to clean his room. But Jack kept putting it off. Then, Joe came over to play. They went to the park. They played ball all day. When Jack came home, he ate a big dinner. Then he went to bed early.

1. Jack did not clean his room because he _____.

- ● went to the park
- ○ read a book
- ○ walked his dog

2. When Jack came home from the park, he was _____.

- ○ excited   ○ sad   ● hungry

3. Jack went to bed early because he was _____.

- ○ happy   ● tired   ○ hungry

4. Did Jack like to clean his room?

- ○ yes   ● no

At Home: Have children predict what Jack will do about his messy room.

Inflectional Endings -er, -est

Add **-er** to compare two things.
Add **-est** to compare three or more things.

Read the word after each sentence. Then add **-er** or **-est** and write the word to complete the sentence.

1. Gail plays the game __faster__ than me.   fast

2. Kate's braid is the __thickest__ of all.   thick

3. My train is __longer__ than yours.   long

Now draw a line from each sentence to the word that completes it.

4. That is the _____ flag pole.   softest

5. This plum is _____ than that one.   fresher

6. Kate's bed is the _____ of all.   tallest

At Home: Work with children to illustrate one of these sentences.

Johnny Appleseed • RETEACH

Long a: ay, ai

Say these words. What sound do you hear that is the same in each word?

play

mail

Circle the word that names each picture.

1. quail **(pail)**

2. **(rain)** rail

3. **(hay)** jay

4. tail **(nail)**

5. sail **(snail)**

6. **(chain)** clay

High-Frequency Words

Complete each sentence with the correct word from the box.

| how | light | little | live | pretty |

1. The __light__ was on.

2. See __how__ I run.

3. I __live__ here.

4. This is a __little__ bug.

5. The kite is __pretty__.

Story Comprehension

Think about "Johnny Appleseed." Write one thing Johnny did that matches each word. **Answers may vary.**

Kind ⟶ **He mended a quail's wing;**

he saved a wolf from a trap.

Happy ⟶ **He always had a big smile;**

he was not sad.

Poor ⟶ **He dressed in rags and**

old sacks; he had no shoes.

Helpful ⟶ **He helped people by planting**

apple trees.

A Chart

This **chart** tells how a plum tree grows. Remember: The steps go in order from left to right.

Look at the Plum Tree chart below.

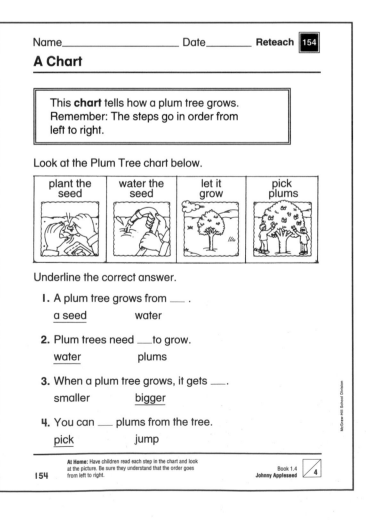

Underline the correct answer.

1. A plum tree grows from ___ .
   a seed   water

2. Plum trees need ___ to grow.
   water   plums

3. When a plum tree grows, it gets ___.
   smaller   bigger

4. You can ___ plums from the tree.
   pick   jump

Johnny Appleseed • RETEACH

Reteach 155

Name_____ Date_____ Reteach 155

Long a: ay, ai

Read these words. How are they the same?

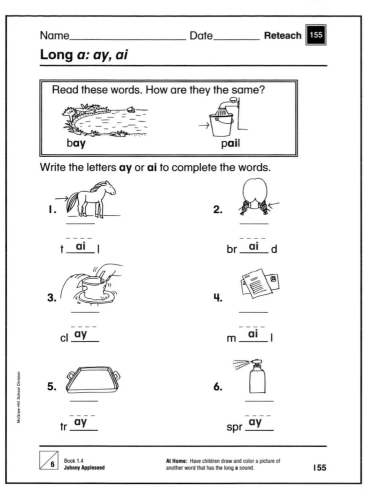

bay   pail

Write the letters **ay** or **ai** to complete the words.

1. t __ai__ l

2. br __ai__ d

3. cl __ay__

4. m __ai__ l

5. tr __ay__

6. spr __ay__

6 Book 1.4
Johnny Appleseed

At Home: Have children draw and color a picture of
another word that has the long a sound.

155

Reteach 156

Name_____ Date_____ Reteach 156

ai, ay; u-e, o-e

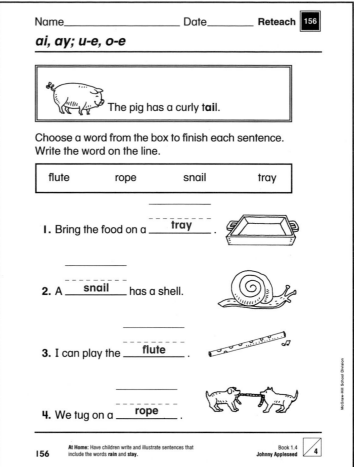

The pig has a curly **tail**.

Choose a word from the box to finish each sentence.
Write the word on the line.

| flute | rope | snail | tray |

1. Bring the food on a ____**tray**____ .

2. A ____**snail**____ has a shell.

3. I can play the ____**flute**____ .

4. We tug on a ____**rope**____ .

156

At Home: Have children write and illustrate sentences that
include the words **rain** and **stay**.

Book 1.4
Johnny Appleseed 4

Reteach 157

Name_____ Date_____ Reteach 157

Make Inferences

You can use what you read and what you
already know to help you better understand
a story.

Read the sentences. Circle the picture that
answers the question.

1. The cook began to cut
the apple. Why was he
mad?

2. The cook put some
bread on the table. Why
was he mad?

3. The cook needed
cheese. Why was he
mad?

4. The cook went to get the
pie. Why was he mad?

5. The cook came to get
carrots. Why was he
mad?

5 Book 1.4
Johnny Appleseed

At Home: Have children explain the answer to each
question.

157

Reteach 158

Name_____ Date_____ Reteach 158

Inflectional Endings -er, -est

Add **-er** to compare two things.
warm + **er** = warm**er**
This lake is warm**er** than that one.

Add **-est** to compare three or more things.
warm + **est** = warm**est**
This is the warm**est** lake in the world.

Circle the words that compare two things.
Underline the words that compare three or more
things.

1. Dave's cab is (newer) than my truck.

2. This is the longest kite in the park.

3. My hair is (shorter) than yours.

4. These grapes are the freshest of all.

5. Kate is (faster) than Jan.

6. I saw the oldest map in the world.

158

At Home: Invite children to illustrate two of the comparisons
made with **-er** and **-est** words above.

Book 1.4
Johnny Appleseed 6

T43

Johnny Appleseed • EXTEND

Long a: ay, ai

Look at each picture. Read the words. Circle the word that matches the picture.

(rain) ran

(snail) snack

train (tray)

hat (hay)

(spray) jam

(mail) may

Choose two of the words that you circled. Use each one in a sentence. **Sentences will vary**

1. _____

2. _____

Book 1.4
Johnny Appleseed

At Home: Invite children to write the words they circled on separate cards. Challenge them to pick one card and name a word that rhymes with the one on the card.

151

High-Frequency Words

| how | light | little | live | pretty |

Read the words in the box. Find them in the puzzle. Circle them.

```
K E I W B (H O W) S V W I T Y
P P G E J T S I (L I V E) J C
S R V (L I T T L E) E U B W X
T E U X I J F K O D N B W I
T X (L I G H T) E C U B E V I
Q T S H E N (P R E T T Y) V W
```

Which word asks a question? _____ **how** _____

Which word means small? _____ **little** _____

What does the sun give? _____ **light** _____ .

At Home: Invite children to create their own word search with the five words. Have children trade puzzles.

Book 1.4
Johnny Appleseed

152

Story Comprehension

How did Johnny Appleseed help others? Complete each sentence. **Sample answers are given.**

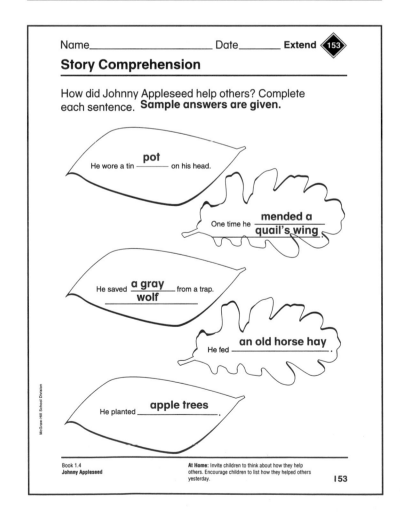

He wore a tin **pot** on his head.

One time he **mended a quail's wing**

He saved **a gray wolf** from a trap.

He fed **an old horse hay**

He planted **apple trees**

Book 1.4
Johnny Appleseed

At Home: Invite children to think about how they help others. Encourage children to list how they helped others yesterday.

153

Use a Chart

Color the pictures. Cut them out. Glue the pictures in the right order on the chart.

How a Cherry Tree Grows

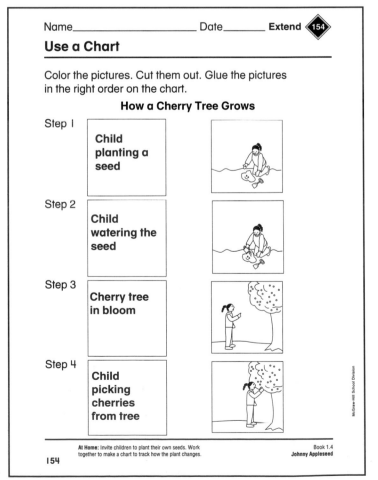

Step 1 — Child planting a seed

Step 2 — Child watering the seed

Step 3 — Cherry tree in bloom

Step 4 — Child picking cherries from tree

At Home: Invite children to plant their own seeds. Work together to make a chart to track how the plant changes.

Book 1.4
Johnny Appleseed

154

Johnny Appleseed • EXTEND

Long *a: ay, ai*

| tray | hay | bay | pail | tail | rail |

Look at the words. Choose a word from the box that
rhymes. Write it on the line. **Sample answers are given.**

1. clay _____**tray**_____

2. pay _____**hay**_____

3. snail _____**pail**_____

4. trail _____**tail**_____

5. say _____**bay**_____

6. mail _____**rail**_____

Book 1.4
Johnny Appleseed

At Home: Invite children to write a poem using some of
the rhyming words.

155

---

ai, ay; u-e, o-e

Color the picture that has the same middle sound
as in the first picture.

snail

tray

cube

rose

At Home: Have children write the word for each answer on one index card
and a drawing of the word on another. Place the cards face down. Have
the child play a memory game and match each word to its drawing.

156

Book 1.4
Johnny Appleseed

Make Inferences

Look at the picture. Underline the sentence that is
true.

It is my first day at school.
It is my birthday.
I got a new bike.

I lost the race.
This is my dog.
I won the race.

It is winter.
It is summer.
It is spring.

I will go to the park.
I am sick.
I will go to the movies.

I am so tired.
My dog likes to go for walks.
I love to dance.

Book 1.4
Johnny Appleseed

At Home: Invite children to look through a magazine.
Encourage them to talk about how the people in the
photographs might feel.

157

Inflectional Endings *-er, -est*

Look at the pictures. Write a sentence about each
one. Use words from the box.
Sample sentences are given.

| bigger | biggest | taller | tallest | faster | fastest |

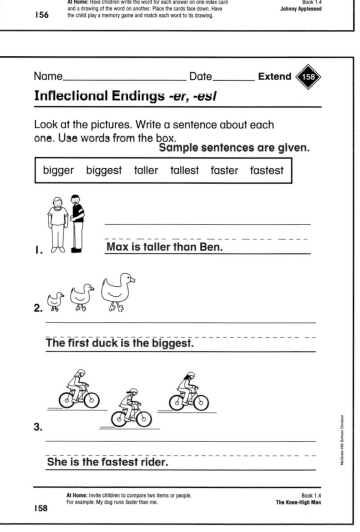

1. **Max is taller than Ben.**

2. **The first duck is the biggest.**

3. **She is the fastest rider.**

At Home: Invite children to compare two items or people.
For example: My dog runs *faster* than me.

158

Book 1.4
The Knee-High Man

Johnny Appleseed • GRAMMAR

See and *Say*

- The verb *see* has a special form to tell about the past.
- Use *see* or *sees* to tell about the present.

  Johnny Appleseed **sees** pink buds.
- Use *saw* to tell about the past.

  He **saw** people going west.

Write the underlined verb so that it tells about the past.

1. Johnny sees the trees. _____ **saw** _____

2. He sees the people. _____ **saw** _____

3. They see his smile. _____ **saw** _____

4. Johnny sees the buds. _____ **saw** _____

5. Then he sees apples. _____ **saw** _____

See and *Say*

- The verb *say* has a special form to tell about the past.
- Use *say* and *says* to tell about the present.
- Use *said* to tell about something that happened in the past.

  I **say** something.   He **said** something.

Write the underlined verb so that it tells about the past.

1. Johnny says the ham was good. _____ **said** _____

2. He says he would rest. _____ **said** _____

3. He says the sun was up. _____ **said** _____

4. He says "I'm Johnny." _____ **said** _____

5. They say, "Hello, Johnny." _____ **said** _____

See and *Say*

- Use *see* or *sees* to tell about the present.

  We **see** pink flowers.
- Use *saw* to tell about something that happened in the past.

  We **saw** pink buds.

Circle the word that makes each sentence tell about the past.

1. Johnny (saw, see, sees) a wolf in a trap.

2. One day, he (saw, see, sees) an old horse.

3. People (saw, see, sees) his pets.

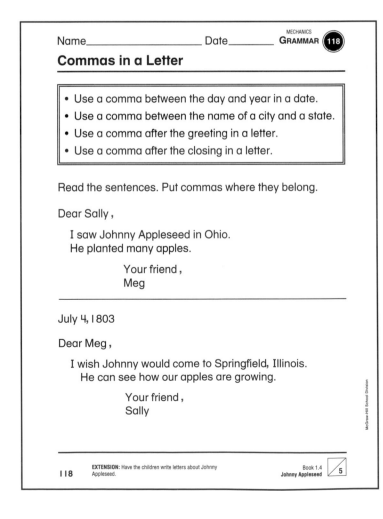

Circle the word that makes each sentence tell about the present.

4. Johnny (saw, see, sees) many plants.

5. He could (saw, see, sees) rain.

6. He (saw, see, sees) many people.

6 Book 1.4
Johnny Appleseed

EXTENSION: Have the children write present or past tense
sentences about seeing apples.

117

Commas in a Letter

- Use a comma between the day and year in a date.
- Use a comma between the name of a city and a state.
- Use a comma after the greeting in a letter.
- Use a comma after the closing in a letter.

Read the sentences. Put commas where they belong.

Dear Sally,

I saw Johnny Appleseed in Ohio.
He planted many apples.

Your friend,
Meg

July 4, 1803

Dear Meg,

I wish Johnny would come to Springfield, Illinois.
He can see how our apples are growing.

Your friend,
Sally

Johnny Appleseed • GRAMMAR

Test

Draw a line under the verb that tells about the present. Circle the verb that tells about the past.

1. Johnny Appleseed (saw) apple trees.

2. Johnny Appleseed <u>sees</u> apple trees.

3. Johnny (said), "Plant apple seeds."

4. Johnny <u>says</u>, "Plant apple seeds."

5. Johnny <u>sees</u> people planting trees.

6. Johnny (saw) people planting trees.

7. Johnny (said) he liked animals.

8. He <u>says</u> he likes animals.

9. The people (said) they liked Johnny.

10. The people <u>say</u> they like Johnny.

More Practice with *See* and *Say*

- Use *see* or *sees* to tell about the present.
- Use *saw* to tell about the past.
- Use *say* or *says* to tell about the present.
- Use *said* to tell about the past.

Read each sentence aloud. Circle the sentences that tell about the past. Underline the sentences that tell about the present.

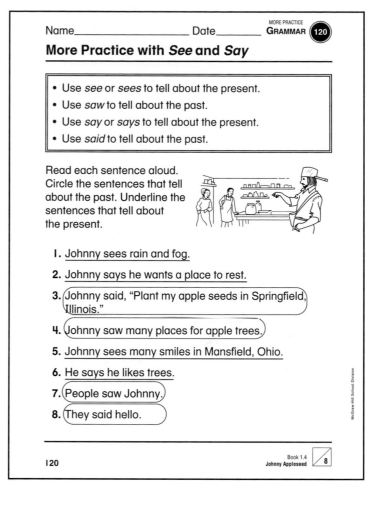

1. <u>Johnny sees rain and fog.</u>

2. <u>Johnny says he wants a place to rest.</u>

3. (Johnny said, "Plant my apple seeds in Springfield, Illinois.")

4. (Johnny saw many places for apple trees.)

5. <u>Johnny sees many smiles in Mansfield, Ohio.</u>

6. <u>He says he likes trees.</u>

7. (People saw Johnny.)

8. (They said hello.)

T47

Johnny Appleseed • SPELLING

Name_____ Date_____

Words with Long a: ai, ay

Pretest Directions
Fold back the paper along the dotted line. Use the blanks to write each word as it is read aloud. When you finish the test, unfold the paper. Use the list at the right to correct any spelling mistakes. Practice the words you missed for the Posttest.

1. _____
2. _____
3. _____
4. _____
5. _____
6. _____

1. rain
2. wait
3. way
4. day
5. say
6. tail

To Parents
Here are the results of your child's weekly spelling Pretest. You can help your child study for the Posttest by following these simple steps for each word on the list:

1. Read the word to your child.
2. Have your child write the word, saying each letter as it is written.
3. Say each letter of the word as your child checks the spelling.
4. If a mistake has been made, have your child read each letter of the correctly spelled word aloud, and then repeat steps 1-3.

Challenge Words
_____
_____
_____
_____
_____

how

light

live

pretty

Name_____ Date_____

Words with Long a : ai, ay

Using the Word Study Steps

1. LOOK at the word.
2. SAY the word aloud.
3. STUDY the letters in the word.
4. WRITE the word.
5. CHECK the word. Did you spell the word right? If not, go back to step 1.

Spelling Tip
When there is a long vowel sound at the beginning or in the middle of a one-syllable word, it usually has two vowels.
rain   say

Word Scramble
Unscramble each set of letters to make a spelling word.

1. nria _____ **rain**
2. yas _____ **say**
3. ady _____ **day**
4. ayw _____ **way**
5. iwat _____ **wait**
6. ilta _____ **tail**

To Parents or Helpers:
Using the Word Study Steps above as your child comes across any new words will help him or her spell well. Review the steps as you both go over this week's spelling words.
Go over the Spelling Tip with your child. Help your child write new one-syllable words that have a long vowel sound at the beginning or in the middle and have two vowels.
Help your child complete the spelling activity.

Name_____ Date_____

Words with Long a : ai, ay

Read the words. Circle the letters that are the same in each set of words.

1. ra(in)   t(ai)l   w(ai)t
2. d(ay)   s(ay)   w(ay)

Write the letters that complete each spelling word.

3. r_____ **ai** _____n
4. w_____ **ai** _____t
5. w_____ **ay**
6. d_____ **ay**
7. s_____ **ay**
8. t_____ **ai** _____l

Read the rhyme. Circle the words that have the long **a** sound as in **may**.

I (wait) in the (rain) on a school (day).
Hoping the bus will come my (way).

Write the words you circled that have the long **a** spelled **ay**.

9. _____ **day**
10. _____ **way**

Write the words you circled that have the long **a** spelled **ai**.

11. _____ **wait**
12. _____ **rain**

Name_____ Date_____

Words with Long a : ai, ay

Complete each spelling word by adding letters that spell the long **a** sound as in **way**.

1. The r_____ **ai** _____n makes plants and grass grow.
2. D_____ **ay** is the opposite of night.
3. The dog wags her t_____ **ai** _____l when she is happy.
4. We w_____ **ai** _____t for the school bus together.
5. We s_____ **ay** "Hi!" to all our friends.
6. Then the bus goes on its w_____ **ay**.

Johnny Appleseed • SPELLING

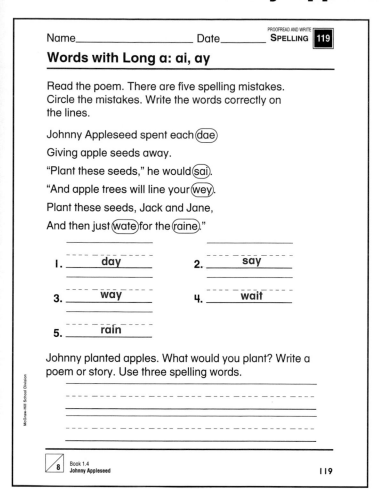

Words with Long a: ai, ay

Read the poem. There are five spelling mistakes.
Circle the mistakes. Write the words correctly on
the lines.

Johnny Appleseed spent each (dae)

Giving apple seeds away.

"Plant these seeds," he would (sai).

"And apple trees will line your (wey).

Plant these seeds, Jack and Jane,

And then just (wate) for the (raine)."

1. _____ day _____
2. _____ say _____
3. _____ way _____
4. _____ wait _____
5. _____ rain _____

Johnny planted apples. What would you plant? Write a
poem or story. Use three spelling words.

_____
_____
_____

8 Book 1.4
   Johnny Appleseed

119

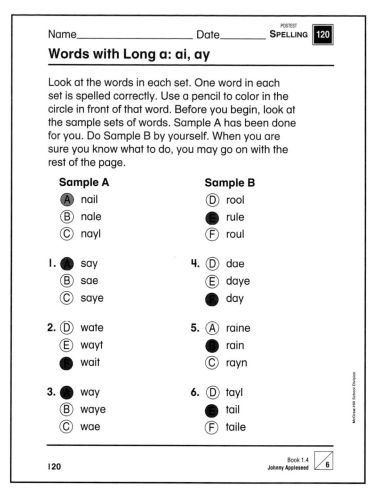

Words with Long a: ai, ay

Look at the words in each set. One word in each
set is spelled correctly. Use a pencil to color in the
circle in front of that word. Before you begin, look at
the sample sets of words. Sample A has been done
for you. Do Sample B by yourself. When you are
sure you know what to do, you may go on with the
rest of the page.

Sample A
- Ⓐ nail ●
- Ⓑ nale
- Ⓒ nayl

Sample B
- Ⓓ rool
- Ⓔ rule ●
- Ⓕ roul

1.
- Ⓐ say ●
- Ⓑ sae
- Ⓒ saye

2.
- Ⓓ wate
- Ⓔ wayt
- Ⓕ wait ●

3.
- Ⓐ way ●
- Ⓑ waye
- Ⓒ wae

4.
- Ⓓ dae
- Ⓔ daye
- Ⓕ day ●

5.
- Ⓐ raine
- Ⓑ rain ●
- Ⓒ rayn

6.
- Ⓓ tayl
- Ⓔ tail ●
- Ⓕ taile

120

Book 1.4
Johnny Appleseed 6

T49

Put Out the Fire • PRACTICE

Practice 159

Name_____ Date_____ Practice (159)

ai, ay; u-e, o-e, i-e, a-e

Write a word from the box to complete each sentence.

| fumes | smoke | spray | ride | rain |

1. The fire made black __**smoke**__.

2. They __**spray**__ water with a hose.

3. I want to __**ride**__ on a truck!

4. Do you smell the smoke __**fumes**__?

5. The __**rain**__ put out the fire.

McGraw-Hill School Division

☐ 5 Book 1.4
Ring! Ring! Ring! Put Out the Fire!

At Home: Have children draw a picture for the following words: **slide, hose, rule, sail,** and **day.**

159

Practice 160

Name_____ Date_____ Practice (160)

High-Frequency Words

Write a word from the box to complete each sentence. The pictures show what each sentence means.

| how | clean | always | work | done |

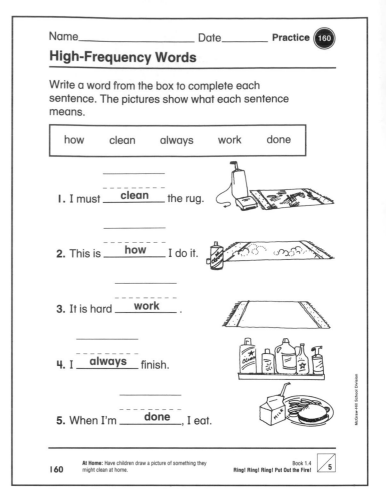

1. I must __**clean**__ the rug.

2. This is __**how**__ I do it.

3. It is hard __**work**__.

4. I __**always**__ finish.

5. When I'm __**done**__, I eat.

McGraw-Hill School Division

160
At Home: Have children draw a picture of something they might clean at home.

Book 1.4
Ring! Ring! Ring! Put Out the Fire! 5

Hen and Snail

Snail went to Hen and asked for a bite to eat and a place to stay.

"From now on you must work." said Hen.

Snail said, "Yes." Hen and Snail became friends.

At Home: Have children talk about why work is important. What kinds of work are there? What kind of work do they like to do?

4

160a

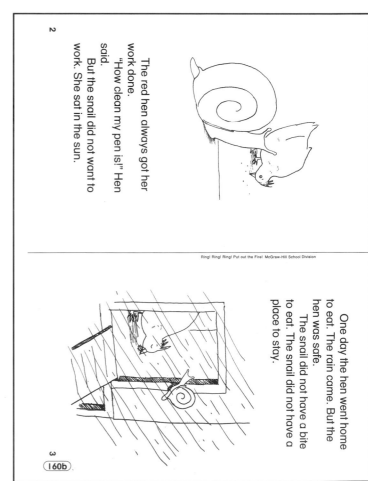

2

The red hen always got her work done.

"How clean my pen is!" Hen said.

But the snail did not want to work. She sat in the sun.

One day the hen went home to eat. The rain came. But the hen was safe.

The snail did not have a bite to eat. The snail did not have a place to stay.

Ring! Ring! Ring! Put out the Fire! McGraw-Hill School Division

3

160b

Put Out the Fire • PRACTICE

Story Comprehension

Circle the sentences that tell what happened in
"Ring! Ring! Ring! Put Out the Fire!"

1. (The fire truck can rush to a fire.)

2. (The fire truck has things to put out a fire.)

3. (The fire hose can spray on a fire.)

4. The fire truck is very small.

5. (Masks help with smoke and fumes.)

A Chart

Jon's class voted about where to go on a picnic.
They chose from four places. This **chart** tells you
how many votes each place got.

Place	Number of Votes
Mill Pond Park	l l l l l l l l l
Fish Creek	l l l l l l l
Sand Beach	l l l l l
Stone Hills	l l l l l l

1. How many votes did Fish Creek get? **seven**

2. How many votes did Stone Hills get? **six**

3. Which place got the most votes? **Mill Pond Park**

4. Which place got the least votes? **Sand Beach**

Cause and Effect

Read the question. Look at the picture. Underline
the answer

Effect | **Cause**

1. Why did the milk spill? | The cup was too full.
The knight bumped the cup.
The cup was too tall.

2. Why did the queen go away? | No one was home.
The king said to go away.
The prince was late.

3. Why did the queen call the knight? | He tells good stories.
She wants the dragon to go away.
The king is missing.

4. Why did the cook run in? | He saw a mouse.
The food was not cooked.
The pot was running over.

Make Inferences

Read the sentences. Circle the word that tells how
the person might feel. Then write the word on the
line.

1. Jill wants a new toy.
Her mom says no.
Jill is _____.
(sad)   happy   excited   **sad**

2. Ann loves animals.
Dad brings her a hamster.
Ann is _____.
sad   mad   (happy)   **happy**

3. Ray wants a snack.
He asks for an apple.
Ray is _____.
silly   (hungry)   happy   **hungry**

4. Dad looks at the clock.
He yawns.
Dad is _____.
sad   happy   (sleepy)   **sleepy**

Put Out the Fire • PRACTICE

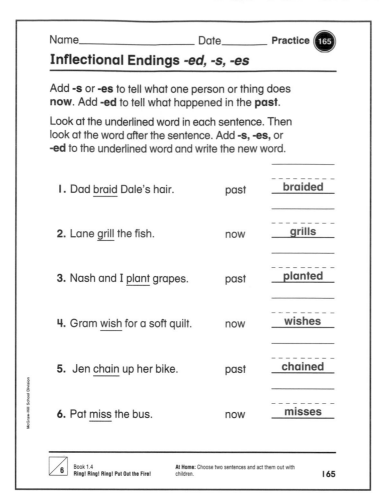

Inflectional Endings -ed, -s, -es

Add **-s** or **-es** to tell what one person or thing does **now**. Add **-ed** to tell what happened in the **past**.

Look at the underlined word in each sentence. Then look at the word after the sentence. Add **-s, -es,** or **-ed** to the underlined word and write the new word.

1. Dad braid Dale's hair. past **braided**

2. Lane grill the fish. now **grills**

3. Nash and I plant grapes. past **planted**

4. Gram wish for a soft quilt. now **wishes**

5. Jen chain up her bike. past **chained**

6. Pat miss the bus. now **misses**

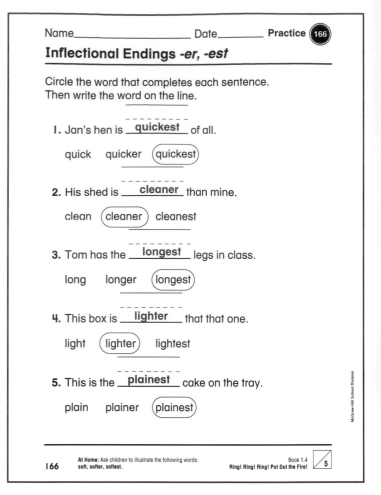

Inflectional Endings -er, -est

Circle the word that completes each sentence. Then write the word on the line.

1. Jan's hen is __quickest__ of all.

   quick quicker (quickest)

2. His shed is __cleaner__ than mine.

   clean (cleaner) cleanest

3. Tom has the __longest__ legs in class.

   long longer (longest)

4. This box is __lighter__ that that one.

   light (lighter) lightest

5. This is the __plainest__ cake on the tray.

   plain plainer (plainest)

Put Out the Fire • RETEACH

Name_____ Date_____ **Reteach** `159`

ai, ay; u-e, o-e, i-e, a-e

Read these words.

| sail | day | cute | globe | time | game |

Draw lines to match the pictures to the words.

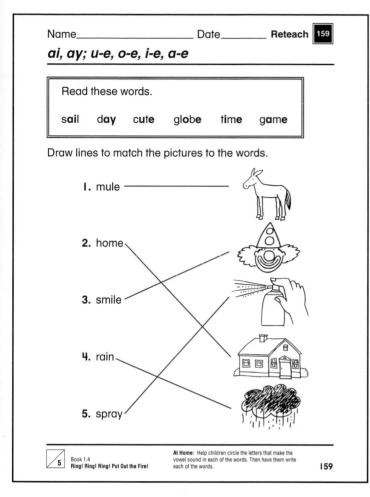

1. mule
2. home
3. smile
4. rain
5. spray

5 | Book 1.4
Ring! Ring! Ring! Put Out the Fire!

At Home: Help children circle the letters that make the vowel sound in each of the words. Then have them write each of the words.

159

Name_____ Date_____ **Reteach** `160`

High-Frequency Words

Underline the word in the sentence that is also in the box. Then write the word.

| how | clean | always | work | done |

1. I <u>clean</u> our house. _____**clean**_____

2. Mom <u>always</u> bakes on Sunday. _____**always**_____

3. The <u>work</u> is fun. _____**work**_____

4. Ken knows <u>how</u> to make cookies. _____**how**_____

5. We eat when we are <u>done</u>. _____**done**_____

160 | **At Home:** Have children write a new sentence using one or more of the vocabulary words.

Book 1.4
Ring! Ring! Ring! Put Out the Fire! | 5

Name_____ Date_____ **Reteach** `161`

Story Comprehension

Draw a line to match the words to the pictures.

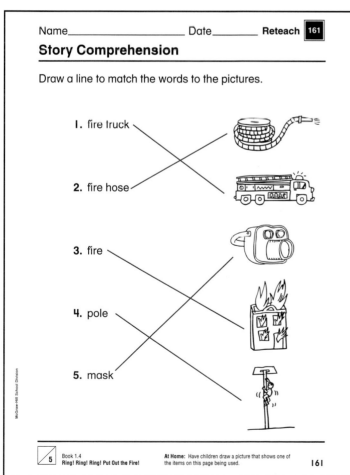

1. fire truck
2. fire hose
3. fire
4. pole
5. mask

5 | Book 1.4
Ring! Ring! Ring! Put Out the Fire!

At Home: Have children draw a picture that shows one of the items on this page being used.

161

Name_____ Date_____ **Reteach** `162`

A Chart

A vote and tally **chart** helps you figure out the results of an election.

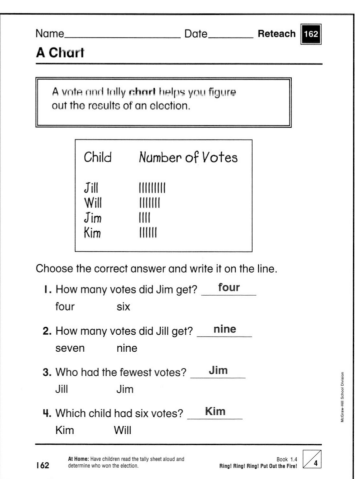

Child	Number of Votes
Jill	IIIIIIIII
Will	IIIIIII
Jim	IIII
Kim	IIIIII

Choose the correct answer and write it on the line.

1. How many votes did Jim get? _____**four**_____
   four   six

2. How many votes did Jill get? _____**nine**_____
   seven   nine

3. Who had the fewest votes? _____**Jim**_____
   Jill   Jim

4. Which child had six votes? _____**Kim**_____
   Kim   Will

162 | **At Home:** Have children read the tally sheet aloud and determine who won the election.

Book 1.4
Ring! Ring! Ring! Put Out the Fire! | 4

Put Out the Fire • RETEACH

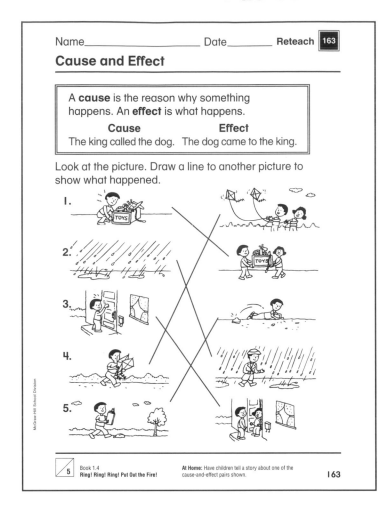

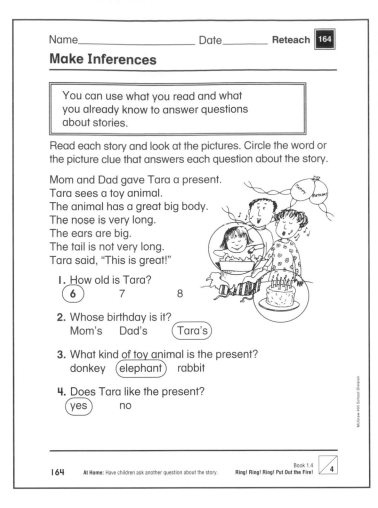

Put Out the Fire • EXTEND

ai, ay; u-e, o-e, i-e, a-e

Red words: Rome, note, home, phone, pole
Color words that have the long **o** sound as in
Rome red.   **Yellow words: say, clay, pay**
Color words that have **ay** as in **say** yellow.
Color words that have the long **i** sound as in
mime green.   **Green words: mime, time, slime**
Color words that have the long **u** sound as in
tune blue.   **Blue words: tune, rude, prune, flute, tube, dune.**

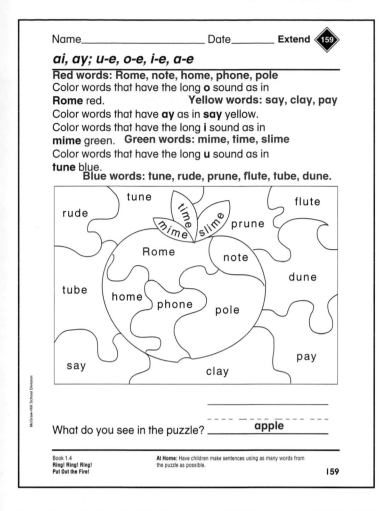

What do you see in the puzzle? _____**apple**_____

High-Frequency Words

Use the words in the box to finish the poem.

how	clean	always	work	done

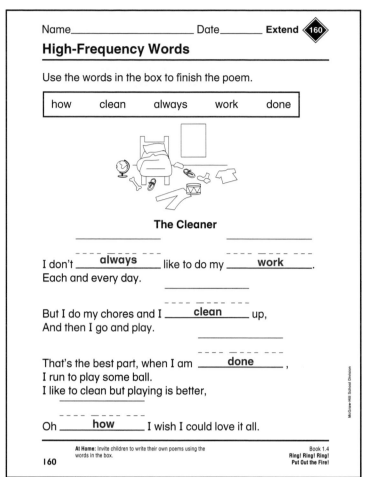

The Cleaner

I don't ____**always**____ like to do my ____**work**____.
Each and every day.

But I do my chores and I ____**clean**____ up,
And then I go and play.

That's the best part, when I am ____**done**____ ,
I run to play some ball.
I like to clean but playing is better,

Oh ____**how**____ I wish I could love it all.

Story Comprehension

Look at the pictures. Put a 1 in the box to show
what happens first. Put a 2 in the box to show what
happens next. Put a 3 in the box to show what
happens last.

3	2	1

What are some other things firefighters do? Draw a
picture.

Use a Chart

What does a firefighter need? Read the list.
Use ✓ check marks to fill in the chart.

Answers may vary.

What Does a Firefighter Need?	A Firefighter Needs . . .	A Firefighter Does Not Need . . .
hose	✔	
cat		✔
fire truck	✔	
iron		✔
fire hat	✔	
horse		✔
sneakers		✔
boots	✔	
lamp		✔
ladder	✔	

Use / tally marks to answer.
How many things does a firefighter need?   ‖‖‖
How many things does a firefighter not need?   ‖‖‖

Cause and Effect

Name_____ Date_____ Extend 163

Look at each picture. ✔ the sentence that happens next.

- ☐ The water turns to ice.
- ☐ The water gets cold.
- ✔ The water gets hot.

- ☐ The bank will fly.
- ✔ The bank will break.
- ☐ The bank will stop in the air.

Look at each picture. ✔ the sentence that happened before.

- ☐ Sam fell off his bike.
- ☐ Sam played with a friend.
- ✔ Sam cleaned his bike.

- ✔ Jane heard a joke.
- ☐ Jane did her homework.
- ☐ Jane ate an apple.

Book 1.4
Ring! Ring! Ring!
Put Out the Fire!

At Home: Take turns playing a **Why/Because** game with children. One person makes a simple statement. The other person asks **Why?** and the first person responds.

163

Make Inferences

Name_____ Date_____ Extend 164

Look at the chart. Read the words. Make the ☐ red if it is a word that tells about a firefighter.

brave	June	trained
strong	good	while
busy	lake	hard-working
when	fast	helpful

Shade in these spaces: brave, strong, trained, good, helpful, busy, hard-working, fast

At Home: Invite children to think about other brave or helpful people. Who are they? Ask children to make drawings of them.

164

Book 1.4
Ring! Ring! Ring!
Put Out the Fire!

Inflectional Endings -s, -es

Name_____ Date_____ Extend 165

Choose the right word. Write it in the blank.

A firefighter can put out a **(fire fires)** ___fire___.

My mom **(smile smiles)** ___smiles___ at me.

How many **(grape grapes)** ___grapes___ can you hold?

The **(fume fumes)** ___fumes___ made me sick.

There were **(flame flames)** ___flames___ in the fireplace.

The firefighter **(chop chops)** ___chops___ down the door.

Book 1.4
Ring! Ring! Ring!
Put Out the Fire!

At Home: On individual index cards, write **-es, -s,** and these base words: **flame, muffin, fire, can, fume,** and **grape.** Turn the word cards face down on a table. Have the child pick a card and point to the correct ending.

165

Inflectional Endings -er, -est

Name_____ Date_____ Extend 166

Name each picture. Use the words in the box to help you.

long longer longest	small smaller smallest
tall taller tallest	big bigger biggest

1. ___long___ ___longer___ ___longest___

2. ___small___ ___smaller___ ___smallest___

3. ___tall___ ___taller___ ___tallest___

4. ___biggest___ ___bigger___ ___big___

At Home: Invite children to make sentences with the words in the box.

166

Book 1.4
Ring! Ring! Ring!
Put Out the Fire!

Put Out the Fire • GRAMMAR

More Contractions with *Not*

> • A **contraction** is a short form of two words.
> • A **contraction** is a short way of saying two words.
> • An **apostrophe** (') takes the place of the letters that are left out.
>
>   was not   wasn't
>   were not   weren't

Read the sentences. Circle the short form of two words.

1. The house (wasn't) on fire.
2. They (weren't) going to a fire.
3. They (weren't) in the truck.
4. There (wasn't) any work to do.
5. He (wasn't) putting out a fire.
6. They (weren't) going down the pole.
7. The pole (wasn't) tall.
8. The trucks (weren't) blue.

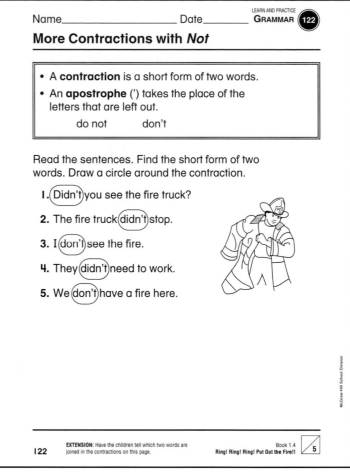

More Contractions with *Not*

> • A **contraction** is a short form of two words.
> • An **apostrophe** (') takes the place of the letters that are left out.
>
>   do not   don't

Read the sentences. Find the short form of two words. Draw a circle around the contraction.

1. (Didn't) you see the fire truck?
2. The fire truck (didn't) stop.
3. I (don't) see the fire.
4. They (didn't) need to work.
5. We (don't) have a fire here.

More Contractions with *Not*

> • A **contraction** is a short form of two words.
> • An **apostrophe** (') takes the place of the letters that are left out.
>
>   was not   wasn't
>   were not   weren't
>   do not   don't
>   did not   didn't

Read the sentences. Circle the two words that make the contraction in each sentence.

1. The firefighters don't always need masks.
   (do not)   was not   did not
2. The firefighters weren't on their way.
   (were not)   was not   do not
3. They didn't rush away.
   (did not)   was not   do not
4. They didn't go down the pole.
   (did not)   was not   do not
5. That wasn't the ladder.
   (was not)   did not   do not

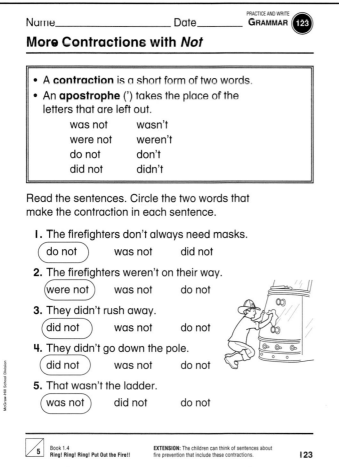

More Contractions with *Not*

> • A **contraction** is a short form of two words.
> • Use an **apostrophe** (') in place of <u>o</u> in a contraction with <u>not</u>.
>
>   was not   wasn't

On the lines, write the contractions for the words in ( ).

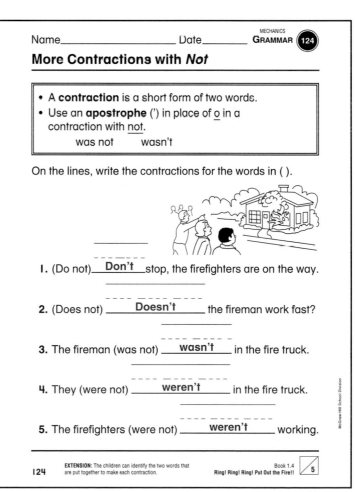

1. (Do not) __Don't__ stop, the firefighters are on the way.
2. (Does not) __Doesn't__ the fireman work fast?
3. The fireman (was not) __wasn't__ in the fire truck.
4. They (were not) __weren't__ in the fire truck.
5. The firefighters (were not) __weren't__ working.

Test

Write the contraction for the underlined words.

1. The house <u>was not</u> on fire.

   _____
   wasn't

2. The men <u>did not</u> rush.

   _____
   didn't

3. <u>Do not</u> go near the fire.

   _____
   Don't

4. They <u>were not</u> at home.

   _____
   weren't

5. She <u>did not</u> see the truck.

   _____
   didn't

5 | Book 1.4
Ring! Ring! Ring! Put Out the Fire!!

125

More Practice With Contractions

- A **contraction** is a short form of two words.
- An **apostrophe** (') takes the place of the letters that are left out.

Look at the picture. Read the sentences about it. Circle the contraction for the underlined words.

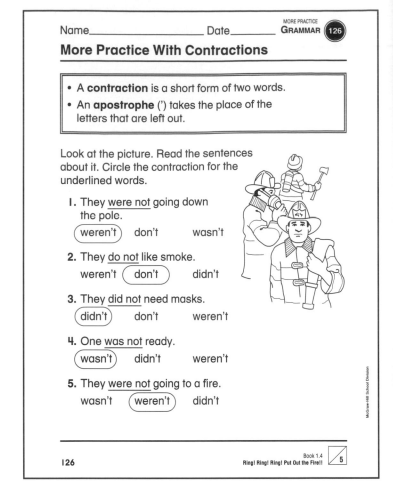

1. They <u>were not</u> going down the pole.

   (**weren't**)   don't   wasn't

2. They <u>do not</u> like smoke.

   weren't   (**don't**)   didn't

3. They <u>did not</u> need masks.

   (**didn't**)   don't   weren't

4. One <u>was not</u> ready.

   (**wasn't**)   didn't   weren't

5. They <u>were not</u> going to a fire.

   wasn't   (**weren't**)   didn't

Put Out the Fire • SPELLING

Page 121

Name_____ Date_____

Words from Science

Pretest Directions
Fold back the paper along the dotted line. Use the blanks to write each word as it is read aloud. When you finish the test, unfold the paper. Use the list at the right to correct any spelling mistakes. Practice the words you missed for the Posttest.

1. _____
2. _____
3. _____
4. _____
5. _____
6. _____

1. truck
2. smoke
3. bell
4. pole
5. ring
6. brave

To Parents
Here are the results of your child's weekly spelling Pretest. You can help your child study for the Posttest by following these simple steps for each word on the list:
1. Read the word to your child.
2. Have your child write the word, saying each letter as it is written.
3. Say each letter of the word as your child checks the spelling.
4. If a mistake has been made, have your child read each letter of the correctly spelled word aloud, and then repeat steps 1-3.

Challenge Words
_____ clean
_____ always
_____ work
_____ done

Book 1.4
Put Out the Fire   121

Page 122

Name_____ Date_____

Words from Social Studies

Using the Word Study Steps
1. LOOK at the word.
2. SAY the word aloud.
3. STUDY the letters in the word.
4. WRITE the word.
5. CHECK the word.
   Did you spell the word right?
   If not, go back to step 1.

Spelling Tip
Keep a notebook with a list of words you have trouble spelling.

Find and Circle
Where are the spelling words?

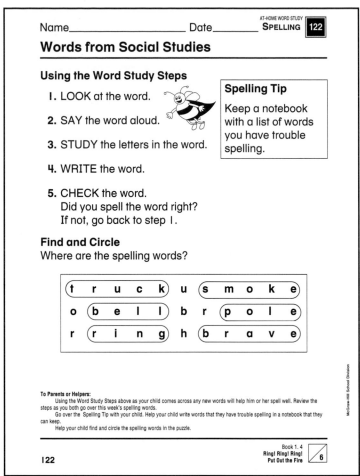

To Parents or Helpers:
Using the Word Study Steps above as your child comes across any new words will help him or her spell well. Review the steps as you both go over this week's spelling words.
Go over the Spelling Tip with your child. Help your child write words that they have trouble spelling in a notebook that they can keep.
Help your child find and circle the spelling words in the puzzle.

122   Book 1.4
Ring! Ring! Ring!
Put Out the Fire

Page 123

Name_____ Date_____

Words from Social Studies

Look at the spelling words in the box. Write each word in the correct helmet.

truck smoke bell pole ring brave

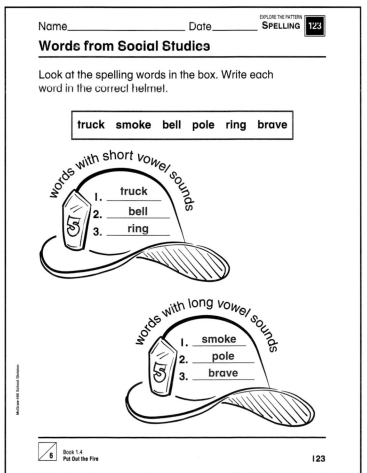

words with short vowel sounds
1. _____ truck
2. _____ bell
3. _____ ring

words with long vowel sounds
1. _____ smoke
2. _____ pole
3. _____ brave

Book 1.4
Put Out the Fire   123

Page 124

Name_____ Date_____

Words from Social Studies

Write the spelling word that goes with each picture.

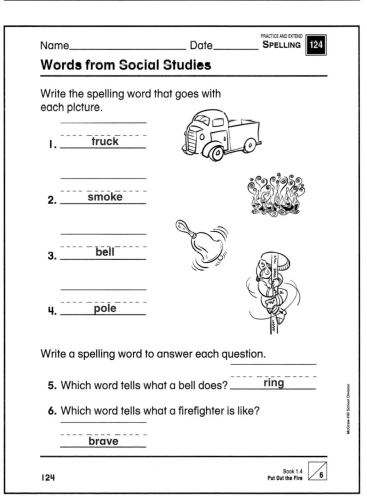

1. _____ truck
2. _____ smoke
3. _____ bell
4. _____ pole

Write a spelling word to answer each question.

5. Which word tells what a bell does? _____ ring

6. Which word tells what a firefighter is like?
_____ brave

124   Book 1.4
Put Out the Fire

T59

Put Out the Fire • SPELLING

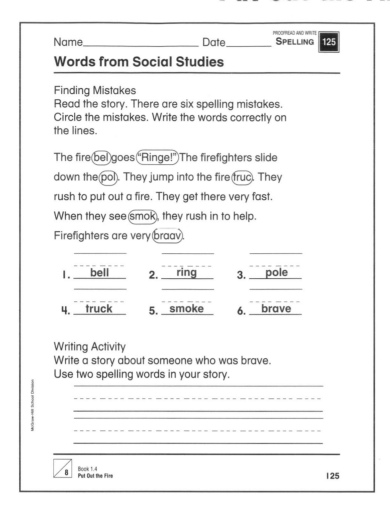

Words from Social Studies

Finding Mistakes
Read the story. There are six spelling mistakes.
Circle the mistakes. Write the words correctly on
the lines.

The fire (bel) goes ("Ringe!") The firefighters slide
down the (pol). They jump into the fire (truc). They
rush to put out a fire. They get there very fast.
When they see (smok), they rush in to help.
Firefighters are very (braav).

1. __bell__   2. __ring__   3. __pole__

4. __truck__   5. __smoke__   6. __brave__

Writing Activity
Write a story about someone who was brave.
Use two spelling words in your story.

_____
_____
_____

Book 1.4
Put Out the Fire   125

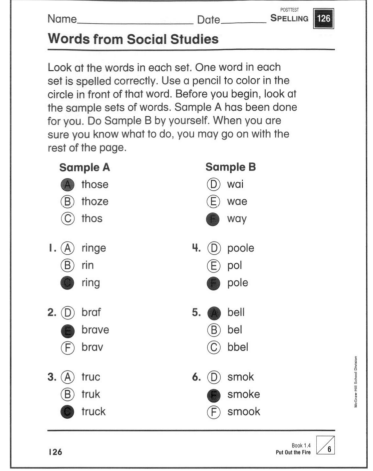

Words from Social Studies

Look at the words in each set. One word in each
set is spelled correctly. Use a pencil to color in the
circle in front of that word. Before you begin, look at
the sample sets of words. Sample A has been done
for you. Do Sample B by yourself. When you are
sure you know what to do, you may go on with the
rest of the page.

Sample A
- (A) those ●
- (B) thoze
- (C) thos

Sample B
- (D) wai
- (E) wae
- (F) way ●

1. (A) ringe
   (B) rin
   (C) ring ●

2. (D) braf
   (E) brave ●
   (F) brav

3. (A) truc
   (B) truk
   (C) truck ●

4. (D) poole
   (E) pol
   (F) pole ●

5. (A) bell ●
   (B) bel
   (C) bbel

6. (D) smok
   (E) smoke ●
   (F) smook

126   Book 1.4
                                    Put Out the Fire 6

Unit 4 Review • PRACTICE and RETEACH

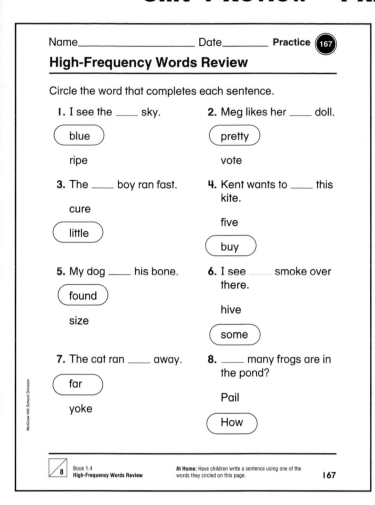

Name_____ Date_____ Practice ⬤167

High-Frequency Words Review

Circle the word that completes each sentence.

1. I see the ____ sky.
   - (blue)
   - ripe

2. Meg likes her ____ doll.
   - (pretty)
   - vote

3. The ____ boy ran fast.
   - cure
   - (little)

4. Kent wants to ____ this kite.
   - five
   - (buy)

5. My dog ____ his bone.
   - (found)
   - size

6. I see ____ smoke over there.
   - hive
   - (some)

7. The cat ran ____ away.
   - (far)
   - yoke

8. ____ many frogs are in the pond?
   - Pail
   - (How)

Book 1.4
8 High-Frequency Words Review

At Home: Have children write a sentence using one of the words they circled on this page.

167

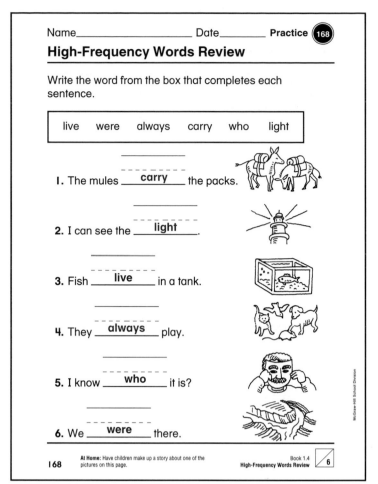

Name_____ Date_____ Practice ⬤168

High-Frequency Words Review

Write the word from the box that completes each sentence.

| live | were | always | carry | who | light |

1. The mules ___carry___ the packs.

2. I can see the ___light___.

3. Fish ___live___ in a tank.

4. They ___always___ play.

5. I know ___who___ it is?

6. We ___were___ there.

168 At Home: Have children make up a story about one of the pictures on this page.

Book 1.4
High-Frequency Words Review 6

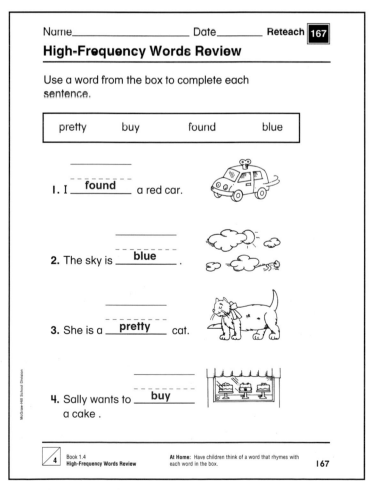

Name_____ Date_____ Reteach 167

High-Frequency Words Review

Use a word from the box to complete each sentence.

| pretty | buy | found | blue |

1. I ___found___ a red car.

2. The sky is ___blue___.

3. She is a ___pretty___ cat.

4. Sally wants to ___buy___ a cake.

4 Book 1.4
High-Frequency Words Review

At Home: Have children think of a word that rhymes with each word in the box.

167

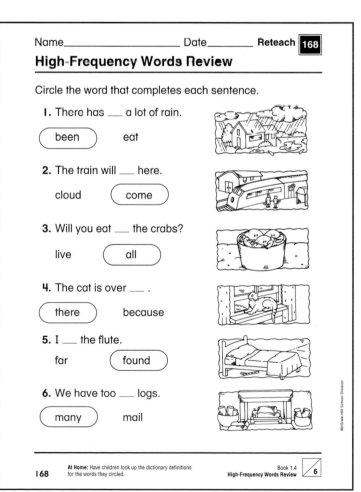

Name_____ Date_____ Reteach 168

High-Frequency Words Review

Circle the word that completes each sentence.

1. There has ___ a lot of rain.
   - (been)
   - eat

2. The train will ___ here.
   - cloud
   - (come)

3. Will you eat ___ the crabs?
   - live
   - (all)

4. The cat is over ___.
   - (there)
   - because

5. I ___ the flute.
   - far
   - (found)

6. We have too ___ logs.
   - (many)
   - mail

168 At Home: Have children look up the dictionary definitions for the words they circled.

Book 1.4
High-Frequency Words Review 6

T61

Unit 4 Review • EXTEND and GRAMMAR

Name_____ Date_____ Extend ◈167

High-Frequency Words Review

Draw a line from the sentence to its picture.

The duck is **after** the dog.

The lake is **blue**.

I use the lamp for **light**.

I **found** a frog.

We **live** in a home.

She is **clean** after a bath.

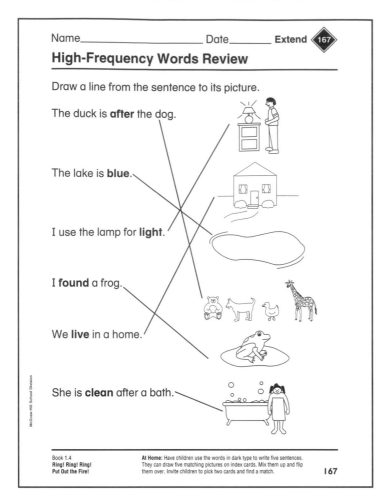

Book 1.4
Ring! Ring! Ring!
Put Out the Fire!

At Home: Have children use the words in dark type to write five sentences. They can draw five matching pictures on index cards. Mix them up and flip them over. Invite children to pick two cards and find a match.

167

Name_____ Date_____ Extend ◈168

High-Frequency Words Review

Read the sentences. Use the words in the box. Write the word on the line. Then write the word in the puzzle.

some	because	who	always

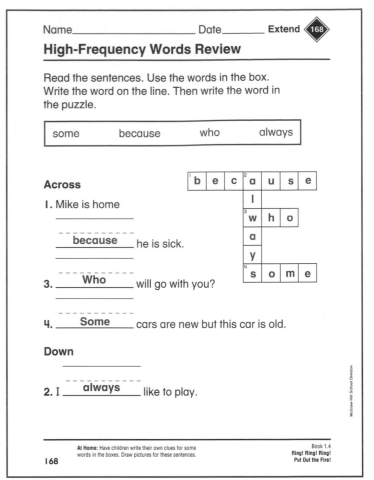

Across

1. Mike is home
   _____

   because ___ he is sick.

3. **Who** _____ will go with you?

4. **Some** _____ cars are new but this car is old.

Down

2. I _____ **always** like to play.

168

At Home: Have children write their own clues for some words in the boxes. Draw pictures for these sentences.

Book 1.4
Ring! Ring! Ring!
Put Out the Fire!

Name_____ Date_____ REVIEW GRAMMAR ●127

More About Verbs

Read the sentences in the box. Look at the part with the line under it. Is there a mistake? How do you make it right? Mark your answer.

Five plums were in a bag. A jar of jam were on the shelf.
(1)

1. (A) Take away *were*.
    ● Change *were* to *was*.
    (C) Do not change.

The child has ducks. The children has many ducks.
(2)

2. ● Change *has* to *have*.
    (B) Take away *has*.
    (C) Do not change.

Yasmin have many ducks. The ducks have a home.
(3)

3. (A) Take away *have*.
    ● Change *have* to *has*.
    (C) Do not change.

Sam went to get help. Sam go up the tree.
(4)

4. ● Change *go* to *went*.
    (B) Take away *go*.
    (C) Do not change.

→ Go on

Book 1.4
Let's Find Out!

127

Name_____ Date_____ REVIEW GRAMMAR ●128

More About Verbs

Sam went to see Bob the Bull. Where do Sam go?
(5)

5. ● Change *do* to *did*.
    (B) Change *go* to *went*.
    (C) Do not change.

Long ago, Johnny says he liked apples. He planted apple trees.
(6)

6. (A) Take away *says*.
    ● Change *says* to *said*.
    (C) Do not change.

People saw apple trees. Johnny see people smile.
(7)

7. ● Change *see* to *saw*.
    (B) Take away *see*.
    (C) Do not change.

We do'nt like smoke. We aren't going to the fire.
(8)

8. ● Change *do'nt* to *don't*.
    (B) Change *do'nt* to *doesn't*.
    (C) Do not change.

128

Book 1.4
Let's Find Out!
◢12

T62 *Annotated Workbooks*

Unit 4 Review • SPELLING

Book 1.4 Unit Review Test

Read each sentence. If an underlined word is spelled wrong, fill in the circle that goes with that word. If no word is spelled wrong, fill in the circle below NONE.

Read Sample A, and do Sample B.

A. The <u>twigs</u> will <u>drope</u> in the <u>snow</u>.
    A   B   C
A. Ⓐ ● Ⓒ Ⓓ NONE

B. <u>When</u> was the <u>class</u> <u>tripe</u>?
    E   F   G
B. Ⓔ Ⓕ ● Ⓗ NONE

1. That dog has a <u>white</u> <u>nose</u> and <u>taile</u>.
            A   B   C
1. Ⓐ Ⓑ ● Ⓓ NONE

2. I <u>hope</u> to fill the <u>tuube</u> with <u>white</u> seeds.
    E   F   G
2. Ⓔ ● Ⓖ Ⓗ NONE

3. The baby at <u>home</u> has a cute <u>pink</u> <u>noize</u>.
           A   B C
3. Ⓐ Ⓑ ● Ⓓ NONE

4. Do not <u>hide</u> your <u>smyle</u> in the <u>smoke</u>.
        E   F   G
4. Ⓔ ● Ⓖ Ⓗ NONE

5. I <u>hope</u> it will not <u>raine</u> on that <u>day</u>.
    A   B   C
5. Ⓐ ● Ⓒ Ⓓ NONE

6. He will <u>hope</u> to find a <u>ring</u> at <u>hom</u>.
        E   F   G
6. Ⓔ Ⓕ ● Ⓗ NONE

Go on →

Book 1.4
Unit Review Test 127

7. <u>Hyde</u> from the <u>smoke</u> in the <u>tube</u>.
    A   B   C
7. ● Ⓑ Ⓒ Ⓓ NONE

8. I <u>hope</u> to see a <u>whyte</u> <u>truck</u>.
    E   F   G
8. Ⓔ ● Ⓖ Ⓗ NONE

9. The <u>smocke</u> came out of the <u>tube</u> in a <u>ring</u>.
      A   B   C
9. ● Ⓑ Ⓒ Ⓓ NONE

10. One <u>daye</u> I will see the <u>truck</u> and <u>smile</u>.
       E   F   G
10. ● Ⓕ Ⓖ Ⓗ NONE

11. We <u>hoppe</u> to know the <u>rule</u> of <u>day</u>.
      A   B   C
11. ● Ⓑ Ⓒ Ⓓ NONE

12. I took the <u>white</u> <u>truk</u> <u>home</u>.
         E   F   G
12. Ⓔ ● Ⓖ Ⓗ NONE

13. I will <u>hide</u> the <u>cute</u> <u>ringe</u>.
       A   B   C
13. Ⓐ Ⓑ ● Ⓓ NONE

14. The <u>rulle</u> of the <u>day</u> is to <u>smile</u>.
       E   F   G
14. ● Ⓕ Ⓖ Ⓗ NONE

15. She has a <u>cuut</u> <u>tail</u> and a small <u>nose</u>.
          A B   C
15. ● Ⓑ Ⓒ Ⓓ NONE

128   Book 1.4
Unit Review Test 15

T63

Phonological Awareness

 OBJECTIVES Children will practice blending sounds, segmenting sounds, and deleting beginning sounds.

Alternate

Blend Sounds

WHAT DO YOU LIKE?

 This activity will help children blend sounds **GROUP** to form words.

- Explain to children that you are going to tell them about something you like to do and say one of the words sound by sound. Children will then blend the sounds to form the word.

- Say to children *I like to ride a /b/-/ī/-/k/. I like to fly a /k/-/ī/-/t/. I like to take a /h/-/ī/-/k/.*

Segment Sounds

COUNTDOWN!

Materials: picture cards and pictures from **PARTNERS** magazines

This activity will help children segment individual sounds in words.

- Organize children into pairs. Give each pair several pictures of objects that represent one-syllable words, such as *bike, five, drive, smile,* or *dime.*

- Have children say the name of each object slowly and segment the name into individual sounds.

- Ask childen to count the sounds. Tell children to place all the pictures that have the same number of sounds in one pile.

Delete Sounds

DOWN THE SLIDE

Use this activity to help children practice deleting beginning sounds.

- Have children practice throwing their arms over their heads and crouching down as though they are going down a slide.

- Give each child a word while he or she is at the "top of the slide."

- As children mimic moving down the slide, have them say the word without its initial sound: *bride/ride, price/rice, spine/pine, flake/lake.*

Long *i*: *i–e*

OBJECTIVES Children will be introduced to words containing the combination of the long *i* sound and silent *e*.

Alternate Activities

Visual

SECRET AGENTS

Materials: outline drawing of a secret agent, crayons, markers, pencils

Use the following activity to introduce children to words containing the combination of long *i* with silent *e*.

- Draw a large outline of a secret agent in a trench coat, sunglasses, and a slouch hat with "silent *e*" written on it.

- Have children color in the drawing.

- Below the drawing, list the following words: *win, hip, din, bin, fin, pin, dip, dim, Tim, gin, lip.*

- Ask children to be "long *i* silent *e* sleuths" and find the words which, when an *e* is added to them, become words with the long *i* sound. ▶**Linguistic**

Kinesthetic

ALL TOGETHER NOW

Materials: cardboard, markers

Have children work with letter cards, combining them to form words with long *i* and silent *e*.

- Make up cardboard cards that have the letters *v, w, m, d, f, l, n,* and *p* printed on them.

- Hand out the cards to eight children, and ask them to hold them up in front of the class.

- Choose eight other children to hold up cards with the word *in* printed on them. Ask these children to pick a letter to stand next to.

- Choose one child to be the "silent *e*." Ask the child to stand at the end of each of the three-letter groups.

- Ask the remainder of the class to read the word that is formed. ▶**Bodily/Kinesthetic**

Auditory

LISTEN FOR THE I

Materials: recordings of popular songs with long *i* words in the lyrics, for example, The Beatles' "I, Me, Mine"

Encourage children to listen to the music and see if they recognize words with the long *i* sound. Have children jot down those words. Then have children share the words they jotted down, distinguishing those that have a silent *e*.

- Play a recording of a popular song which contains some long *i* words (*mine, fine, line, etc.*).

- Ask children to listen for the long *i* sound.

- Have children say the words and list them on the chalkboard. Ask volunteers to underline the silent *e* on the end of the words. ▶**Musical**

Phonics CD-ROM

See Reteach 127, 131, 132, 140, 148, 159

Charts

Alternate Activities

Visual

HEIGHT CHARTS

 Materials: examples of charts, large sheet of paper, markers, tape

Draw a chart on the chalkboard to show the heights of all the children. Have them fill it in and then use it and other charts as models to make their own height charts.

- Have on display in the classroom various charts for children to view.

- Using large sheets of paper taped to the wall, measure the heights of all children in the class. Ask each child to label his or her name and height on the chart you have drawn on the chalkboard.

- Ask children to return to their seats and create a chart of their own showing statistics for four of their classmates. ▶**Spatial**

Kinesthetic

PHYSICAL CHART

 Materials: masking tape, cardboard, markers, index cards

Help children learn to interpret chart information by creating a "physical chart."

- Make a grid with masking tape on the floor. Explain to children that you are making a physical chart of different types of shoes children are wearing.

- Ask a child wearing patent leather shoes to stand in one square, a child wearing sneakers to stand in one square, a child wearing black shoes to stand in one square, and so on.

- Ask each of the children standing in a square to count the number of children in the class who fit the criterion of his or her square.

- Give each child standing in a square a card with the number of children who fit the category written on it.

- Talk the class through ways of interpreting the data on the chart. ▶**Logical/Mathematical**

Auditory

CHART THIS

 Materials: examples of charts, paper, markers

Give children additional practice with interpreting information on charts by having groups make up their own charts.

- Divide the class into small groups, and hand out examples of charts for them to study and discuss.

- Ask groups to decide on something within the classroom to chart and a format to copy from the examples in the handouts.

- Have groups share their charts with the class. Ask the class questions that can be answered by using the information on the charts. ▶**Spatial**

See Reteach 130, 138, 146, 154, 162

Cause and Effect

OBJECTIVES Children will learn to recognize cause and effect.

Alternate Activities

Visual

CAN YOU PREDICT?

Materials: magazines, scissors, pencils

ONE Use magazine illustrations to help children understand cause and effect.

- Provide children with magazines that have a lot of illustrations.

- Explain the meaning of cause and effect by discussing everyday examples, such as: *If you knock over the glass of milk, the milk will spill.*

- Ask children to look through magazines for photographs which demonstrate cause and effect. Explain that although both the cause and the effect may not be apparent in the photos, the child may be able to make up either the cause or the effect. For example, if one photo shows a glass of milk, the student can invent the scenario of knocking it over.

WRITING Have children cut out the photographs and write a cause-and-effect statement under them. ▶**Logical/Mathematical**

Kinesthetic

ACT IT OUT

PARTNERS Have children work in pairs to demonstrate cause and effect.

- Ask one child in each pair to be the CAUSE and the other child to be the EFFECT.

- Ask each pair to come up with a pantomime of a cause-and-effect situation, such as: *John tickles Joe, and Joe giggles.*

- Have the pairs act out their scenarios, and ask the audience to state the cause and effect.
  ▶**Bodily/Kinesthetic**

Auditory

ONE CAUSE, MANY EFFECTS

Materials: large sheets of paper, pencils

GROUP Use this activity to show children that one cause may have several different effects.

- Ask children to think of several cause-and-effect situations. They may be drawn from the book they have just read or from real-life observations.

 Ask one child to say a cause. The classmate WRITING on their left says a plausible effect of that cause.

- Have the next child state another plausible effect to match the initial cause.

- Do this several times, then begin the process again with other children. ▶**Interpersonal**

See Reteach 133, 141, 163

Inflectional Endings -s, -es

OBJECTIVES Children will review making plurals by adding -s and -es.

Alternate Activities

Visual

TRADING LISTS

 PARTNERS Have children work with partners to make plural words.

- Ask children to make lists of ten words in their singular form.

- Assign each child a partner, and have partners exchange lists.

- Ask each child to write the plural of the words on the partner's list. Remind children that some plurals require just an -s, and others need an -es.

- To ensure that some of the words will require the less common -es ending, you can suggest several words (*ax, box, fox, etc.*) which should be included on everyone's list. ▶**Linguistic**

Kinesthetic

LABELS

ONE **Materials:** blue and white index cards

Review -s and -es endings by having children write the plurals of the names of objects in the classroom.

- Ask children to use white index cards to label items in the classroom.

- Have children write on the card the name of the object and tape it to the surface of the object if possible.

- Once the labels are in place, ask children to use blue index cards to label each object with the word in its plural form. For example, if the white index card says *window,* the blue index card would say *windows.*

- Suggest several items in the classroom whose names require -es to form the plural, such as *box.*
  ▶**Bodily/Kinesthetic**

Auditory

WORD CARDS

 PARTNERS **Materials:** index cards or white paper

Have children make word cards, and then have partners take turns quizzing each other about the words' plurals.

- Write the words *fox, box, mix, cat, dog, ball,* and *hat* on the chalkboard.

- Ask children to copy each word onto an index card or slip of white paper.

- Ask children to write on the back of each card whether the word requires -s or -es to make it plural.

- Have children work in pairs, taking turns holding up the cards and asking each other the following: *What is the word, and how do you make it plural?*
  ▶**Linguistic**

See Reteach 134, 165

Phonological Awareness

 OBJECTIVES Children will practice blending sounds, segmenting sounds, and deleting beginning sounds.

Alternate Activities

Blend Sounds

MOLE IN THE HOLE

Materials: construction paper, paper cups, craft sticks

ONE

This activity will help children blend sounds to form words.

- Have children make a small mole out of construction paper and attatch it to a craft stick to make a mole puppet. Children should be able to move the mole up and down inside of its "hole."

- Tell children that the mole only looks out of his hole when he hears other animal names. Say words such as the following: /p/-/i/-/g/; /n/-/ō/-/t/; /b/-/ō/-/n/; /f/-/i/-/sh/, /h/-/o/-/p/, /s/-/n/-/a/-/k/, /b/-/i/-/k/, /m/-/i/-/s/. Children blend the sounds to form the words. Children should move the mole up when they hear another animals name.

- Tell children to have their mole pop out of his hole when he hears the name of an animal.

Segment Sounds

DOGGIE, DOGGIE, WHERE'S YOUR BONE?

 Materials: construction paper cut into bone shape

GROUP

This activity will help children segment individual sounds in words.

- Play "Doggie, Doggie, Where's Your Bone?" with children.

- Choose a child to be the "doggie." Have the "doggie" close his or her eyes while you hide the paper bone behind another child.

- The "doggie" then makes three guesses as to who has the bone hidden behind him. The "doggie" must amke a guess by segmenting the individual sounds in a child's name.

- Continue by letting everyone have a chance to be the "doggie."

Delete Sounds

ICE CREAM CONES

 Materials: construction paper cut into triangles and circles

PARTNERS

This activity will help children practice deleting beginning sounds.

- Give partners a construction paper triangle and four circles to make an ice cream cone.

- Tell children to listen carefully as you say the following words: *spoke, stone, smile, bride,* and *crate.*

- Repeat the words, and ask children to delete the initial sound from each word. After children successfully delete the sound, tell them to take away a scoop of ice cream from their cones.

T69

Long *o: o-e*

OBJECTIVES Children will be introduced to words containing the long *o* sound.

Alternate Activities

Visual

LOOKING FOR LONG *O*'S

 Materials: books, magazines, newspapers, paper, pencils or crayons

Use this activity to introduce words with long *o* and silent *e,* helping children recognize these words in books, magazines, and newspapers.

- Have each child draw the letter *o* several times on a sheet of paper, leaving plenty of space between them to add letters.

- Have children decorate each *o* to look like an eye by adding a pupil and eyelashes.

- Ask children to use their eyes to look through books, magazines, and newspapers in search of long *o* words with silent *e* endings.

- Have children write the words on their sheet of paper, using the eyes to represent the *os* in the words. ▶**Spatial**

Kinesthetic

ADD THE SILENT *E*

 Materials: index cards, bulletin board, thumbtacks

Have children tack on silent *e*'s to review words with the long *o* sound.

- Ask children to help make a list of long *o* words with silent *e* endings. If children suggest words which have the long *o* sound but not the silent *e,*

such as *soap,* make a separate list of those words, and discuss them afterward.

- Write the long *o* words on cards, leaving off the final *e,* and use thumbtacks to attach the cards to a bulletin board.

- Make cards with only the letter *e* on them, and hand these out to children.

- Ask children to tack on the final *e* to the words on the bulletin board. Pronounce the words correctly aloud. ▶**Linguistic**

Auditory

IS IT OR ISN'T IT?

 Materials: cardboard, markers

Have children use letter cards to help them listen for words containing long *o* and silent *e.*

- Read a passage from *Yasmin's Ducks,* making sure to choose a section which has words containing the long *o* sound and silent *e* on the end.

- Ask children to make up two cards, one which has long *o* on it and one which has an *e* on it.

- Ask children to listen to the passage and to raise their long *o* cards when they hear a long *o* word.

- When they raise their cards, ask: *If you think this word has a silent* e *on the end, raise your* e *card.*

- Write the word on the chalkboard so they can see the spelling. ▶**Linguistic**

 **CD-ROM**

See Reteach 135, 139, 140, 148, 156, 159

Phonological Awareness

✓BJECTIVES Children will practice blending sounds, segmenting sounds, and substituting beginning and ending sounds.

Alternate Activities

Blend Sounds

TRUE OR FALSE

 This activity will help children blend sounds to form words.

- Tell partners they are going to play the game "True or False."

- Ask one partner to think of a fact and then say it in a statement. Ask that child to segment the individual sounds in a key word in the sentence for their partner to blend together. For instance, say: *After May comes /j/-/ū/-/n/. True or False? A /m/-/ū/-/l/ has two legs. True or False?*

- The other partner should blend the sounds together to form the word. Then he or she should answer by saying *true* or *false*.

- Repeat by having partners switch roles.

Segment Sounds

CLAY TIME

 Materials: modeling clay or play dough
This activity will help children segment the individual sounds in words.

- Give each child a small ball of clay.

- Use the following words: *tune, June, cube, stove, state, flute, lake, rude.*

- Say a word. Ask children to name the individual sounds in the word, as they take off a small piece of clay for each sound. Tell children to count the pieces of clay to determine the number of sounds in the word.

Substitute Sounds

CHANGE THE SOUND

Materials: Phonics Picture Cards: *rope, cane, cube*

This activity will help children substitute the beginning and ending sound of a word.

- Invite a volunteer to choose a Phonics Picture Card. Ask children to name the beginning sound of the picture name.

- Have children substitute new beginning sounds to form both real and nonsense words. Do the same with other Phonics Picture Cards.

- Follow the same procedure by having children substitute new ending sounds for the words.

Long *u: u–e*

OBJECTIVES Children will be introduced to words with the long *u* sound.

Alternate Activities

Visual

WORD GRID

Materials: paper with grid drawn on it, pencils

To introduce children to words containing long *u* and silent *e*, have them create word grids.

- Provide each child with a nine-box grid. On the chalkboard, write the following words: *rule, use, June, cute, tune, tube, mule, flute.*

- Ask children to write one of the words in each square, in any order they choose.

- Read a word from the list, and ask children to find the word on their grid.

- Once they have located the word, ask children to say the word out loud and then to underline the silent *e* in the word.

- Continue until all of the words have been called. ▶**Logical/Mathematical**

Kinesthetic

GONE FISHING

Materials: construction-paper fish, pencils or markers

Play *Go Fish* with words containing long *u* and silent *e*.

- Cut out fish shapes from colored construction paper.

- Have each child write on the fish: *rule, mule, rude, dude, tube, huge, use, fuse, fume, plume, dune, June, tune, prune, cute, lute, flute.*

- Children pick a partner and combine their fish.

- Have each pair play *Go Fish* with the words.

- Explain the rules. Each player starts with three fish. A player asks for a particular word. If the other player doesn't have it in his or her hand, then the first player must draw a fish from the pile. The player with the most word pairs is the winner. ▶**Interpersonal**

Auditory

LISTENING FOR THE LONG *U*

Materials: oak tag, markers

Have children use smiling and frowning faces when they hear words with the long *u* sound.

- Ask children to draw two pictures, one on either side of a piece of oak tag. One side has a smiling face, the other a frowning face.

- Read the following list of words: *rule, rub, use, mule, mud , tube, tub, huge, hug, fuss, fume, plum, June, prune, run, fun, flute, sun.*

- Ask children to hold up the happy face when they hear a long *u* word and to hold up the sad face when they hear a word that does *not* have the long *u* sound. ▶**Bodily/Kinesthetic**

 **CD-ROM**

See Reteach 143, 147, 148, 156, 159

Make Inferences

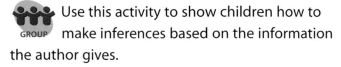

OBJECTIVES Children will be introduced to making inferences.

Alternate Activities

Visual

WHAT DO YOU REALLY KNOW?

 Use this activity to show children how to make inferences based on the information the author gives.

* Explain that authors do not always tell readers everything.

* Write the following statement on the chalkboard: *John picked up his pen and thought very, very hard.*

* Ask children the following: *What information has the author given you?* (The person's name is John; He has a pen; He is thinking.)

* Explain that an inference is something which is implied, rather than stated directly.

* Ask children: *What inferences can you make based on that sentence?*

* Encourage children to ask "why" questions. For example, *Why did John pick up the pen?* (He is about to write something.) *Why is John thinking very, very hard?* (He is trying to decide what to write about.) ▶**Logical/Mathematical**

Kinesthetic

INFERENCE CHARADES

 Have children play a game of *Charades* and make inferences.

* Write out a series of simple actions for children to act out (*pick up the book, close your eyes*).

* Have a child act out the action. Have the class tell what the action is: *He is picking up the book.*

* On the bottom of each action statement, add another statement, such as *you want to read a story, you are angry,* or *you are in a hurry.*

* Ask the child to repeat the action, including the second statement in the pantomime.

* Based on the action, have the class guess how the child feels.

* Encourage children to ask "why" questions: *Why is he picking up the book?* (He wants to read a story.) ▶**Bodily/Kinesthetic**

Auditory

DID THE AUTHOR TELL US?

 Show children how to make inferences using the "Five Ws."

* Ask children to listen to a passage as you read aloud from the featured text.

* After you have read the passage, write the following question words on the chalkboard: *Who? What? Where? When? Why?*

* Ask children to ask and answer questions about the text using the words on the chalkboard.

* List the answers on the chalkboard and ask: *Did the author tell us this, or did we figure it out on our own?* ▶**Interpersonal**

See Reteach 149, 157, 164

T73

Inflectional Endings *-er, -est*

OBJECTIVES Children will be introduced to the concept of adding *-er* and *-est* to compare objects.

Alternate Activities

Visual

FILL IN THE BLANKS

 Materials: duplicate sheets, as described below

Use this activity to introduce the inflectional endings *-er* and *-est*.

- Hand out duplicate sheets with charts consisting of three boxes in a row. In the top row of boxes write the words *big, bigger,* and *biggest.*

- In each subsequent row, one of the boxes will contain a word, and the other two boxes will be blank. For example, box 1 would be blank, box 2 would contain the word *faster,* and box 3 would be blank.

- Ask children to fill in the blank boxes.

- When they have completed their charts, ask children to underline *-er* and *-est* in the comparative forms. ▶**Linguistic**

Kinesthetic

THREE OF A KIND

 Materials: paper, markers
Have children show the differences between *big, bigger,* and *biggest* by drawing comparative pictures.

- Have each child draw three pictures illustrating the concepts of *big, bigger,* and *biggest.*

- Encourage children to share their illustrations with the class, using comparative words when describing the three drawings. For example, *The first bear is big. The second bear is bigger. The third bear is the biggest.* ▶**Spatial**

Auditory

BIG, BIGGER, BIGGEST

 Materials: boxes or baskets, items to be compared

Have children review the inflected endings *-er* and *-est* by comparing various objects.

- Gather several three-object sets that can be easily compared; for example, use three pencils of varying lengths.

- Place three baskets or boxes on a table.

- Box 1 has no label, box 2 is labeled *-er,* and box 3 is labeled *-est.*

- Ask children to place the objects in the boxes according to the criterion by which they are categorizing them, for example, *long, longer, longest.* ▶**Logical/Mathematical**

- Hold up the objects and ask: *Which one is long? Which one is longer? Which one is longest?* (Substitute appropriate adjectives.)

See Reteach 150, 158, 166

Phonological Awareness

OBJECTIVES Children will practice blending sounds, segmenting sounds, and substituting middle sounds.

Alternate Activities

Blend Sounds

GET ON THE TRAIN

 Materials: pictures of the following objects: pail, chain, nail, duck, man, tray, pen, rain

This activity will help children blend sounds to form words.

- Have children choose a picture and blend the sounds to form the word that names it.

- Ask children to tell whether or not the object they have shosen can get on the train. Explain that only those objects whose names have the /a/ sound can get on the train.

Segment Sounds

PICTURE IT

 Materials: pictures of objects, such as train, rope, nine, snail, cube, chain

This activity will help children segment individual sounds in words.

- Have children work with a partner. One child says the name of the object. His or her partner then tells the individual sounds in the word.

- Have partners switch roles. Then challenge children to think of other words to say and segment.

Substitute Sounds

STAND UP FOR SOUNDS

 This activity will help children substitute the middle sound of a word.

- Have three children stand together. Assign each child a sound. For example, for the word pail, ask one child to say the /p/ sound, the second child to say the /ā/ sound, and the third child to say the /l/ sound. Ask children to blend the sounds together and say the word.

- Ask the second child to substitute the /ī/ sound for the /a/ sound.

- Have children blend the sounds together. Ask them what the new word is. (pile)

- Repeat the activity with other children using words such as the following: *tail, kite, like, note, tune, cake, take.* Suggest a vowel sound to substitute for each word.

Long *a: ai, ay*

OBJECTIVES Children will be introduced to words with the long *a* sound spelled *ai* or *ay*.

Alternate Activities

Visual

AY OR AI?

Materials: index cards, two shoe boxes

Use index cards with long *a* words to help children distinguish words spelled *ai* from those spelled *ay*.

- On the chalkboard, tack up index cards with the following words written on them: *bay, day, hay, lay, may, pay, play, ray, say, way, aid, paid, laid, maid, raid, paint, saint, pain, gain, main, rain.*

- Ask children to read a word, remove it from the chalkboard and place it in one of two boxes—one marked "*ay* words" and one marked "*ai* words."

- After all cards have been removed, draw them out of the boxes and read them aloud one at a time.

- Ask children whether it is an *ay* word or an *ai* word. If they answer correctly, put the card back on the chalkboard. If they answer incorrectly, put it back in the box.

- Continue until all of the cards are back on the chalkboard. ▶**Logical/Mathematical**

Kinesthetic

THE LONG *A* TEAM

Have children work in teams to decide whether *ai* or *ay* is used in spelling words with the long *a* sound.

- Divide the class into two teams—the *ai* team and the *ay* team.

- Read sentences containing one of the following words: *bay, day, hay, lay, may, pay, play, ray, say, way, aid, paid, laid, maid, paint, pain, gain, main, rain.* After you've read the sentences, repeat the word with the long *a* sound.

- Alternating teams, choose one player to decide whether the long *a* sound in the word you read is represented by the letters *ai* or *ay*.

- If the player guesses correctly, he or she writes the word on the chalkboard, and his or her team gets one point. If the player guesses incorrectly, the other team writes the word on the chalkboard and gets the point. ▶**Interpersonal**

Auditory

WHICH IS IT?

 Review *ai* and *ay* by having children list words with the long *a* sound.

- Read a passage from the featured text or a newspaper article, or write and read a passage of your own which contains both *ai* and *ay* words.

- Ask children to raise their hands when they hear a word with the long *a* sound.

- If the word they hear has *ai* or *ay* in it, ask children to write it on a piece of paper.

- Review the list with the whole group. ▶**Intrapersonal**

 CD-ROM

See Reteach 151, 155, 156, 159

Notes

Writing Readiness

Before children begin to write, fine motor skills need to be developed. Here are examples of activities that can be used:

- **Simon Says** Play Simon Says using just finger positions.
- **Finger Plays and Songs** Sing songs such as "Where Is Thumbkin" or "The Eensie, Weensie, Spider" or songs that use Signed English or American Sign Language.
- **Mazes** Use or create mazes, especially ones that require moving the writing instruments from left to right.

The Mechanics of Writing

POSTURE

- Chair height should allow for the feet to rest flat on the floor.
- Desk height should be two inches above the elbows.
- There should be an inch between the child and the desk.
- Children sit erect with the elbows resting on the desk.
- Letter models should be on the desk or at eye level.

PAPER POSITION

- **Right-handed children** should turn the paper so that the lower left-hand corner of the paper points to the abdomen.

- **Left-handed children** should turn the paper so that the lower right-hand corner of the paper points to the abdomen.

- The nondominant hand should anchor the paper near the top so that the paper doesn't slide.
- The paper should be moved up as the child nears the bottom of the paper. Many children won't think of this.

The Writing Instrument Grasp

For handwriting to be functional, the writing instrument must be held in a way that allows for fluid dynamic movement.

FUNCTIONAL GRASP PATTERNS

- **Tripod Grasp** The writing instrument is held with the tip of the thumb and the index finger and rests against the side of the third finger. The thumb and index finger form a circle.
- **Quadrupod Grasp** The writing instrument is held with the tip of the thumb and index finger and rests against the fourth finger. The thumb and index finger form a circle.

INCORRECT GRASP PATTERNS

- **Fisted Grasp** The writing instrument is held in a fisted hand.

- **Pronated Grasp** The instrument is held diagonally within the hand with the tips of the thumb and index finger but with no support from other fingers.

- **Five-Finger Grasp** The writing instrument is held with the tips of all five fingers.

- **Flexed or Hooked Wrist** Flexed or bent wrist is typically seen with left-handed writers but is also present in some right-handed writers.

- To correct wrist position, have children check their writing posture and paper placement.

TO CORRECT GRASPS

- Have children play counting games with an eye dropper and water.
- Have children pick up small objects with a tweezer.
- Do counting games with children picking up small coins using just the thumb and index finger.

Evaluation Checklist

Formation and Strokes

☑ Does the child begin letters at the top?

☑ Do circles close?

☑ Are the horizontal lines straight?

☑ Do circular shapes and extender and descender lines touch?

☑ Are the heights of all upper-case letters equal?

☑ Are the heights of all lower-case letters equal?

☑ Are the lengths of the extenders and descenders the same for all letters?

Directionality

☑ Do the children form letters starting at the top and moving to the bottom?

☑ Are letters formed from left to right?

Spacing

☑ Are the spaces between letters equidistant?

☑ Are the spaces between words equidistant?

☑ Do the letters rest on the line?

☑ Are the top, bottom and side margins on the paper even?

Handwriting

Write the Alphabet

Trace and write the letters.

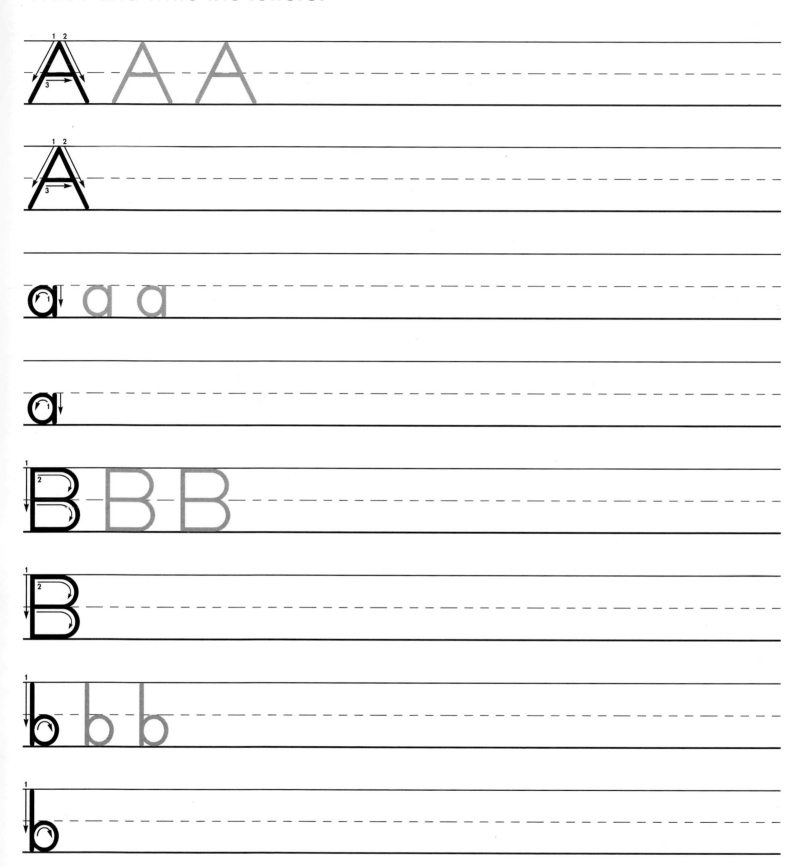

Trace and write the letters.

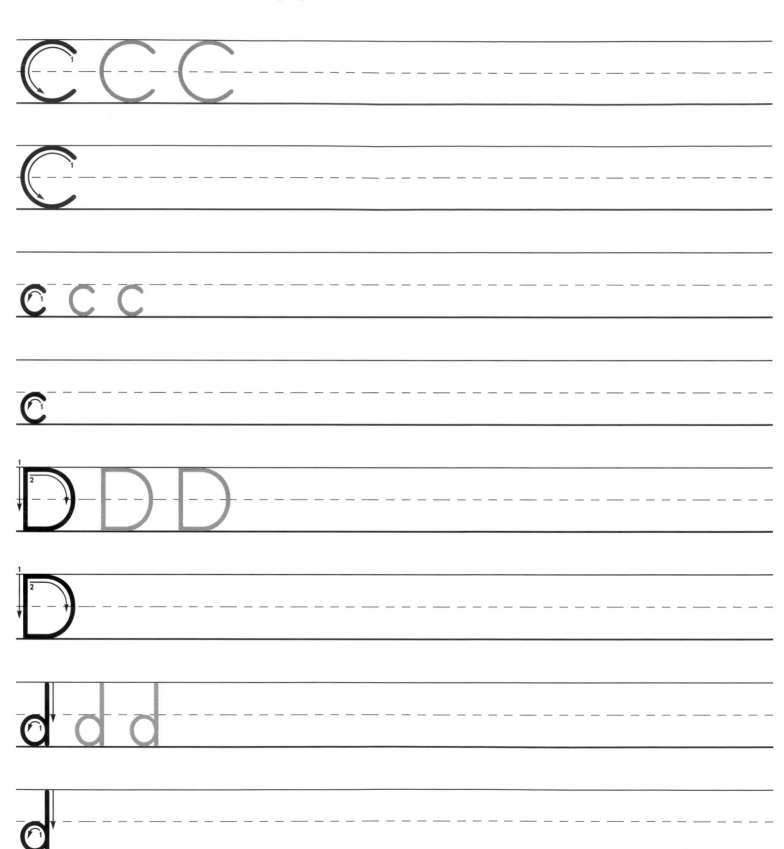

Trace and write the letters.

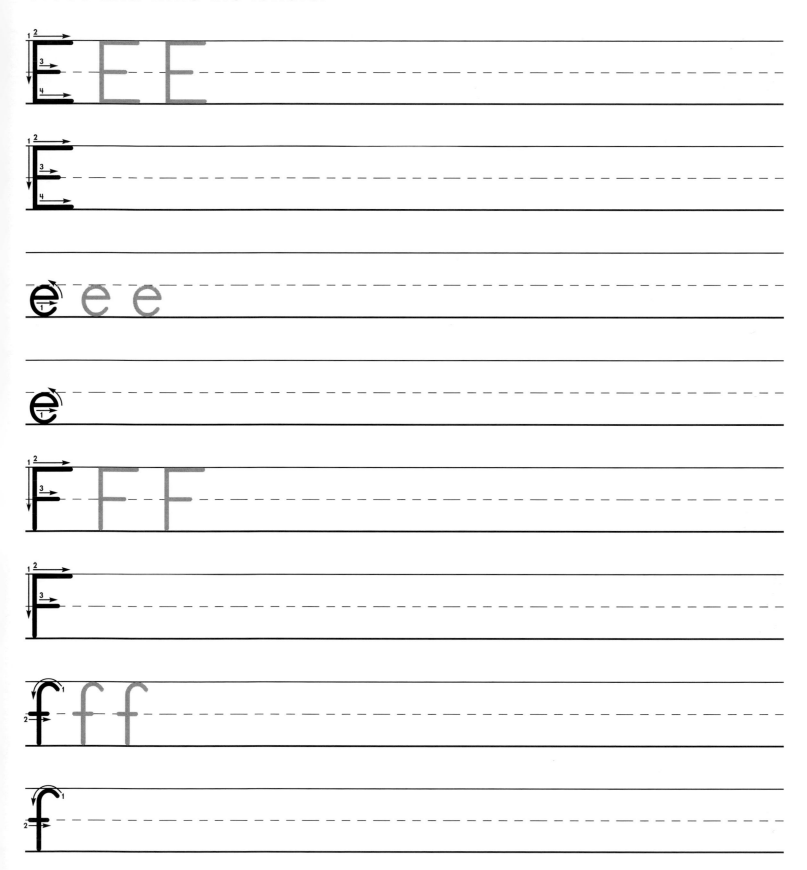

Trace and write the letters.

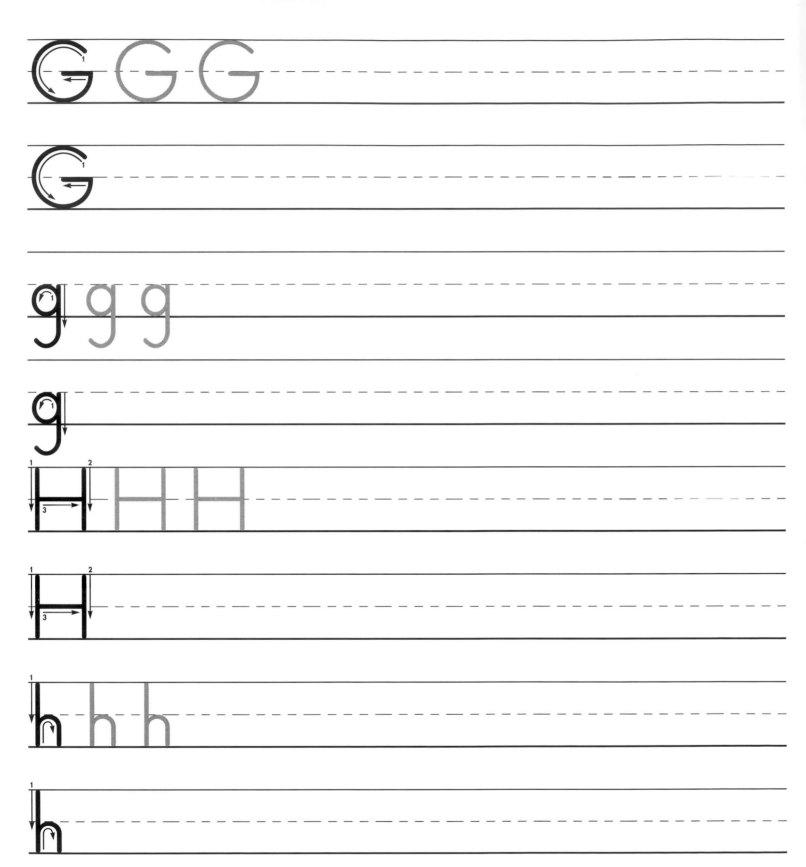

Trace and write the letters.

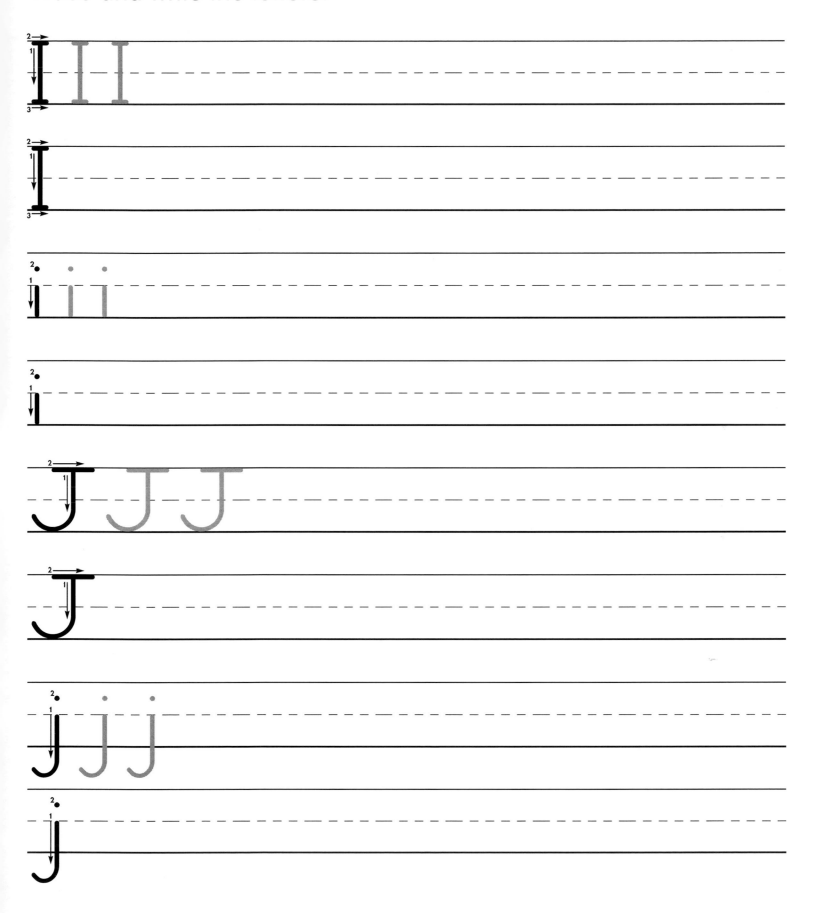

Trace and write the letters.

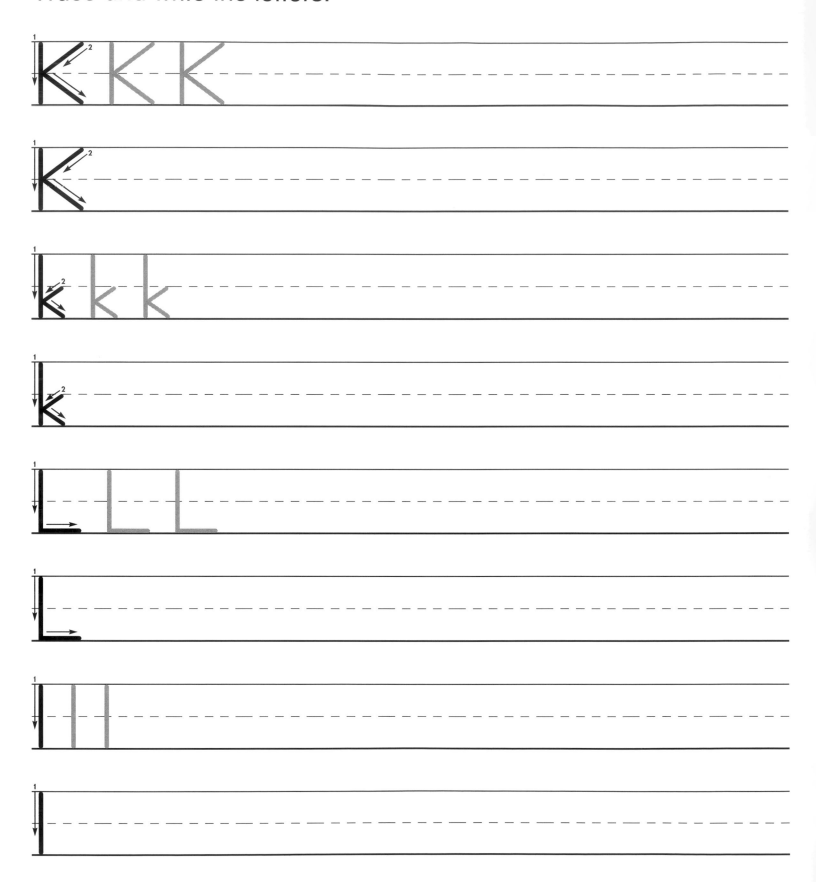

Trace and write the letters.

M M M

M

m m m

m

N N N

N

n n n

n

Trace and write the letters.

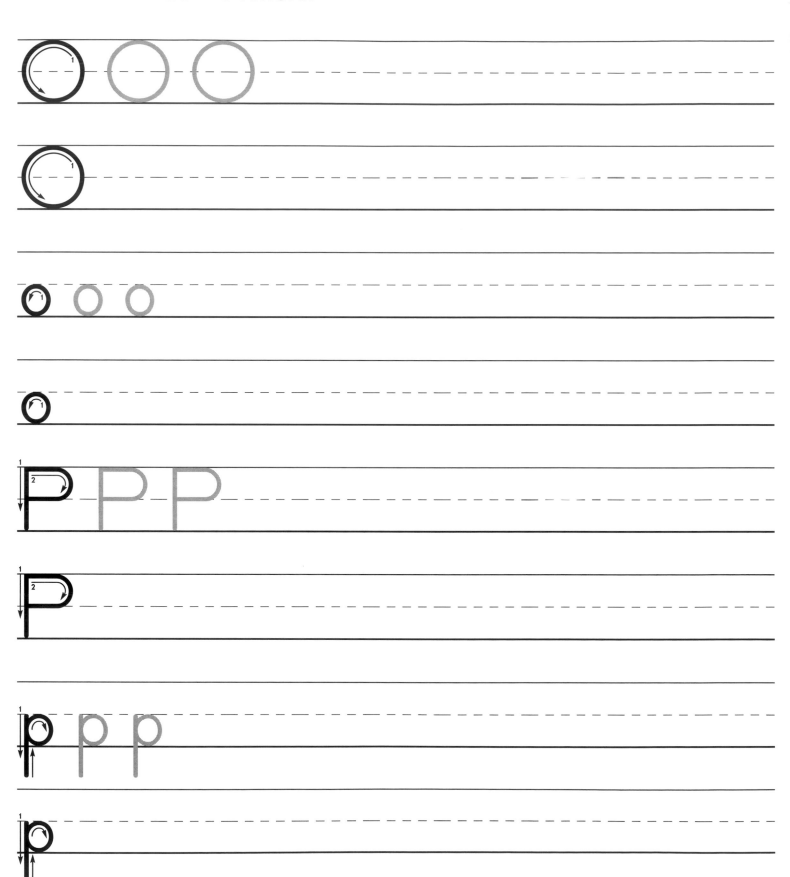

Trace and write the letters.

Q Q Q Q

Q

q q q

q

R R R R

R

r r r

r

Trace and write the letters.

S S S

S

S S S

S

T T T

T

t t t

t

Trace and write the letters.

U U U

U

u u u

u

V V V

V

v v v

v

Trace and write the letters.

W W W

W

w w w

w

X X X

X

x x x

x

Trace and write the letters.

Y Y Y Y

Y

y y y

y

Z Z Z

Z

Z Z Z

Z

Handwriting Models—Slant

A B C D E F G H

I J K L M N O P

Q R S T U V W

X Y Z

a b c d e f g h

i j k l m n o p

q r s t u v w

x y z

Handwriting Practice

Selection Titles

Honors, Prizes, and Awards

QUACK
Book 1, p. 30
by *Judy Barrett*

Author/Illustrator: *Judy Barrett*, winner of IRA-CBC Children's Choice Award (1978) for *Cloudy With a Chance of Meatballs*

WHAT DOES PIG DO?
Book 1, p. 50
by *Angela Shelf Medearis*
Illustrated by *Barbara Reid*

Author: *Angela Shelf Medearis*, winner of IRA-Teachers' Choice Award (1995) for *Our People*
Illustrator: *Barbara Reid,* winner of Canada Council Award (1985) for Children's Illustrations for *Have You Seen Birds?;* Ezra Jack Keats Award (1988); Mr. Christie Book Award (1991) for the *Zoe* series; ALA Notable (1994) for *Two By Two;* IBBY Honor List (1996) for *Gifts;* Governor General's Award for Illustration (1997) for *The Party*

A YEAR LATER
Book 1, p. 102
by *Mary Ann Hoberman*

Poet: *Mary Ann Hoberman*, winner of American Book Award Paper Picture Book Award (1983) for *A House Is a House for Me*

ONE GOOD PUP
Book 2, p. 10
by *Frank Asch*

Author/Illustrator: *Frank Asch*, winner of American Book Award Pick of the List Award (1997) for *Barnyard Animals*

WHAT BUG IS IT?
Book 2, p. 98
by *Pat Cummings*

Author/Illustrator: *Pat Cummings*, winner of Coretta Scott King Award (illustration; 1984) for *My Mama Needs Me;* National Council of Teachers of English Orbis Pictus Award, Boston Globe-Horn Book Award (1992), ALA Notable (1993) for *Talking with Artists;* ALA Notable (1996) for *Talking with Artists, Vol. 2*

Selection Titles	Honors, Prizes, and Awards
STAN'S STUNT Book 3, p. 10 by **Lynn Plourde** Illustrated by **Pam Levy**	**Illustrator: Pam Levy,** winner of 1996 Society of Children's Book Writers and Illustrators Magazine Merit Award for *Cricket* magazine
GREG'S MASK Book 3, p. 40 by **Ann McGovern**	**Author: Ann McGovern**, winner of Boston Globe-Horn Book Honor (1975) for *Scram Kids*
THE SHOPPING LIST Book 4, p. 10 by **Gary Apple** Illustrated by **Shirley Beckes**	**Illustrator: Shirley Beckes,** winner of The 39th Annual Book Exhibit, The Chicago Book Clinic Honor Book Certificate Award for *Irwin the Sock*
THE KNEE-HIGH MAN Book 4, p. 68 by **Ellen Dreyer** Illustrated by **Tim Raglin**	**Illustrator: Tim Raglin,** winner of Silver Medal by the Society Illustrators, 39th Exhibition

Selection Titles	Honors, Prizes, and Awards
BABY CHICK Book 5, p. 8 by **Aileen Fisher**	**Poet: *Aileen Fisher***, winner of National Council of Teachers of English Award for Excellence in Poetry for Children (1978)
SHRINKING MOUSE Book 5, p. 48 by **Pat Hutchins**	**Author/Illustrator: *Pat Hutchins***, winner of Boston Globe-Horn Book Honor (1968) for *Rosie's Walk;* New York Times Best Illustrated (1972) for *You'll Soon Grow Into Them, Titch;* IBBY Honor Award (1974); ALA Notable (1997) for *The Doorbell Rang*
YOU CAN'T SMELL A FLOWER WITH YOUR EAR! Book 5, p. 84 by **Joanna Cole**	**Author: *Joanna Cole***, winner of ALA Notable (1983) for *Bony-Legs* and *Cars and How They Go;* ALA Notable, Golden Kite Honor Book (1984) for *How You Were Born;* Boston Globe-Horn Book Honor (1987) for *The Magic School at the Waterworks;* Texas Blue Bonnet Master List (1995) for *On the Bus with Joanna Cole;* IRA-CBC Children's Choice (1997) for *The Magic School Bus Blows Its Top: A Book About Volcanos*
OWL AND THE MOON Book 5, p. 120 by **Arnold Lobel**	**Author/Illustrator: *Arnold Lobel***, Caldecott Honor (1970) for *Frog and Toad Are Friends,* (1972) for *Hildilid's Night;* Christopher Award (1972) for *On the Day Peter Stuyvesant Sailed Into Town;* Newbery Honor (1973) for *Frog and Toad Together;* Christopher Award (1977) for *Frog and Toad All Year;* Caldecott Medal (1981) for *Fables;* ALA Notable, Caldecott Honor (1982), Boston Globe-Horn Book Honor, New York Times Best Illustrated (1981) for *On Market Street;* Boston Globe-Horn Book Honor (1984) for *Rose in My Garden;* ALA Notable (1984) for *Book of Pigericks/Pig Limericks;* ALA Notable (1986) for *Three Day Hat;* Golden Kite Award Book (1987) for *The Devil and Mother Crump*

Selection Titles	Honors, Prizes, and Awards

 **NEW SHOES FOR SILVIA**
Book 5, p. 194
by *Johanna Hurwitz*
Illustrated by *Jerry Pinkney*

Author: *Johanna Hurwitz*, winner of Texas Blue Bonnet Award (1987) for *The Hot and Cold Summer;* ALA Notable (1984) for *Rip-Roaring Russell;* Texas Blue Bonnet Master List (1996–97) for *Birthday Surprises: Ten Great Stories to Unwrap*

Illustrator: *Jerry Pinkney,* winner of Coretta Scott King Award, ALA Notable, Christopher Award (1986) for *Patchwork Quilt;* Newbery Medal, Boston Globe-Horn Book Honor (1977) for *Roll of Thunder, Hear My Cry;* Boston Globe-Horn Book Honor (1980) *Childtimes: A Three Generation Memoir;* Coretta Scott King Award (1987) for *Half a Moon and One Whole Star;* ALA Notable (1988) for *Tales of Uncle Remus: The Adventures of Brer Rabbit;* ALA Notable, Caldecott Honor, Coretta Scott King Award (1989) for *Mirandy and Brother Wind;* ALA Notable, Caldecott Honor, Coretta Scott King Honor (1990) for *Talking Eggs: A Folktale for the American South;* Golden Kite Award Book (1990) for *Home Place;* ALA Notable (1991) for *Further Tales of Uncle Remus: The Misadventures of Brer Rabbit, Brer Fox ...;* ALA Notable (1993) for *Back Home;* ALA Notable, Boston Globe-Horn Book Award, Caldecott Honor (1995) for *John Henry;* ALA Notable, Blue Ribbon (1997) for *Sam and the Tigers;* ALA Notable, Christopher Award, Coretta Scott King Award, Golden Kite Honor Book (1997) for *Minty: A Story of Young Harriet Tubman;* Aesop Prize (1997) for *The Hired Hand;* National Council for Social Studies Notable Children's Book Award (1998) for *The Hired Hand* and *Rikki-Tikki-Tavi;* Rip Van Winkle Award (1998); 1998 Hans Christian Andersen nominee

MY MAMI TAKES ME TO THE BAKERY Book 5, p. 304
by *Charlotte Pomerantz*

Poet: *Charlotte Pomerantz,* winner of Jane Addams Book Award (1975) for *Princess and the Admiral;* ALA Notable (1994) for *Outside Dog*

Theme Bibliography

THE SHOPPING LIST	YASMIN'S DUCKS

Trade Books

Additional fiction and nonfiction trade books related to each selection can be shared with children throughout the unit.

THE SHOPPING LIST

Don't Forget the Bacon
Pat Hutchins (William Morrow, 1994)

A young boy goes shopping for his mother and tries very hard to remember her instructions.

To Market, To Market
Anne Miranda, illustrated by Janet Stevens (Harcourt Brace, 1997)

Starting with the familiar Mother Goose nursery rhyme, this tale then takes off to describe a series of unruly animals that run amok.

Bunny Money
Rosemary Wells (Dial Books for Young Readers, 1997)

When Max and his sister Ruby go shopping for Grandma's birthday gift, they almost run out of money before they find the right present.

YASMIN'S DUCKS

Building a House
Byron Barton (Greenwillow Books, 1981)

The steps in building a house are briefly described and colorfully illustrated.

Ducks
Gail Gibbons (Holiday House, 2001)

The author/illustrator gives us a great deal of information about all kinds of ducks: where they live, their habits, and their physical characteristics.

The Art Lesson
Tomie dePaola (G. P. Putnam's Sons, 1989)

Tommy learns that the art lesson in school is very different from drawing at home.

Technology

Multimedia resources can be used to enhance children's understanding of the selections.

Alexander Who Used To Be Rich (AIMS Media) Video, 14 min. When Alexander's grandparents give him five dollars, Alexander discovers more ways to spend his money than to save it.

Money Town (Simon and Schuster/Davidson) CD-ROM, Macintosh and Windows. Players earn money to keep the Greenstreet Town Park open. Teaches money identification, adding, and making change.

Adventure Enough (Phoenix/BFA) A young boy's trip to the grocery store is anything but usual.

Living or Nonliving? (National Geographic Educational Services) Video, 16 min. Teaches the differences between living and nonliving things. Explores how living things are nourished, grow, and respond to the world around them.

Discovering Art: Discovering Lines (BFA Educational Media) Video, 17 min. Shows children the different ways that a line can record movement.

THE KNEE-HIGH MAN

The Very Small
Joyce Dunbar, illustrated by Debi Gliori (Harcourt, Inc., 2000)

A baby bear finds a Very Small something and brings it home. It takes a big bear sneeze to help Very Small get back to his own home.

What Can You Do?
Shelly Rotner and Sheila Kelly (Millbrook Press, 2001)

"What can you do well?" asks the author, who names many of the abilities children have, while comparing individual differences in a non-competitive way.

So What!
Miriam Cohen, illustrated by Lillian Hoban (Bantam Doubleday Dell Books for Young Readers, 1988)

After much insecurity, a first grader learns to accept himself as he is.

JOHNNY APPLESEED

One Bean
Anne Rockwell, illustrated by Megan Halsey (Walker, 1998)

Watch what happens to a bean when it is soaked, planted, and watered, and eventually produces pods.

The Giving Tree
Shel Silverstein (Harper & Row, 1964)

The story of a boy who loved a tree throughout his entire life and how the tree responded to his love.

The Apple Pie Tree
Zoe Hall, illustrated by Shari Halpern (Scholastic, 1996)

Two sisters describe the changes that occur as they watch an apple tree grow in their backyard. A recipe for apple pie is included at the end of the story.

TIME FOR KIDS
RING! RING! RING! PUT OUT THE FIRE!

Fire Engines
Anne Rockwell, (E. P. Dutton, 1986)

The parts of a fire engine and how firefighters use them are described.

Fire Truck
Peter Sis (Greenwillow Books, 1998)

Matt loves fire trucks so much that one day he turns into one and saves the community with his heroic deeds.

Fire Fighters
Norma Simon, illustrated by Pam Paparone (Simon & Schuster Books for Young Readers, 1995)

The vehicles, equipment, and procedures used by firefighters are described and illustrated.

Express Yourself (National Geographic Educational Services) Video, 15 min. An edition of the Me and You Series. Children discover how to express feelings in a constructive manner.

Jack and the Beanstalk (Great Tapes for Kids) Video. In this English folktale, young Jack sells his family cow for a handful of magic beans and lands in a misadventure with a giant.

Johnny Appleseed (Weston Woods) Video or cassette. Narrated by Garrison Keillor, this video tells the story of naturalist Johnny Appleseed's life of goodwill.

The Giving Tree (SVE/Churchill) Video, 10 min. Shel Silverstein narrates his classic story of the many lessons of giving and receiving.

Trees for Life (National Geographic Educational Services) Video, 22 min. Children discover the profusion of life that lives in a tree and how trees are important to life on Earth.

The Fire Station (National Geographic Educational Services) Video, 13 min. Children learn about the important work of firefighters and paramedics.

The Police Station (National Geographic Educational Services) Video, 15 min. Find out the multitude of ways in which police officers serve their communities.

Tonka Search and Rescue (Hasbro Interactive) CD-ROM, Macintosh and Windows. Teaches following directions and listening.

Abdo & Daughters
4940 Viking Drive, Suite 622
Edina, MN 55435
(800) 800-1312 • www.abdopub.com

Aladdin Paperbacks
(Imprint of Simon & Schuster Children's
Publishing)

Atheneum
(Imprint of Simon & Schuster Children's
Publishing)

**Bantam Doubleday Dell Books for
Young Readers**
(Imprint of Random House)

Blackbirch Press
260 Amity Road
Woodbridge, CT 06525
(203) 387-7525 • (800) 831-9183 •
www.blackbirch.com

Blue Sky Press
(Imprint of Scholastic)

Boyds Mills Press
815 Church Street
Honesdale, PA 18431
(570) 253-1164 • Fax (570) 253-0179 •
(800) 490-5111 • www.boydsmillspress.com

Bradbury Press
(Imprint of Simon & Schuster Children's
Publishing)

BridgeWater Books
(Distributed by Penguin Putnam)

Candlewick Press
2067 Masssachusetts Avenue
Cambridge, MA 02140
(617) 661-3330 • Fax (617) 661-0565 •
www.candlewick.com

Carolrhoda Books
(Division of Lerner Publications Co.)

Children's Press (Division of Grolier, Inc.)
P.O. Box 1795
Danbury, CT 06816-1333
(800) 621-1115 • www.grolier.com

Child's World
P.O. Box 326
Chanhassen, MN 55317-0326
(612) 906-3939 • (800) 599-READ •
www.childsworld.com

Chronicle Books
85 Second Street, Sixth Floor
San Francisco, CA 94105
(415) 537-3730 • Fax (415) 537-4460 •
(800) 722-6657 • www.chronbooks.com

Clarion Books
(Imprint of Houghton Mifflin, Inc.)
215 Park Avenue South
New York, NY 10003
(212) 420-5800 • (800) 225-3362 •
www.houghtonmifflinbooks.com/clarion

Crowell (Imprint of HarperCollins)

Crown Publishing Group
(Imprint of Random House)

Dial Books
(Imprint of Penguin Putnam Inc.)

Dorling Kindersley (DK Publishing)
95 Madison Avenue
New York, NY 10016
(212) 213-4800 • Fax (212) 213-5240 •
(888) 342-5357 • www.dk.com

Doubleday (Imprint of Random House)

E. P. Dutton Children's Books
(Imprint of Penguin Putnam Inc.)

Farrar Straus & Giroux
19 Union Square West
New York, NY 10003
(212) 741-6900 • Fax (212) 741-6973 •
(888) 330-8477

Four Winds Press
(Imprint of Macmillan, see Simon &
Schuster Children's Publishing)

Greenwillow Books
(Imprint of William Morrow & Co, Inc.)

Grosset & Dunlap
(Imprint of Penguin Putnam, Inc.)

Harcourt Brace & Co.
6277 Sea Harbor Drive
Orlando, FL 32887
(407) 345-2000 • (800) 225-5425 •
www.harcourtbooks.com

Harper & Row (Imprint of HarperCollins)

HarperCollins Children's Books
1350 Avenue of the Americas
New York, NY 10019
(212) 261-6500 • Fax (212) 261-6689 •
(800) 242-7737 •
www.harperchildrens.com

Holiday House
425 Madison Avenue
New York, NY 10017
(212) 688-0085 • Fax (212) 421-6134

Henry Holt and Company
115 West 18th Street
New York, NY 10011
(212) 886-9200 • (212) 633-0748 • (888)
330-8477 • www.henryholt.com/byr/

Houghton Mifflin
222 Berkeley Street
Boston, MA 02116
(617) 351-5000 • Fax (617) 351-1125 •
(800) 225-3362 •
www.houghtonmifflinbooks.com

Hyperion Books
(Division of ABC, Inc.)
77 W. 66th Street, 11th Floor
New York, NY 10023
(212) 456-0100 • (800) 343-4204 •
www.disney.com

Ideals Children's Books
(Imprint of Hambleton-Hill Publishing, Inc.)
1501 County Hospital Road
Nashville, TN 37218
(615) 254-2451 • (800) 327-5113

Joy Street Books
(Imprint of Little, Brown & Co.)

Just Us Books
356 Glenwood Avenue
E. Orange, NJ 07017
(973) 672-7701 • Fax (973) 677-7570 •
www.justusbooks.com

Alfred A. Knopf
(Imprint of Random House)

Lee & Low Books
95 Madison Avenue, Room 606
New York, NY 10016
(212) 779-4400 • Fax (212) 683-1894

Lerner Publications Co.
241 First Avenue North
Minneapolis, MN 55401
(612) 332-3344 • Fax (612) 332-7615 •
(800) 328-4929 • www.lernerbooks.com

Little, Brown & Co.
3 Center Plaza
Boston, MA 02108
(617) 227-0730 • Fax (617) 263-2864 •
(800) 759-0190 • www.littlebrown.com

Lothrop Lee & Shepard
(Imprint of William Morrow & Co.)

Macmillan
(Imprint of Simon & Schuster
Children's Publishing)

Marshall Cavendish
99 White Plains Road
Tarrytown, NY 10591
(914) 332-8888 • Fax (914) 332-1888 •
(800) 821-9881 •
www.marshallcavendish.com

Millbrook Press
2 Old New Milford Road
Brookfield, CT 06804
(203) 740-2220 • (800) 462-4703 •
Fax (203) 740-2526

William Morrow & Co.
(Imprint of HarperCollins)

Morrow Junior Books
(Imprint of HarperCollins)

Mulberry Books
(Imprint of HarperCollins)

National Geographic Society
1145 17th Street, NW
Washington, DC 20036
(202) 857-7345 • (800) 638-4077 •
www.nationalgeographic.com

Northland Publishing
(Division of Justin Industries)
P.O. Box 1389
Flagstaff, AZ 86002
(520) 774-5251 • Fax (800) 744-0592 •
(800) 346-3257 • www.northlandpub.com

North-South Books
1123 Broadway, Suite 800
New York, NY 10010
(212) 463-9736 • Fax (212) 633-1004 •
(800) 722-6657 • www.northsouth.com

Orchard Books (A Grolier Company)
95 Madison Avenue
New York, NY 10016
(212) 951-2600 • Fax (212) 213-6435 •
(800) 433-3411 • www.grolier.com

Owlet (Imprint of Henry Holt & Co.)

Penguin Putnam, Inc.
375 Hudson Street
New York, NY 10014
(212) 366-2000 • Fax (212) 366-2636 •
(800) 631-8571 •
www.penguinputnam.com

Willa Perlman Books
(Imprint of Simon & Schuster
Children's Publishing)

Philomel Books
(Imprint of Penguin Putnam, Inc.)

Puffin Books
(Imprint of Penguin Putnam, Inc.)

G. P. Putnam's Sons Publishing
(Imprint of Penguin Putnam, Inc.)

Random House
1540 Broadway
New York, NY 10036
(212) 782-9000 • Fax (212) 302-7985 •
(800) 200-3552 •
www.randomhouse.com/kids

Scholastic
555 Broadway
New York, NY 10012
(212) 343-7500 • Fax (212) 965-7442 •
(800) SCHOLASTIC • www.scholastic.com

Charles Scribner's Sons
(Imprint of Simon & Schuster Children's
Publishing)

Sierra Club Books for Children
85 Second Street, Second Floor
San Francisco, CA 94105-3441
(415) 977-5500 • Fax (415) 977-5793 •
(800) 935-1056 • www.sierraclub.org

Simon & Schuster Children's Books
1230 Avenue of the Americas
New York, NY 10020
(212) 698-7200 • (800) 223-2336 •
www.simonsayskids.com

Smith & Kraus
177 Lyme Road
Hanover, NH 03755
(603) 643-6431 • Fax (603) 643-1831 •
(800) 895-4331 • www.smithkraus.com

Teacher Ideas Press
(Division of Libraries Unlimited)
P.O. Box 6633
Englewood, CO 80155-6633
(303) 770-1220 • Fax (303) 220-8843 •
(800) 237-6124 • www.lu.com

Ticknor & Fields
(Imprint of Houghton Mifflin, Inc.)

Usborne (Imprint of EDC Publishing)
10302 E. 55th Place, Suite B
Tulsa, OK 74146-6515
(918) 622-4522 • (800) 475-4522 •
www.edcpub.com

Viking Children's Books
(Imprint of Penguin Putnam Inc.)

Walker & Co.
435 Hudson Street
New York, NY 10014
(212) 727-8300 • (212) 727-0984 •
(800) AT-WALKER

Watts Publishing
(Imprint of Grolier Publishing;
see Children's Press)

Whispering Coyote Press
300 Crescent Court, Suite 860
Dallas, TX 75201
(800) 929-6104 • Fax (214) 319-7298

Albert Whitman
6340 Oakton Street
Morton Grove, IL 60053-2723
(847) 581-0033 • Fax (847) 581-0039 •
(800) 255-7675 • www.awhitmanco.com

Workman Publishing Co., Inc.
708 Broadway
New York, NY 10003
(212) 254-5900 • Fax (800) 521-1832 •
(800) 722-7202 • www.workman.com

Multimedia Resources

AGC/United Learning
6633 West Howard Street
Niles, IL 60714-3389
(800) 424-0362 • www.unitedlearning.com

AIMS Multimedia
9710 DeSoto Avenue
Chatsworth, CA 91311-4409
(800) 367-2467 •
www.AIMS-multimedia.com

BFA Educational Media
(see Phoenix Learning Group)

Broderbund
(Parsons Technology;
also see The Learning Company)
500 Redwood Blvd
Novato, CA 94997
(800) 395-0277 • www.broderbund.com

Carousel Film and Video
260 Fifth Avenue, Suite 705
New York, NY 10001
(212) 683-1660 • e-mail:
carousel@pipeline.com

Cloud 9 Interactive
(888) 662-5683 • www.cloud9int.com

Computer Plus (see ESI)

Coronet/MTI
(see Phoenix Learning Group)

Crayola (Binney Smith)
1100 Church Lane
Easton, PA 18042
(800) 272-9652 • www.crayola.com

Davidson (see Knowledge Adventure)

Direct Cinema, Ltd.
P.O. Box 10003
Santa Monica, CA 90410-1003
(310) 636-8200

Disney Interactive
(800) 900-9234 •
www.disneyinteractive.com

DK Multimedia (Dorling Kindersley)
95 Madison Avenue
New York, NY 10016
(212) 213-4800 • Fax: (800) 774-6733 •
(888) 342-5357 • www.dk.com

Edmark Corp.
P.O. Box 97021
Redmond, WA 98073-9721
(800) 362-2890 • www.edmark.com

Encyclopaedia Britannica Educational Corp.
310 South Michigan Avenue
Chicago, IL 60604
(800) 522-8656 • www.eb.com

ESI/Educational Software
4213 S. 94th Street
Omaha, NE 68127
(800) 955-5570 • www.edsoft.com

GPN/Reading Rainbow
University of Nebraska-Lincoln
P.O. Box 80669
Lincoln, NE 68501-0669
(800) 228-4630 • www.gpn.unl.edu

Great Tapes for Kids
P.O. Box 954
Middlebury, VT 05753
(888) 543-8273 •
www.greattapes.com/cart/home.phtml

Hasbro Interactive
(800) 683-5847 • www.hasbro.com

Humongous
13110 NE 177th Pl., Suite B101, Box 180
Woodenville, WA 98072
(800) 499-8386 • www.humongous.com

IBM Corp.
1133 Westchester Ave.
White Plains, NY 10604
(770) 863-1234 • Fax (770) 863-3030 •
(888) 411-1932 •
www.pc.ibm.com/multimedia/crayola

ICE, Inc.
(Distributed by Arch Publishing)
12B W. Main St.
Elmsford, NY 10523
(914) 347-2464 • (800) 843-9497 •
www.educorp.com

Knowledge Adventure
19840 Pioneer Avenue
Torrence, CA 90503
(800) 542-4240 • (800) 545-7677 •
www.knowledgeadventure.com

The Learning Company
6160 Summit Drive North
Minneapolis, MN 55430
(800) 395-0277 • www.learningco.com

Listening Library
One Park Avenue
Greenwich, CT 06870-1727
(800) 733-3000 • www.listeninglib.com

Macmillan/McGraw-Hill
(see SRA/McGraw-Hill)

Maxis
2121 N. California Blvd
Walnut Creek, CA 94596-3572
(925) 933-5630 • Fax (925) 927-3736 •
(800) 245-4525 • www.maxis.com

MECC
(see the Learning Company)

Microsoft
One Microsoft Way
Redmond, WA 98052-6399
(800) 426-9400 • www.microsoft.com/kids

National Geographic Society Educational Services
P.O. Box 1041
Des Moines, IA 50340-0597
(800) 225-5647 •
www.nationalgeographic.com

National School Products
101 East Broadway
Maryville, TN 37804
(800) 251-9124 • www.ierc.com

PBS Video
1320 Braddock Place
Alexandria, VA 22314
(800) 344-3337 • www.pbs.org

Phoenix Films
(see Phoenix Learning Group)

Phoenix Learning Group
2348 Chaffee Drive
St. Louis, MO 63146
(800) 221-1274 • e-mail:
phoenixfilms@worldnet.att.net

Pied Piper (see AIMS Multimedia)

Scholastic New Media
555 Broadway
New York, NY 10003
(800) 724-6527 • www.scholastic.com

Simon & Schuster Interactive
(see Knowledge Adventure)

SRA/McGraw-Hill
220 East Danieldale Road
De Soto, TX 75115
(888) 772-4543 • www.sra4kids.com

SVE/Churchill Media
6677 North Northwest Highway
Chicago, IL 60631
(800) 829-1900 • www.svemedia.com

Tom Snyder Productions (also see ESI)
80 Coolidge Hill Rd.
Watertown, MA 02472
(800) 342-0236 • www.teachtsp.com

Troll Associates
100 Corporate Drive
Mahwah, NJ 07430
(888) 998-7655 • Fax (800) 979-8765 •
www.troll.com

Voyager (see ESI)

Weston Woods
12 Oakwood Avenue
Norwalk, CT 06850
(800) 243-5020 • Fax (203) 845-0498

Zenger Media
10200 Jefferson Blvd., Room 94,
P.O. Box 802
Culver City, CA 90232-0802
(800) 421-4246 • (800) 944-5432 •
www.Zengermedia.com

BOOK 1

	Decodable Words			Spelling	Vocabulary

MAX, THE CAT

Short *a* (Decodable Words)

am	ham	**Pam**
and	**has**	pan
as	hat	pat
at	jam	rag
bad	Jan	ran
bag	lap	**sad**
bat	**mad**	Sam
cab	man	sat
can	map	tag
cap	**mat**	tan
cat	**Max**	tap
dad	nag	van
Dan	Nan	wag
fan	**nap**	wax
fat	pad	yam
had		

Short *a* (Spelling)

bad
can
had
hat
mat
pan

High-Frequency Words

give
likes
one
this

QUACK

Digraph *ck* (Decodable Words)

back	**pack**	rack
Jack	**packs**	sack
Mack	**quack**	tack

Digraph *ck* (Spelling)

back
pack
quack
rack
sack
tack

High-Frequency Words

on
they
what
your

WHAT DOES PIG DO?

Short *i* (Decodable Words)

bib	is	pin
big	it	pit
bin	jig	quick
bit	Jim	quit
Dick	**kick**	quiz
did	**kicks**	rib
dig	kid	Rick
digs	Kim	rip
dip	kit	sick
fin	lick	Sid
fit	lid	sip
fix	Lin	sit
hid	lip	six
him	mix	tick
hip	Nick	Tim
his	nip	tin
hit	**pick**	tip
if	**picks**	**wig**
in	**pig**	win

Short *i* (Spelling)

dig
kick
pick
pig
pin
win

High-Frequency Words

does
her
look
there

Boldfaced words appear in the selection.

BOOK 1

	Decodable Words			Spelling	Vocabulary
A Path on the Map	**Digraphs *sh, th***			**Digraphs *sh, th***	**High-Frequency Words**
	bath	math	that	dish	**be**
	cash	**path**	thick	**path**	**could**
	dash	rash	thin	**shack**	**down**
	dish	**shack**	**this**	that	**see**
	finish	shin	thrash	thin	
	fish	ship	wish	wish	
	mash	than	with		
Time for Kids: Ships	**Phonics Review**			**Words from Social Studies**	**Review High-Frequency Words**
				bus map	**look** **one**
				fast **ship**	**this** **what**
				go stop	

BOOK 2

	Decodable Words			Spelling	Vocabulary
One Good Pup	**Short *u***			**Short *u***	**High-Frequency Words**
	buck	hum	shut	buck	**no**
	bud	hush	sub	**but**	**out**
	bug	hut	suck	cut	**ride**
	bun	jug	sum	duck	**small**
	bus	luck	sun	rug	
	but	mud	sup	**tug**	
	cub	mug	thud		
	cup	nut	**tub**		
	cut	**pup**	tuck		
	duck	rub	**tug**		
	dug	rug	up		
	fun	run	us		
	gum	rush	yum		
	hug	rut			
The Bug Bath	**Short *o***			**Short *o***	**High-Frequency Words**
	Bob	job	pop	hop	**saw**
	box	jog	pot	**hot**	**two**
	cob	jot	rock	lock	**very**
	cot	lock	**rocked**	**not**	**want**
	dock	log	rod	rock	
	Don	lot	shock	**top**	
	dot	mom	sob		
	fog	mop	sock		
	fox	nod	tock		
	got	**not**	Tom		
	hog	**on**	**top**		
	hop	ox	tot		
	hot	pod			

BOOK 2

	Decodable Words		Spelling	Vocabulary

SPLASH!

Decodable Words — Short e

bed	led	**pets**
beg	leg	**red**
Ben	**legs**	Rex
bet	let	set
Beth	**Meg**	**shed**
Deb	men	Ted
deck	met	ten
den	**neck**	**them**
fed	Ned	**then**
get	net	vet
hem	peck	web
hen	peg	**wet**
Jen	pen	yes
jet	pet	yet
Ken		

Spelling — Short e

hen
pet
red
shed
then
wet

Vocabulary — High-Frequency Words

away
good
into
put

WHAT BUG IS IT?

Decodable Words — Blends and Double Consonants

bass	**hill**	**slim**
bell	hiss	slip
Bess	huff	slit
bill	hull	slob
buzz	ill	slop
cuff	**Jill**	slot
doll	kiss	slug
dull	lull	slush
fell	mass	**smack**
fill	mess	smash
flap	mill	smell
flash	**Miss**	smock
flat	muff	smug
flesh	**Nell**	snack
flick	**pass**	**snag**
flip	pill	**snap**
flock	puff	sniff
flop	quill	snip
fluff	ruff	snob
fresh	sell	snug
frill	sill	tell
frock	slam	thrill
frog	slap	till
fuss	slash	well
gill	slick	**will**
gull	slid	yell

Spelling — Blends and Double Consonants

doll
flat
miss
pass
puff
snap

Vocabulary — High-Frequency Words

about
again
around
use

TIME FOR KIDS: A VET

Decodable Words — Phonics Review

Spelling — Words from Social Studies

cat	job
help	pat
hog	**vet**

Vocabulary — Review High-Frequency Words

small	**good**
out	**want**

BOOK 3

	Decodable Words	Spelling	Vocabulary

STAN'S STUNT

Decodable Words

Blends

asked	melt	spend
bang	mend	spent
belt	milk	spill
bend	mint	spin
bent	mist	splash
best	must	spot
bump	nest	stab
camp	pant	stack
can't	past	staff
damp	pest	stamp
dent	pond	**Stan**
dump	pump	**Stan's**
dust	quilt	stand
end	raft	stem
fang	ramp	step
fast	rang	stick
felt	rent	stiff
fist	rest	still
fling	ring	sting
flung	risk	stomp
gang	rung	**stop**
gasp	rust	stub
gift	sand	stuck
gust	sang	stuff
hang	scab	stump
held	scat	stung
help	scuff	**stunt**
hint	self	**stunts**
hump	send	sung
hung	sent	swift
hunt	shelf	swim
jest	shift	swing
jump	sift	swung
just	silk	task
Kent	sing	tend
king	skid	tent
lamp	skill	test
last	skimp	theft
left	skin	**thing**
lend	skip	thump
lent	skit	tilt
lift	skull	trust
limp	slant	vent
lint	soft	vest
list	span	**went**
loft	spat	west
lump	speck	wilt
lung	sped	wind
mask	spell	wing

Spelling

Blends

bump
jump
spell
spill
tent
went

Vocabulary

High-Frequency Words

fall
their
try
would

BOOK 3

Decodable Words				Spelling	Vocabulary

GREG'S MASK

Blends

black	clasp	drift	plot
blast	**class**	drill	plug
blend	click	**drip**	plum
blimp	cliff	**drop**	plump
blob	cling	drum	plus
block	**clip**	glad	press
blond	clock	glass	print
blot	clog	Glen	prop
bluff	club	**glob**	track
blush	cluck	grab	tramp
Brad	clump	grand	trap
brag	crab	grant	**trash**
brand	crack	grasp	trick
brass	craft	grass	trim
brick	cramp	**Greg**	trip
bring	crash	Greg's	trot
brisk	crib	grill	truck
brush	crisp	grip	trust
clack	crop	gruff	twig
clam	crush	grump	twin
clamp	crust	grunt	**twist**
clang	draft	plan	
clap	drag	plant	
clash	dress	plop	

Blends (Spelling)

clap
class
dress
drop
track
trip

High-Frequency Words (Vocabulary)

any
grow
new
old

SAM'S SONG

ch, wh, nk

bank	chip	link	stink
bench	chomp	lunch	such
blank	chop	**much**	sunk
branch	**Chuck**	munch	tank
brunch	chunk	pinch	thank
bunch	clank	pink	**think**
Chad	clunk	plank	trunk
champ	crank	**plink**	whack
chant	**crunch**	pluck	**when**
check	drank	**plunk**	**which**
chess	drink	prank	whip
chest	Frank	punch	**whish**
Chet	French	ranch	whisk
chick	Hank	rank	**wink**
chill	honk	**sank**	yank
chimp	hunk	**sink**	
chin	inch	spank	

ch, wh, nk (Spelling)

chick
chin
sink
think
when
wink

High-Frequency Words (Vocabulary)

eat
now
together
too

BOOK 3

	Decodable Words	Spelling	Vocabulary
SNAKES	**Long *a: a-e***	**Long *a: a-e***	**High-Frequency Words**

SNAKES

Long *a: a-e*

bake	gate	save
base	gave	scale
blame	gaze	**scales**
brake	grade	shade
brave	grape	shake
cake	grate	shame
came	hate	shape
cane	Jake	shave
cape	Jane	skate
case	Kate	**snake**
cave	**lake**	**snake's**
chase	lane	state
crate	late	take
date	**made**	tale
Dave	**make**	tame
daze	mane	tape
drape	name	trade
fade	pane	vase
fake	plane	wade
fame	plate	wake
flake	rake	wave
flame	**safe**	whale
frame	sale	
game	same	

Spelling

Long *a: a-e*

came
lake
made
name
shade
snake

Vocabulary

High-Frequency Words

know
under
where
why

TIME FOR KIDS: LET'S CAMP OUT!

Phonics Review

Words from Science

fire	**sticks**
mud	**sun**
snow	**twigs**

Review High-Frequency Words

old
eat
together
under

BOOK 4

	Decodable Words	Spelling	Vocabulary

THE SHOPPING LIST

Decodable Words — Long *i: i-e*

bike	lime	**smile**
bite	line	**smiled**
bribe	live	snipe
bride	**Mike**	spike
chime	**Mike's**	spine
chive	mile	stride
crime	mime	strike
dime	mine	stripe
dine	mite	swine
dive	Nile	swipe
drive	nine	tide
file	pike	tile
fine	pile	**time**
fire	pine	tire
five	pipe	tribe
glide	pride	vile
grime	prime	vine
gripe	prize	while
hide	quite	whine
hike	ride	**white**
hire	**ripe**	**wide**
hive	shine	wife
jive	side	wine
kite	size	wipe
life	slide	wire
like	slime	

Spelling — Long *i: i-e*

bite
hide
smile
while
white
wide

Vocabulary — High-Frequency Words

after
always
blue
were
who

YASMIN'S DUCKS

Decodable Words — Long *o: o-e*

bone	home	rose
broke	**hope**	scope
choke	hose	shone
chose	**hoses**	slope
clone	**joke**	smoke
close	mope	spoke
clove	**nope**	stole
code	nose	stone
coke	note	stove
cone	poke	strode
cope	pope	stroke
cove	pose	those
dome	probe	throne
dove	prone	tone
drone	prose	vote
drove	quote	woke
globe	rode	yoke
grove	**Rome's**	zone
hole	rope	

Spelling — Long *o: o-e*

hole
home
hope
nose
rope
those

Vocabulary — High-Frequency Words

because
buy
found
some
work

BOOK 4

	Decodable Words			Spelling	Vocabulary
THE KNEE-HIGH MAN	*Long u: u-e*			*Long u: u-e*	**High-Frequency Words**
	brute	dune	prune	cute	**been**
	cube	flute	pure	flute	**carry**
	cure	fume	rude	mule	**clean**
	cute	fuse	**rule**	**rule**	**done**
	dude	**June**	tube	tube	**far**
	duke	**mule**	tune	tune	
JOHNNY APPLESEED	*Long a: ai, ay*			*Long a: ai, ay*	**High-Frequency Words**
	bail	**jays**	sail	**day**	**how**
	bait	laid	**sailed**	**rain**	**light**
	bay	lay	**say**	say	**little**
	braid	maid	snail	tail	**live**
	brain	mail	Spain	**wait**	**pretty**
	chain	main	sprain	**way**	
	clay	**May**	spray		
	day	nail	stain		
	days	paid	stay		
	drain	pail	strain		
	explained	pain	stray		
	fail	pay	sway		
	faint	plain	tail		
	frail	play	trail		
	Gail	praise	train		
	gay	quail	tray		
	grain	**quail's**	vain		
	gray	raid	wail		
	hail	rail	wait		
	hay	**rain**	**way**		
	jail	raise			
	jay	ray			
TIME FOR KIDS: RING! RING! RING! PUT OUT THE FIRE!	**Phonics Review**			**Words from Social Studies**	**Review High-Frequency Words**
				bell **ring**	**work**
				brave **smoke**	**always**
				pole **truck**	**done**

BOOK 5, UNIT 1

	Decodable Words	Spelling	Vocabulary

SEVEN SILLIES

Decodable Words — Long *e: e, ee*

be	green	**sheep**
bee	greet	sheet
beef	he	sleep
beep	heel	sleet
beet	jeep	speech
bleed	keep	steel
cheek	Lee	steep
cheep	me	steer
creek	meet	street
creep	need	sweep
deed	peek	sweet
deep	peel	tee
deer	peep	teen
fee	queen	**three**
feed	reef	tree
feel	screech	tweet
feet	screen	we
flee	**see**	weed
fleet	seed	week
free	seek	weep
freed	seem	wheel
freeze	seen	
greed	she	

Spelling — Long *e: e, ee*

bee
she
sheep
three
tree
we

Vocabulary — High-Frequency Words

all
four
many
over
so

SHRINKING MOUSE

Decodable Words — Long *e: ie, ea*

beach	field	read
bead	**fields**	scream
beak	flea	sea
bean	grief	seal
beast	heal	seat
beat	hear	shield
bleach	heat	sneak
cheat	Jean	speak
chief	lead	squeak
clean	leak	steal
clear	leap	steam
cream	least	streak
deal	meal	stream
Dean	mean	tea
dear	meat	teach
dream	near	team
each	neat	tear
ear	pea	thief
east	peach	weak
eat	peak	year
fear	reach	yield
feast	**reached**	

Spelling — Long *e: ie, ea*

fields
leaf
piece
reached
read
sea

Vocabulary — High-Frequency Words

before
come
off
our
right

BOOK 5, UNIT 1

	Decodable Words	Spelling	Vocabulary
You Can't Smell a Flower with Your Ear!	**Long *o: o, oa, oe, ow*** blow · glow · **opening** blown · go · **pillow** boat · goal · road bold · goat · roast **both** · **goes** · roll bow · groan · row bowl · grow · scold coach · grown · show coal · **hold** · shown coast · **holding** · slow coat · Joan · snow **cold** · Joe · so croak · load · soak crow · loan · sold don't · low · throat float · moan · toad flow · **moment** · toast flown · most · toe foal · mow · told foam · no · toll fold · oat · won't follow · old	**Long *o: o, oa, oe, ow*** boat **cold** **goes** **hold** road show	**High-Frequency Words** **by** **find** **kind** **high** **more**
Owl and the Moon	**Long *i: i, y, igh*** blind · grind · sigh bright · high · sight by · **I** · **sky** child · **kind** · slight cry · **light** · sly dry · might · tight fight · mild · try find · mind · why flight · **my** · wild fly · **night** · wind fright · **right** fry · shy	**Long *i: i, y, igh*** child **my** **night** **shy** **sky** tight	**High-Frequency Words** **everything** eyes gone head room
Time for Kids: The Night Animals	**Phonics Review**	**Words from Science** **bugs** · **owl** frog · pond logs · **rat**	**Review High-Frequency Words** **many** **off** **all**

BOOK 5, UNIT 2

	Decodable Words	Spelling	Vocabulary

A Friend for Little Bear

/ü/oo — Decodable Words

bloom	fool	pool	spoon
boo	groom	proof	stool
boom	hoop	**roof**	stoop
boot	hoot	**room**	too
booth	loom	root	tool
broom	loop	scoop	tooth
cool	moo	shoot	troop
doom	mood	snoop	zoo
droop	moon	soon	zoom
food	noon	spool	

/ü/oo — Spelling

cool
fool
moon
roof
soon
zoo

High-Frequency Words — Vocabulary

called
friend
only
pulled
these

New Shoes for Silvia

/ä/ar — Decodable Words

ark	chart	mark
arm	Clark	park
art	dark	part
bar	dart	shark
bark	**far**	sharp
barn	farm	spark
Bart	hard	star
car	harm	start
Carl	harp	tart
cart	Lark	yard
charm	march	yarn

/ä/ar — Spelling

bark
car
dark
park
part
star

High-Frequency Words — Vocabulary

every
morning
once
or
took

The Story of a Blue Bird

/ûr/ir, ur, er — Decodable Words

bird	first	squirt
birds	fur	stir
birth	girl	**surprised**
burn	her	term
churn	herself	third
clerk	hurt	thirst
curb	jerk	turn
curl	shirt	twirl
dirt	sir	verb
fern	skirt	whirl
fir	stern	

/ûr/ir, ur, er — Spelling

bird
burn
first
girl
hurt
serve

High-Frequency Words — Vocabulary

brother
from
mother
sister
walked

BOOK 5, UNIT 2

	Decodable Words	Spelling	Vocabulary

YOUNG AMELIA EARHART

Decodable Words

/ou/ou, ow; /oi/oi, oy

boil	frown	plow
bound	gown	point
bow	grouch	pound
boy	ground	pout
boys	growl	proud
broil	hound	prowl
brow	**how**	round
brown	howl	Roy
cloud	**Howland**	scout
clown	join	soil
coin	joint	sound
couch	joy	sour
count	loud	south
cow	moist	spoil
crown	mound	sprout
down	mount	town
drown	mouth	toy
flour	now	wound
foil	oil	
found	our	
fowl	out	

Spelling

/ou/ou, ow; /oi/oi, oy

boys	sound
mouse	town
noise	toy

Vocabulary

High-Frequency Words

father
horse
people
should
woman

TIME FOR KIDS: ON THE GO!

Phonics Review

Words from Math

feet	miles
five	sum
less	**ten**

Review High-Frequency Words

from	**or**
these	horse
called	**people**

Listening, Speaking, Viewing, Representing

LISTENING	K	1	2	3	4	5	6
Learn the vocabulary of school (numbers, shapes, colors, directions, and categories)							
Identify the musical elements of literary language, such as rhymes, repetition, onomatopoeia, alliteration, assonance							
Determine purposes for listening (get information, solve problems, enjoy and appreciate)							
Understand and follow directions							
Listen critically and responsively; recognize barriers to effective listening							
Ask and answer relevant questions (for clarification; to follow up on ideas)							
Listen critically to interpret and evaluate							
Listen responsively to stories and other texts read aloud, including selections from classic and contemporary works							
Connect and compare own experiences, feelings, ideas, and traditions with those of others							
Apply comprehension strategies in listening activities							
Understand the major ideas and supporting evidence in spoken messages							
Participate in listening activities related to reading and writing (such as discussions, group activities, conferences)							
Listen to learn by taking notes, organizing, and summarizing spoken ideas							
Know personal listening preferences							

SPEAKING	K	1	2	3	4	5	6
Uses repetition, rhyme, and rhythm in oral texts (such as in reciting songs, poems, and stories with repeating patterns)							
Learn the vocabulary of school (numbers, shapes, colors, directions, and categories)							
Use appropriate language, grammar, and vocabulary learned to describe ideas, feelings, and experiences							
Ask and answer relevant questions (for clarification; to follow up on ideas)							
Communicate effectively in everyday situations (such as discussions, group activities, conferences, conversations)							
Demonstrate speaking skills (audience, purpose, occasion, clarity, volume, pitch, intonation, phrasing, rate, fluency)							
Clarify and support spoken messages and ideas with objects, charts, evidence, elaboration, examples							
Use verbal communication in effective ways when, for example, making announcements, giving directions, or making introductions							
Use nonverbal communication in effective ways such as eye contact, facial expressions, gestures							
Retell a story or a spoken message by summarizing or clarifying							
Connect and compare own experiences, ideas, and traditions with those of others							
Determine purposes for speaking (inform, entertain, compare, describe, give directions, persuade, express personal feelings and opinions)							
Recognize differences between formal and informal language							
Demonstrate skills of reporting and providing information							
Demonstrate skills of interviewing, requesting and providing information							
Apply composition strategies in speaking activities							
Monitor own understanding of spoken message and seek clarification as needed							

VIEWING	K	1	2	3	4	5	6
Demonstrate viewing skills (focus attention, organize information)							
Understand and use nonverbal cues							
Respond to audiovisual media in a variety of ways							
Participate in viewing activities related to reading and writing							
Apply comprehension strategies in viewing activities, including main idea and details							
Recognize artists' craft and techniques for conveying meaning							
Interpret information from various formats such as maps, charts, graphics, video segments, technology							
Knows various types of mass media (such as film, video, television, billboards, and newspapers)							
Evaluate purposes of various media, including mass media (information, appreciation, entertainment, directions, persuasion)							
Use media, including mass media, to compare ideas, information, and points of view							

REPRESENTING	K	1	2	3	4	5	6
Select, organize, or produce visuals to complement or extend meanings							
Produce communication using appropriate media to develop a class paper, multimedia or video reports							
Show how language, medium, and presentation contribute to the message							

Reading: Alphabetic Principle, Sounds/Symbols

☑ Tested Skill

☐ Tinted panels show skills, strategies, and other teaching opportunities

PRINT AWARENESS	K	1	2	3	4	5	6
Know the order of the alphabet							
Recognize that print represents spoken language and conveys meaning							
Understand directionality (tracking print from left to right; return sweep)							
Understand that written words and sentences are separated by spaces							
Know the difference between individual letters and printed words							
Understand that spoken words are represented in written language by specific sequence of letters							
Recognize that there are correct spellings for words							
Know the difference between capital and lowercase letters							
Recognize how readers use capitalization and punctuation to comprehend							
Recognize the distinguishing features of a letter, word, sentence, paragraph							
Understand appropriate book handling							
Recognize that parts of a book (such as cover/title page and table of contents) offer information							

PHONOLOGICAL AWARENESS	K	1	2	3	4	5	6
Listen for environmental sounds							
Identify spoken words and sentences							
Divide spoken sentence into individual words							
Produce rhyming words and distinguish rhyming words from nonrhyming words							
Identify, segment, and combine syllables within spoken words							
Blend and segment onsets and rimes							
Identify and isolate the initial, medial, and final sound of a spoken word							
Add, delete, or substitute sounds to change words (such as *cow* to *how*, *pan* to *fan*)							
Blend sounds to make spoken words							
Segment one-syllable spoken words into individual phonemes							

PHONICS AND DECODING	K	1	2	3	4	5	6
Alphabetic principle: Letter/sound correspondence	☑	☑	☑				
Blending CVC words	☑	☑					
Segmenting CVC words	☑						
Blending CVC, CVCe, CCVC, CVCC, CVVC words	☑	☑	☑				
Segmenting CVC, CVCe, CCVC, CVCC, CVVC words and sounds	☑	☑	☑				
Initial and final consonants: /n/n, /d/d, /s/s, /m/m, /t/t, /k/c, /f/f, /r/r, /p/p, /l/l, /k/k, /g/g, /b/b, /h/h, /w/w, /v/v, /ks/x, /kw/qu, /j/j, /y/y, /z/z	☑	☑					
Initial and medial short vowels: *a, i, u, o, e*	☑	☑	☑				
Long vowels: *a-e, i-e, o-e, u-e* (vowel-consonant-e)		☑	☑				
Long vowels, including *ay, ai; e, ee, ie, ea; o, oa, oe, ow; i, y, igh*		☑	☑				
Consonant Digraphs: *sh, th, ch, wh*		☑					
Consonant Blends: continuant/continuant, including *sl, sm, sn, fl, fr, ll, ss, ff*		☑					
Consonant Blends: continuant/stop, including *st, sk, sp, ng, nt, nd, mp, ft*		☑					
Consonant Blends: stop/continuant, including *tr, pr, pl, cr, tw*		☑					
Variant vowels: including /ù/oo; /ô/a, aw, au; /ü/ue, ew		☑	☑				
Diphthongs, including /ou/ou, ow; /oi/oi, oy		☑	☑				
r-controlled vowels, including /âr/are; /ôr/or, ore; /îr/ear			☑				
Soft *c* and soft *g*			☑				
nk		☑	☑				
Consonant Digraphs: *ck*	☑	☑					
Consonant Digraphs: *ph, tch, ch*			☑				
Short *e: ea*			☑				
Long *e: y, ey*			☑				
/ü/oo		☑	☑				
/är/ar; /ûr/ir, ur, er		☑	☑				
Silent letters: including *l, b, k, w, g, h, gh*			☑				
Schwa: /ər/er; /ən/en; /əl/le;			☑				
Reading/identifying multisyllabic words		☑	☑				
Using graphophonic cues							

Reading: Vocabulary/Word Identification

WORD STRUCTURE	K	1	2	3	4	5	6
Common spelling patterns							
Syllable patterns							
Plurals		☑					
Possessives		☑					
Contractions		☑					
Root, or base, words and inflectional endings (-s, -es, -ed, -ing)		☑	☑	☑		☑	
Compound Words		☑	☑	☑	☑	☑	☑
Prefixes and suffixes (such as un-, re-, dis-, non-; -ly, -y, -ful, -able, -tion)			☑	☑	☑	☑	☑
Root words and derivational endings				☑	☑	☑	☑

WORD MEANING	K	1	2	3	4	5	6
Develop vocabulary through concrete experiences, word walls, other people							
Develop vocabulary through selections read aloud							
Develop vocabulary through reading							
Cueing systems: syntactic, semantic, graphophonic							
Context clues, including semantic clues (word meaning), syntactical clues (word order), and graphophonic clues	☑	☑	☑	☑	☑	☑	☑
High-frequency words (such as the, a, and, said, was, where, is)	☑	☑					
Identify words that name persons, places, things, and actions							
Automatic reading of regular and irregular words							
Use resources and references (dictionary, glossary, thesaurus, synonym finder, technology and software, and context)							
Classify and categorize words							
Synonyms and antonyms			☑	☑	☑	☑	☑
Multiple-meaning words			☑		☑	☑	☑
Figurative language			☑	☑	☑	☑	☑
Decode derivatives (root words, such as like, pay, happy with affixes, such as dis-, pre-, un-)							
Systematic study of words across content areas and in current events							
Locate meanings, pronunciations, and derivations (including dictionaries, glossaries, and other sources)							
Denotation and connotation							☑
Word origins as aid to understanding historical influences on English word meanings							
Homophones, homographs							
Analogies							☑
Idioms							

Reading: Comprehension

PREREADING STRATEGIES	K	1	2	3	4	5	6
Preview and predict							
Use prior knowledge							
Set and adjust purposes for reading							
Build background							

MONITORING STRATEGIES	K	1	2	3	4	5	6
Adjust reading rate							
Reread, search for clues, ask questions, ask for help							
Visualize							
Read a portion aloud, use reference aids							
Use decoding and vocabulary strategies							
Paraphrase							
Create story maps, diagrams, charts, story props to help comprehend, analyze, synthesize and evaluate texts							

(continued on next page)

☑ Tested Skill

Tinted panels show skills, strategies, and other teaching opportunities

SKILLS AND STRATEGIES

Skill	K	1	2	3	4	5	6
Recall story details, including character and setting	☑	☑					
Use illustrations	☑	☑					
Distinguish reality and fantasy	☑	☑	☑				
Classify and categorize	☑						
Make predictions	☑	☑	☑	☑	☑	☑	☑
Recognize sequence of events (tell or act out)	☑	☑	☑	☑	☑	☑	☑
Recognize cause and effect	☑	☑	☑	☑	☑	☑	☑
Compare and contrast	☑	☑	☑	☑	☑	☑	☑
Summarize	☑	☑	☑	☑	☑	☑	☑
Make and explain inferences		☑	☑	☑	☑	☑	☑
Draw conclusions		☑	☑	☑	☑	☑	☑
Distinguish important and unimportant information				☑	☑	☑	☑
Recognize main idea and supporting details	☑	☑	☑	☑	☑	☑	☑
Form conclusions or generalizations and support with evidence from text			☑	☑	☑	☑	☑
Distinguish fact and opinion (including news stories and advertisements)				☑	☑	☑	☑
Recognize problem and solution			☑	☑	☑	☑	☑
Recognize steps in a process		☑	☑	☑	☑	☑	☑
Make judgments and decisions				☑	☑	☑	☑
Distinguish fact and nonfact				☑	☑	☑	☑
Recognize techniques of persuasion and propaganda							☑
Evaluate evidence and sources of information, including checking other sources and asking experts							☑
Identify similarities and differences across texts (including topics, characters, problems, themes, cultural influences, treatment, scope, or organization)							
Practice various questions and tasks (test-like comprehension questions)							
Paraphrase and summarize to recall, inform, and organize							
Answer various types of questions (open-ended, literal, interpretive, test-like such as true-false, multiple choice, short-answer)							
Use study strategies to learn and recall (preview, question, reread, and record)							

LITERARY RESPONSE

Skill	K	1	2	3	4	5	6
Listen to stories being read aloud							
React, speculate, join in, read along when predictable and patterned selections are read aloud							
Respond to a variety of stories and poems through talk, movement, music, art, drama, and writing							
Show understanding through writing, illustrating, developing demonstrations, and using technology							
Connect ideas and themes across texts							
Support responses by referring to relevant aspects of text and own experiences							
Offer observations, make connections, speculate, interpret, and raise questions in response to texts							
Interpret text ideas through journal writing, discussion, enactment, and media							

TEXT STRUCTURE/LITERARY CONCEPTS

Skill	K	1	2	3	4	5	6
Distinguish forms and functions of texts (lists, newsletters, signs)							
Use text features to aid comprehension							
Understand story structure							
Identify narrative (for entertainment) and expository (for information)							
Distinguish fiction from nonfiction, including fact and fantasy							
Understand literary forms (stories, poems, plays, and informational books)							
Understand literary terms by distinguishing between roles of author and illustrator							
Understand title, author, and illustrator across a variety of texts							
Analyze character, character's motive, character's point of view, plot, setting, style, tone, mood		☑	☑	☑	☑	☑	☑
Compare communication in different forms							
Understand terms such as *title, author, illustrator, playwright, theater, stage, act, dialogue,* and *scene*							
Recognize stories, poems, songs, myths, legends, folktales, fables, tall tales, limericks, plays, biographies, autobiographies							
Judge internal logic of story text							
Recognize that authors organize information in specific ways							
Recognize author's purpose: to inform, influence, express, or entertain							
Describe how author's point of view affects text				☑	☑	☑	☑
Recognize biography, historical fiction, realistic fiction, modern fantasy, informational texts, and poetry							
Analyze ways authors present ideas (cause/effect, compare/contrast, inductively, deductively, chronologically)							
Recognize literary techniques such as imagery, repetition, flashback, foreshadowing, symbolism							

(continued on next page)

(Reading: Comprehension continued)

☑ Tested Skill

☐ Tinted panels show skills, strategies, and other teaching opportunities

VARIETY OF TEXT	K	1	2	3	4	5	6
Read a variety of genres and understand their distinguishing features							
Use expository and other informational texts to acquire information							
Read for a variety of purposes							
Select varied sources when reading for information or pleasure							
Know preferences for reading literary and nonfiction texts							
FLUENCY							
Read regularly in independent-level and instructional-level materials							
Read orally with fluency from familiar texts							
Self-select independent-level reading							
Read silently for increasing periods of time							
Demonstrate characteristics of fluent and effective reading							
Adjust reading rate to purpose							
Read aloud in selected texts, showing understanding of text and engaging the listener							
CULTURES							
Connect own experience with culture of others							
Compare experiences of characters across cultures							
Articulate and discuss themes and connections that cross cultures							
CRITICAL THINKING							
Experiences (comprehend, apply, analyze, synthesize, evaluate)							
Make connections (comprehend, apply, analyze, synthesize, evaluate)							
Expression (comprehend, apply, analyze, synthesize, evaluate)							
Inquiry (comprehend, apply, analyze, synthesize, evaluate)							
Problem solving (comprehend, apply, analyze, synthesize, evaluate)							
Making decisions (comprehend, apply, analyze, synthesize, evaluate)							

Study Skills

INQUIRY/RESEARCH AND STUDY STRATEGIES	K	1	2	3	4	5	6
Follow and give directions							
Use alphabetical order							
Use text features and formats to help understand text (such as boldface, italic, or highlighted text; captions; headings and subheadings; numbers or symbols)							
Use study strategies to help read text and to learn and recall information from text (such as preview text, set purposes, and ask questions; use SQRRR; adjust reading rate; skim and scan; use KWL)							
Identify/frame and revise questions for research							
Obtain, organize, and summarize information: classify, take notes, outline, web, diagram							
Evaluate research and raise new questions							
Use technology for research and/or to present information in various formats							
Follow accepted formats for writing research, including documenting sources							
Use test-taking strategies							
Use text organizers (book cover; title page—title, author, illustrator; contents; headings; glossary; index)		☑	☑	☑	☑	☑	☑
Use graphic aids, such as maps, diagrams, charts, graphs, schedules, calendars		☑	☑	☑	☑	☑	☑
Read and interpret varied texts, such as environmental print, signs, lists, encyclopedia, dictionary, glossary, newspaper, advertisement, magazine, calendar, directions, floor plans, online resources		☑	☑	☑	☑	☑	☑
Use print and online reference sources, such as glossary, dictionary, encyclopedia, telephone directory, technology resources, nonfiction books		☑	☑	☑	☑	☑	☑
Recognize Library/Media center resources, such as computerized references; catalog search—subject, author, title; encyclopedia index		☑	☑	☑	☑	☑	☑

Writing

MODES AND FORMS	K	1	2	3	4	5	6
Interactive writing							
Descriptive writing			☑				
Personal narrative			☑	☑	☑	☑	☑
Writing that compares		☑	☑	☑	☑	☑	☑
Explanatory writing			☑	☑	☑	☑	☑
Persuasive writing				☑	☑	☑	☑
Writing a story		☑	☑	☑	☑	☑	☑
Expository writing; research report		☑	☑	☑	☑	☑	☑
Write using a variety of formats, such as advertisement, autobiography, biography, book report/report, comparison-contrast, critique/review/editorial, description, essay, how-to, interview, invitation, journal/log/notes, message/list, paragraph/multi-paragraph composition, picture book, play (scene), poem/rhyme, story, summary, note, letter							

PURPOSES/AUDIENCES							
Dictate sentences and messages such as news and stories for others to write							
Write labels, notes, and captions for illustrations, possessions, charts, and centers							
Write to record, to discover and develop ideas, to inform, to influence, to entertain							
Exhibit an identifiable voice							
Use literary devices (suspense, dialogue, and figurative language)							
Produce written texts by organizing ideas, using effective transitions, and choosing precise wording							

PROCESSES							
Generate ideas for self-selected and assigned topics using prewriting strategies							
Develop drafts							
Revise drafts for varied purposes, elaborate ideas							
Edit for appropriate grammar, spelling, punctuation, and features of published writings							
Proofread own writing and that of others							
Bring pieces to final form and "publish" them for audiences							
Use technology to compose, revise, and present text							
Select and use reference materials and resources for writing, revising, and editing final drafts							

SPELLING							
Spell own name and write high-frequency words							
Words with short vowels (including CVC and one-syllable words with blends CCVC, CVCC, CCVCC)							
Words with long vowels (including CVCe)							
Words with digraphs, blends, consonant clusters, double consonants							
Words with diphthongs							
Words with variant vowels							
Words with r-controlled vowels							
Words with /ər/, /əl/, and /ən/							
Words with silent letters							
Words with soft c and soft g							
Inflectional endings (including plurals and past tense and words that drop the final e and double a consonant when adding -ing, -ed)							
Compound words							
Contractions							
Homonyms							
Suffixes such as -able, -ly, -ful, or -less, and prefixes such as dis-, re-, pre-, or un-							
Spell words ending in -tion and -sion, such as station and procession							
Accurate spelling of root or base words							
Orthographic patterns and rules such as keep/can; sack/book; out/now; oil/toy; match/speech; ledge/cage; consonant doubling, dropping e, changing y to i							
Multisyllabic words using regularly spelled phonogram patterns							
Syllable patterns (including closed, open, syllable boundary patterns)							
Synonyms and antonyms							
Words from Social Studies, Science, Math, and Physical Education							
Words derived from other languages and cultures							
Use resources to find correct spellings, synonyms, and replacement words							
Use conventional spelling of familiar words in writing assignments							
Spell accurately in final drafts							

(continued on next page)

(Writing continued)

☑ Tested Skill

☐ Tinted panels show skills, strategies, and other teaching opportunities

GRAMMAR AND USAGE

Skill	K	1	2	3	4	5	6
Understand sentence concepts (word order, statements, questions, exclamations, commands)							
Recognize complete and incomplete sentences							
Nouns (common, proper, singular, plural, irregular plural, possessives)							
Verbs (action, helping, linking, irregular)							
Verb tense (present, past, future, perfect, and progressive)							
Pronouns (possessive, subject and object, pronoun-verb agreement)							
Use objective case pronouns accurately							
Adjectives							
Adverbs that tell how, when, where							
Subjects, predicates							
Subject-verb agreement							
Sentence combining							
Recognize sentence structure (simple, compound, complex)							
Synonyms and antonyms							
Contractions							
Conjunctions							
Prepositions and prepositional phrases							

PENMANSHIP

Skill	K	1	2	3	4	5	6
Write each letter of alphabet (capital and lowercase) using correct formation, appropriate size and spacing							
Write own name and other important words							
Use phonological knowledge to map sounds to letters to write messages							
Write messages that move left to right, top to bottom							
Gain increasing control of penmanship, pencil grip, paper position, beginning stroke							
Use word and letter spacing and margins to make messages readable							
Write legibly by selecting cursive or manuscript as appropriate							

MECHANICS

Skill	K	1	2	3	4	5	6
Use capitalization in sentences, proper nouns, titles, abbreviations and the pronoun *I*							
Use end marks correctly (period, question mark, exclamation point)							
Use commas (in dates, in addresses, in a series, in letters, in direct address)							
Use apostrophes in contractions and possessives							
Use quotation marks							
Use hyphens, semicolons, colons							

EVALUATION

Skill	K	1	2	3	4	5	6
Identify the most effective features of a piece of writing using class/teacher-generated criteria							
Respond constructively to others' writing							
Determine how his/her own writing achieves its purpose							
Use published pieces as models for writing							
Review own written work to monitor growth as writer							

Handwriting, 65M, 95M, T78–T91

High–frequency words, 10B–C, 37A–C, 40B–C, 55, 65A–C, 68B–C, 77, 95A–C, 98B–C, 123A–C, 126B–C, 133A–C
after, 10B–C, 37A–C
always, 10B–C, 37A–C
because, 40B–C, 65A–C
been, 68B–C, 95A–C
blue, 10B–C, 37A–C
buy, 40B–C, 65A–C
carry, 68B–C, 95A–C
clean, 68B–C, 95A–C, 126B–C
done, 68B–C, 95A–C, 126B–C
far, 68B–C, 95A–C
found, 40B–C, 65A–C
how, 98B–C, 123A–C, 126B–C
light, 98B–C, 123A–C
little, 98B–C, 123A–C
live, 98B–C, 123A–C
pretty, 98B–C, 123A–C
some, 40B–C, 65A–C
were, 10B–C, 37A–C
who, 10B–C, 37A–C
work, 40B–C, 65A–C, 126B–C

High–utility vocabulary, 10B–C, 37A–C, 40B–C, 65A–C, 68B–C, 95A–C, 98B–C, 123A–C, 126B–C, 133A–C

Idioms, 85

Illustrations, using, 13, 15, 18, 22, 30, 37A, 37B, 42, 48, 49, 57, 59, 69, 79, 81, 82, 88, 95J, 116, 133A

Independent reading, 8B, 37B, 38B, 65B, 66B, 95B, 96B, 123B, 124B, 133B

Inferences, making, 12, 16, 17, 19, 20, 28, 31, 34, 42, 51, 58, 59, 62, 71, 79, 86, 95B, 95C, 95I–J, 96G, 98–123, 123A–C, 123I–J, 127, 128, 129, 130, 133G–H, T73

Inflectional endings, 37K–L, 65K–L, 123K–L, 133K–L, T67, T71

Informal assessment, 8J, 37F, 37H, 37J, 37L, 48J, 65F, 65H, 65J, 65L, 66J, 95F, 95H, 95J, 95L, 96J, 123F, 123H, 123J, 123L, 124J, 133F, 133H, 133J, 133L

Integrated language arts. *See* Cross-curricular.

Internet connection, 6J, 20, 22, 35, 37D, 44, 48, 63, 65D, 72, 80, 86, 93, 95D, 100, 106, 121, 123D, 129, 131, 133D, 135

Intervention/prevention. *See* Prevention/intervention.

Johnny Appleseed, 98–119

Journal writing, 8/9, 33, 37D, 37N, 37R, 38/39, 61, 65D, 65N, 65R, 66/67, 91, 95N, 95D, 95R, 96/97, 119, 123D, 123N, 123R, 124/125, 129, 133D, 133N, 133R

Knee–High Man, 68–95

Language arts link, 8G, 96G, 124G

Language control, 140C

Language support, 10A, 11, 13, 15, 16, 19, 23, 28, 30, 37N, 37O, 37Q, 47, 53, 57, 65J, 65K, 65L, 65N, 71, 79, 82, 85, 95N, 107, 109, 115, 116, 123N, 133N, 140B

Learning styles
auditory, 10B, 24, 37F, 40B, 68B, 98B, 124G, 126A, 126B, T64–76
interpersonal, 65H, 95J
kinesthetic, 8J, 10A, 37H, 37J, 38G, 40A, 68A, 76, 86, 95F, 95H, 96I, 98A, 102, 104, 124G, 133J, T64–76
linguistic, 8J, 10A, 20, 24, 37F, 37H, 40A, 44, 65F, 65H, 65J, 68A, 80, 86, 95H, 95J, 96I, 98A, 106, 123H, 123J, 123L, 133H, 133J
logical, 42, 44, 48, 65J, 76, 110
spatial, 12, 38J, 58, 65F, 95F
visual, 8G, 12, 20, 22, 37J, 37L, 40A, 42, 48, 58, 72, 80, 84, 96G, 104, 106, 123H, 123J, 123L, T64–76

Leveled books, 8B, 37A–D, 38B, 65A–D, 66B, 95A–D, 96B, 123A–D, 124B, 133A–D

Liatsos, Sandra, 6–7

Limited English proficiency. *See* Language support.

Listening and speaking activities, 8G, 10A, 10B–C, 32, 33, 37D, 37N, 37O, 38G, 40A, 40B–C, 60, 61, 65D, 65N, 65O, 66G, 68A, 68B–C, 90, 91, 95D, 95N, 95O, 96G, 98A, 98B–C, 118, 119, 123D, 123N, 123O, 124G, 126A, 126B–C, 128, 129, 133D, 133N, 133O. *See also* Speaking and listening activities, Presentation ideas.

Listening library, 6, 8A, 38A, 66A, 96A, 124A

Lists, making, 6J, 10A, 35, 37C, 37F, 37R, 40A, 65M, 65R, 75, 78, 86, 95M, 95R, 123F, 123M, 123R, 133R, 134

Literacy support. *See* Language support.

Literary devices, 135
rhyme, 135

Literary genre, 6–7, 8G, 10, 11, 38G, 40, 41, 66G, 68, 69, 96G, 98, 99, 124G, 126, 127, 134

fable, 38G
folktale, 66G, 96G
informational story, 41, 134
legend, 99
narrative nonfiction, 127
play, 69, 134
poetry, 6–7, 8G, 124G
story, 11

Literary response, 7, 33, 37A–C, 61, 65A–C, 91, 95A–C, 119, 123A–C, 129, 133A–C, 135

Long vowels and phonograms, 8C, 8I–J, 8/9, 10–33, 37A–C, 37E–F, 37G–H, 38C, 38I–J, 38/39, 40–61, 65A–C, 65E–F, 65G–H, 66I–J, 66/67, 68–91, 95A–C, 95E–F, 95G–H, 96C, 96I–J, 96/97, 98–119, 123A–C, 123E–F, 123G–H, 124C, 124I–J, T69, T70, T71, T72, T75, T76
long *a: a-e,* 37G–H, 65G–H, 95G–H
long *a: ai, ay,* 96I–J, 96/97, 98–119, 123A–C, 123E–F, 123G–H, 124I–J, T75, T76
long *i: i-e,* 8I–J, 8/9, 10–33, 37A–C, 37E–F, 37G–H, 65G–H, 95G–H, 124I–J, T64, T65
long *o: o-e,* 38I–J, 38/39, 40–61, 65A–C, 65E–F, 65G–H, 95G–H, 123G–H, 124I–J, T69, T70
long *u: u-e,* 66I–J, 66/67, 68–91, 95A–C, 95E–F, 95G–H, 123G–H, 124I–J, T71, T72
See also Phonics and decoding.

Main idea/supporting details, identifying, 59, 89, 100

Math link, 8D, 12, 48, 66D, 76, 110

Mechanics and usage, 37P, 65P, 95P, 123P, 133P
apostrophes in contractions, 117P
commas in letters, 123P
proper nouns, 37P, 95P
sentence punctuation, 65P
See also Grammar, mechanics and usage.

Meeting Individual Needs
for comprehension, 37J, 65J, 95J, 123J, 133F, 133H
for phonics, 8J, 37F, 37H, 38J, 65F, 65H, 66J, 95F 95G, 96J, 123F, 123H, 124J
for study skills, 36, 64, 94, 122, 132
for vocabulary, 37L, 65L, 95L, 123L, 133J, 133L
for writing, 37N, 65N, 95N, 123N, 133N
grouping suggestions for strategic reading, 10, 34, 40, 64, 70, 94, 100, 122, 128, 136
leveled books, 8B, 37D, 38B, 65D, 66B, 95D, 96B, 123D, 124B, 133D
resources for, 6F, 8B, 38B, 66B, 96B, 124B

Scoring Chart

The Scoring Chart is provided for your convenience in grading your students' work.

- Find the column that shows the total number of items.
- Find the row that matches the number of items answered correctly.
- The intersection of the two rows provides the percentage score.

TOTAL NUMBER OF ITEMS

N↓ / Items→	1	2	3	4	5	6	7	8	9	10	11	12	13	14	15	16	17	18	19	20	21	22	23	24	25	26	27	28	29	30
1	100	50	33	25	20	17	14	13	11	10	9	8	8	7	7	6	6	6	5	5	5	5	4	4	4	4	4	4	3	3
2		100	66	50	40	33	29	25	22	20	18	17	15	14	13	13	12	11	11	10	10	9	9	8	8	8	7	7	7	7
3			100	75	60	50	43	38	33	30	27	25	23	21	20	19	18	17	16	15	14	14	13	13	12	12	11	11	10	10
4				100	80	67	57	50	44	40	36	33	31	29	27	25	24	22	21	20	19	18	17	17	16	15	15	14	14	13
5					100	83	71	63	56	50	45	42	38	36	33	31	29	28	26	25	24	23	22	21	20	19	19	18	17	17
6						100	86	75	67	60	55	50	46	43	40	38	35	33	32	30	29	27	26	25	24	23	22	21	21	20
7							100	88	78	70	64	58	54	50	47	44	41	39	37	35	33	32	30	29	28	27	26	25	24	23
8								100	89	80	73	67	62	57	53	50	47	44	42	40	38	36	35	33	32	31	30	29	28	27
9									100	90	82	75	69	64	60	56	53	50	47	45	43	41	39	38	36	35	33	32	31	30
10										100	91	83	77	71	67	63	59	56	53	50	48	45	43	42	40	38	37	36	34	33
11											100	92	85	79	73	69	65	61	58	55	52	50	48	46	44	42	41	39	38	37
12												100	92	86	80	75	71	67	63	60	57	55	52	50	48	46	44	43	41	40
13													100	93	87	81	76	72	68	65	62	59	57	54	52	50	48	46	45	43
14														100	93	88	82	78	74	70	67	64	61	58	56	54	52	50	48	47
15															100	94	88	83	79	75	71	68	65	63	60	58	56	54	52	50
16																100	94	89	84	80	76	73	70	67	64	62	59	57	55	53
17																	100	94	89	85	81	77	74	71	68	65	63	61	59	57
18																		100	95	90	86	82	78	75	72	69	67	64	62	60
19																			100	95	90	86	83	79	76	73	70	68	66	63
20																				100	95	91	87	83	80	77	74	71	69	67
21																					100	95	91	88	84	81	78	75	72	70
22																						100	96	92	88	85	81	79	76	73
23																							100	96	92	88	85	82	79	77
24																								100	96	92	89	86	83	80
25																									100	96	93	89	86	83
26																										100	96	93	90	87
27																											100	96	93	90
28																												100	97	93
29																													100	97
30																														100

NUMBER CORRECT

Writing That Compares: Writing a Letter

Scoring Rubric: 6-Trait Writing

6. Exceptional

- **Ideas & Content** crafts a strong argument that could affect a reader's opinion; thoughtful details support the writer's position.
- **Organization** well-planned structure allows a reader to follow each point of the argument; has an inviting beginning and a solid ending.
- **Voice** shows originality and deep involvement with the argument; matches a genuine personal message to the purpose and audience.
- **Word Choice** makes creative use of new and everyday words; advanced vocabulary conveys a strong opinion.
- **Sentence Fluency** varied sentences flow naturally and add interest to the argument; writing is easy to follow and read aloud.
- **Conventions** is skilled in most writing conventions; proper use of the rules of English enhances clarity and meaning; editing is largely unnecessary.

5. Excellent

- **Ideas & Content** creates a detailed argument that could influence a reader.
- **Organization** creates a careful strategy, in an order that helps the reader follow the argument's logic; has a solid beginning and ending.
- **Voice** shows originality and strong involvement with the topic; brings a personal message to the topic and audience.
- **Word Choice** makes thoughtful use of both new and everyday words; message is clear and interesting.
- **Sentence Fluency** crafts well-paced sentences with a variety of lengths, beginnings, and patterns that fit together well.
- **Conventions** is skilled in most writing conventions; proper use of the rules of English enhances clarity and meaning; editing is largely unnecessary.

4. Good

- **Ideas & Content** presents a solid, clear argument, with details that help the reader understand the main idea.
- **Organization** presents facts and ideas in a logical order; has a clear beginning and ending; reader can follow the writer's logic.
- **Voice** attempts to convey a real personal message; shows involvement with the topic; message matches the argument, and attempts to reach an audience.
- **Word Choice** uses a variety of words that fit the argument; explores some new words, or makes fresh use of familiar words.
- **Sentence Fluency** careful, easy-to-follow sentences vary in length, beginnings, and patterns; writing is easy to read aloud.
- **Conventions** may make some errors in spelling, capitalization, punctuation, or usage but these do not interfere with understanding the text; some editing is needed.

3. Fair

- **Ideas & Content** attempts to argue a position; may include ideas or details which are not clear, or do not fit the topic.
- **Organization** attempts to argue a position, but the logic is sometimes hard to follow; some ideas don't belong where they are placed; beginning and ending may be too short or may ramble.
- **Voice** may not show involvement with the topic; opinion comes across, but may not convey who is behind the writing.
- **Word Choice** states the argument, but in an ordinary way; may try to use a variety of words, but some do not fit; may overuse some words/expressions.
- **Sentence Fluency** most sentences are readable, but are limited in lengths and patterns; some rereading is necessary to follow the meaning; some sentences are choppy or overlong.
- **Conventions** has basic control of conventions, but makes enough errors to interfere with a smooth reading of the text; significant editing is needed.

2. Poor

- **Ideas & Content** has little control of task to persuade, or seems unsure of the topic; ideas are vague; details are few, repeated, or inaccurate.
- **Organization** has no clear structure; order of ideas is hard to follow; details don't fit where they are placed; beginning and ending are missing or undeveloped.
- **Voice** is not involved in sharing ideas with a reader; writing may be lifeless, with no sense of who is behind the words.
- **Word Choice** does not choose words that convey a clear opinion; some words may detract from the meaning or impact of the argument.
- **Sentence Fluency** sentences may be incomplete or awkward; patterns are similar or monotonous; text may be hard to follow or read aloud.
- **Conventions** makes frequent errors in spelling, word choice, punctuation and usage; paper is difficult to read; needs extensive revision and editing.

1. Unsatisfactory

- **Ideas & Content** does not state an opinion; writer is unsure of what s/he wants to say.
- **Organization** has an extreme lack of structure; ideas and details are disconnected; details, if given, are inaccurate or vague.
- **Voice** does not address an audience at all; does not show a sense of sharing a personal message or style.
- **Word Choice** uses words that do not fit, or are vague and confusing; no new words are attempted.
- **Sentence Fluency** uses incomplete, rambling, or confusing sentences that make the text hard to follow and read aloud.
- **Conventions** makes severe errors in most conventions; spelling errors may make it hard to guess what words are meant; some parts of the text may be impossible to follow or understand.

0: This piece is either blank, or fails to respond to the writing task. The topic is not addressed, or the student simply paraphrases the prompt. The response may be illegible or incoherent.

Writing That Compares: Writing a Letter

8-Point Writing Rubric

8	7	6	5	4	3	2	1
The writer	The writer	The writer	The writer	The writer	The writer	The writer	The writer
• presents an exceptionally well-constructed letter, containing vivid descriptions.	• crafts a well-organized letter with fine descriptions.	• presents an organized letter with descriptions.	• attempts an organized, detailed letter.	• has made an adequate attempt at a letter.	• attempts a minimally-successful letter.	• makes a largely unsuccessful attempt at writing a letter.	• makes little attempt at writing and exhibits a lack of awareness of the topic.
• uses interesting facts and finely observed or researched description to elaborate each aspect.	• elaborates with facts and observations.	• uses facts that present a clear picture.	• elaborates with some facts and description.	• may not consistently elaborate on the facts or observations.	• exhibits organizational problems, such as an illogically-structured list of facts without a beginning, middle, or end.	• exhibits organizational problems great enough to interfere with comprehension of the text.	• lacks any sense of organization.
• uses sophisticated language and compelling images to enhance the facts.	• uses sophisticated vocabulary and interesting images to highlight the facts.	• chooses vocabulary and images that highlight the facts.	• may vary word choice but doesn't include personal observation.	• may show lapses in logical ordering of ideas.	• may not elaborate on factual information.	• has not used pertinent facts or descriptions about a place.	• has used only generalities, with no attempt to include specific facts, descriptions, or observations.
• uses a logical structure with an intriguing beginning, detailed middle, and apt end.	• clearly presents a logical structure with a beginning, middle, and ending.	• presents a logical structure.	• may exhibit organization difficulty with lapses in conventions.	• exhibits recurring problems with conventions.	• may exhibit limited control of grammar, mechanics, and usage.	• may show repeated errors in basic grammar, mechanics, and usage.	• shows serious and repeated errors in basic grammar, mechanics, and usage.
• reaches a well-thought out conclusion based on facts and reasons.	• reaches a thoughtful conclusion based on the facts.	• reaches a conclusion.	• may not offer an entirely logical conclusion.	• may not offer a relevant conclusion.	• may not draw a pertinent conclusion.	• does not draw a conclusion or concludes with a comment unrelated to facts, reasons, or the topic itself.	• leaves writing unfinished without even an attempt at a conclusion.

0: This piece is either blank, or fails to respond to the writing task. The topic is not addressed, or the student simply paraphrases the prompt. The response may be illegible or incoherent.